We Knew
Mary Baker Eddy

Mary B. G. Eddy

We Knew
Mary Baker Eddy

EXPANDED EDITION

VOLUME II

The Christian Science Publishing Society
210 Massachusetts Avenue, Boston, Massachusetts 02115 USA

The Christian Science Publishing Society

210 Massachusetts Avenue, Boston, Massachusetts, 02115 USA

www.christianscience.com

Several abbreviations appear in credits and
copyright notices throughout this book:
CSPS: The Christian Science Publishing Society
TMBEC: The Mary Baker Eddy Collection
TMBEL: The Mary Baker Eddy Library

Frontispiece and jacket of Mary Baker Eddy by J. A. J. Wilcox, © CSPS,
photo H. G. Smith © TMBEC
Illustrations on the front dust jacket and pages 300 and 479 by Joan Wolcott
Book design by Jerry Rutherford

Library of Congress Cataloging-in-Publication *(Provided by Quality Books, Inc.)*
We Knew Mary Baker Eddy. Volume 2.—Expanded ed.
    v. cm.
    Includes bibliographical references and index.
    LCCN 2013930790
    ISBN-13: 978-0-8751-0485-0 (v.1)
    ISBN-13: 978-0-8751-0490-4 (v.2)

    1. Eddy, Mary Baker, 1821-1910. 2. Christian Scientists—Biography.
I. Christian Science Publishing Society.

BX6995.W4 2011   289.5'092
               QBI13-600014

G750B51421EN

Printed in the United States of America
1 3 5 7 9 10 8 6 4 2

First Edition

Contents

Introduction

If names and numbers, facts and dates, make up history's melody, people's perspectives turn that melody into symphony.

Readers of the first volume in the expanded edition of *We Knew Mary Baker Eddy* saw how multiple accounts of the same experience can enrich the historical record. Take June 29, 1903, for example, when Mary Baker Eddy addressed a large gathering from the balcony of her home in New Hampshire. Her talk, with one sentence added, was later published, and a few pictures, still extant, give some sense of the considerable crowd. That's the melody pure and simple.

Fortunately, that first volume includes several accounts of this event told from different vantage points. In particular, John Lathrop offers an interesting perspective from behind the scenes, where he listened to Eddy's address from inside her room. He describes her as "radiantly happy" when she reenters the room. Then he explains what happens next:

> The maid removed her wrap and bonnet, and she sat down in her big chair, folded her hands, and said to me, "Wasn't it a wonderful occasion?" Then she asked me, "What are they doing?" I looked below and told her they were having silent prayer. "We will pray, too," she said. "Now what are they doing?" she asked. "They are singing your hymn 'Shepherd,' Mother." After that they repeated "the scientific statement of being" (see *Science and Health*, p. 468).
>
> Then they quietly dispersed, and when I told her, she said, "Now I will see what God says about it." She took up her Bible and opened it at random to read the

first passage her eyes would light upon. It was Isaiah, thirty-fifth chapter, tenth verse: "And the ransomed of the Lord shall return, and come to Zion with songs and everlasting joy upon their heads: they shall obtain joy and gladness, and sorrow and sighing shall flee away." "See," she said, "how God is always with me. That verse I will add to my address."[1]

Lathrop's account, by itself, turns this event's historical "melody" into a multilayered musical composition. Add other accounts, and we approach a symphony.

That same type of amplification occurs in this volume as well—for events as commonplace as meals and as substantive as Eddy's final class. This collection of distinct yet overlapping accounts—from metaphysical workers, maids, housekeepers, secretaries, students, and church workers—broadens and deepens our view of one of the most well-known women in late-nineteenth- and early-twentieth-century America.

The timeframe of the narratives is significant, too. Collectively, the writers' acquaintance with Eddy spans nearly twenty-five years (1886–1910)—and not just any twenty-five years. In the course of them, Eddy reorganized her Church, giving it the name it carries today (The First Church of Christ, Scientist); she secured the Church's spiritual foundation with her *Church Manual* and ordained the Bible and *Science and Health with Key to the Scriptures* as the Church's pastor; the Original Mother Church and its Extension were built; early workers in the movement introduced Christian Science across the United States and beyond its borders; Eddy founded the *Christian Science Sentinel, Der Herold der Christian Science* (*The Herald of Christian Science*, first published in German), and *The Christian Science Monitor*; and vigorous efforts to unseat her as the

Church's Leader were definitively defeated. Learning of Eddy from those who knew her during this extremely demanding and productive period provides insight not only about her as a Leader but about the Cause she led. In addition, readers get to know key members of the movement whose contributions earned them lasting recognition—Adam Dickey, Septimus Hanna, and Clara Shannon, for example.

In sharing their memories, the twenty-two authors included here became historians—not students of history but chroniclers of it. None of them takes this role lightly; each is deeply concerned with recording his or her experiences accurately. For example, Adelaide Still assures us that she has "taken every possible care to be accurate" (see p. 457). And Anna Baker's reminiscence begins with this note: "The material in this book is authentic. It has been compiled from a journal kept during long residence in Mrs. Eddy's home, from notes verified by her, or from references taken verbatim" (p. 288).

Yet despite their best efforts, the authors' memories fail them on occasion. Such is the nature of reminiscences. Instead of weakening the writers' credibility, however, these little lapses make them all the more believable (and endearing) because we can relate to them. Who doesn't have vivid memories—with holes in them? When experiences touch us deeply, what matters most stays with us even if names and dates fade. So it is with these authors, all of whom were profoundly touched by Eddy.

Some of the writers found their lives not only changed but literally saved by the healing truth Eddy discovered. Others saw family members freed from what appeared to be hopeless suffering through Christian Science treatment or the sufferer's own study of Eddy's writings. Either way, decisive physical healing sets the stage for most of these writers' first encounters with Eddy, for their boundless gratitude for her, and for their devotion to her Cause.

The authenticity of these accounts is further confirmed by a remarkable consistency across reminiscences. Time and again, the authors' descriptions of Eddy's appearance, demeanor, high expectations, firmness, humor, warmth, and wisdom echo each other, so much so that, in the course of the book, an impression of Eddy emerges that feels not only reliable but familiar. By the time William Rathvon describes her in the penultimate paragraph as "like the rest of us in many things, and in others ... as far above any of us as the stars above the earth," we know enough from earlier chapters to understand how Eddy fits both ends of this spectrum.

Thanks to the voices in this volume—each like an instrument in an orchestra—Eddy's history as a woman, Leader, teacher, healer, and student of the Science she herself revealed is far more symphony than simple melody.

Yet for all they add to the historical record, these accounts are no substitute for Eddy's own writings. Through *Science and Health* and her other published works, Eddy alone definitively explains the Science of Christ. The authors in this volume shared their reminiscences not to focus thought on their Leader's personal past but to direct attention to the timeless truths she lived and loved. Rathvon said as much outright. "Think of her in terms not of the past but of the present," he urged. "See her as speaking to you now through her books and her writings, which need no date, for their truths can never grow old and yet were never new" (p. 587).

We Knew Mary Baker Eddy first appeared as a series of four volumes published in 1943, 1950, 1953, and 1972, respectively.

The series comprised eighteen reminiscences, ten of which were delivered as talks in The Mother Church Extension between 1937 and 1946 and then published in the Church's weekly periodical, the *Christian Science Sentinel*. Most of the other reminiscences were presented publicly for the first time in the four-volume series. In 1979, the series was published as a single volume, still titled *We Knew Mary Baker Eddy*. No new material was added.

The first volume of the expanded edition was published in 2011. It included the original series; additional material from the reminiscences of Julia Bartlett, Annie Knott, and John Lathrop; as well as material from four reminiscences never published before—those by Alfred Farlow, John Salchow, Laura Sargent, and Hermann Hering.

With only a few exceptions, none of the reminiscences in this second volume of the expanded edition has been published before. The accounts are arranged chronologically according to the date of each author's first significant encounter with Eddy, and subheads have been added as a means of breaking the text into briefer, more accessible sections. Minor changes in spelling, capitalization, and punctuation have been made when necessary for clarity or to bring terms into consistency with the current Stylebook of the *Journal*, *Sentinel*, and *Herald* Editorial Department. Changes or insertions of a substantive nature are noted in brackets. Since, in most cases, the material was excerpted from much longer reminiscences, it was not practical to indicate deletions with ellipses.

These reminiscences in their entirety as well as the vast majority of primary source material referenced in the endnotes are held at The Mary Baker Eddy Library in Boston, Massachusetts. The library's collections are available for public research.

JENNIE E. SAWYER *(1847–1932)*

Born in Wisconsin, Eunice J. Passage married Silas J. Sawyer in 1867. For the first fifteen years of the couple's married life, Jennie suffered from illnesses so severe that she became an almost helpless invalid. Then in 1883, her husband learned of Christian Science and purchased Science and Health.[2] *The Sawyers met Mary Baker Eddy in December of that year and, within days of that meeting, took Primary class instruction from her. Soon afterward, Sawyer was completely healed, and two months later both she and her husband were listed in* The Christian Science Journal *as practitioners in Milwaukee, Wisconsin.*

Sawyer took another Primary class from Eddy in 1884 and a Normal class from her in 1886.[3] Along with her healing work, Sawyer was active in establishing Christian Science in Milwaukee. She began teaching Christian Science in 1905 or 1906.

Taking Class with Mary Baker Eddy

JENNIE E. SAWYER

Christian Science has been a Cause which has enlisted my most earnest effort up to the present time, never having lost my first enthusiasm and conviction of its being the [t]ruth; and I have ever held an abiding certainty that Christian Science has taught us how to approach God that He may restore unto us the liberty which we have in Christ Jesus.

Dr. S. J. Sawyer, my husband, and myself had three separate courses of instruction with Mrs. Mary Baker G. Eddy—our first Primary course in December 1883. We took up the work unitedly, continuing our work together until Dr. Sawyer passed on in 1905. He had given twenty-two years of continuous service to Christian Science, giving up a lucrative practice in dentistry that he might give his whole time and energy unreservedly to the Cause under Mrs. Eddy's personal supervision and direction, holding himself ever ready to go at any time or on any mission Mrs. Eddy might desire.

These were pioneer days in planting the thought of

Christian Science in different localities and placing the literature in public libraries, teaching the Science wherever there were inquiring minds and receptive thought; he gave public talks on the subject when there was a demand for so doing. In fulfilling these various duties, it necessitated his being away from home much of the time, thereby leaving the healing work and holding the meetings, together with the various duties of the home work, to my personal effort to meet. And from those early days my individual interest has continued—from 1883 to 1930, the present time—forty-seven years of unremitting labor of love for the Master, our Lord Jesus Christ, and the Cause of Christian Science.

My years of invalidism

Previous to the year 1883, I, Jennie E. Sawyer, had been an invalid for fifteen years, pronounced incurable as I had chronic and organic diseases that would not yield to medicine or treatment of any material nature. On three separate occasions my life had been despaired of and I had faced death—but had rallied and continued suffering until a relapse into another hopeless and dangerous condition.

Thus, life had become an endless torture. Physicians gave me no hope of recovery as medicine seemed to poison the system, so there came a time when they recommended only fresh air, pure water, and sunshine, together with absolute quiet, as the only hope of relieving the body of constant suffering and pain. There was no waking moment that I was not enduring pain, and life had become a grievous burden until my constant prayer was that I might die, thinking thereby I should enter into eternal rest. Finally I was sent to a resort, or rest cure, where no medicine was given, and patients were required to do nothing but lie out in the sunshine or shade, ride in row boats on artificial ponds, read, or remain idle as they chose. At first I was too utterly weary to even avail myself of these privileges. It seemed an amazing thing that one could be so tired and utterly weary that even breathing exhausted them, and still I lived!

But gradually, after gaining a degree of strength, I was able to sit up a portion of the day, wear my clothes a few hours at a time, and avail myself of a few moments of boat riding or of lying out on the porch. But before I was able to rely on myself at all—after about seven weeks—a letter came from my husband informing me that several friends had been urging him to try a mental method of healing which included no medicine and no physical exertion on the part of the patient—and even mentally they did not require the patient to accept it until relief came and [he or she] could better understand it.

Some people from Boston were visiting friends of ours and had brought these vague statements regarding a method of healing they had heard about, but [they] could give no definite idea of what it was except that a lady in Boston, through what was supposed to be a silent prayer, was healing people. [My husband] finally purchased *Science and Health* by Mary Baker G. Eddy, relating to her own experience of years of invalidism and of her method of healing, which he could not understand but which seemed more Christian and spiritual than the ordinary faith of the church. And he, knowing that I firmly believed that the only ease I obtained was from God, suggested that we go to Boston and consult with Mrs. Eddy.

Our decision to visit Mrs. Eddy

The very thought of such a proposition caused a relapse. I was opposed to the idea of attempting such a journey, feeling I could not endure it nor hope to reach the journey's end alive. But my husband, through reading *Science and Health*, had gained a thought that had deeply impressed him as wholly different from any other Christian faith; it seemed a practical, workable, demonstrable faith, and he desired to meet the author personally. I had not seen, nor was I able to read, the book; I was too weak physically or mentally to read or remember anything very long. So a month or two passed before arrangements could be made to move me or I could gain courage or strength to attempt such a journey. It required closing his dental office and discontinuing business during our absence, but finally the trip was accomplished and we arrived in Boston one evening about the middle of December of 1883.

Dr. Sawyer, leaving me at the hotel, called at once on Mrs. Eddy at 571 Columbus Avenue, where her home and College were situated; he gained an appointment for me the following morning. On his return to the hotel from this first call on Mrs. Eddy, I remember he said, "I don't know what you will think! She seemed very much of a lady and very sincere in her faith. She talked of God and of man's relation to God in a manner we are not familiar with; her talk seemed sensible and convincing and very interesting, but very strange and unusual. She did not even inquire specially about your physical symptoms or condition, but in some way I feel there is help for you in it."

The following morning, on seeing Mrs. Eddy, I felt

favorably impressed with her sincerity and womanly, motherly kindness; there seemed no opposition in my thought to trying this method of healing. She did not apparently diagnose my case, nor did she act as though I were an invalid. There was no talk of sickness. It was a strange experience, for my appearance plainly showed that I was a constant sufferer. Even at that very moment, I was too weary to listen or to grasp hold on what she was saying. Still, there was something attractive and alluring in the idea of gaining rest and health through abiding in God's omnipotence, and in the sure confidence and trust that she presented as possible.

One earlier glimpse of God

During my invalidism I had [had] one answer to my prayer, but I did not know just what thought had brought it about, nor could I gain or reproduce the same result again. It was at the time of a critical turn in my disease; I had most fervently prayed [to] God to help me endure my suffering (holding to it as material and real), but I remember I suddenly realized that "whether I live or whether I die, I am the Lord's," and at once I found a sudden surcease of pain. All fever left me, and I was free of that unnatural weariness and fear. This wonderful calm remained with me for about ten hours; both mind and body were at ease. I knew it was God-given, but I did not realize that I had momentarily yielded my false sense and thereby gained the blessing. And with those about me thinking it might be merely preceding the final dissolution, I could not hold the calmness or gain freedom from the return of pain.

I feel that this experience had largely to do with my [eventual] desire to know, and my acceptance of, Christian Science.

For while I, as a professed Christian of many years, had never gained a knowledge of how to approach God with any degree of certainty that my prayer would be answered, I often gained a mental assurance and indefinite belief that I was cared for; but I could not tell what thought brought about the change. But here was Mrs. Eddy presenting a solved problem of faith and trust bringing out a sure result as practical as a problem solved in mathematics. The wonder of it all caused both Dr. Sawyer and me to desire further enlightenment.

Surprises on the road to healing

The only hesitation I felt [about] being healed was the dread of an invalid's convalescent state—of gradually, slowly, gaining a degree of strength, and then through some cause suffering a relapse, then again gaining a hope of health, and then dying. That was more appalling to me than to die at once. I said to Mrs. Eddy, "If I gain my health, it will be such a slow process, and then I must sooner or later die. I would rather go now as I feel willing and ready to die." Mrs. Eddy assured me there would be no convalescent state if I were healed in Christian Science. She also startled me by saying, "If you die, you will awaken to the realization that you are not dead and still have your problem to solve, for Life is from everlasting to everlasting."

The most astounding thing was that she did not physically diagnose my case nor ask what the different physicians had thought my trouble was. She did not give me any treatment but rather questioned my thought about God and mankind and Life. And finally she said, "I would advise you to sit in my class and let me teach you." That was the most astonishing thing, for I had not been able to remember three lines of anything I had read for months! I was too tired to think, and the presence and conversation of people wearied me almost beyond endurance. Physicians had repeatedly told me there was nothing to build on and had warned me that I was liable to die at any moment. But she paid not the slightest attention to the doctors' verdicts but answered, "Your husband is in good health, and together you might gain a thought that would heal you." At that time to imagine that a "thought gained" would heal incurable, hopeless, organic disease seemed almost an insane idea. Up to that time I had been unable to bear the weight of my clothes but a few hours each day; still she assured me, "You will be able to sit in this class, for as you learn your true relationship to God, you will forget these things that now trouble you."

Mrs. Eddy at this time was a woman past sixty years of age, a well-preserved, beautiful woman—not so much because of her physical charm as because there was discernible an inward light or reflection of thought that shone through her countenance that was an entirely new expression of being. This had its own influence—one felt drawn to a better Life just from being in her presence. This realization of Life that she possessed gave impulse to her every action, word, and speech. She was prepossessing, attractive, and kind in her manner, and most considerate in guiding the thought of the members of this class away from discussions in relation to matter as the only tangible evidence of life.

Primary class instruction

Mrs. Eddy guided the argumentative beliefs wisely into an acceptance of infinite Mind's power and presence, and this became a time marked by an absolute change of consciousness regarding Life and its demand, together with its motive, purpose, desire, and aim, thereby changing the whole current of thought from a material, mortal mind basis to a spiritual perception of man and the universe as reflecting God and His handiwork in the world—and thereby enabling one to recognize God's ever-presence, protection, and care in every way, at all times, and under all circumstances.

In those early days of Christian Science teaching, the world at large had not accepted so mental a basis to work from, and this class was loath to let go of material power, physical sensation, and mortal life as realities, so arguments and discussions occupied many hours of time until a higher light dawned on the consciousness. To one who had suffered and accepted physical sense as real, it seemed like being cast into the sea without rudder or compass to guide or control. Our former faith had led us to plead and beg for help and salvation from sin, sickness, and death, while those false methods were to be replaced by a faith that took hold on God's promises without faltering because of a firm reliance on Christ's redeeming grace and a recognition of God's ability to save to the uttermost.

It was not easy to realize that letting go of a self-sustaining sense of force and the belief of one's own energy, and taking hold on divine might, power, and presence, was the secret of one's standing in line to reflect the all-sufficiency of God's divine leading. As one would catch a glimpse of Mrs. Eddy's spiritual meaning, her face would become actually radiant with the spiritual uplift, and one would become conscious of the inspiration of thought imparted from God through her words and realize it was a divine utterance and message—not her personal belief.

This experience was like being born again from above into the kingdom of ever-present Love and care of our heavenly Father. It was a glimpse into a better [l]ife, a glorious awakening from the falsities and educated beliefs concerning life and body, into a realization of the kingdom of God's reign and rule on earth as in heaven, thus not only teaching us man's true relationship to God, but enabling us to discern man's true embodiment as a mental manifestation of God's attributes—strength, power, action—the true reflection of Mind's dominating power, [and] the possibility of having dominion over the work of His hands.

Mrs. Eddy gave us about three weeks of time [in this class]. She told Dr. Sawyer and me that we were the first students to have come from the West for instruction with her, and she formed this class especially to accommodate us as we had come so great a distance.

The unsettling effect of truth

Our faith and trust [were] so vague and uncertain compared with her grasping hold on God's promises that it was literally like being born again. Learning to abide in the kingdom of Truth and Love seemed a mighty effort and created [such] a fever of fear and unrest and disquietude that she claimed it were better to discontinue her explanations for a few days until the balance was adjusted on the side of trust and assurance. I felt I could not discontinue or cease learning more, as I was not well enough established in the new way to treat or pray in Christian Science, and my former way of praying I could not go back to. She noticed my unrest and asked before the class disbanded, "Mrs. Sawyer, do you ever stir yeast when it is rising?" I answered, "No, but what has that to do with this?" She answered, "God's hand is leading you, and I would not do more just now." I did not understand it and could not repress my tears. She sent one of her older students to meet me as I went from the classroom alone, and he said, "Mrs. Eddy wants you to know that you are in the most favorable condition of mind of anyone in the class." I said, "This is too serious a matter to say anything like that. I don't know what I am here for; I cannot grasp it, and I cannot go back to my old faith." He said comforting words that were wholly lost on me, and although I do not cry easily, I went out sobbing.

I remember taking *Science and Health* and thinking I will read until I know where and what God is. Suddenly, as I was reading in the chapter "Footsteps of Truth," it dawned on me that I was reaching far out for God as though He were a long way off—unapproachable and difficult to find. And out of that darkness and bewilderment, an illumination of thought encircled me, and I felt and knew and realized God's ever-presence. It was like a conversion—a remarkable experience of "God with us" at all times, under all circumstances. My eyes were open to the Truth of Being, and from that day to the present time, it has been a daily, hourly realization that my eyes need not be holden but may at all times recognize the bountiful mercy, love, and care of our heavenly Father that the Christ-thought brings to our consciousness if we but turn our faces God-ward and realize His ever-presence. Mrs. Eddy made a private appointment for that evening and gave us many new ideas and comforting thoughts. We scarcely realized what a privilege we had in these private talks with her, but later on we learned to treasure the words given.

The class members were of different church affiliations, and to this day it does seem astonishing that so mixed a thought of different denominational religious beliefs could be brought into unison and conformity on so vital a question as one's Christian faith; but at the close of the class we "were all of one accord in one place" [see Acts 2:1], established in God as our only source of supply.

Sharing Christian Science despite resistance

At this time Mrs. Eddy was holding services in Hawthorne Hall in Boston. She not only gave an address, but she answered questions to all inquiring minds. One could readily realize that Christian Science was not well

Hawthorne Hall and a handbill for services in the "Hawthorn [sic] Rooms"

THE
Church of Christ
respectfully invites you to attend their services at

No. 2 Park St.
HAWTHORN ROOMS.
EVERY SUNDAY,
At 3 P. M., and learn how to heal the sick with Christianity.
LECTURE by
Mrs. M. B. Glover Eddy

known nor fully accepted. Many were misunderstanding the true import of her thought, and foolish impractical questions were asked and much time consumed in Mrs. Eddy's patiently guiding their thought rightly.

At this time the churches were speaking very pointedly against it. Many people spoke derisively and with contempt of it, but none of them knew actually what it was that they were condemning. That was an astonishing thing to find our ministers and Christian people, [whose judgment] we had always felt could be relied on as just and true, preach[ing] and talk[ing] against it as a wicked pernicious evil, warning people against it and against those who believed in it. They were entirely ignorant of the subject and would not be informed or gain any knowledge concerning it.

This ignorant prejudice of thought only heightened our esteem and love for Christian Science, and at the end of the class, when Mrs. Eddy asked Dr. Sawyer if he would go to different cities and establish the work under her directions and teach the Science wherever he found receptive minds, he accepted the call although he knew it would array public thought against him. He closed a lucrative business and followed along the line of Christian Science endeavor the remainder of his earth-life. Mrs. Eddy then asked me what I thought of it and what I was going to do with the thought she had imparted to me. I answered, "I am filled with a wonderful Truth. I don't know what I am to do with it!" She said in a most convincing manner, "You are going to heal with it!" She seemed to foresee the future and felt that I would apply the knowledge gained to heal others whether present or absent. She assured me that I was practically healed of my infirmities and apparent disease; that had not quite dawned on me, and it seemed almost incredible to think there would be no return of those ailments.

I realized that to practice Christian Science would place me where I would be a target for severe criticism among my home friends and church people, but I also realized that I had left my home and friends in a hopeless, dying condition that none could help, and my life had been prolonged and saved, and my health restored, and my faith renewed through and by this revelation of the Christ-healing taught by my teacher, Mrs. Mary Baker G. Eddy. I could not do less than make a solemn compact with God to give my remaining days to His service. I promised to do all in my power to help others to understand this blessed Truth of Christian Science.

The start of our healing practice

We arrived home early in January 1884 and at once began healing whoever desired help. My first case was a young girl of about twenty years, born of a consumptive mother. She had never been strong and at this time was suffering from inflammatory rheumatism, which [had] rendered her right arm and hand useless. I began the treatment on Friday evening and did absent work until Monday morning, when she called and said, "See what I can do!" and she lifted a large heavy atlas with her right hand! This girl had been afflicted with a double curvature of the spine from her birth, and through the treatment, her back was straightened and healed in twenty-three days.

These healings seemed so marvelous to us that I at once wrote to Mrs. Eddy, asking if it were possible that God through our small effort and limited understanding could have brought about this wonderful change. Mrs. Eddy answered, "I would not dare do otherwise than claim it for God!" Oh, this was too wonderful to believe as possible, and it humbled me to think of all the years wasted in a futile blind faith of asking for blessings, while infinite Love could and would come so near as to answer our prayer for another who was only seeking personal help and physical relief without once recognizing the help received as more than mortal mind could have done for her, never once recognizing God's blessing to her.

I personally got the blessing and took this healing so to heart that nothing could shake my faith in Christian Science healing. In all these years of having professed Christianity, I had never before realized that an actual possession of a living faith in our God could or would bring such a blessing into one's experience!

At first only the chronic and apparently incurable cases came for treatment, and for several months we worked without compensation. As suffering was relieved for one, they would tell another of [the] benefit received. Thus, in time, a practice was established, and in a lesser way, we were pioneers of our teacher's method of treating. Hundreds of miles away from her, we were endeavoring to practice Christian Science.

Loss and gain in our pursuit of truth

Planting a new thought, especially if it be of a religious nature, is not wholly a thing of joy or happiness, except in one's own consciousness of right action. We had at once called on our own minister and physician, feeling sure they would appreciate this spiritual truth and rejoice in the recovery of health. [But] our minister and church friends immediately turned a cold shoulder on us, and many would not even allow an explanation in any direction, fearing it was of a mesmeric nature and in some way they could be made to believe in it without desiring to do so. They felt we had been innocently led astray by Mrs. Eddy's thought, and even the friends who had urged Dr. Sawyer to take me to Boston for this healing dropped us socially. They simply judged it must be wrong because no minister had ever, in all his study of the Scriptures, discovered any such rendering of thought.

Our physician was more lenient and kind and had to admit I seemed well, but he warned me that the moment "that woman's thought"—meaning Mrs. Eddy's thought—"was off from me," I would pass out, as it was but a mesmeric effect. He emphatically said he knew my physical condition and I could not be healed! Both minister and physician watched my case for several years, but there was no relapse, and I have outlived most of these friends.

In all of these trials, we had letters of guidance and cheer from Mrs. Eddy that sustained and comforted us. There were also Association meetings each year; we had joined Mrs. Eddy's Association after our first Primary class and had also taken two other courses of lectures since 1883— one in 1884 and our Normal course in 1886—and had gradually gathered about us inquiring minds who desired to know more of Christian Science.

After that third, or Normal, class, Mrs. Eddy had detained me privately and requested me to teach, as my husband was at this time doing personal work for her in New York and Boston and in several other states. I frankly said I did not want to teach but would greatly prefer doing healing work; I did not feel competent to meet the public and explain this mighty Truth. When she had told me on leaving the Primary class that I would do healing work, I did not then realize what the import of such a thought would be.

Our former Clerk of The Mother Church, Mr. William B. Johnson, once asked me if I "would have had the courage to have taken up the Science had I foreseen just what I had to face?" Yes, I think so! There is a sustaining grace in healing and teaching Christian Science that no other religion possesses.

The public healing was rendered more difficult as the charging for services rendered seemed quite beyond my ability to do. I had for several months given my time and effort unlimited to those who did not offer to pay, and I was burdened by work and unable to gain respite or relief, and I hadn't the courage to present a bill. Finally Mrs. Eddy advised charging for the treatment, as that would give me more time for those who were earnestly seeking the Science and would cull out those who were merely gaining relief for themselves. Thus she guided and directed in establishing the early work; and in a few months others were seeking instruction from Mrs. Eddy personally, and the knowledge of Christian Science had gained a foothold beyond one's possible imagination.

[For a while] we held meetings in our own home. Our minister objected to this. We offered to meet with the officers of the church and tell them frankly what we understood Science to be [and] also tell them of my healing, but Rev. Ide would not even listen himself nor consent to others meeting with us. He felt that would be a very dangerous proceeding as some innocent person might be persuaded to accept it as we had been misled, without purposely intending to go wrong. Finally he preached a sermon on "How to treat a member who had gone astray," and he advised "ignoring them until they returned to the church."

Of course this left us apparently stranded and caused a separation and change in our social and church relations which was not expected; and only [because] we were absorbed in doing the Master's work according to our highest light could we have endured those strenuous days, for even our own relatives judged our position harshly. I recall but two friends who had known me since childhood who wrote me kindly, but guardedly, saying, "It can't be wrong or you would not be in it"; that was comforting, although they allowed we might later on regret being influenced in accepting it.

We were devoting our whole time, energy, and ability, [and] also our earthly possessions to the Cause and service of Christian Science, giving up our private home life for the meetings and class work and patients, until we were sufficiently well established to rent a hall. Our Sunday and mid-week meetings were conducted about the same as today [with] reading from the Bible and selections from *Science and Health*; we did not have the *Quarterly* at that time. We had a short address, and at the evening meetings, readings, testimonials, and answered questions. In the meantime, as organizations were formed in different parts of the country, Mrs. Eddy formed Students' Christian Science associations as branches of her Association in Boston. Ours is Number Eleven, as Dr. Sawyer's and my students were meeting together as we worked unitedly under one charter.

Discord within the movement

We were so absorbed in our labors that we had not noticed the unrest or disturbance throughout the Field in the different churches, and our amazement was great on finding there could be such disloyalty and unfairness among those professing to understand Christian Science.[4]

We had much to learn in meeting all these phases of belief that had not been demonstrated, in uniting people in working impersonally together in oneness of Mind and [in] the putting out of self and sense in serving God in [s]pirit and in [t]ruth. Finding that this error of ambition and self-seeking was entering our own organization was a grievous thing. It had grown through an envious desire [among some] to occupy positions that they had not demonstrated sufficiently to properly fill, and instead of building on their own individual work, they were deliberately usurping and undermining the work of others who, through demonstration, had been more successful than themselves. Thus the labor and work of the more faithful Scientists was again interfered with.

Many of these people had united with these different churches throughout the Field without having studied the Science except as their own personal sense had rendered it by reading *Science and Health*. When voting on any question, they invariably voted from a personal sense standpoint, as they formerly would have done as members of an orthodox church, without possessing a demonstrable thought of working it out according to God's direction or divine leading.

This unscientific rendering of Christian Science, this lack of the understanding of God's blessed [t]ruth through and by demonstration, has led up to a disruption of many churches, and our church together with many others was apparently undone, although no one, nor anything, can disrupt or undo our work done for our heavenly Father.

Reflecting on a lifetime of healing

[Looking back], we account the very earliest work the most wonderful and the happiest of all these many years of service. We were then but a small band of Scientists meeting together, their thought reaching out for the highest light possible to be gained, aiming for no selfish personal position, desiring only God's divine leading. These early struggles brought us into a closer relation with our teacher and with one another than otherwise could have existed. Mrs. Eddy guided, and she helped and encouraged us; she gave personal instruction on how to meet an emergency or to cover a need that would have required long practice and experience to have recognized and met.

To have learned that it is mortal mind's false picture that seems to be material life but that it can be erased the same as the false solving of an example—[this] lifts the weight of fear and produces a change in the outward appearance. This change of consciousness was very apparent in Mrs. Eddy. Although her body showed age in many ways, still, her countenance was often radiant with this inward light, which she possessed to a marked degree; her eyes and expression of face showed that her thought and life were not bound to a sense of fleshly personality. She lived quite apart and superior to [a] mortal sense of being, and toward the last of her earth-life, this grew more and more apparent. At one time twelve years had elapsed since I had seen her, and in this one respect the change was remarkable: she did not look as though she lived in her body, showing how truly thought depicts or makes a likeness of itself. Her very presence rebuked error without a spoken word; one wanted to be and do better simply from having come in contact with her.

It is now forty-seven years of continuous practice and teaching of Christian Science, and it has been one glorious experience of endeavor to undo self and sense and thereby serve God, the Giver of every good and perfect gift.

Excerpts from Sawyer's association addresses[5]

1905: Mrs. Eddy has said, "To never be found *thinking* on the wrong side of any question would solve the problem."

1910: I once heard Mrs. Eddy say, "It is not the student who can quote *Science and Health* the most readily, or who can talk the most glibly of Science, that does the best healing work; but those who silently before God use the thought gained bring out the best fruit for the Master's use."

1913: Mrs. Eddy once said with great force and vehemence of manner, "God is the only talker!"

1914: I once heard Mrs. Eddy say, "If one was foolishly sensitive or had a sense of pride as regards gaining help from another, that was the time they should ask for it." She never hesitated about asking students to work for her, even when they were very young in Science.

1914: Mrs. Eddy has said [that] this appearance to the human sense is but a shadow of a shadow—it is but a shadow of our perception of the ideal man, and the glimpse we momentarily catch of the Truth of being is but a shadow of itself. We see as in a glass darkly, but this glimpse held onto firmly resolves itself into a clearer perception, which brings out a better appearance to the human sense, but at no time is human being the image and likeness of God, no matter how beautiful an appearance.

1915: Mrs. Eddy once said, "We are but incidental to the healing, and we have no right to intercept or misdirect that blessing."

1916: In Mrs. Eddy's class instruction to teachers, she has said:

> Practitioners of Christian Science should keep informed of the new names that the medical world is constantly giving to the different ailments the human body is subject to, for each name conveys to the mind of the patient an increased sense of fear and danger—as though some dread and deadly disease had been discovered. The Christian Scientist, knowing that the name imparts added fear, must be on the alert to meet and undo the old claim under its new name, otherwise the patient's fear is so far increased that the practitioner's treatment does not overcome the supposed new disease.

1916: Mrs. Eddy was asked, "Does Christian Science deny the existence of disease germs or merely assert man's superiority over such forces?" She answered, "It denies the existence thereof."

1918: Mrs. Eddy once said, "I find the Science of Mind disposes of all evil, while to believe in evil as a reality is to bring out the effects of evil."

1918: I once received a treatment from Mrs. Eddy that

unfolded to my thought a realization of the God-Love manifest in the world, so widely different from any human sense of love that I have never found words to express the enlightenment, the uplift, it brought to my consciousness. I was able for weeks to treat those who appealed to me for help with the realization I [had] gained of that one characteristic, that one attribute, of our heavenly Father's protection and care. It came to me as an effulgence of light, not as a personal thing at all; one could readily recognize that Love must be reflected from an infallible source, for no human sense could hold or express so vast a thing as the divine ever-presence.

1921: In the Primary class with Mrs. Eddy, this thought of identity was a wonderful revelation; it seemed to open to our consciousness the possibilities and power of *reflection* as nothing else had ever done. It lifted us out of harm's way, established us as children of God, and taught us that we, as individuals, represent the whole of Life—all its attributes.

1921: I am often reminded of Mrs. Eddy's encouraging words in this direction: when one's faith faltered in meeting a difficult case, she would say, "Jesus did it and left the example for you; and the promise was given that the followers of Jesus would do greater works as the result of increasing revelation or power to reflect Life, Truth, and Love."

1926: Mrs. Eddy said in class, "Always clinch your argument against evil by saying, 'It cannot abide, it cannot harm, for God fills all space, all time. God is the *only* presence.'"

1926: Mrs. Eddy tells us, "When we awaken from the dream of life in matter, we shall learn this grand truth of being—that there is but one side to God; it has no evil side. God is All-in-all."

1929: Mrs. Eddy has said, "If a *negative thought* comes to

you, rise to your feet immediately and declare the Truth aloud."

1930: On meeting Mrs. Eddy, I was deeply impressed by her abiding in God's presence, as it were, in a natural manner. Where we had always reached out for God as though He were a long way off, beseeching Him to help us endure things beyond our ability to stand, she seemed to stand alongside, as it were, and feel the security of His ever-presence. She dwelt in her true relationship as a child of God, accepted the certainty of her inheritance, and seemed to draw others seeking the understanding of Science into this nearness she felt in the Father's presence.

1931: Mrs. Eddy once said, "God knows your thought better than you are able to express it, and He answers the desire of the heart."

VICTORIA H. SARGENT *(1848–1930)*

*A native of Maine, Victoria Adams moved with her family
to Fort Howard (now known as Green Bay), Wisconsin,
while still a child. In 1866 she married Henry Sargent,
and the couple's first daughter, Minerva (nicknamed
Minnie), was born about three years later. By 1870, the
family had moved to Oconto, Wisconsin, and had several
relatives from both sides of the family living with them.
About thirteen years later, the couple's second daughter,
Elizabeth (nicknamed Bessie), was born. Meanwhile,
Sargent's sister, Laura, had married James Sargent,
Henry's brother.*

*In 1883, Victoria learned about Christian Science when
Laura was healed. In May 1884, Laura took Primary
class instruction with Mary Baker Eddy in Chicago
and then began holding worship services in Oconto with
Victoria and others interested in Christian Science.
That summer, Victoria was healed by reading* Science
and Health; with a Key to the Scriptures,[6] *and in*

December of that year, both sisters took Primary class instruction with Eddy in Boston. Victoria took Normal class with Eddy in 1886, and that fall the first edifice in the world built for Christian Science services was erected in Oconto for $1,137.20. The opening service was held October 31, 1886; the building was dedicated less than four months later.

Victoria Sargent was listed in The Christian Science Journal *as a practitioner by March of 1889 and taught her first class in 1895. She went to Concord, New Hampshire, for several weeks in 1907 at Eddy's request to support her in prayer concerning the "Next Friends" suit. In 1915, she became custodian of Eddy's Chestnut Hill home but continued healing and teaching. At least one of her daughters, Minnie, became a Christian Science practitioner.*

Lessons from Our Leader

VICTORIA H. SARGENT

I first met our revered Leader, Mary Baker Eddy, in May 1884, while she was teaching the class in Chicago. In my first conversation with Mrs. Eddy, I was greatly impressed with these words: "Man is the image and likeness of God." Mrs. Eddy was the first Christian Scientist I ever saw, and I bought my first copy of *Science and Health* from her. It was then in the eighth edition, in two volumes. As she handed them to me, she said, "This is the same healing that Jesus did." In my search in reading the book to see how Jesus healed, I was perfectly healed of a complication of diseases.

In December 1884, I came to Boston to take the Primary class with Mrs. Eddy in the Massachusetts Metaphysical College at 571 Columbus Avenue. At that early date, she took more than two weeks for the twelve lessons, as she occasionally gave us a day between the lessons to digest or assimilate what she had given us.

Mrs. Eddy's insistence on handling error

In Mrs. Eddy's wonderful teaching of God and His creation, she had taken us up on the mountaintop, and when she began to teach us about the error—animal magnetism— we did not want to hear it. I recall the morning when she asked one of the class to tell her how she would handle a belief of disease. The student affirmed the [t]ruth, and Mrs. Eddy said, "If it did not yield, what would you do?" The student answered, "Oh, but it would yield!" Mrs. Eddy smiled and said, "We will suppose it did not yield. Wouldn't you handle animal magnetism?" Then she asked another the same question and received the same answer, and she again asked, "Wouldn't you handle animal magnetism?" Then she said to the class, "I want every one of you to say these words, 'animal magnetism.'" It was time for the class to close, and she said, "We shall continue this lesson tomorrow."

The next morning, when she came into the classroom, she said, "I have told God this morning that I will make you understand animal magnetism if I keep you here two weeks longer. Animal magnetism is the name God gave me to give to you by which to handle the error; it covers all error; it is malicious now because it is fighting the Truth." She then said, "Handle this first in your treatment."

Our Leader's healing practice

One member of the class asked Mrs. Eddy if she might tell what happened when she went with her to buy some chairs. Mrs. Eddy said she might, and she told the following story. She went with Mrs. Eddy to a furniture store to help her select some dining room chairs. The clerk who waited on them had a bandage over one eye. Mrs. Eddy seemed absorbed in thought while they were being shown the chairs and, when asked which she liked best, said, "Anything we can sit on, dear." The student told the clerk they would decide and let him know the next day. When questioned about the chairs, Mrs. Eddy said, "Could I buy chairs from a man with his eye tied up?" When the student went back the next morning, the clerk said, "Who was the lady with you yesterday? When you came in, I had an abscess on my eye, and when you went out, I removed the bandage and there was nothing left of it."

Mrs. Eddy told me she was called to treat a child. When she went in, the mother was holding it and thought it had passed on. Mrs. Eddy said, "Let me take the babe." She did, and the mother went into the next room. In about ten minutes, she put the child down and it walked toward the door. Mrs. Eddy opened the door, and when the mother saw the child walking (it had never walked before), she screamed and the babe sat down, and Mrs. Eddy said, "I saw I had another patient on my hands."

Mrs. Eddy said, "If my students would come to me in the right thought, I would pour right out to them, but they come to me with their thoughts filled with sin, sickness, and death, and it shuts me right off." I remembered these words when Mrs. Eddy invited me to visit her and my sister at Pleasant View, and for weeks before I went, I worked to clear my thought of a sad experience. A few days after I arrived, while Mrs. Eddy was talking with me so sweetly, she suddenly stopped and, in a very sharp voice, said, "What do I feel in your thought?" I answered, "I don't know, Mrs. Eddy. What is it? What is it?" She paused a moment and then, in her usual sweet voice, said, "Well, dear, I feel a sense of sorrow, of grief, and I don't want to feel it there." I was healed and learned a great lesson.

Notes taken over the years

Editor's note: with the exception of the first entry, these notes are not dated:

+ Mother's lesson in the morning, August 15, 1903: God knows that I live. I am not in the body and the body cannot talk to me.

This, she told me, was the way to escape from the belief of pain and flesh.

+ Mother[7] called us and told us the secret of Christian Science healing was in these words, "All things are possible with God."

And another time she said, The rule for healing is "All things are possible to God, and He worketh with you to will and to do of His good pleasure" [see Philippians 2:13].

In treating, be sure to cover the lie which says you make your patient worse instead of better. Truth has all effects for good, and the lie has no effects but to destroy itself.

+ "Do not give [l]ife to evil by attaching [it] to person or thing; it cannot live without a body. Man is immortal one. Evil cannot attach itself to man, and you deceive yourself when you believe that it can." M.B. Eddy

✦ "Hypnotism cannot touch the minds of the world or us to stir up one element of discord. It is not in the focal distance of God, and therefore *is not*, for God is infinite." M.B.E.

✦ God, good, Spirit is ever present, and man is His image and likeness. Mother said this was a rule that would solve every problem.

✦ Every lying argument of hypnotism, Theo[sophy], esoteric magic, etc., is reversed in its effect. Guard this statement of [t]ruth by knowing that it cannot be reversed. Their arguments bless us and do us good because the reversal of them does us good, and "All things shall work together for good to those that love God" [see Romans 8:28]. M.B.G.E.

✦ Mrs. Eddy said, What is Atonement? "It is the self-sacrifice that finds the way for others through the experience that meets and overcomes the error and then shows this way to others who have slept to save them a similar experience."

✦ Mrs. Eddy said, "Evil, disease, or poison cannot be poured into our thought when we are asleep to be brought out in action when we awake."

JANETTE E. WELLER *(1840–1925)*

*Born in Lyman, New Hampshire, Janette Gibson
lived only a few years in her parents' home before they
separated and she and her siblings were scattered. Weller
was sent to live with her father's sister in Lyman. She
may also have lived for a while with relatives as far away
as Illinois. After finishing high school in Littleton, New
Hampshire, Weller spent two spring terms at an academy
in Vermont, but by the time she was 17, she was on her
own. She taught school for a while in Littleton and then,
at age 20, began working for a tailor there. She learned
quickly, becoming a skilled seamstress.*

*In 1861, Weller married Copeland Franklin George
Weller, a painter, coach, and photographer. Their
daughter, Fontenella, was born in 1867; then Weller's
husband passed on in 1877. Three years later, she and
her daughter were living in a boarding house in Littleton.
Also residing there was Fred Robinson, whom Weller
married in 1882.*

Janette Weller Robinson learned of Christian Science in 1884 and was quickly healed of a decades-long struggle with tuberculosis after three weeks of reading Science and Health; with a Key to the Scriptures.[8] *She met Mary Baker Eddy in Boston that spring and took Primary class from her in September. Robinson then took the Obstetrics class from Eddy in 1887 and a Normal class from her in 1889. Just before the Normal class, Robinson was listed in* The Christian Science Journal *as a practitioner in Littleton, but that year and the next, she traveled, helping to establish Christian Science in Philadelphia, Pennsylvania, and Binghamton, New York, as well as in Littleton. In 1890, Robinson's husband filed for divorce, and the proceedings turned into an attack on Christian Science. Robinson moved to Spokane, Washington, where her daughter, now married, was living. While there, Robinson helped establish Christian Science and taught her first class.*

Soon after her daughter and infant granddaughter passed on in 1892, Robinson went back to using her first married name (Weller) and lived for the most part in Littleton until called by Eddy to Boston. Weller worked for several months from late 1896 to early 1897 in Eddy's home putting her seamstress skills to use and creating clippings of Eddy's Journal *articles as part of the preparation for publishing* Miscellaneous Writings: 1883–1896. *Following her service to Eddy, Weller remained in the Boston area working as a Christian Science practitioner.*

The Human Side of Mrs. Eddy

JANETTE E. WELLER

In March 1884, I first heard of Christian Science and its healing work. I immediately purchased a copy of the seventh edition of *Science and Health*, by Mary B. G. Eddy, and read it through carefully, giving most of my time for three weeks to its study. I had not heard that the reading of the book healed the sick, but before these three weeks had passed, I awoke to find that all the claims of disease and pain from which I had suffered for more than twenty years had vanished and that I was free as a bird. I was about to visit Boston, and after my experience while reading *Science and Health*, my greatest desire was to meet and converse with its author. Soon after arriving in Boston, I called at her home, 571 Columbus Avenue. I had previously heard, through one of Mrs. Eddy's students, that she received no callers except by appointment. But as this student was living with Mrs. Eddy at the time, I told the maid who answered the doorbell that I wished to see Miss Blank.

The maid replied, "She is not in."

I then asked if I might see Mrs. Eddy.

"Have you an appointment?" the maid inquired.

Of course, I said, "No."

Without the least hesitancy and quite firmly, she said, "Then you cannot see her."

Then I asked what time Miss Blank would be in, and the maid replied that she did not know, for Miss Blank was out of the city. My hopes of an interview seemed shattered, and I stood on the steps hesitatingly, waiting, trying to think what to do next, when the maid, evidently realizing my keen disappointment, said, "You might see some of the others."

Having heard of but two Christian Scientists, the student whom I had met and the author of the wonderful book *Science and Health*, which had healed me, I quickly asked, "Who's here?"

The maid then gave the names of three or four persons who were there for the purpose of receiving callers. As I knew nothing of any of them, I repeated one of the names which she had spoken and was shown into the back parlor, the only occupant of which was the aforesaid gentleman. He seemed pleasant and kind, and I suppose that he answered all my questions, but I never remembered a word that he said except that I could not see Mrs. Eddy unless by appointment and that her orders were particularly strong that she should not be disturbed on that day. I then asked if they had a picture of her and was told that there was a good crayon portrait of her in the front room which I might see when I [left]. I made quite an extended call, but at last ceased my questioning and arose to go.

Mrs. Eddy's study was on the floor above, directly over the front parlor. As we proceeded along the hall, a portion of which separated the front from the back parlor, I said to him, "I want to see that picture," and he opened the parlor door and stepped over the threshold into the room. Halting, he said smilingly, "Beg pardon; I did not know you were here."

"Walk right in," said Mrs. Eddy, rising.

"But I have a lady here who is anxious to see you," said he.

I was close behind him and already in the room. Mrs. Eddy, coming forward with her right hand extended, grasped mine with much warmth of welcome and these words: "What a power of mind it was that brought me downstairs. I was at my desk, writing as busily as ever I was in my life when, suddenly, I laid aside my pen, came down here, and waited—I did not know what for."

Today I can recall little of that detailed conversation but know that it largely pertained to sickness. Mrs. Eddy inquired of what I had been healed, and I rehearsed to her something of my long struggle with fears of consumption. I was proceeding rather minutely when Mrs. Eddy startled me with the following remark, which she emphasized with an emphatic tapping of her foot upon the floor: "If mortal mind had said that you breathed with your *toes*, you'd have breathed with your toes."

Out of that day's conversation with Mrs. Eddy, this was almost the only statement which has always remained with me. However, I do know surely that, as I was coming away, she said to me, "I shall book you for my next class, which will convene about the first of September." I was also told of the Sunday services which were held at the Massachusetts Metaphysical College, which was likewise her home, and Mrs. Eddy invited me to attend the next regular service on the first Sunday in May 1884.

Formal instruction from Mrs. Eddy

One Saturday morning, I received a telegram which read, "Come to class which convenes at the College Tuesday morning at 10 o'clock." I was there promptly.

569 and 571 Columbus Avenue, Boston, home of the Massachusetts Metaphysical College

Besides myself, there were only eight others in that class. The class included twelve lessons, and we met on Sunday just as upon weekdays. Upon that day, Mrs. Eddy gave us the spiritual interpretation of the first chapter of John.

During the five months that had intervened between my first introduction to Mrs. Eddy and my call to the class the following [September], I gave most of my spare time to the study of *Science and Health*. The more I read, the more I wanted to read. In fact, I literally hungered and thirsted for the righteousness which is taught so simply, and made so practical, on every page of that inspired book. Several times during the summer, people almost *accusingly* acknowledged to me that I had made them feel better, curing them of headaches and so forth, while I conversed with them. These experiences puzzled me, for I had no idea how to apply what I had been reading to the healing of sickness, [so] when I was really summoned to class, my joy was great.

I think it was at the close of the eighth or ninth lesson that Mrs. Eddy said to the class, "Now, you all know somebody who is sick, and I want you to heal a case of sickness before the next lesson, which will be on the day after tomorrow."

The friend with whom I was staying had made frequent complaints, and I said to myself, "There's my case." After I had reached her home and had had my dinner, I repaired to my room to go to work and was immediately confronted with the fact that Mrs. Eddy had given the class eight lessons and had not yet told us how to heal the sick or even said anything about sickness. So, what was I to do in such a dilemma? Then I began to recall what she *had* talked of during those eight lessons and found that it had all been about God and His image and likeness, man, and that there was no sickness in *either* of *them*. My patient quickly responded to that realization and was healed.

A surprising discovery

One day in class, I asked if it were possible that what little I had learned from reading *Science and Health* the previous summer had really destroyed the result of an accident—a blow on a man's forehead from the butt of an ax—and Mrs. Eddy replied earnestly, "Certainly; always give credit to Truth." I called this man by name, Mr. Patterson, as I asked the question, and after she had answered, Mrs. Eddy said, "Was that man a dentist?"

I replied, "No, but there used to be a man by that name who was a dentist in that town."

Then she remarked, "I heard that he is dead."

At once I thought to myself, "Now, here's someone who knows that man. If I have an opportunity, I'll ask Mrs. Eddy about him."

That opportunity came after the close of the class, when we were all in Mrs. Eddy's study, where she was herself attending to the receiving of the payment from the students. Sometime during the transaction of this business, it came to me to tell Mrs. Eddy that I wanted to know something about this man. In reply, she said to me that after teaching a class and having her thought so filled with the Truth, she did not like to come down to commonplace or unpleasant matters. [A little later] she inquired of me, "Can you come to see me tomorrow?"

Ten o'clock [the next day] found me at her door. We were soon seated in the parlor, and Mrs. Eddy at once asked me to tell her what people had thought of Dr. Patterson. I answered truthfully that he had done many puzzling things which had aroused suspicion regarding his morality. Mrs. Eddy had asked me only three or four questions when she made the astounding statement, "He was my husband."

I have no words to express the feelings that I had. The association of those two persons together caused such a revulsion of feeling that it seemed to me I could not hear more. When Mrs. Eddy saw how I felt, she said, "If it had not been for that man, I should never have given the world Christian Science."

Mrs. Eddy [also] talked of her childhood. She told me of the mysterious calls which she had heard. This was in 1884, years before she wrote down these experiences in *Retrospection and Introspection* [see pp. 8–9]. She said that she had become so accustomed to these voices that she had ceased to heed them; but going to her mother one day, [after having] been in another room with her cousin Mehitable Huntoon, who had also heard the call, she said, "Mitty heard it this time, Mother."

When her mother told Mary to answer on the next occasion of hearing these voices, as had the infant Samuel, Mrs. Eddy recalled that she had said, "Then I'll die, won't I, Mama?" And Mrs. Baker, probably fearful herself, had reassured the child as well as she could. Recalling the day when she did, at last, answer as her mother had told her to, waiting until the call came a third time, Mrs. Eddy said to me, "I have no *words* to describe *what* I saw, but I saw heaven."

My start as a Christian Science practitioner

On the following Saturday I returned home. I began at once my healing work, as was Mrs. Eddy's wish. She had said that her instruction was to enable us to "go into the world and heal the sick."

In January, following my class instruction in Boston, Mrs. Eddy wrote me this letter:

571 Columbus Avenue

Boston, Mass.

Jan. 26, 1885

My dear Student:

Do you find any difficulty in healing? If so, strike for the higher sense of the *nothingness* of *matter*. Do not care to search into causation there, for there is no cause and no effect in matter; *all is Mind*, perfect and eternal. Whenever you treat a patient, include in your understanding of the case that no ignorant or malicious mind can affect the case and there *is no relapse*. Science tells us this in all it manifests. *Progress* is the law of the Infinite, and finite views [are] but supposition and belief. Now *realize* this, and be a law to every case—when you commence treating it—that there is but *one Mind* and this one governs your patient; that there are no *minds* to interfere. Error is not *Mind*, has *no power* over *you* or the patient. These are the rules for you to work out every hour of your life. Realize constantly that no mortal mind (so-called) can affect you or make you believe you cannot *cure* your patients. There is *no malice, no envy, no will power;* all is Love and Truth. *Argue this* clearly.

Lovingly yours,
M.B.G. Eddy

Thanksgiving with Mrs. Eddy

It was my privilege to have many pleasant and profitable interviews with Mrs. Eddy. On one visit to Boston, about one or two or three years after I first took class instruction from her, I called at the [Massachusetts Metaphysical] College, and Mrs. Eddy invited me to take Thanksgiving dinner with her, telling me that her guests would consist of a sister-in-law, the widow of her eldest brother, Samuel, a Reverend Mr. Gill, his wife and little daughter, and myself. This Orthodox clergyman was a recent student of hers and at that time was preaching for her and also assisting her in editing *The Christian Science Journal*.

After partaking of a good New England Thanksgiving dinner, we retired to the parlor, and I was much interested in the conversation which was carried on between Mrs. Eddy and the clergyman. He was constantly plying her with questions from a theological standpoint, but he never seemed to grasp her metaphysical statements. Suddenly she turned to him as they were sitting on the sofa and said, "Brother Gill, you will *never* understand these things until you heal the sick."

That remark struck home to me, for I saw that *that* was a vital point in Christian Science, not only to the Reverend Mr. Gill but to myself and to every other student of the Science.

On three other occasions, I dined with Mrs. Eddy at

Pleasant View on Thanksgiving Day. Once there were five others there besides myself; none of us had homes of our own, and she playfully called us "orphans" whom she had "called to Mother's home for dinner." The conversation was of a general social nature, and we had a merry time.

Letters concerning the Cause

The following letter from Mrs. Eddy, which I received in 1887, proves that she was not only willing but eager that her students should be able to take up the work which she had started and carry it on—that she was not arbitrary and insistent upon doing everything herself, as has sometimes been imagined.

Massachusetts Metaphysical College

571 Columbus Avenue

Boston, Mass.

March 23, 1887

My dear Student and your Students:

The tender testimonial from you and my native state fills me with gratitude, and sympathy so generous encourages me to press on still in the thickest of the battle that has been a war of *21 years*. Am I not a veteran[,] and ought not I to have a place more serene on the retired list, and you that are willing, hardy soldiers to fill my place?

Our Father is keeping guard over these hours. He knows them only to reach them by the eternal law of right and justice. His laws and His love sustain us.

With tender regard, thanks, and a prayer
for blessing on you all, I am most sincerely
yours,

M.B.G. Eddy

Come all of you to our National C.S.A. in Boston.[9]

The Christian Science pathway, while leading heavenward, is not always strewn with flowers, and like all other religious denominations, its followers are not always of the same
mind. At one time a difference in opinions and methods of
work arose between two students with whom I happened to
be associated, and while affairs were being adjusted, I received
the following letter from Mrs. Eddy, which brings out some
of the many wonderful characteristics of her mentality:

> Massachusetts Metaphysical College
> 571 Columbus Avenue
> Boston, Mass.
> August 5, 1888

My darling Student:

What a great matter a little fire kindleth.
What an unruly member is the tongue—what a
mischievous thing is the pen if not governed in
wisdom. Both these students are *peculiar*; both
have their good qualities. One is over-anxious
about her own—or what she claims; the other is
naturally prone to step on people's toes. Both are
doing good. I have not my eyes closed, as one of
them represents; I see what I seldom say I see....
She has done nobly in the midst of the last overt

acts of seceders and kept straight all the way.

Now, dear, this is my advice: Associate with all my good students. Help each other. In union is strength. But it is best not to take the opinion of any student on points of Science, especially when they concern your happiness at home. A loss of affection is a great evil. A wife can lead the element of love up higher from the basement into the upper chamber. Let God alone direct here. This unfortunate affair between these two is another put-up job, to end as the others have ended by setting one or the other apart from me because I will not abuse either one. You have so much good sense that you will do justice in the end, so much Christianity that God will guide you and all will come out right. Darling, good-bye. Father, keep thine own.

M.B.G. Eddy

The discord referred to above extended over some months, and later there followed another letter, [excerpted] below:

Massachusetts Metaphysical College
571 Columbus Avenue
Boston, Mass.
November 9, 1888

My dear Student:

Was rejoiced to hear from you in the way you wrote. To leave all for Christ is leaving *nothing* and finding *all*. Keep out of your reading all that worketh or maketh a lie; then you will be forming the right human concept of the diviner life and love. In no other way can this be done. I wish you would get those letters of dear Miss _____ and see that they are burned up, and then let the dead bury the dead....

I am building up fast again in Boston. The last Christian Science Association was the best conducted one by the students we ever had. The first meeting this autumn, I put as many new members into the Christian Science Association as the error had taken out.

Lovingly,
M.B.G. Eddy

Mrs. Eddy's generosity and gratitude

I attended the Obstetrics class [in 1887] and the following May was called to the Normal class. I had no money to pay my tuition for the latter and so gave Mrs. Eddy my note instead. And whenever I could spare a few dollars, I sent them to her. I kept no account of my payment, but when I had paid the face of the note, she sent it to me receipted. Until then I was not aware that I had paid even the principal and, of course, was much surprised that she had exacted no interest of me, for I knew she was far from wealthy in those days. *Science and Health* was then in its eighteenth edition, and that was her only book; no other appeared until seven years later. However, I said to myself, "She'll get that interest some time, if it's possible for me to pay it."

The opportunity came in the autumn of 1893, when I sold my home in New Hampshire and received the money for it. I well remember how happy I felt when I immediately computed the interest on the note and sent a check for it to Mrs. Eddy. The following letter expressed her appreciation of that transaction:

Pleasant View
Concord, N.H.
Dec. 23, 1893

My beloved Student:

Will you pardon me for forgetting to answer your letter that gave me great pleasure, and thanking you beyond words for such conscientiousness when I by no means required it of you.

Well, such signs are most encouraging and rare. I do thank God for your prosperity and am not in the least surprised at it. He tried you in the fire. He loves to deliver [H]is children from the depths. He chooses them not in worldly prosperity, but in the midst of affliction. Thus has He accepted you, dear one. Oh, praise Him and follow this Divine Love closely, and watch and wait thankfully and joyfully on all His providences. Wishing you much joy at this and all seasons.

Yours ever lovingly,
Mary B.G. Eddy

Personal trials and spiritual growth

I returned to my home in March, as I was notified that my husband had sued for divorce. I had no wish to oppose him but, being entirely ignorant of the law in such cases, was induced to attend the first hearing that I might learn on what grounds he based his claims for separation. But, alas, I soon learned that I had unwittingly committed myself as his opponent and for seven days was compelled to listen to strange tales by good neighbors and former friends, every one of whom testified that they "had nothing to say against this woman until she took up this Science business." Often I was cross-examined on the doctrines of Christian Science and was several times asked to tell the court (and all the townspeople who could get into the courtroom) how I gave mental treatments to sick persons. I gladly acquiesced in this requirement and earnestly hoped that someone in the audience might see and accept the Christliness of Christian Science and be blessed thereby.

During these years, I was constantly tormented with a burning desire to be justified before the world. It seemed to me that I could not endure to be misjudged and misunderstood. This intense longing for self-justification kept up for many months [until], suddenly at a Sunday service, the thought came to me that *my* justification would mean *another's* condemnation, and a new light dawned in my consciousness. I was then and there convinced that a desire for self-justification was the highest sense of revenge one could entertain.

When I told Mrs. Eddy this, she replied that my

conclusions were correct, and she emphasized her statement with many helpful and illuminating thoughts along this point. She comforted me once by saying, "I am afraid of a Christian Scientist who is never sick, for if he is doing his work, he will have plenty to meet."

Fourth of July at Pleasant View

The following invitation was joyfully accepted:

> Pleasant View
> Concord, N.H.
> July 2, 1895

Mrs. Weller: My dear Student:

Come and see me on July 4th. Take the 9 o'clock train.

Yours truly,
M.B. Eddy

This visit with Mrs. Eddy on that July 4th was one of the pleasantest of my whole experience. She was very happy over the completion of The Mother Church building, which had been dedicated the previous January. Also, her first public address given in The Mother Church, May 26, 1895 (see *Miscellaneous Writings: 1883–1896*, pp. 106–110), had been most kindly received by her Church, and the press had widely quoted it. In fact, Christian Science was in a most prosperous condition. After dinner, we retired to the library, and I remember distinctly how firmly she made this declaration: "Christian Science is the last revelation that will ever come to humanity. It has come now in books and is established in the world, and it can never be destroyed."

Ready forgiveness and genuine appreciation

The following letter indicates how careful Mrs. Eddy always was to be perfectly just; in fact, she literally "ran to meet" every repentant one who had wandered from the fold of Christian Science:

> Pleasant View
> Concord, N.H.
> October 24, 1895

My dear[,] dear Student:

> Oh, let us bury out of sight all error. I am sorry for what was said of two persons. God will care for them, and a letter from one of them indicates repentance and reform. I love your habit of saying nothing of anyone unless you can say some good of them. This I so love to do. But it is not always apparent at the moment how much needs to be said to save others, or how little. Bury the dead[,] and let us love those that hate us and despitefully use us. Know in your argument that _____ cannot harm your practice or hinder it. You must not treat her for this; only treat yourself.

With love,
Mother M.B. Eddy[10]

No one could appreciate or express more gratitude for favors than did Mrs. Eddy, as is shown by the following letters:

Pleasant View
Concord, N.H.
March 29, 1896

My precious Student:

When you were last here, you seemed so
near my heart that I did not need to speak
to you. This is a phenomenon that always,
since I discovered Science, has followed me
in Science. When a student comes to see me
and I find them so right, if anyone else is with
them, I can only talk to them that are not so
clear; but if I followed my inclination, I should
turn to the one that is needing me less and
give my attention there where I could rest.
My life is made up of self-sacrifices. I only
seem to achieve the little that I do accomplish, not for myself, but for the students.

Pleasant View
Concord, N.H.
April 23, 1897

My precious Student:

For your dear letter I thank you and take
courage. Press on; the rest in labor is sweet
and the journey is long.

With love, Mother
M.B. Eddy

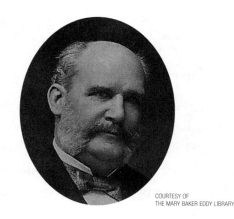

CAPTAIN JOSEPH S. EASTAMAN *(1836–1910)*

*The son of a sea captain, Joseph Eastaman was born at sea
en route from Spain to St. Andrew, Louisiana, near New
Orleans. (His parents were returning from a visit to his
mother's family.) By age ten, Eastaman was working on
his father's ship as a cabin boy; he continued working in
various capacities for his father and other captains until
he became a captain himself at the age of twenty-one.
For nearly thirty years, Eastaman commanded ships at
sea, overcoming difficulties of all sorts through reliance
on God. He wrote of these exploits in a series entitled
"The Travail of My Soul," published across five issues of*
The Christian Science Journal.[11] *This reminiscence is
excerpted from that series.*

*Eastaman married in 1870, and he and his wife, Mary,
who was severely ill for much of their early married life,
set up house in Chelsea, Massachusetts. When Eastaman
returned from sea in 1884 and found his wife near
death, he learned of Christian Science and sought help*

in person from Mary Baker Eddy. She encouraged him to enroll in her upcoming Primary class to learn how to heal his wife himself. He attended the class, which began December 22, 1884, and after the first week of instruction, he began treating his wife through prayer. She improved dramatically and took class with Eddy a few months later. Soon afterward, Eastaman's wife was completely healed and became a Christian Science practitioner and later a teacher.

Eastaman had planned to return to sea, but at Eddy's encouragement, he opened an office as a Christian Science practitioner instead. In 1887, he took an Obstetrics class from Eddy and became a teacher; however, the primary focus of his life's work was healing. Eastaman was a member of the first Christian Science Board of Directors and was one of the original twelve First Members of The Mother Church.[12]

From Seafaring to Healing

CAPTAIN JOSEPH S. EASTAMAN

After an interval of five years, each month of which furnished material for a chapter by itself, I started on my way home from Peru to save, if possible, the life of my wife, who for six months had been very low and under the doctor's care. On my arrival, I found her much lower than I had supposed, and the consultation of physicians, immediately secured, only made it apparent that she could not live long. In anxiety and distress I then added my own knowledge of medicine—of necessity quite good to have enabled me so many years properly to care for both passengers and crews. This also failing to prove of use, my extremity was reached, and God's opportunity arrived.

One evening as I was sitting hopeless at my wife's bedside, a lady friend called and asked, "Captain, why don't you get a Christian Scientist to treat your wife?" To my inquiry as to what that was, she replied that she did not know but had heard that they healed many cases without medicine. "Anything that will heal my wife I will get, if it takes all I own in the world," I replied.

In the room, at the time, was my nephew who also was under medical treatment. At close of the lady's call, he exclaimed, "Uncle, if Christian Science is good for Manie, it must be good for me too!" I assented, and in a day or two his wife took him (he could not see his way) to a Scientist, under whose treatment he at once placed himself. His teeth, salivated by free use of mercurial remedies, had restricted him entirely to the use of a spoon-diet, but on his return from the first treatment, he gritted them together and exclaimed, "There, Uncle! I can eat something now." This renewed my determination to look into the matter, in spite of my wife's protests and fears that it was spiritualism. Accordingly, I accompanied him on his next visit to the Scientist's and myself had a talk with the healer.

At this interview I learned, for the first, the existence in Boston of a College whose president and principal, the Rev. Mary B. G. Eddy, was the Founder of Christian Science; also, that Christian Science was not for one or two chosen only, for other practitioners were to be found. To my nephew I said, "If this healer can do so much, his teacher must heal instantly. I will take you there; then when you are healed, Manie will see what it is, and I will get the Founder to come to the house and heal her." So, like a drowning man grasping at a straw, with alternating hopes and fears besieging me on the way, I led him to the College.

A gentle challenge from Mrs. Eddy

In answer to my request for a personal interview, Mrs. Eddy kindly granted us an extended audience, though to my appeal for help, she made the gentle announcement that she herself did not now take patients but had instructed students who were well qualified to heal. At this, my heart failed utterly, for I felt that none less than the Founder was equal to the healing necessary in our case. As I was about to leave, she turned to me and, with much earnestness, asked, "Captain, why don't you heal your wife yourself?" I stood spellbound. Never for one moment had the possibility of *my* becoming a healer dawned upon me. I did not know what to say, or think. Finally, I stammered out, "How can I heal my wife! Have I not procured the best medical aid—and, to leave nothing untried, added to that my own medical knowledge? What more can I do?" Gently she said, "Learn how to heal." Without hesitation, I returned to the parlor for particulars. It seemed, then, that it must require years of study to learn Christian Science, and she whom I was trying to save would not long be here, but when I heard that the entire term required but three weeks, I gathered courage and asked about tuition fees, which proved to be very reasonable. In twenty minutes more, I had arranged to enter the class about to open on the third day following.

My wife proved much averse to the plan, having, in addition to her fears with regard to spiritualism, due caution on account of the already heavy financial drain occasioned by her prolonged illness. I was ready to spend every dollar to save her, however, and continued firm in my resolve to go through the class. Thus, the 22nd of December 1884, ended "the travail of my soul" since it proved to be the day of my birth in Christian Science.

The class included many highly cultured people, all more or less conversant with the rudiments of Christian Science, while I, a sailor, with only a seaman's knowledge of the world, and no faintest inkling of the field to be opened up before me, felt very much out of place indeed. However, God had called me there, and I had long since been schooled to say, "Thy will be done." To that first and last and most important question, "What is God?," the students replied variously, according to their own thought or to the technicalities of *Science and Health*,[13] which I had not yet procured. When the question came to me, I stammered out, "God is all, with all and in all; everything that is good and pure—I don't know, but it is the very breath I draw." The teacher smiled encouragingly as my answers followed one after another, and I was strengthened to go on.

Every day during the term, questions were asked and answers made that puzzled me not a little, but to all of my own simple and earnest queries, the patient teacher replied clearly and satisfactorily. The many laughs enjoyed by the class at my expense did not trouble me, therefore; for evidently my teacher knew that I would not profess to understand when I did not. The simpler my questions, the more pains she took to explain clearly, and thus were brought forward and cleared up many points that otherwise might not have been touched upon. In consequence, that has been admitted to be one of the best classes, as a whole, that has ever graduated from the College. All, except one, went into active work in the Master's Cause, and the majority bid fair to remain "faithful to the end." For myself, I am sure I did not want Christian Science in part; I wanted every bit of it.

Immediate proofs of progress

How much was due to my own changed thought, I cannot tell, but after Christian Science was recognized in our home—even before I entered the College—my wife began to recover. Soon as I understood the rudiments, I began to treat her, and so quickly did she respond to the treatment that she was able to avail herself of the kind invitation of the teacher to accompany me to the final session. That one lesson dispelled her every doubt as to whether Christian Science had any kinship with mesmerism or spiritualism— for which she had strong antipathies. She became, then and there, a staunch friend to the Cause, eager to join the next class, that she too might become a Christian Scientist and help to bless mankind.

As to myself, I had always been temperate as to [the] use of both liquor and tobacco but was not a total-abstinence man. When [I was] about to enter [the] College, the president asked if I drank; I said, "Very seldom." Did I use tobacco? "Oh, yes!" I replied, "have done so from my boyhood." The next day, I was unaccountably dissatisfied with my choice brand of cigars, while the second day found all desire for tobacco completely and forever gone. Christian Science had healed me of the abnormal appetite for tobacco.

My start in the practice

Like most other students, I became at once very enthusiastic about Christian Science, and my naturally impulsive temperament added somewhat to it, no doubt. This impulsiveness often got me into [the] belief of trouble, but the discipline of Christian Science has brought me safely through thus far and will guide me all along. My first active efforts in the Cause, aside from healing my wife, were made among my personal acquaintances, ship owners, and merchants. In response to my friendly arguments, some let me relieve their suffering while others only laughed at me for enlisting in such foolishness. My first patient was a wealthy ship owner having complicated beliefs. He was happy over the success in getting rid of his ailments, but pride made him keep the good news to himself instead of aiding others by his experience. Next, however, he engaged me to treat his wife and daughter, who, on recovery, freely introduced me to their suffering friends. Here virtually, though I knew it not, began my practice.

In a few weeks, my wife had fully recovered; then, beginning to look about me for work, and not caring specially for marine service, I bethought me of an excellent offer made me on my way up from Peru, by the Panama R.R. Company. I accordingly engaged passage to Aspinwall but on the last day was reminded of a promise made [to] my teacher. I at once wrote her of my plans, asking if [they were] wise, and received immediate counsel not to go. Packed, and passage taken, here was a dilemma! Still, I was ready to be rightly guided and wrote again, asking what I should do. [Mrs. Eddy's] reply came: "Take an office."

This, certainly, was the last thing I should have thought of doing, for I could see no way to clear personal expenses, to say nothing of meeting the added rent in an essentially central location. However, the command had come, and the birthright in Christian Science required obedience— even though to me it did look like throwing away time and means. I dimly perceived that Christian Science was a "pearl of great price" and somehow felt I had to remain in it or sink, for often a "still small voice" told me, "Your prayer for so many years is granted; only be guided by Wisdom." This "prayer" had been the unconquerable longing to find on land some occupation that would benefit not only me but my fellow human beings. I could not disobey. Besides, since class, my former habitual despondency and forebodings had entirely passed away, and I had come to look on the bright side of things, so I set about office hunting.

Thanks to the kindly aid of a brother Scientist, I soon found just the place needed—and where I now have been for seven years. I at first wished to take it on trial, but a voice kept telling me that I would do better to take a lease for at least a year. I did as directed, and it is well I did, for mortal mind soon tried to drive me away, and apparently at times the obligations of the lease, only, held me firm. Christian Science at that time being comparatively a new method of healing, it is not strange that some months were required to establish a practice based upon justice as well as generosity, but work away I did, whether or no. Before the year was out, with no advertising except what my work gave me, I had all I could do.

Proving error's nothingness

About this time, I began to work upon the problem of how to meet and overcome the adversary, so needful for all to know. One who expects to remain in Christian Science practice will find it necessary to *work* out his own salvation. Unless faithfulness and energy are at the helm, there is and can be no permanent success. Each must diligently work, and watch his *own* work—not that of others—here as well as elsewhere, if he would succeed. I myself never worked so hard, even at stowing cargoes in the West India service, as during the past seven years, but I can say with equal sincerity, never did I find, in any other work, the abiding happiness that is mine in the service of suffering, sin-sick humanity.

I have proven beyond all doubt that errors of every sort, whether foolish or malicious, are cowards. An incident that occurred years ago, when I was [an] ordinary seaman on shipboard, and before I had ever heard of such a thing as mesmerism, shows the cowardliness of these claims so clearly, that I venture to give it.

A few days out on a trip from Havana to London, it was generally admitted by passengers and crew that our ship was haunted. Strange noises had been heard, and though we had none on board, a large black dog had distinctly been seen running about the deck at a certain hour in the evening, frightening some very badly. I saw it [along] with the rest and resolved to kill it, and so rid the ship of the disturbance. Two chums joined me in my watch, sitting in the passage where he was wont to pass before disappearing. After about four evenings [of] fruitless waiting, the dog again appeared at the usual hour and walked calmly over our legs, but when we each grabbed him, there was nothing in our arms! After an evening or two, the same thing was repeated, but this time I ran aft to catch it. The dog disappeared, as before, at the booby hatch, but one of the passengers, with elbows on the rail and face between his hands, stood laughing ready to burst. With no thought of the consequences or of what I was doing, I ran to him, put my large sailor's knife to his temple, and exclaimed: "If you don't stop these monkey tricks, I'll put this into you!" Astonished at the fearlessness of so young a lad, the man drew back and, without a word, entered the cabin—but that was the last of the dog and the noises.

It afterwards proved that lie was a mesmerist experimenting for his own amusement—being of the sort to have a good laugh *at* the fears of others instead of saving them *from* their fears, as Christian Scientists are taught and have enlisted to do. Of all my early experiences, this one most clearly represents the nothingness of error's claims, whatever their seeming magnitude. I have seen cancers, tumors, and insanity disappear before the sword of Truth as effectually and permanently as both the dog and the man before the sailor-lad's knife.

MARY F. EASTAMAN *(1848–1924)*

*A first-generation American, Mary Frances Barry
was born in Massachusetts. She was often ill not only
as a child but well into her adult years, including the
first fifteen years of her marriage to Captain Joseph
Eastaman, a sailor. The couple lived in Chelsea,
Massachusetts, though he was often at sea.*

*Joseph Eastaman visited Mary Baker Eddy in 1884 to
ask her help for his wife. Eddy recommended that he
take her Primary class instruction and learn how to
treat his wife himself, which he did. Under her husband's
treatment, Mary began to improve and took Primary
class from Eddy the following year. By that December,
both Eastamans were listed in* The Christian Science
Journal *as practitioners in Chelsea. In 1887, Mary
took Normal class from Eddy and became a Christian
Science teacher. She had always wanted to be a
schoolteacher but ill health had prevented it. When
Eddy learned this, she told Mary, "But now, dear,*

you are a teacher and will lead many into the paths of righteousness and peace."

In 1892, Mary Eastaman became one of the first twelve First Members of The Mother Church.[14] She and her husband moved to Somerville, Massachusetts, in 1896. Two years later, Eddy appointed Eastaman to the Bible Lesson Committee; she served in that capacity for twenty-four years, in addition to her work as a healer and teacher.

This selection interweaves excerpts from Eastaman's own reminiscence with those from an account she wrote about her husband.

Lives of Glad Devotion

MARY F. EASTAMAN

Captain Joseph S. Eastaman was born at sea a short time before the vessel that his father commanded arrived at New Orleans. His home was in St. Andrew, a suburb of New Orleans, where his father owned a plantation with a number of slaves.

Captain Eastaman's mother was the daughter of a Spanish gentleman, a ship broker in Barcelona, Spain. His father was a most devout Christian and a Presbyterian by faith. When he married, he promised to take his wife home once a year to visit her parents. He kept his promise, hence the reason for their son's birth at sea.

Having been left motherless at an early age, Joseph went to sea with his father until he was ten years old. He then started out as a cabin boy. Years passed, and at the age of twenty-one, he was a captain commanding a vessel. For nearly thirty years he held the position of captain, honored and respected for his integrity, honesty, and uprightness. His business ability was recognized by ship owners in Boston and other parts of the world and testified to in certificates and credentials presented by them. During all these years spent at sea, Captain Eastaman never lost a vessel nor a man—a most remarkable record.

On his way home from Valparaiso, [Chile], during his last voyage, Captain Eastaman stopped at Colon, then known as Aspinwall, a seaport on the Atlantic coast of Panama. There he was offered a position in a ship brokerage business. Upon reaching home, however, he found me critically ill, and consequently all business operations were temporarily suspended. The position referred to above remained open for his future acceptance.

Our introduction to Christian Science

The early years of my married life were saddened by frequent periods of extreme illness which increased as the years went on until, in October 1884 after an illness of several months, I patiently awaited the summons. My minister, who was away on his vacation, came many miles to see me. As he felt he could not make the journey again, he asked that my folks have someone else officiate when I passed on.

In this hour of greatest need, a friend asked my husband if he had ever heard of Christian Science. The friend did not know much about it but had heard of wonderful cures, one in particular in Chelsea. When asked to try Christian Science, I expressed the fear that it was not of God but some "ism" opposed to God's law and commandments.

A young man, a member of the family who was almost totally blind, decided to try Christian Science. He had been a year in this condition and was steadily growing worse. To protect his eyes, he wore a black bandage and a shade. He had been in a dark room for three months with blinds and shades closed and a heavy covering over the window. From strong medicines, his teeth had loosened so that he partook only of liquid nourishment. He was pronounced incurable by the best oculists in Boston. His wife led him to a Christian Science practitioner. He returned from the visit with teeth firmly set and ate the first meal [in] months. The healing of the eyes also began.

My husband sought Mrs. Eddy on Columbus Avenue and took the young man to her, hoping she would heal him instantaneously and then heal me. This proof he thought would cause me to believe. Mrs. Eddy replied that she took no patients. Crushed and burdened with sorrow, he turned to go. Mrs. Eddy called him back and asked, "Why not study Christian Science and heal your wife?" She explained about class teaching, the length of term, and the price. My husband replied, "Do you think that I could learn it?"

"Yes," she replied, "but I must ask you three questions."

The following questions were asked, and my husband answered them:

"Do you love God?" (I do.)

"Do you use alcohol in any form?"

(I do not.)

"Do you use tobacco?" (Yes, I smoke.)

To the last, Mrs. Eddy replied, "That appetite will be taken away." Truly enough, from the first day he entered class, the desire never returned.

Persuaded by Christ, Truth

Class opened December 22, 1884. Meantime my husband kept urging me, and I consented to try a practitioner. I did not continue because the lady who called could give no light on the Scriptures as to the truth of Christian Science, and as I had been a lover of the Bible from early childhood, I could not accept what she offered. [With her] simply repeating that God never made sin, sickness, or death, and giving no foundation or hope on which to build, I could not continue.

One day while visiting me, she placed a copy of *The Christian Science Journal* on my bed. When alone, I found that glorious hymn [that begins] "Saw ye my Saviour," written by our beloved and revered Leader, Mary Baker Eddy. A great peace and sense of joy came to me. I said, "This must be of God because they believe in Jesus." My attitude of thought changed but not sufficiently to have help.

At the end of the first week of study, Mrs. Eddy told my husband to begin work and to report to her. Knowing his purity and goodness of character, I was willing to accept his help. These were testing times, a trial of faith, but I persevered, and a change was soon evident. Gradually the healing continued, and the light began to dawn upon my consciousness that the healing power of Christ had returned to bless mankind.

In the earlier days, Mrs. Eddy gave two Sunday talks to her students. The last Sunday, she asked my husband to [bring] me. As I had not been on the street for months, it seemed impossible. Truth impelled me so strongly I couldn't resist the desire to go. I was too weak to stand up to be dressed, but, dressed in a chair with the aid of my mother and husband, I made ready to go. With great difficulty I made the journey, walking very slowly up two flights of stairs. At the proper time, the teacher entered the room. I looked at her and a sense of joy filled my entire being.

I heard the words, "This is God's message to this age," and I rested in God's love and promises. I state here, now, and forever that never in thirty-four years has even a shadow of doubt come to my consciousness that our beloved and revered Leader and teacher was called and chosen by God to bring to weary sinning humanity the promised comfort which Jesus said should come and which has come and which we know and have proved to be Christian Science. The return home was made with less effort, and instead of going to bed, I ate with the family. It seemed like a miracle to them, but I had heard the words spoken from heaven-enthroned harmony and beheld God's messenger. Therefore I knew what had wrought the mighty change. My nephew was entirely healed of blindness and lives today rejoicing in what the [t]ruth did and has done in his family during the past thirty-four years.

My husband's devotion to Truth

Mrs. Eddy quickly recognized the spiritual status of her student, Captain Eastaman, and realizing that with the return of my health he would, no doubt, be asked to take up the work previously offered him, requested him at the close of the class not to accept any business offer without first consulting her. The promise was readily given.

The necessity for decision soon presented itself. Accordingly, one day during my convalescence, he referred to the possibility of soon being able to accept the position awaiting him. I asked him if he had consulted Mrs. Eddy. He replied that he would do so at once. In the course of the interview, Mrs. Eddy replied, "I wish you to take an office and enter the practice of Christian Science healing." Obedient to her command, he took an office at No. 3 Park Street, which office he held until he passed onward and upward.

In the early days patients were not plentiful, and many had no money with which to pay. Our financial resources were greatly reduced, and it seemed at times as though some other work was needed that would add somewhat to the necessary income without interfering with the practice of Christian Science. During this time, Captain Eastaman was offered three different positions by the United States Department of Customs in Boston, Massachusetts. He did not consider the first two, but the third was very lucrative, would permit of his being at home, and was just what he wanted. Desiring to accept it, he wrote to Mrs. Eddy. She replied:

> My Beloved Student,
>
> No, a thousand times no. Better be a doorkeeper in the house of the Lord than to dwell in the tents of wickedness.[15]
>
> Affectionately your teacher,
> Mary Baker Eddy

In response to this admonition he rose higher in the understanding and demonstration of Christian Science. Captain Eastaman applied himself prayerfully to the problem which confronted him. In speaking of this experience, he says:

> I entered my office one afternoon, opened *Science and Health with Key to the Scriptures* by Mary Baker Eddy to the platform of Christian Science (see pp. 330–340), and spent two hours in prayerful study.

Words cannot do justice to the illumination which followed. I soon had ample proof of the fact that the demonstration was made. My practice increased rapidly, and the Scripture, "Seek ye first the kingdom of heaven and its righteousness, and all these things will be added unto you," was certainly fulfilled [see Matthew 6:33].

Captain Eastaman always said that he worked for one-third of his patients for love, expecting no remuneration but rejoicing in their healing and acceptance of Christian Science. In after years, as God had prospered them, the expressions of gratitude, monetary and otherwise, from many of these patients [were] very gratifying and beautiful. He never hesitated to sow the seed and leave the rest to God.

My turn to learn and practice the truth

In February 1885, Mrs. Eddy desired me to enter her class and learn more fully the truth of Christian Science teaching. At that time I was not fully healed, but longing to see again the teacher that I believed was sent from God, I made [the] effort to be present at the opening of the class. Words cannot express my joy at the wonderful revelations of the Scriptures that followed day after day until the close of class. My questions were answered regarding different portions of the Scriptures, and one day, no longer able to contain my sense of gratitude, I said to Mrs. Eddy, "Surely this is sitting together in heavenly places in Christ Jesus" [see Ephesians 2:6]. She made no reply but gave me such a look of ineffable peace that I can never forget it.

Days passed, class closed, and our beloved Leader and

teacher placed her hand on my shoulder and, looking into the very depths of my heart, said, "You have your armor on and are ready to go forth." To me those words came as a divine summons and benediction, and I felt I dared not disobey, although I had fully determined never to take up the practice of Christian Science for the reason that I had been reared in a conservative manner and did not enjoy meeting people. [During class] I had been fully convinced of the absolute truthfulness of Christian Science and understood that God was omnipresent and ever present, the author of all good; that He must be understood, adored, and demonstrated by healing the sick and sinful according to the teaching of Christ Jesus; and that the promised Comforter was Christian Science, which could be and would be proved by every honest, sincere, faithful follower of our revered Leader, our teacher, Mary Baker Eddy.

To my surprise, when called to the first case, I went with joyful step. My patient, a man lying perfectly helpless, at times suffering great agony, had had three physicians. After the second day, there was no return of pain. He had been allowed no food except milk. I asked him if he would eat if a meal was prepared for him. He looked doubtful but said, "If you think I can eat, I will try." The day following, his wife said that he hadn't eaten. The reason I found out was that the steak was not good. The family, being poor, had not been able to pay for a better quality. After doing my metaphysical work for him, I surprised my mother by asking her to prepare a plateful of dinner for my patient. I returned with stuffed roast veal, mashed turnip, potato, and bread and butter. He ate it all with evidence of real enjoyment. In ten days he was back at work and during that time never lacked proper nourishment.

When that patient was healed, I most willingly and unreservedly gave myself to God and the work of Christian Science. I can plainly recall my attitude of thought as I voiced audibly, "This is God's work, and I am ready for it."

Many years have passed since then, and, if necessary, pages could be written and testimonies given of the work of the early students of Mrs. Eddy, but the same Truth is here today, and the holy, sacred work continues—healing the sick, giving comfort to the sorrowing, and reforming the sinful. Surely nothing but the power of God, as taught in Christian Science by our beloved Leader, could do the mighty works that have been done, that continue to be done, and that will continue until every child of God comes home to the true home, divine Mind where naught can enter "that defileth, neither whatsoever worketh abomination, or maketh a lie," for God is All-in-all [Revelation 21:27].

The Captain's love for our Leader

Captain Eastaman received instruction from our beloved Leader, Mary Baker Eddy, in the Primary, Normal, and Obstetrics classes and became a teacher of Christian Science as well as a practitioner. He was actively associated with the Cause of Christian Science during the early years of the movement, serving as a director of The Mother Church, apart from the healing and teaching work. Later, at the request of Mrs. Eddy, he gave himself up wholly to the healing work. In asking him to do this, she said, "It is not that I do not wish to have you continue what you have been doing, but we need healing, and you are the one who is doing the healing."

Captain Eastaman's great love for our beloved and

revered Leader, Mary Baker Eddy, and the Cause of Christian Science with its attendant blessings, as well as his inherent spirituality, are best described in the following letter written by him to Mrs. Eddy in July 1910:

> Boston, July 1, 1910
>
> Rev. Mary Baker Eddy
>
> My Precious Teacher,
>
> You and your priceless teaching in Christian Science have been, are, and will ever be present in my thoughts to keep me in remembrance of the many blessings I have received from God through Christian Science. I write these few lines to my dear Teacher and friend, not to keep dates, times, and seasons, but to acknowledge you as my best friend and guide and to thank you over and over again for the many good advices you have given me. You told me more than twenty-five years ago to take an office and to go to work on Christian Science healing. I did as you told me and took this room on lease. It is just twenty-five years today since I began the most holy work (to my sense), and, oh, Beloved Teacher, how many are the people that I have been the instrument to heal and help in that time, and how many are the people that are living in comparative health today who were given up by the medical profession and through my efforts

in Christian Science to save them are today
well and praising God for Christian Science.

You know me better than anybody in
this world, because you have tried me and I
think have found me all you expected. You
judge me by your experience of me. God led
me to you in the hour of most need. I said
then I should never turn away from you and
have never done so, and I never will, so help
me God. Don't you remember, my precious
Teacher, how many hard battles against the
belief of error we fought in days gone by
and won them all by God's help and your
wise counsel[?] The old captain always did
love you and always will, mainly because,
through your sound teachings in Christian
Science, you saved my precious wife from
the belief of death and the grave. She was
given up to die by a number of doctors and
by myself, too, who as a sea captain had to
be a doctor and practice medicine to protect
my passengers and crews. But God has
always kept the best before me, so [He] gave
me the chance to rise above the ordinary
sailor and kept my feet from falling into the
pit which the sailors usually fall into unless
they are alert to the guidance of God.

For more than sixty years, my prayer,
so simple and brief, has been, "God help
me, God help me, God help me!" With
this little prayer in my thought, I have

conquered attacks of pirates in the China
Seas, the mutinies of sailors on board
the ship, hard gales, hurricanes, tempests
on the high seas, disasters, shipwrecks,
lee shores, lack of provisions and water,
and worst of all, the enmity of men.

To me there is no greater prayer than
those few words, and I can say from actual
experience [that] I have gone for hours
and weeks, yes, and for months, repeating
that prayer mentally, and the result has
always been alike—the answer has always
come, and I was brought out from my
distresses.... This letter is from my heart
and is to cheer you by reminding you of
good work done years ago, and also is, and
mainly so, to give thanks unto the Lord for
His mercies which have endured till today.

My wife, too, and my daughter
join me in sending our love, which
I know you will accept.

Lovingly,
J. S. Eastaman

My devotion to the Cause

I have now entered my thirty-fifth year of Christian
Science study and practice and can speak from experience
of the purity, holiness, and absolute truthfulness of the
teaching received in the Primary, Normal, and Obstetrics
classes and their application to all forms of disease and sin

and their results. We are clearly taught that strict adherence to the teaching of the Gospels and our own textbook, *Science and Health*, and other works of our Leader, Mary Baker Eddy, will [ensure] the success of every student and place his feet firmly on the rock, Christ, Truth, which cannot be shaken, even though envy, malice, hatred, and persecution beset the pathway. Those who have faced the enemy and borne persecution patiently have indeed learned a precious lesson and can say with the prophet Isaiah, "For thou hast been a strength to the poor, a strength to the needy in distress, a refuge from the storm, a shadow from the heat, when the blast of the terrible ones is as a storm against the wall" (25:4). Still another lesson they have learned: "The way which leads to Christian Science is straight and narrow. God has set His signet upon Science, making it coordinate with all that is real and only with that which is harmonious and eternal" (*Science and Health*, p. 472).

JULIA E. PRESCOTT *(1849–1924)*

*Born in North Berwick, Maine, Julia Hall belonged for
many years to the Baptist church her father helped build.
In 1870, she married Samuel W. Came and moved with
him to Portsmouth, New Hampshire, where he and his
brother operated a carriage factory. Not long afterward,
the factory burned, and in 1873, her husband passed
on. Four years later, she married George H. Prescott
in Boston. Their first son did not survive infancy, but a
second son, Carleton, was born in 1881. The family lived
for a while in New Hampshire until Prescott became ill, at
which point they moved to Reading, Massachusetts, near
the town where her parents lived.*

*Prescott learned of Christian Science from a relative
in 1885, and soon after contacting a Christian
Science practitioner for treatment, both she and
her son were healed of long-standing ailments.
Prescott took Primary class instruction from Mary
Baker Eddy in 1885, advertised as a practitioner in*

The Christian Science Journal *in 1895, and began teaching Christian Science in 1896. She was also instrumental in the establishment of First Church, Reading, which so appreciated her work as a healer, teacher, and church member that, after she passed on, the church's Executive Board adopted a resolution saying, in part, "that we will strive to emulate this noble example." Prescott served in Eddy's household from August 1905 through February 1906 and numerous times for shorter periods in 1907.*

Seeking and Finding God

JULIA E. PRESCOTT

From my earliest recollection I longed to know God. I so often asked my mother why the people did not love Jesus. If he were only here now, I told my mother, I would go to him and tell him all my fears and troubles, and would love and obey him. When about 15 years of age, I talked with the pastor of the church—told him of my great desire to know God and asked him what I could do. He said I must be converted and join the church. I inquired how I could find this change of heart I so longed for. He replied that I must give up all for God and show the world my desire to be a Christian; then [I should] join the church. All this I did and tried to find the light and assurance that I was God's child. After a while I told the pastor that I had not found God and asked him what I should do. He told me that I must wait and continue to pray. This I did also but never found my prayers answered until I found the Truth in the Christian Science textbook, *Science and Health with Key to the Scriptures* by Mary Baker Eddy.

The answer in my search for truth

In March 1885, I came to Reading, Massachusetts, to live, and in July of that same year, I first heard of Christian Science and how it healed. I asked a lady who was at that time under treatment to tell me something about Christian Science, and her reply was, "I have just commenced treatment myself, but this I know, that it is all of God." This was a great joy to me! I was then asked why I did not try Christian Science treatment for my child, four years of age, who had not been well for more than two years. I talked with a practitioner about having treatment for my child, and she said she would have to treat me, as the mother-thought was so anxious and fearful.

My next step was to obtain the textbook, *Science and Health*, and I read and read from it. While I did not understand what it said, I could not let it alone, and in one week's time I knew that the understanding of God for which I had always longed was in that book. I found it true. The more I read it, the more convinced I was of the truths contained therein. I could never describe the happiness it brought into my life. It not only healed my child but also healed me of incurable troubles which I had had since eight years of age. I had told the practitioner I did not think that I could ever be helped by Christian Science, for the doctors had always told me I could never be better; but if my child could only be healed, it was all I asked.

A few months later, when I told the practitioner of my deep gratitude for the healing brought into my home, to my child and myself, she said, "Now you can trust God in all conditions, I am sure." I answered, "In all but one." Then

I told her of a severe trouble which always came to my child when the cold winter nights came on and of the law the doctors had laid down which filled me with torturing fear. Not long after this incident, my fear was made manifest by the appearance of the disease upon the child. The practitioner worked all through the night and there was some improvement, but the case was not met. The practitioner said it was all my fear, and as she was to go away the next morning, I was left alone to find God.

I prayed all day and until ten o'clock that night. I was weary and almost in despair, and in my extremity I resorted once more to the old medical remedies and used them just as I had for months every winter before. But the child continued to grow worse until, at six o'clock the next morning, I cried out to God for help and laid the child down and left the house, saying as I rushed out, "I will never come back until I find my God." As I looked up to the stars, these words came: "Abide in me and I will abide in you." Instantly the whole world changed to me from a sense of agony to one of peace and rest. I went back to the house, knowing that the child was well, though it had seemed, when I went out, that he could not live another ten minutes. He was perfectly normal when I returned and never had another attack.

An invitation to study with Mrs. Eddy

The practitioner related my experience to Mrs. Eddy, and she told the practitioner to have me come to her, for she would like to talk with me. I went one evening and was so happy when told that I could enter her next class and receive instruction from her in Christian Science healing. The gentleness and loving interest I felt from her that evening made me feel that I could not wait to sit at her feet and be taught of God. This was only a few months after my healing. Mrs. Eddy was so interested in all my answers to her questions. When she found that I loved music and had spent all my early life in studying it, she invited me to play and sing for her. When the visit was over, she asked if I would be obliged to return to my home alone and if someone would meet me at the railroad station. I was almost overcome with her kindly interest in me, a stranger. Several months later, I went through her class.

Mrs. Eddy's teaching was wonderful! Two things impressed me beyond words to express: First, that Love was our only weapon and would destroy all error that might come to our consciousness. Second, that all Bible passages that came to us in times of great need were messages direct from Him. This made me know that it was the voice of God that had come to me and had destroyed my fear on that morning when my child seemed to be passing on. Mrs. Eddy gave to the meetings of her students' Association such wonderful truths about seeing the error. She told us to always know it was the "adversary" that Jesus came to destroy, not personality. Many of her students could not understand this but felt she was talking about persons and, consequently, turned away from her teaching, saying she was un-Christian. Such Christianity and compassion I could never believe one could manifest, save the Master, until I saw it through our Leader!

Church services and healings in Reading, Massachusetts

Soon after leaving the Massachusetts Metaphysical College, I asked the friend who was healed at the same time that I was to come to my home in Reading with her child and join me with my little boy, and study the *Christian Science Quarterly* Bible Lessons. This she did, and not long after, we procured a small hall in the town, and there we started public meetings. Healing work was being accomplished and, consequently, more people joined us there. This necessitated our procuring a more commodious hall, the largest in the town, in fact. Our numbers increased continually and there came a demand for class instruction. In 1899 I taught my first class and have taught a class every year since then. Many of my students have become good practitioners and have brought out many wonderful truths through their work in Christian Science.

Some years following the organization of the church in Reading, we started a fund to be used for the erection of a church edifice of our own. On two subsequent occasions we contributed the entire amount in our Church Building Fund to assist in the completion of the Original Mother Church in Boston.

In July 1905, our Leader called me to come and live with her at her home at Pleasant View in Concord, New Hampshire. This was the result of her reading a testimony of healing in the *Christian Science Sentinel*, the case of a young man who was healed of appendicitis. His wife came to me asking me to treat her husband, as he was seemingly very ill. A physician had pronounced the case to be appendicitis and had stated that a surgical operation must be performed at once. The case was healed in a few days, and the young man, a blacksmith, went back to his daily occupation. After reading this testimony, Mrs. Eddy wrote to the young man, seeking to learn the name of the practitioner. Mrs. Eddy also wrote to a Christian Scientist in Boston, asking him to investigate the case for her. He called upon the physician who had attended the case before help had been sought in Christian Science and was assured that the young man had had appendicitis.

Mrs. Eddy's healing work

While I was living with Mrs. Eddy at Pleasant View, she told many wonderful things, proving more and more the power of her healing work through Christian Science. She told us, on one occasion, that she had been called to see a man who had been in a very severe accident—using her own words, "He was in pieces." But [through] her sense of God's creation being perfect and man [as] His image and likeness, the man was completely healed in a very short time.

At another time she told us of the case of a child who was born helpless. While out walking one day, Mrs. Eddy observed a small boy drawing another and younger child in a little cart. She inquired of the older boy what was the matter with the little fellow. He replied, "He is my brother and he has never walked." Mrs. Eddy looked into the sweet face and beautiful blue eyes of the little boy lying flat on his back in the cart, his legs dangling over the edge, limp and helpless. In relating the incident, she said the sense of the perfect child of God was so clear to her that the boy slid out of the cart and went running down the street, saying, "See me yun (run)!" He reached his home, which was nearby, crying out, "Mamma, see me yun! See me yun!"

One day when Mrs. Eddy was taking her daily drive, she passed an old acquaintance on the street. He could scarcely walk with a cane, but her sense of God and the perfect man was so strong that he was healed. This was his statement in a letter following the incident, and which I heard our Leader read: "I have been very ill lately, and have suffered a great deal, but was entirely healed the day you passed me on the street. I am grateful to God."

Mrs. Eddy loved little children and would often tell us, on returning from her drives, how the dear little children would wave their hands and throw kisses to her. This was such a joy to her, and she said to us, "I always returned them."

She delighted to give always in every direction. When a young girl, she gave her own lunches to the little, poor children in school. Sometimes her mother would ask, noticing that she was very hungry, "Mary, didn't you have lunch enough?" She would reply, "I gave my lunch to the children. I knew I would have enough when I got home, and perhaps they would not."

Prayer during the "Next Friends" suit

I was with our Leader during the trial of the "Next Friends."[16] It certainly was a trial to Mrs. Eddy in many ways because it took her precious time that she was so anxious to give for the good of the world. One day while the lawyers were at Pleasant View, one of them asked to see me, thinking that I would be a witness on the stand. After talking and asking me a number of questions, he inquired, "What are you here for?" I avoided answering. A few minutes later the lawyer repeated the question, but I still avoided answering him. The third time he said, "And what did you say you were here for?" Commencing to realize that I must give a direct answer, I said, "I will tell you what I am here for. Mrs. Eddy [told] me many years ago to love my enemies. Now she has called me here to teach me how to do it."

As the time was approaching for the climax of the trial, Mrs. Eddy told us we must know that there was but one side, and that was the right side. She told us also that we must know that no one could hurt us, nor be made to, and that we could not hurt anyone, nor be made to; that we could not hurt ourselves, nor be made to, for we all love and help each other, and God loves and helps us all. Such lessons as I learned while

Household workers in the summer house at Pleasant View, from left: Miss Grace Long, Mrs. Mary Blain, Mrs. Julia Prescott

PHOTO COURTESY OF THE MARY BAKER EDDY LIBRARY

living with her, and the spirit of Love which she manifested! I could hear her praying as I passed her study door during the trial: "Father, love my enemies." She knew that God did love her enemies and all mankind, but her human heart was reaching out to God. Another sweet little prayer I would often hear her repeat: "I love everyone and everyone loves me. Father, show me what love is and how to love."

One day Mrs. Eddy called me into her study, and the sense of God was so great that tears came into my eyes. She noticed that I was affected, and she asked, "Why those tears, dear? Are you homesick?"

"Oh no," I responded. "But I feel that you are an angel."

She asked, "You don't mean my personality?"

"Oh no," I answered. "I mean that you give us messages from God."

She concluded: "You mean that I am the window. We are right under the focus of [d]ivine Love."

I went to my room, feeling that all the world was filled with God, Good.

The climax and conclusion of the trial

On the morning we expected the masters to come to Pleasant View to examine our Leader in connection with the trial, she said to one of her secretaries, "Tell Minnie (the cook) to make the best lemonade for them that she ever made, and I want them to use the Bohemian glasses," a set that had been given to her by a student. As a number of men were expected, the secretary replied, "This is a team, Mother, and don't you think we had better use the cut glass tumblers? They are larger." Dear Mrs. Eddy looked disappointed and said, "I only wanted them to have the best, but you know what is right."

The masters came that afternoon. The day was extremely warm, but Mrs. Eddy never complained and answered all of the questions put to her. When one of her interrogators said, "We feel it wrong to question you anymore," she answered, "Oh, I love to talk with you."

One of them said, "I have a mother 85 years old."

"Oh, have you?" Mrs. Eddy responded. "Give my love to her."

If these people had been her best friends, Mrs. Eddy could not have been more loving and kind. After the interview, one of the lawyers, as he was descending the stairs, said, "My, she is smarter than a steel trap."

As we all know, this examination finished the trial of the "Next Friends," and we were all grateful and felt it was another proof of God's care.

My class instruction with our Leader, and my great privilege of living with her at different times, has been the greatest blessing of my life. My highest desire is to follow her teaching.

EMMA A. ESTES *(1853–1942)*

Emma Estes was baptized in the Congregational church but later found Christian Science when she was desperate for a cure for her mother, Julia C. Estes. Though physicians had offered no hope of recovery, her mother was completely healed through Christian Science. Soon both women were healing others, and by the early 1890s they were listed in The Christian Science Journal *as practitioners.*

Emma Estes took both a Primary and a Normal class with Mary Baker Eddy in 1887. For part of that year, she also served as assistant secretary in Eddy's household before leaving, with Eddy's blessing, to work in the Field. She served the Cause briefly in New York and then at length in Cincinnati, where she was instrumental in the establishment of Christian Science. Estes's mother worked alongside her there.

Proving the Truth of Christian Science

EMMA A. ESTES

When a mere school girl, I joined the Congregational church, and after baptism and communion services were over, each of the new communicants was given a card on which was written [a] Bible text. The one given me was Psalms 54, verse 4: "Behold, God is mine helper." Little did I then realize to what extent in the future I would be required to prove the truth of that statement.

About that time my mother's health began to fail, and the best of medical aid did not benefit [her] in the least, except temporarily, and we were well-nigh in despair, although I clung as best I knew how to the text before quoted. One day a lady came to call and, drawing me aside, said cautiously, "Why don't you take your mother to a Christian Science practitioner? That will heal her." I at once eagerly inquired, "What is Christian Science?" for I had never heard of it. The lady did not know much about it but said her little boy had been cured of heart trouble and that God was the healer. That impressed me greatly, and while I had been told by several physicians that my mother was beyond human aid, I believed that God could cure her if He would, although my prayers in her behalf had been unavailing.

Christian Science brings peace and healing

As soon as possible I secured the services of a practitioner of Christian Science, and I shall never forget the beautiful sense of peace that came to me at that first interview. It was as though a great burden had been lifted from my heart and a holy calm had come there to abide forever, and I said in hushed tones, "Will it last, this wonderful peace? It was the effect of your prayer, was it not?" The practitioner replied [that] it was not a prayer of beseeching God to heal but a recognition of His loving presence.

I was eager to learn more of this wonderful teaching. We at once procured the textbook of Christian Science, *Science and Health with Key to the Scriptures*, and devoted every spare moment to the study of that wonderful book, whose spiritual significance opened up its treasures to us, revealing a new sense of God, whose love healed the sick, a new religion capable of daily demonstration, a God who was truly a present help in trouble. Through the earnest, faithful study of that precious book, one by one the dreadful physical ills began to disappear, and health and strength were slowly restored. I made a vow after my first day's experience that if Christian Science restored my mother's health, I would devote my life to the study and practice of its teachings, and that vow has been and is still being sacredly fulfilled.

Sharing the truth with others

Shortly after that, we went to a little town in Michigan

to visit our relatives, taking the precious book with us. We found one or two members of the family sick and under the care of the doctors. I unhesitatingly told them that if they would dismiss the doctors and destroy the medicine, God would heal them through Christian Science, and on the second day these healings were accomplished. The news soon spread abroad in the little town, and many people began coming for help—and were not sent home without it.

One day a lady who had heard of the healings came, begging us to go home with her to see her husband, who was too ill to come. When we reached the house, we found him groaning in agony, tears rolling down his cheeks. I said to him, "God can help you if you will let Him." "I don't believe in God," he replied. "But," I said, "you surely will when you are helped."

Soon the groans became less and less, and inside of twenty minutes had ceased altogether, and when I looked at him, he was gazing at me in wild-eyed astonishment, free from pain, and his first question was, "Will it last?" The next day he greeted me with a smile, saying he had slept all night, the first time in years. The third day, his wife, meeting me at the door, began to cry, "Oh, he is going to die, isn't he?" And when I asked why she thought so, she replied, "He asked me this morning if there was a Bible in the house." I laughingly replied, "No, that is a sure sign that he is going to live and live aright." The next day he asked if he might say grace at the table, and the following week he went to the Baptist prayer-meeting and testified of his healing.

In a few days the minister of that church called, asking what had accomplished the change in that man, saying that he had tried for ten years to get him to come to church but he had never entered the door, and now in a week's time he had been converted and healed, "soul and body," as he expressed it in his testimony. "How did you do it?" I told him that God did it, not I, that I was only a channel for God to work through.

He then invited me to join his church and work with him, but I told him Christian Science was not for Baptists only, but for all of God's children. Shortly after this, a member of his family who had not walked for years applied for help and was healed.

And so the good work went on until the M.D.'s were aroused, as one by one the cases they had pronounced incurable were cured, and they lost no time in holding a session in which they determined to run us out of town or have us arrested for practicing medicine without a license. There was one doctor present at that conference, however, who had himself sent cases to us that he had failed to heal, and to his amazement one case which he had worked on for six weeks was healed in one treatment. So this doctor was convinced there was something about it he did not understand, and he was too broad-minded to condemn after such convincing proof. He told the other M.D.'s they were jealous and they had better let those little women alone.

Class instruction and employment with our Leader

Shortly after this Mrs. Eddy sent for me, and in January 1887 I took the Primary course of instruction at the [Massachusetts] Metaphysical College, which was then located at 571 Columbus Avenue. I was ready to make any material sacrifice to gain more spiritual understanding, and Mrs. Eddy told me [that] because of this attitude of thought, I would be more receptive of the truth she had to impart. One who has not had such an experience can never know what a wonderful spiritual blessing it was to sit for days at the feet of that gifted, God-crowned woman and drink in the spiritual drafts of refreshment from the fount of love. It was a blessing no one could then fully appreciate but which has grown clearer and dearer with all the passing years. This was the beginning of my acquaintance with that remarkably gifted woman whose spiritual teachings are revered today by thousands and thousands of staunch adherents into whose lives have come the benedictions of health, harmony, and happiness.

On my way back I stopped at a little town in New York. Much healing was accomplished, and many were started to seeking truth in their Bibles and [in] *Science and Health*.

In March of 1887, after I had been home a short time from the Primary class, our Leader sent for me to come to Boston to be a helper in her household, as assistant secretary. This opportunity I gladly accepted, rejoicing to be of service in any capacity to one who was doing so much to lessen humanity's woes. During this sojourn with our Leader, many helpful lessons were daily learned. The whole tenor of my life was turned to Truth.

It was a pleasure to Mrs. Eddy's evenings, after dinner, for the little group in her household to sing hymns. Among her favorites were "Sowing Seeds of Kindness" and "When the Clouds Have Rolled Away." One day an urgent call for help came from a gentleman living not far away, and Mrs. Eddy turned to me and said, "You go, child." I began to protest, but she quietly said, "You have only to be a transparency for Truth." I was obedient, and the man was healed.

Serving the Cause around the country

After I'd fulfilled my duty as assistant secretary for Mrs. Eddy for some time, a call came from Brooklyn for helpers, and the principal of the Institute[17] requested Mrs. Eddy to let me come to help her, and it was there, in the absence of the principal, that I was called upon to address the meetings that were being held each week for the rapidly increasing seekers for Truth.

In August of 1887, Mrs. Eddy gave her consent for me to come to Cincinnati where some good healing work had been accomplished but no classes taught. An Institute was established under the laws of the State of Ohio, and weekly meetings were held.[18] In October of 1887, I was called to the Normal class at the College, where we were again thoroughly taught and examined as to our qualifications to impart to others this grand [t]ruth. After proving our ability in healing and teaching for three years, we were entitled to the degree of C.S.D., provided we had also taken the Primary course at the College under Mrs. Eddy's instruction.

Words fail to express my gratitude for having been spiritually alert enough to have received these blessings before the College closed in 1889. After 1889 the Association prospered and increased greatly through the healing work. At this time there were no church organizations anywhere except The Mother Church at Boston, of which Mrs. Eddy was the pastor.[19] Soon the various cities began holding regular Sunday services, and we decided to open our Institute for such services in addition to those we were having each week.[20] At the first regular church service, there were just two present—mother and myself—but as soon as it was announced, our rooms were filled to overflowing in an incredibly short time, and we were obliged to obtain larger rooms.

In an editorial in the February *Journal* of 1889 were these words: "The Sunday class in Science is, after the Association, the germ of church organization." We did not, however, advertise our services in *The Christian Science Journal* until we had obtained our state charter as First Church of Christ, Scientist, of Cincinnati, Ohio.

Steady progress toward Truth

I have not written the history of the many trials, heartaches, and persecutions long endured at the hands of the enemies of Truth during the establishment of the Cause nor of the cruel injustice perpetrated by those who permitted themselves to be used as channels for error. These sorrows and troubles fade into nothingness when I remember those our Leader encountered in establishing the kingdom of heaven on earth through Christian Science. Our Leader forewarned us, saying, "The trials encountered by prophets and apostles await in some form every pioneer of truth" [see *Science and Health*, p. 28], and I am sure we have all proven it true in greater or lesser degree.

Through all these years the sunshine of God's love has been ever present, and always the loving, patient guidance and tender care of my [t]eacher, Mary Baker Eddy, was my own for the asking until I could tread alone the thorny pathway from sense to Soul.

In 1889 when Mrs. Eddy wrote me [that] I might come to Boston to heal and teach, and I replied about our needs here, our Leader came to the rescue with [a] dear letter, which melted away the cloud of false witnesses.[21]

After the passing on of our revered Leader, I have always had the just and staunch support of those whom she left in official capacity to care for our Cause, and at all times and in all ways, my many loving and loyal students from all over the country have nobly done their part as Readers and practitioners, and shown much proficiency in every department of activity in the Cause of Science.

After my first perusal of *Science and Health*, I never doubted for an instant but that its author was divinely endowed to bring the liberating thought to humanity to free them from the thralldom of sin, sickness, and death. Thousands are rising up today to call her blessed, the God-crowned woman whose crown is illuminated with gems of blessings from liberated humanity. Words seem inadequate to properly express the beauty of holiness. Our daily faithfulness to its teachings must prove our sincerity.

LIDA W. FITZPATRICK (1857–1933)

Lida Fitzpatrick was born in Ohio and raised a Methodist. She began studying Christian Science in 1887 and took Primary class twice that year from two different teachers, both of whom were Mary Baker Eddy's students.[22] She healed her husband of diabetes that year as well. The following year, she took Normal class from Mrs. Eddy and was listed in The Christian Science Journal *as a practitioner and teacher in Cleveland, Ohio, where she lived the rest of her life, except when serving in Eddy's household. Fitzpatrick's first marriage ended in divorce.*

Fitzpatrick was a charter member of First Church, Cleveland, where she served as Second Reader. A decade later, in 1901, she helped organize Second Church, Cleveland. She served in Eddy's Pleasant View home several times—for six months in 1903, three months in 1904, and approximately six months in 1907. Fitzpatrick's reminiscence is excerpted from notes she took on lessons Eddy gave her workers.

Gems of Instruction and Encouragement

LIDA W. FITZPATRICK

May 13, 1903

One lesson in divinity
  Is there any darkness in Light? No.
Is there any evil in Good? No.
What tells you there is? Belief, my false sense.
Have you a false sense? No. *There.*
Is there any belief? No. Then *know* it.

Sight, hearing, memory, action, cannot be lost; they are eternal, of God. Eyes do not see, it is Mind; then if I have lost my sight, God has lost His. If I have lost my hearing, God has lost His.

You do not have to sleep. Mind is always active; cessation of thought is not what is needed, but the ever-presence.

All we have to meet is sin; it is a sin to believe a lie and we know it. Now you know what to do with sin.

My suffering (Mrs. Eddy's) is from believing other people's thoughts affect me. I say, Mary, it is not other people's sin; it is your own thought. Nothing can *make* you sin; you do it your-self. There is no prenatal belief that can make you believe you believe it; there is nothing but God and His idea.

The devil tempted Jesus, said, "Come down and I will give you all you see"; and the devil had not an acre of ground to give and has nothing to give you. Jesus did not stop to argue with a lie (argument of error), did not say, "Now, Mr. Devil, I will argue with you about it." He said, "Get thee behind me, Satan" [Luke 4:8]. He "spake the word and it was done" [see Psalms 33:9]. Shut it all out.

You do not have to argue; *know.*

Know God and His idea, and not argue about sin.

A lady in Lynn was so angry at me she would not speak to me after healing her daughter because she said I spoke disrespectfully to her dying daughter. The physicians had said there was only a piece of her lung left and she was dying. I was called and there were *spiritualists* around; I tried to reach her thought but no, could not get at it, so I said, "Get up out of that bed." Then I called to those in the other room, "Bring her clothes." The girl got up and was well, never even coughed again; [she] is living yet for all I know. I have never heard otherwise, but her mother has never spoken to me since.

I speak sharply sometimes, but the thought must *move.*

What is a demonstration? Proof.

Well, the proof already is. I never say I have had a demon-stration, for it was always done.

May 18, 1903

We are told the world will be destroyed; how? By malice. By cyclones, electricity, and be burned up. What is a cyclone?

It is a condition of mortal mind-malice. What burns up[?] Malice. It is all malice, and our textbook tells us, Christian Scientists will hold such things in check. God never made them and they can be overcome just the same as sickness. It is all within.

Now, when there is the claim that the weather is sultry, handle it and you will see a breeze spring up. If it is cold, handle it; it is all in Mind, ever the same, harmonious. God did not make sultry weather, etc. Then, if we through belief have made it, we must unmake it. When it looks like thunder and lightning, handle it; there is no sultry atmosphere to cause thunder and lightning. When I first came to Concord (before hypnotism and mesmerism joined hands to work upon me), there was no snow the first winter at all and no thunderstorms the first year. When [it was] sultry, I would close my eyes for a moment [and] then open them, and the leaves would all be stirring; a breeze had sprung up. We make our own atmosphere. These things are easier handled than sickness. I used to handle them until I forgot about it. Lately I have attended to the work and only kept above the effects. When Clara [Shannon] was here, I would speak about the thunderstorms, and she would work alone and they would all disappear. You can do this, and if you are not at first successful, do not get discouraged; keep on trying. When you have the first indication, forestall it.

May 21, 1903

The true Science—divine Science—will be lost sight of again unless we arouse ourselves. This demonstrating to make matter build up is not Science. The building up of churches, the writing of articles, and the speaking in public is the old way of building up a cause. The way I brought this Cause into sight was through *healing*; and now these other things would come in and hide it, just as was done in the time of Jesus. Now this Cause must be saved, and I pray God to be spared for this work. (I have always stood for God alone.) Now you see what we have to do for the world—be a transparency for *Spirit*. Things must turn and overturn, until He whose right it is shall reign.

We must show the difference between the healing of Christian Science and quackery. Healing is demonstration, nothing else is.

May 23, 1903

"He that *endureth* unto the *end* shall be *saved*" [see Matthew 10:22]. Jesus endured; after he disappeared from their view, he endured. The Lord delayed his coming, so the disciples went back to their nets. He endured; he showed the same nail prints and the same body after as before, showing it was the same Jesus. And so shall we be saved if we endure.

May 25, 1903

Jesus said, "Can ye not watch with me one hour?" [see Matthew 26:40] And they were asleep. Now, *watch*. You may sit in your chair all day and say over beautiful words, and it does not amount to anything; it is the *spirit* that is needed.

Our blessed Master did not have the Science of it; that is, [he] did not *give* the premise, the conclusion, and the logical reasoning as this is. He had the spirit of it and gave it to the disciples. You cannot enter eternity until you have broken the law (or sense) of time. There is no collapse; neither is there any relapse.

May 27, 1903

Handle the thought of reversal. You can do it. The reign of harmony is; you can make it rain; it can water the earth. Is there a devil that can reverse God's government? *No*. Then have faith as a grain of mustard seed. You can.

May 28, 1903

Do not take up [your prayer, saying], there is no thunder and lightning; know that God governs the elements and there is nothing destructive or harmful. God sends the rain that watereth the earth. Human will cannot come in and govern.

You would not argue diphtheria if the case was consumption; neither do you argue thunder and lightning when it is sin (malice). If thunder and lightning come, then know forces are of God and not destructive.

May 29, 1903

Anything that comes from the body is human will; that which comes not from the body and can only do good is the Divine. I (Mrs. Eddy) am only a window pane through which the Light comes. You are helping yourselves more than you help me, for I am *helping* you; the Discoverer has to discover the way to meet these things. You will not have that to do. You are *learning now* how to meet them; I have had to discover it.

June 1, 1903

You do not have to wait for your patient to tell you all about what to meet; you should see it and meet it. Break the law that *after* the treatment is given, the patient is worse.

Break [the] law that you are worse every hour. You are better every hour—so is everyone in the house.

June 4, 1903

God does not come and go; it is the dream that does that. God *stands*, and we are one with Him; we cannot be shaken.

June 5, 1903

You must have the balance on the right side; a row of ciphers without the numeral 1 is nothing. Now have your I with God. There is *no evil*; God is all. There is nothing (cipher) that can weigh against God.

June 12, 1903

In working for the weather, never say, there is no wind, there is no lightning, no rain, etc., for if you do, it will act like mesmerism. It will break out in some other phase; but know the elements are in *God's* hands (His fists). They are not destructive but [are] governed by harmony and express harmony; God gave us dominion over the earth, but it is His dominion. The loving Father gives us what is for us and nothing else can; He is Love and Love controls the elements and all things.

If I say to you, "There is no thunder and lightning," [and] then I say, "Do not say there is no thunder and lightning but know they cannot be destructive," am I inconsistent? No. If I say to a dyspeptic, "You have no stomach," [and] then say, "Eat food and it does you good," am I inconsistent? No. Absolute Science you cannot prove yet; that is, if you try to work that there is no thunder and lightning, you will get into trouble, for it keeps coming and others believe it purifies the atmosphere. So you can see it has no power to harm, is not destructive, can only be harmonious. The dyspeptic, if you tell him to eat and the food does him good, will brighten up and be healed, [whereas] if you declared no stomach, no food, you could not prove it yet (see *Science and Health with Key to the Scriptures*, p. 442, 268th edition).[23]

We can know that God governs *all* harmoniously.

June 14, 1903

"Owe no man any thing, but to love one another" [Romans 13:8]. I (Mrs. Eddy) have all the way in Christian Science when I wanted to do anything "sat down and counted the cost."

Why is it a student will be so brave in the work in one direction and not in another? Because there is not enough Love in the heart; it should be *ever* present, always ready. Love is not person but *love*; it is always present for all occasions.

June 19, 1903

"Lovest thou me?" Yes. "Feed my sheep" [John 21:17].

Can you separate the Principle from its idea? No. Can you love the Principle and not its idea? No. Can you love the idea and not the Principle? No. Jesus was teaching this all the way along. It is the same today—that is the handle.

The Babylonish woman in the Apocalypse has thrown wormwood into the waters to turn trusting thoughts to hatred against me, the idea; handle this and you will find your patients healed. Love and its idea are *one*.

You would declare you love me, when underneath is the hatred nagging; kill it and go on loving.

June 21, 1903

We can feel encouraged in the overcoming of error, but do not feel satisfied until you "awake in His likeness" (see *Science and Health*, p. 4). Every spiritualized thought is that much in this direction.

July 8, 1903

"'Peace, be still' [Mark 4:39]. '*Peace* I leave with you, my peace I give unto you' [John 14:27]; you are in the arms of Love which shields you from everything." These words must be accompanied by the [s]pirit of them.

This was to show how to handle a case when many minds were at work on a case, which would be like wild beasts fighting, locking horns. This realization of peace is needed at such times; [it] will unlock the horns, will stop the discord.

The higher one senses harmony, the more sensitive he is to discord; the same [is true] in music. "The greatest wrong is but the supposititious opposite of the highest right" (see *Science and Health*, p. 368).

July 12, 1903

When we detect error as unreal and God as all, we will be immortal.

July 18, 1903

Theosophists [malpractitioners] profess to make a law that will hold good for six months; they do not sit up nights to work.

Now break these laws; then when that is accomplished and you go out from here, you are ready for the next that is to be met, and when the need is to come here, you will come back again. But if you do not meet it and go out from here, you are not ready for the next and so cannot come back. This is the divinity. In healing a patient, do not try to regenerate the whole; be like a carpenter—strengthen the weak places first, and while [you are] doing so, the patient will be helped mentally. You cannot take the whole structure until you have reached that point. I am now doing the work of meeting the sin of the world.

July 29, 1903

Break the so-called laws which say you cannot heal, you cannot help the patient, the patient will relapse, etc. Work at it every day until they are destroyed; [do] not wait until you have it to meet with the patient, but work every day just as hard as though the patient was dying until you have the mastery. Then they will never have dominion over your work. Look to God, whose only law is harmony.

July 31, 1903

The drunkenness produced by belief in wine is not to be compared with the drunkenness in thought—mental darkness. "Drunken, but not with wine" (Isaiah 51:21).

Keep awake by loving more; love the idea of God and you will love God. You can only love God as far as you love His idea, and love will be *expressed*. What would you think of one who says he loves but never expresses it? Love does express itself; it *heals*. If you do not heal, you have not enough love. Prove your love. Love is God and expresses itself.

August 1, 1903

Do not treat the weather as though a storm could go

around and let our neighbor have it. When I take it up, I face the clouds and see God's face, Love, shining right through; then the clouds scatter, and there is no storm to break upon anyone.

August 7, 1903

It is not enough to smile and look pleasant when talking to the devil; speak with authority, stamp your foot if necessary and command it to come out of him, as Jesus did. The smile and pleasantness will be alright when you are out of the flesh, but in the flesh you must *strive*.

Mesmerism will smile and be pleasant and all the while [be] doing some mischief.

August 9, 1903

Good is all. Evil is not Mind, has no intelligence, is powerless, and falls by its own weight.

August 11, 1903

Humility is the door, honesty is the way, and spirituality is the summit.

Oh! If we could only see ourselves in God—"In him we live, and move, and have our being" [Acts 17:28]—we would have no other consciousness.

August 18, 1903

The world is to us as we see it. The five senses (material) are lies and can only repeat lies; now rise above them to Spirit—the real. That is where health is and freedom from limitation. The lies will disperse as we have seen the clouds disappear; there is no such thing. God is all. You do not have to delve into matter, the body, to know how things are; Spirit shows us things as they are.

Keep your thought up there—this will heal. It is all that is necessary.

When you are "on the housetop do not go down into the house to take anything out" [see Matthew 24:17].

August 19, 1903

Mr. K[24] asked, "When you reach a place where you have done everything you know to do or what to do, desiring, striving for divine guidance, and it does not seem to come, and discouragement comes in and causes you to doubt your ability to grasp it, what do you do?" Mrs. Eddy replied, "Shut out the senses and take the side with God; if it comes to you that you do not know which is the side with God, turn to Him *alone*, shutting out everything else. This is the way."

We must learn that we do not depend upon material food for health and Life; Spirit—not matter—sustains us and we must prove it.

It is not necessary to eat as much as we do even now.

Mrs. Eddy was called to a case of fever where two physicians present said the man could not live; he had refused to eat *anything* for a week. As she went to his door, he was saying, "This tastes good and that tastes good," and he did not have any food in the room. Mrs. Eddy said, "With that consciousness, he can live without eating." The physicians laughed at it. "Well then, he can eat," she said, and instantly he was in his right mind, recognized someone in the room, and called for something to eat. They brought him a bountiful supply, and he ate it all, dressed himself, went out in the yard, and was entirely well.

Mrs. Eddy did not think about the physical, just "God is all," and shut out what the physicians had said and everything else from the sense side. She at first demonstrated health in the flesh; now she is demonstrating health outside the flesh, she said.

August 28, 1903

The students who are called here do not come to this house for glory; when they come here, they come to the cross. The first step is willingness to leave all, then the cross, *then* "Enter thou into the joy of thy Lord" [Matthew 25:21]. You cannot gain the crown except by "taking up the cross and following."

September 8, 1903

We are all drunk without wine, in the senses; sleep is one of its phases, and Spirit will compel us some time to give it up. False gods, etc., must go, cannot enter the kingdom; each has this work to do.

The teaching should be more in the line of showing the students how to overcome the evil than by examining with the letter, smoothing over, making things pleasant, and taking the money. There must always be the *cross* before the crown; the cross cannot be smoothed over. It is the plucking out of the eye and cutting off [of] the hand. A student of *Science and Health* who has the Spirit, [but] when he goes to a patient does not know the letter to gabble over, is better off than to be filled with the letter and not the Spirit.

Each one must work out of matter, for it is wrong in every way, from the hair on the head to the toe. If I were teaching a class now and there was one in it [who] would get angry if I rebuked her before the others, [and] her pride would not let her receive it, I would tell her to walk out of the class; such a one would not be ready to help others out of the same difficulty.

There is no power in evil; the reverse is true—God is the power; He is infinite. Then your work is the Christ-power against nothingness; hold there—*know* it, and there is nothing else. *Know* it is with power, and what else is there? Nothing; then the work is done; God did it.

September 9, 1903

If you have a patient who does not respond, would you say, I have done the best I could, and give up? No; it is the opportunity to rise higher and meet the demand.

September 12, 1903

Science does not ameliorate error; it *destroys* it.

September 13, 1903

Charity is good and peaceful, but it must not cover iniquity. Just as long as you compromise with error, just so long will the error stick to you. In teaching students, I have always uncovered the error to them; that is what should be done, and not all the pleasant things said only. "He that covereth iniquity (his sins) shall not prosper" [see Proverbs 28:13].

The error that is holding them must be uncovered to students so they can overcome it.

September 15, 1903

God governs all; this is the way Jesus stilled the tempest. There is no person and no persons that have any control over us; that belief is all illusion. God is all; we must prove this. We learn through suffering, as the Scripture reads: "My *rod* and my staff they comfort me" [see Psalms 23:4] and "Whom the Lord loveth he chasteneth, and scourgeth every son whom he receiveth" (Hebrews 12:6). Am not I an example?

September 24, 1903

"When you are on the housetop, don't go down to take anything out of the house" [see Matthew 24:17]. I am a great way out of the house (body), and it will not do for me to go down into the house (argument); I gain more by holding to God. If you are *in* the house, you will have to heal others (argue) and so get out of the house. One who has suffered sickness or discord, I have always found more tractable in Science than one who has always been well.

Do we have to be sick to work out? Not if you can get out without; health in matter must be given up for health in God. If one is a tenant and is satisfied, he will remain there; the owner may want him out of the tenement and so takes out the windows, boards up the doors, and makes it so uncomfortable for him [that] he finally gets out. God is the owner; if one is comfortable in the material tenement, he must be made uncomfortable in it to get out, but if he gets out without being made uncomfortable (sick, etc.,), all right. I have never seen one who did. The Bible continually speaks of tribulation. If you are well, heal the sick, and so get out of the material tenement (matter) and learn health in God; do not court sickness but get out of material belief. I have come so far through tribulation.

Do not think you are out because comfortable; do not *think* you are out when you are not. A pupil may work out an example on the blackboard wrong and think he is right. The teacher is out of it and sees the mistake; then the pupil must be made to see it in order to get out. Spirit is the way; it will take you out.

September 25 and 26, 1903

You must watch, as Jesus said, if you would not have the house broken open; you think you are watching, but are you when the house is broken open? What would be thought of a watchman who would let the place watched be burglarized? Would he be the right kind of a watchman? That is just why I named our paper *Sentinel* and on it, "Watch." Now, how should we watch? A guard who was watching on the side of the Union soldiers in time of the war was walking up and down while on duty when he suddenly *felt* the approach of the enemy—danger. So he began to sing, "Jesus, lover of my soul, Let me to thy bosom fly, etc.," and the verse that did the work was "Other refuge have I none, Hangs my helpless soul on thee, etc." He gave up to God. Afterward, he talked with the man who said he approached with his gun to his shoulder to shoot the guard, and he said his arm fell and the rifle with it; he could not shoot. That was watching. We must *feel* the danger and lift our thought to God; He will save us.

If we do not feel the danger and go right on as though everything was all right, declaring you are all right, you cannot die, etc., when the seeming is all wrong, you will not be watching with God.

When we *feel* the danger, then we earnestly turn to God.

When one is drunk without wine—mesmerism, apathy— he will talk with a thick tongue, something like a drunken man. I can always tell it; they must arouse out of such a sense. I (Mrs. Eddy) was in a street car once when a drunken man came in and sat down. I said mentally, "You are a fool and don't know it." I kept thinking that and nothing else; in a few moments that man was perfectly sober. It had roused his dormant sense to the situation, and when he *saw*, that was the end of it. Keep awake—watch, the right kind of watching.

October 1, 1903

Do not tell anyone he can't die, can't be sick, until you can prove it to him. I (Mrs. Eddy) used to look away from the patient sometimes until I would get the thought and the patient would vanish right out of my thought, and when I would look back at him, he would be *well*. I never told them they could not die until I could see it; then when I spoke, it was *done*. But we must keep at it, declaring it to ourselves until we can see it.

It used to be easy healing sickness—anything, a man all cut to pieces. But now we are meeting sin; I would rather have a man with his head cut off to heal, rather than sin. In *Science and Health*, I wrote, "Sin will make deadly thrusts…" [see p. 458] and "Christian Scientists will hold crime in check…" [see p. 97], and I knew no more than a babe what it meant when I wrote it; now I do.

December 7, 1903

What we most need is wisdom.

We must take advantage of time, not time of us. There is a time to do everything—a time to speak to students, a time to speak to the world—and we must have wisdom and know when to speak and act. Jesus said, "Can ye not discern the signs of the times?" [Matthew 16:3]

When student[s] [are] wrong, if it is not deep sin, I (Mrs. Eddy) walk with them away to help them out—even when they are working right against me sometimes—walk with them away and open their eyes to the error; then when they see, the error is gone. Not go at them denouncing them, pouncing upon them.

I love; one will ask, Who[m] do you love? I answer, I love. What do you love? I love.

If you love, you can raise the dead. Love will heal death; that is the way I have raised the dead, by Love—Love that is above the human.

December 9, 1903

The earth is spiritual—not material, a compound idea (see *Science and Health*, p. 585). Matter is a subjective state of mortal mind, a thought projected.

In teaching I bring out the facts clearly, get down to the bottom of things and not mix them up by comparisons. The distinct line between matter and Spirit must be drawn.

What moves your arm? Mind. What mind? Mortal mind. Is there a mortal mind? No. Then you have come back to—nothingness. God does not know anything about the moving of your hand. If you can control your hand, move it out and back, can you not control the clouds also? Yes. I am now speaking from the material sense. In immortal Mind there are no clouds and no storms. When the workmen could not finish their work if it rained (and it did not rain for three weeks) and [when] my neighbor could not furnish milk because his well was dry (and the next morning he found three or four feet of water in his well and it had not rained and he asked if we were witches or prophets here), I did not depend on clouds or storms but upon the higher power.

The material senses are lies; the spiritual sense is the real.

The spiritual sense *destroys* the material.

When you move with human will and think through human will, that is not Christian Science; it is working with the objective instead of the subjective.

The question was asked, "How did I heal the other day when I felt so helpless to do for someone who saw so far above me?" The answer was, "Through that helplessness you let Truth in, and it was Christian Science which healed the case, not your own exertion."

You are under no law but God's law.

When I first came to Christian Science, I was lifted right out of the belief of sickness into the belief of perfect health; since then I am working out of that belief in health into the Science of health, and it would have been easier if I had never been in that belief, just as it is with one who sings by ear, which is not the science of music and afterward learns the science of music. It would have been easier to have commenced right in the first place than to have to unlearn and learn over again.

December 15, 1903

The preachers speak of Jesus as though he was always so placid, never ruffled, while really he was very stern. The Scriptures speak of him as saying to his disciples, "Get thee behind me, Satan"; and just before he ascended, he called them "fools" [Luke 24:25]. I used to be very amiable before coming into Christian Science—was a peacemaker at home when arguments about temperance, politics, and philosophy would arise—but now I am *stern*.

December 17, 1903

My students will place themselves in conditions which to carry through would strike at their life, [and] then they will throw it all on to me; then I have to give the master stroke.

It was not the material cross that killed Jesus, but it was the desertion of his students that killed him (this is the reason he gave up quicker than the malefactors with him), knowing the loss that desertion meant to the Cause which was so dear to him; but he did not lose it, and he came back and proved that he had not. God was with him.

December 24, 1903

Let us take "heart" as a token of our Christmas—the great heart of Christ. It is the palpitating presence encircling the universe; it is the only intelligence, and that is what? Love. Could there by anything greater?

December 26, 1903

You have dominion over all. Elijah made a cloud to come; he made it rain. If he could make it rain, he could make it snow. You can do the same.

You are not a Christian Scientist until you do control the weather.

I cannot produce sickness. I experimented one time; a student went into another room and I argued sickness for him as hard as I could. He said he kept feeling better and better. Then he argued for me, and I began to feel pain right away. I am working now to overcome sin and not feel others' thoughts. You can see by the above I cannot be a malpractitioner. I feel others' thoughts mentally, but I am trying to work out of that; [I] do not want to feel them.

December 28, 1903

Jesus read the minds of his students; he saw their sins but did not believe it was their [m]ind, and this did the healing.

January 3, 1904

I love. What do you love? I don't know; I *love*. Do you love all? Yes, all or nothing.

How have I gained what I have? By being honest, being "faithful over a few things, and I will make you ruler over many"; then "Enter thou into the joy of thy lord" [see Matthew 25:21]. These are the steps.

Lida, God loves you; He loves you much. He loves you dearly. You have endured affliction; "Whom the Lord loveth he chasteneth" [Hebrews 12:6]. Now you return that love by giving out to others, bringing rest and peace to the world, and yourself.

January 5, 1904

The negation will not do the work, i.e., arguing no disease, etc. It is the Truth that does the work—standing on the right side [and] keeping the two commandments, "Have no other gods before me" [see Exodus 20:3] and "There is no life, truth, intelligence, nor substance in matter" [*Science and Health*, p. 468].

The moment you are pleasant with or in error, that moment you can do nothing with it. There must be *authority*. It is not seeking but *striving* that enables us to conquer.

January 8, 1904

Jesus said, "Watch and pray" [Matthew 26:41]. The watching comes first. You must watch, see the enemy before it comes and strikes, destroy before it approaches.

January 12, 1904

Is there death any more than sickness? No. Now, go and prove it.

You cannot be made to believe you cannot heal; you do heal. There are a few laws to be broken; then we will be free.

January 17, 1904

Learn what *watching* means. *Nothing* material belongs to Spirit; all materiality must be given up to get into heaven. There is no other way; you cannot take any of it with you.

I have watched all these years for you and the world; do you think anyone else in the world would have done as I have, held on through everything and not given up? I left everything, father, (Mother had gone), brother, relatives, everything; and because I held to this, my relatives would not speak to me, said I had disgraced them. [They] would ride along in their carriage, and I would be on the sidewalk, and they would not speak to me. All these have I given up, and I work on without a cent for it except from books—although I always advocate, "The labourer is worthy of his hire" [Luke 10:7]. Now, you watch; be always on duty—on guard.

If we were to pass on right here now in this room, we would waken right here, and nothing would be changed any more than you see it now.

January 23, 1904

All is Mind. If you do not heal, it is because you have not reached the realization in your treatment or—[you have not handled] reversal. *Science and Health* page 412 says, "To prevent disease or to cure it, the power of the divine Spirit must *break* this dream of the material senses.... Conform the argument so as to destroy the *evidence* of disease."[25] Also page 417 says, "When you silence the witness against your plea, you destroy the evidence, for the disease disappears."

January 29, 1904

Is it necessary that one eat and sleep? No. Then do not talk about eating and sleeping being a normal condition. Know that we depend upon *God* for everything, and then the emerging gently will take care of itself. Leave that with God. A musician would not call a discord a c[h]ord one time any more than another; neither must we mix Spirit and matter. What is this body you see? A belief of mortal mind. Are there any clouds? No. Any weather? No. Atmosphere? No, simply beliefs. Then haven't you dominion over the weather and clouds (beliefs) as you have over the body? Yes. Now, prove it.

Wrongs are done to me, and yet I turn right around and do them a kindness—not because I intend to do so, but I cannot help it, do it without thinking.

January 31, 1904

I used to heal with a word. I have seen a man yellow

because of disease, and the next moment I looked at him, his color was right; [he] was healed.

I knew no more how it was done than a baby—only it was done every time; I never failed, [and] almost always in one treatment, never more than three. Now God is showing me how, and I am showing you.

All we have to do is one thing: keep the First Commandment [see Exodus 20:3]—Thou shalt have none other gods before (beside) me, infinite Mind, and that is infinite Love. There is no evil mind; that sweeps away error. There is infinite Mind—Good. Infinity is all. There is no other intelligence, life, or love. Now, work out your problem from this standpoint. If we do not keep the First, we cannot keep the Second—to love one another. If ye love not man (your brother) whom you have seen, how can you love God whom you have not seen? [See I John 4:20]. You only love God as far as you love man.

February 8, 1904

When I say you are not doing a thing and you contradict—you say you are when there is no manifestation of it—you *think* you are, but belief is talking the louder, and the patient feels the belief instead of the [t]ruth and feels worse. You go right on arguing as fast as you can and think you are doing something; the way to do at such a time is to turn from the mesmerism to God, knowing He is all and there is nothing else. The above described condition of mesmerism is lack of faith in your treatment and in what I tell you. Know that the treatment is with power, for all power is God.

February 16, 1904

The Bible would seem to contradict itself, but it does

not when you know what it means. "Answer not a fool according to his folly" and "Answer a fool according to his folly" [Proverbs 26:4, 5]. They say my book (*Science and Health*) contradicts itself, but it does not when you understand it.

The Bible says, "Honor thy father and thy mother: that thy days may be long ..." [Exodus 20:12]. Then it says in Luke 14:26, "If any man come to me, and hate not his father, and mother, and wife, and children, and brethren, and sisters, yea, and his own life also, he cannot be my disciple." This would look like a direct contradiction of the words just quoted but is not; after we have honored our father and mother, then comes the next step—forsaking the flesh for Spirit.

We must be Christian Scientists and do as we say we believe or else be hypocrites. We *say* Spirit is all, and then when we have to take our choice between Spirit and the flesh, we cry, "The flesh, the flesh." God is coming very near to us, is making demands on us. Mr. Frye made his choice twenty-one years ago and since then has been having his experiences, and if he should pass now, [he] would waken to glorified being. Those who choose the flesh will yet have all the experience to go through. What is the result of forsaking all for Spirit? Dominion over the earth.

February 20, 1904

God is Love and Love is infinite. Realize this and you are safe from harm; nothing can touch you.

February 22, 1904

Do not let self-justification cloud over the [p]rinciple of right doing.

February 24, 1904

Do not work *against* error, but *feel* the Love that dissolves it.

February 26, 1904

If you can do a thing right once, you can every time.

February 15, 1907

[Do] not arrange things and then go to God, but go to God first. Then followed the reading of Luke 24:1–16 (about the resurrection). These things are occurring again. My words seem as "idle tales" to you; but I speak Truth.

February 17, 1907

There are no lies. All is Mind and governs. What is matter? Nothing. Mortal mind is matter; it cannot talk. Then hold to Mind, and the rest will take care of itself—the rest is nothing; this (material) is all nothing.

Life is Divine, immortal, and there is no other life. That is all the Life there is and is ours.

February 23, 1907

Stand with God and you will stand with Mother; stand with Mother and you will stand with God.

February 26, 1907

There is but one way through and only one way through, and that is to unself.

It is my unselfed love that has made a success of this Cause for the world.

Can you get rid of a lie and not get rid of it? No. Is it a lie that there is Life, substance, and intelligence in matter? Yes.

Then unself it. Everyone must do this. There is too much looking out for self instead of others. This is the trouble with the teaching of today, and [the reason] there is so much erroneous teaching being done; [it is] not unselfed enough.

You cannot *teach* Christian Science in that way. You can say over the words, but unless you prove it, you are not *teaching* (imparting). Prove it in healing the sick and casting out sin.

I pray and watch in the little details; someone must, as Good is expressed in the minutiae of things.

March 7, 1907

What is the one evil? Animal magnetism. Yes. Is it person? No. Is it anything? No. Then we cannot be harmed by it. That is what I mean by the one evil.

March 9, 1907

What is a way shower? There is a human and a divine meaning. A way shower is that which shows the way; it must be some *thing* or some *one*. Jesus was the Way-shower, the Christ with him, and if he had not been, where would we be? He showed the way as the masculine idea of Principle; then woman took it up at that point—the ascending thought in the scale—and is showing the way, thus representing the male and female Principle (the male and female of God's creating).

Is there anything in the world of more importance than holding up the hands of the Way-shower? No. If they had all done that with Jesus, we would be in the millennium. We must become unselfed.

Can you heal a disease by holding it or its symptoms before you? No. Then hold to the opposite (absolute Science) which does the healing.

March 13, 1907

God talks to me through this book (the Bible) as a person talks to another, and [He] has for forty years.

March 15, 1907

We must be resurrected from the dead—dead in trespasses and sin; the belief of life in the body, of matter, of life, substance, and intelligence in matter; the proclivities of the parents manifested through a belief in heredity, etc. We must be resurrected from all this, for what does Paul say, "Except ye have part in the resurrection, my preaching is vain" [see I Corinthians 15:12-14].

March 16, 1907

The hour is the acme of hate against Love, and Love alone can meet it. God *demands* God. *Truth* destroys error.

March 17, 1907

In balancing a pencil on the finger, if you put anything on one side, you take from the other. God is infinite, all, and has no opposite. Then the way to do is to hold with God; if not, what have we? Nothing. We must give up *all* for Christ, Truth, and not say, I have bought a farm, or a yoke of oxen, or married a wife and cannot come. 1 and 1 are 2; you cannot deviate from it one iota and have a correct answer; neither can you deviate from the law of God, or take the opposite of what the Scriptures say, and have a correct result. Error cannot get into the kingdom, so we must divest ourselves of it. We must hold with God alone.

I need to say before going before an audience, Now dear God, here I am, use me; I am absent from the body and present with Thee in consciousness. Love uses me in its own good way. I would lift myself right out of the material sense of self and audience, and let God use me.

March 20, 1907

My revelations for 40 years have come through the Scriptures; study them yourselves.

March 22, 1907

Stop denying error, and place all the balance on the right side, the side of God. You can negative [i.e., negate] error without individualizing it so much.

March 27, 1907

The disciples followed Jesus up to a certain point and then deserted him, and darkness followed. Follow the Way-shower, and you will follow the divine idea; turn away from the Way-shower, and you turn away from the divine idea—like [when] turning away from the window pane, you turn away from the light. It is not my personality you are following or that you love. You are being turned from the person to the idea. When this is accomplished, then you will be free in health to go on and do for the world.

March 29, 1907

We must give up *all* for Christ and Christian Science. We must come to see we do not depend upon eating, sleeping, etc., for Life and health, but depend on Mind. The spiritual cannot be touched.

Jesus did not make the demonstration over death but yielded to it—because of the desertion of his disciples. If they had stood by him, we should now be in the millennium.

That demonstration must be made, or the world will again be left in darkness. The students must hold up the hands of the Way-shower. They will say *you* have no need, but *you* can see the need.

March 31, 1907, Easter—Resurrection

We must be resurrected, must put off the old man and put on the new.

If you dress for Easter, your clothes are all in keeping, are clean. You do not put on some clean ones and some soiled ones. Neither can you put on part of the new man and part of the old; you must put on the whole of the new man, the spiritual idea.

If you put a new patch on an old garment, you will have the old garment.

There is a time when you take off your old garments before you put on the new. Now, if we patch up this body, try to make a better eye, a better limb, etc., we are not putting on the new.

We want to say, "Eye, you cannot talk to me. I have put you off." Rise to the spiritual sense, [and] then your body will respond; then take no thought what you eat, your clothes, etc., for "your heavenly Father knoweth ye have need of these things" [see Matthew 6:32]. This is the resurrection. The resurrection is not to be resurrected from matter, dust. There never was any Life in matter to be resurrected. The resurrection is seeing the real man that was never in matter; he never was sick to be made well. That is the way I did the healing; I never saw the material man before me, but the real man, perfect, and this healed instantaneously, and [with] no relapse. This is the way Jesus healed, as in *Science and Health* it reads, "Jesus beheld the perfect man ..." [see pp. 476-477]. This is the resurrection.

April 8, 1907

In healing you either have to know the allness of God, where there is no sickness, as I used to do, or else you must know what the disease is and argue it down. The same way with healing sin; you heal it with knowing there is no sin, for God is all, or you must know what the sin is and heal it that way.

In healing sickness, fear is back of it; destroy the fear and the case comes right up, out of it. In healing sin, hate is back of it (meaning hatred [of] Truth), so you must destroy the hate, and keep at it and keep at it until it is destroyed.

It is not of any use to want to die to get out of this constant struggle, for if you should do so, you would still have to keep at it until accomplished, and even more so because you would have to overcome not having done it when you could—a lost opportunity.

Lida, you have done beautifully since you have been here, have helped me *so much*.

April 9, 1907

When we *realize* the allness of God, that He is Life, Truth, Love, omnipotent, omnipresent, infinite Principle, all will be accomplished.

You have a belief about God—I have a belief about God.

April 18, 1907

The Way-shower must explore the way. You learn that way

by that experience. You are learning now from my experience. Old age is just as much of a claim to be overcome as cancer or any other belief. You have not come to it yet, but you will.

Overcome the belief in it *now*; you have it to do sometime.

When I let my thought down, I can hear the mental arguments of error, or the devil (there is no devil); it cannot hide from me when I want to know what it is doing.

I can lift my thought right above it and shut it all out, or I can find out what it is doing.

If there was an assassin which could overpower you, it would be better for you to know what he was doing so as to be better prepared to meet it.

If the work had been done in the time of Jesus, it would not have to be done now, but the disciples did not do their part. They were not obedient to him; they questioned what he was doing—did not understand—and it was not done. So it must be done now.

We can enter into immortality here on earth, now, and overcome death. We must do it. "Bear ye one another's burdens, and so fulfil the law of Christ" [Galatians 6:2].

April 20, 1907

After reading from the gospel of St. John, [Mrs. Eddy] said, this talk from the Bible is as plain as though the person, John, were present speaking to us because [t]ruth is impersonal.

There are no personalities, for God is *im*personal and to personalize ourselves, to say *I*, etc., is to selfishize ourselves. To personalize others is to selfishize others. This is not Christian Science.

The neighbor is one with the Father, so are we all one in Spirit. The "I" is one, infinite. This one who sees this and abides in it—becomes unselfed and is then ready to do for his neighbors—is a Christian Scientist. "Inasmuch as ye have done it unto one of the least of these my brethren, ye have done it unto me," said Jesus [Matthew 25:40].

When you rebuke sin, you cannot be nice to the sinner. Jesus said, "Get thee behind me, Satan," and called them *fools*, hypocrites. He [Jesus] did not palaver and smile and [was not] nice to them.

May 3, 1907

We must rise above the religion of the Hebrew, the Greek, the Catholic, and the Protestant to Christian Science. You only know as far as you demonstrate, as far as you prove. It is not Science to be too thin or too fleshy; either is a state of fear, for flesh manifests mind.

May 7, 1907

There is one thing needed all over the Field which is only supplied here and might not be supplied in the Field in centuries; that is, to have but one God, divine Principle, and its *demonstration*. (There is nothing [that] can prevent it.) To have one God—[then] father, mother, wife, children, [and] lands can have no claim upon you.

May 24, 1907

There are three things to keep before us continually: "to have one God"—one Mind [see Exodus 20:3]; "to love our neighbor as ourselves" [see Matthew 22:39]; and "do unto others as we would have others do unto us" [see Luke 6:31].

To have one Mind means for all to work alike—not you work in your work and I in my work, but work *together*. It is time for us today to *be* Christian Scientists and keep these points before us before doing anything.

May 25, 1907

God is all. To have God is to have all—harmony. Discord comes from looking away from all, thinking there is something else. You heal disease by knowing there is none. You heal sin in the same way. The prodigal goes into a far country thinking there is something there. I go after them thinking they have gone after something, and so it goes. But we must look to the spiritual as Paul says in 2 Corinthians 4:17, 18: "For our light affliction, which is but for a moment, worketh for us a far more exceeding and eternal weight of glory; while we look not at the things which are seen, but at the things which are not seen: for the things which are seen are temporal; but the things which are not seen are eternal."

May 26, 1907 (Divinity lesson)

What I am teaching is the spiritual. The material fights it and I fight the material; it will do it to you. The more spiritual the thought, the more will you be fought. That which takes the place of God and creates man and woman, and sees everything material, will fight the spiritual. We must see everything spiritual.

To sense, I am on the cross. Am I? No. What makes me on the cross? The belief that I am there. What would kill? The belief of being killed. See me (all right) (and others) as a spiritual idea and not on the cross; then you will see me as I am.

If I tell the truth of a lie, have I lied? Yes. If I tell a lie about the truth, have I lied? Yes. [T]alk is material. I sometimes think argument hinders the work by materializing the thought. Hold to the spiritual.

Knowing you do not depend upon the action of bowels or stomach, eyes to see, ears to hear, and sleep for rest, will rest you more than sleep. I have demonstrated this.

May 30, 1907

God's laws are eternal. They cannot be reversed; they *stand.* In your work you declare the [t]ruth about things; know those declarations *cannot* be reversed. I have for forty years stood with God through all this effort to reverse my work. If I had allowed the devil to reverse my work, where would it have been? *No.* I have stood and carried this Cause in spite of it, and all of you can do the same.

JOSEPH G. MANN *(1864–1932)*

Joseph Mann was born in Connecticut, the son of German immigrants. In 1886, he was healed through Christian Science after his brother-in-law accidentally shot him in the heart. Following this healing, Mann and his siblings became actively interested in Christian Science. Mann took Primary class from Mary Baker Eddy in 1888 and for the next five years lived off and on in Junction City, Kansas, where two of his brothers, Frederick and Christian, lived. During his time in Junction City, Mann helped organize a branch church and was listed there as a practitioner in The Christian Science Journal. *He also taught about 20 students in the area, though the majority of his teaching took place in Connecticut beginning in 1907.*

In 1894, Mann relocated his healing practice to Boston, Massachusetts. His sister, Pauline, joined him to keep house in a property on the site where the Original Mother Church would eventually be built. To help with finances, they rented rooms to Christian Scientists. After they moved and the Church had been built, they again opened their home to early workers in the movement, including Calvin Hill, Emma Easton Newman, and Annie Knott.

Mann attended Mary Baker Eddy's final class in 1898 and worked in her Pleasant View home from June 1898 to June 1902, as well as for shorter stints as late as 1907. Pauline worked for a time in Eddy's household as well. By 1904, however, both Joseph and Pauline had established residence in New Britain, Connecticut, and Mann was listed in The Christian Science Journal *as a practitioner there. Beginning in 1907, he also taught Christian Science in New Britain. In 1920, five years after Pauline passed on, Mann married Mrs. Alice Temple Newman, a Christian Science practitioner who had emigrated from England in 1905. In 1924, they moved to West Haven, Connecticut, and took up their healing work there.*

Privileged to Serve Our Leader

JOSEPH G. MANN

I should despair of doing justice to Mrs. Eddy's closet-life through the medium of word-painting, and were I able to write what I know, the world would regard my portrayal as a canonizing idealism. From my honest recounting of her daily life, even Christian Scientists might ascribe miraculousness to Mrs. Eddy rather than the ideality of a demonstrated spiritual reality whose every breath overcame the human with the divine.

My introduction to Mary Baker Eddy came in the classroom. I was one of a class of forty or fifty students taught by Mrs. Eddy in the Massachusetts Metaphysical College—the only chartered college in the world for teaching the Science of Christian Science Mind-healing—founded by Mary Baker Eddy, of which she was president, and in which she was then sole teacher.

Mrs. Eddy in the classroom

Our class, probably, was no exceptionally cosmopolitan

body, for always Mrs. Eddy's classes were as large in numbers as she would permit and as varied in personnel as the wide world afforded.

Before our large class of mature students (of whom I was the youngest in years, having only passed into my twenties) sat Mary Baker Eddy, natural and queenly. I witnessed with deepest interest the registration of the mental moods of the class in Mrs. Eddy's beautiful face. Her teaching was not from the intellectual standpoint of the letter or cold logic, or even a human sense of Science, but out of the spontaneity of the depth of Soul itself.

Another instance of her natural spiritual penetration is illustrated in the case of an old soldier-student in my class. This student had fought in the Civil War and, like many other soldiers, had come out of the army with an old chronic trouble which neither surgery nor materia medica had healed.

Mrs. Eddy one day suddenly turned to him and said, "Mr. So-and-so, you joined the army because of your love of right, to fight for the right and save the Union, did you not?"

The student, hesitating, disconcerted, instantly convicted, replied, "I don't know, Mrs. Eddy; I think I

PHOTO © THE MARY BAKER EDDY LIBRARY

CLASS RULES.

Students must take no notes
of their lessons.

They must not treat patients
during the term.

They must not treat each
other under ordinary
circumstances.

Massachusetts Metaphysical College class rules posted in the classroom

joined the army for the bounty that was offered."

Again Mrs. Eddy laughed with such heavenly satisfaction as to make me feel that the whole world was laughing with her, while my Grand Army[26] classmate blushed with confusion, no longer wondering why he was still selfish enough to be ailing.

A sharp rebuke to error brings healing

The class term included several lessons on the subtlety of malicious animal magnetism. During one of those lucid lessons, Mrs. Eddy gave the class a very vivid exposure of the dangers of hidden sin, or the secret workings of evil in the name of good. In short, she illustrated the need [for] the wisdom which is wiser than the wisdom of the serpent, whose instinct is to hide—even the divine Wisdom, which brings the serpent out of its hole, or hiding, to its self-destruction. During Mrs. Eddy's fearless uncovering of the serpent, [a] classmate suddenly cried out in wild fear of the exposed serpent [she] supposed to be crawling about the room, "Oh! Mrs. Eddy, I'm so afraid of the serpent!"

Quick as lightning from heaven, Mrs. Eddy rebuked the malicious evil she had uncovered; and her words "There is no serpent!" accompanied by a stamp of her foot, which shook the platform and reverberated over the classroom, were more powerfully thunderous to the victim—to her arousal and instant restoration—than is the thunder following the lightning flash which self-shatters the threatening storm cloud.

Reporting for duty at Pleasant View

Having learned of the need of additional helpers at Pleasant View, and after much earnest prayer, I volunteered my services to Mrs. Eddy in whatever capacity she might see fit to use me. I reported for duty at Pleasant View in the year 1898. After my arrival Mrs. Eddy called me to her for the purpose of outlining in a general way what she hoped I might do to relieve Mr. Frye of growing [outdoor] duties.

Pleasant View comprised many acres with a very pleasant, indeed natural, southern outlook, though at that time the estate was still in the making. When Mrs. Eddy purchased it, Pleasant View was within her own conscious-ness—her own mental concept of divine possibilities to be humanly evolved by that transformation of an abandoned

Haying with a horse-drawn wagon at Pleasant View

PHOTO BY CALVIN FRYE © THE MARY BAKER EDDY COLLECTION

New England farm into a well-ordered, simple estate.

I entered upon my duties at Pleasant View as superintendent, a capacity of service which involved not only the care of the farm, the garden, the stable, the greenhouse, and the help needed in the care of these, but also the making of such improvements as Mrs. Eddy would outline from time to time.

Being a stranger in Concord and at Pleasant View, having just come out of the Field of Christian Science practice in Boston, I quite naturally felt at a loss as to just how best to begin in my new sphere of duties. I was sure of only one thing—that I had come to Pleasant View to help our beloved Leader in such ways as I might, to lighten her burden by being as selfless in serving her, as she, under God, was the unacknowledged faithful servant of the whole world.

Mrs. Eddy lovingly expressed to me her hope that I [would] look after everything about the place as if it were my own. I promptly assured her that I would be most glad to do so, and incidentally I remarked, "While I am getting acquainted with the requirements of my new calling, I shall feel free to ask Mr. Frye about matters not known to me." But Mrs. Eddy immediately interposed, "No, dear, don't ask Mr. Frye—ask God."

In all my later years at Pleasant View, I witnessed how truly Mrs. Eddy realized in daily living the truth of her initial sentence to the preface of her God-inspired textbook, *Science and Health with Key to the Scriptures*: "To those leaning on the sustaining infinite, to-day is big with blessings" [p. vii].

Lively kindness—and firmness

It is not an exaggeration to say that without doubt, in her time, Mrs. Eddy was the busiest woman on earth. Yet I recall an instance which illustrates the fact that Love is never too busy to be kind and considerate. The painters were at work painting the house. The day was cold and quite cheerless. Mrs. Eddy called her maid to her and asked her to provide hot coffee with cream and sugar for the painters.

Mrs. Eddy herself drank neither tea nor coffee, but always as hostess, she preferred considerately and lovingly to draw her guests to her. To Mrs. Eddy, nothing that her ever wide-awake Love-sense could see to do was of minor importance. Though preoccupied with the largest world problems, she constantly surprised me with her intimate knowledge of everything in daily affairs about her.

[Another time], with her characteristic aliveness, Mrs. Eddy once thunderingly rebuked her household with the query, "Have you no God?"—arousing us out of a self-mesmeric barrenness resulting from a very liberal use of the letter quite devoid of the quickening Spirit; that is, devoid of the grace of God-with-us.

What she wrote in *Science and Health* was clearly her ideal of Christian striving. She says: "The notion that animal natures can possibly give force to character is too absurd for consideration, when we remember that through spiritual ascendency our Lord and Master healed the sick, raised the dead, and commanded even the winds and waves to obey him. Grace and Truth are potent beyond all other means and methods" [p. 67].

Spiritual impulsion and intuition

Mrs. Eddy became the modern pioneer Christian not from human choice but by reason of divine necessity. What Mrs. Eddy did was the overflow of a selfless, spiritual naturalness. Only those humanly near could appreciate the practical sweetness and severity of her spontaneous God-governed and -directed life. I never doubted Mrs. Eddy's providential direction—her right and rightness—even when it was sometimes humanly hard to understand.

Mrs. Eddy one day called the attention of the carpenter to a slight discrepancy in the height of the ends of the balustrade surrounding the balcony just outside the bay window of her study. To her sense the balustrade was at least an inch lower at the end toward her window. It was only after measuring that the carpenter, to his chagrin, was convinced that Mrs. Eddy was right and that the intuitive measurements of pure Mind are truer than expert, trained human judgment.

I remember with gratitude a most meaningful lesson which Mrs. Eddy very tenderly and lovingly gave me. Our long row of healthy apple trees had yielded much more choice fruit than Pleasant View needed. Out of our bounty, I gave a barrel of her nice apples as a special thanks from Pleasant View to the obliging boys at the express office, having in mind their always willing heart and hand. Quite incidentally and innocently, I told Mrs. Eddy of it. She was glad I had been generously thoughtful of the boys and said so, but added so very motherly, "The next time, dear, you will tell Mother before you do even a kindness in her name?"

I once heard Mrs. Eddy illustrate [a] particular point of watchfulness before about one hundred of her students whom she had invited to visit her at Pleasant View. She sat in her large reception room with her students crowding about her and spoke to them with that quiet earnestness which impresses itself indelibly upon the receptive thought. [She said], "My students think they do well when they discover the burglar after he has broken in and then succeed in throwing or driving him out; but Mother watches and sees his intent before he gets in and, by faithfully locking the doors and windows, keeps him from getting in." Mrs. Eddy always guarded against the too-human tendency [to] blindly do evil in the hope of doing good.

An inspired—and inspiring—reader

I recall the natural beauty of Mrs. Eddy's reading of the Scriptures, as I have often heard her read to her household, or to me, to share some special point of inspiration that had come to her. As she read, both reader and the word were quite lost sight of in her natural fervor of heart-appeal. It is impossible to describe in words with what musical modulation and inflection the genuine pleading of her reading was the reflection of God-with-us.

Often she would preface some morning Scripture-reading with the confiding invitation, "Come and hear what God said to me this morning," and then she would read as God's ambassador. There was nothing of the assumed or artificial in all her reading; she read with the unaffected grace of a heart overflowing with humility and understanding, even as she spoke from demonstration as one who had suffered and who had a right to speak.

Mr. Frye and I, by her special and impromptu appointment one Sunday, read for Mrs. Eddy and her household the universal Lesson-Sermon; this was the first time that Mrs. Eddy had heard the reading of the services which she had instituted for her Church, over which the impersonal pastor, the Bible and *Science and Health with Key to the Scriptures*, ordained by her, was presiding.

I venture to say that two readers have never had so interested and interesting a listener as Mrs. Eddy on that memorable Sunday at Pleasant View. At the close of the heavenly little home-service, Mrs. Eddy thanked the readers most heartily for their part; she expressed her joy in the sermon and gave a special word of praise to the reader of the Scriptures, assuring him lovingly, that she had never heard the Bible read more understandingly.

Our Leader's ageless beauty

Mrs. Eddy's demonstration of her inspired concept of beauty proved to me that it is impossible for the unreal veil of sense to hide the radiance of Soul. One could not see Mrs. Eddy and think of her as growing old. It were easier to imagine sunlight affected by shadows, than to think that age could mar her "charms of being" [*Science and Health*, p. 247].

Even under the weight of earth's most cruel wickedness, Mrs. Eddy bore her daily cross with Christian dignity and godly poise. There were no unlovely and useless years in Mrs. Eddy's life; on the contrary, I knew her only as always about the Father's business with the glow of His inspiration so self-evident upon her as to naturally confirm the truth of her own words: "Love never loses sight of loveliness" [*Science and Health*, p. 248].

To human sense, age implies helplessness. In Mrs. Eddy's increasingly Soul-governed life, the opposite was true. She allowed neither multiplying years nor time's vicissitudes to interfere with her usefulness. Her riper years only added wisdom to her ability to do, while age but added to the stateliness of her womanhood, as she emulated with her increasing spirituality the demonstration of Christ Jesus, who to the end lived to minister, "not to be ministered unto" [Matthew 20:28].

I intuitively recognized that to truly serve Mrs. Eddy, I must demonstrate an aliveness to duty which amounted to a spontaneity of wisdom in action that was akin to the godliness in which she rested. It was, therefore, my living prayer to be so alive to the originality of God-with-me as to enable me to do harmoniously and quickly the things of which I knew she had need and, whenever possible, to bring to her the joy of good fruitage before she knew I had planted.

Pure spirituality and stern affection

As Mrs. Eddy, on the watchtower of spiritual understanding, was always keenly alive not to be deceived by the works of the darkness that appears to be light, so she taught that not all apparent healing in the name of Christian Science is true Christian healing. On this same basis Mrs. Eddy rejoiced not so much in whatever was accomplished as in the manner of its accomplishment.

To Mrs. Eddy the ideal was not transcendental. Her life did not elevate God above the world, but she made appreciable the Revelator's vision that God dwells with men and so shall be their God and they His people [see Revelation 21:3]. Mrs. Eddy was a true friend in that she had the moral courage to wound when the necessity for sin-healing demanded it.

The following letter written to me during my first year of serving at Pleasant View, hints [at] the [l]ove that healed after it had wounded:

> Pleasant View
> Concord, New Hampshire
> July 8, 1899

My beloved Son:

You know Mother wrote *Science and Health* under [d]ivine orders. When I left the room the last day you were here[,] I thought I had done speaking to you. But when I opened the Bible[,] I felt *impelled* to return and knew not why!

What I said I now know but little of. Why I said it *God alone knows*.

But from experience I must believe it was needed or I should not have been so led. I remember only your kind care for me and my place. I remember never a word or act of yours that was not kind. I remember that God is Love and that He loves us all and knows best what we most need—so let His will be done.

With [l]ove,
Mother
M.B. Eddy

The Godlike glory of our beloved Leader's natural, spiritual affection revealed to me the demonstrable fact that Love itself is sweet or bitter to us, just in the degree that we ourselves are saints or sinners. A saint's heaven is a sinner's hell.

A gracious hostess

It was my good fortune while at Pleasant View to meet men and women of note—lights of the professions of business and of letters—who regarded an interview with Mrs. Eddy as a privilege. Invariably, distinguished callers, whom it was often my pleasure after the visit to take to the station, expressed in glowing terms their admiration of Mrs. Eddy. Lawyers, for instance, were surprised at her understanding grasp of law; businessmen marveled that a woman should manifest such an enterprising capacity for business. Leading lights generally were astounded by her comprehensive knowledge of world problems and her deep, motherly heart-interest in the weal of the world.

At supper one evening, the conversation was turned to the subject of cooking. Various general remarks were made by different members of the family relative to the fine points of scientific requirements as to proper seasoning, delicate flavoring, the human differences of taste, et cetera. Mrs. Eddy naively contributed to the conversation, saying, "My students tell me that nobody can make cocoa that tastes quite like that which Mother makes, but I don't know why it is so, unless it is that Mother stirs more [l]ove into it."

It is also inspiring to recall and to accent an especially noteworthy bent in the life of our Leader—her always selfless and loving consideration of others. This was most pronounced in her home life, where, in conversation with her guests, she considerately interested herself in subjects and things which most interested them. As dear as the living subject of Christian Science was to her heart, I never knew her to introduce it to visitors or guests who were not Christian Scientists.

Mrs. Eddy, ever tenderly watchful, always practiced far more than she preached, demonstrating what all true followers who emulate her know—that divine Love consistently lived on earth as it is in heaven makes a Christian Scientist a ministering angel. This heaven-born spirit pervaded the atmosphere of her home, of which she was the exemplary center.

Refined sensibilities and sincere humility

When a mere girl, blooming into young womanhood, Mrs. Eddy's inborn purity asserted itself quite appreciably to a young man who was as thoughtless or discourteous as to smoke in her presence. Before the company of young friends who had come to bid her farewell, she snatched a cigar from his mouth and to his rebuke threw it out of the car window.

Her refined, purity-loving nature naturally shrank from a world reeking in sensuousness. She never regarded herself especially favored of God, except as she construed her human suffering resulting from her inherited delicate constitution, or as David recognized God's hand upon him when he said, "thy rod and thy staff, they comfort me," [Psalms 23:4].

I happily recall how, upon an informal occasion, Mrs. Eddy inadvertently ruminated aloud, with sweet, childlike wonderment, saying, "I don't understand, Joseph dear, how it is that people press upon me so, why they want to see me, why even lords and ladies come from across the sea to call upon me—me, an antiquated old fossil!"

[In a more formal setting, during a class,] Mrs. Eddy [once] asked, "Does anyone in the world understand

Science and Health?" One student answered in the affirmative; whereupon Mrs. Eddy asked, "Who?"

The student replied, "Mrs. Eddy."

But Mrs. Eddy, with an earnestness which amounted to solemnity, shaking her head emphatically, said, "No! No! A thousand times No!"

Divinely impelled leadership

Mrs. Eddy was preeminently a Leader, the strength and glory of whose leadership lay in her own consecrated following of the Christ, a Leader [who was] herself irresistibly divinely led. Humanly she could not have compelled others to follow her. In humility she could teach and lead them through Love demonstrated in healing, but she could not personally rule.

The greatness of Mrs. Eddy's leadership was best seen in the naturalness of her closet-home life. Here we witness her leadership of Love, practically demonstrated—Love amounting to law, divinely not humanly enforced.

An earnest, honest, consecrated student protesting his appreciation of her leadership, said to her, "Mrs. Eddy, I'll follow you faithfully, as far as I can see!" Her swift reply, rebuking his limited sense, was, "You can't see; you will have to walk by faith."

Mary Baker Eddy did not vie with the ages in imposing architectural church splendor when she inspired the building of The Mother Church. But she was mindful of the "one thing needful" [see Luke 10:42], according to the Master, and prayed to outshine the church builders of the old world not in magnificence of cathedrals but in the simplicity of the spiritual building in which she humbly led—even the spiritual building which overcomes "the world, the flesh, and the devil," for whose superstructure of self-sacrifice Christ Jesus laid the foundation.

One day as I was about to leave her presence, she arose from her comfortable chair, clasped my hand firmly, and resting her venerable head on my shoulder, mused aloud, oh, so tenderly: "Joseph, dear, Mother is homesick for heaven."

My first Christian Science healing

To God, through Mrs. Eddy, belongs the credit of that which to benighted believers seemed a miracle of healing. The four physicians called to my death-bed, after a final consultation, agreed that nothing more could be done for me. I had been accidentally shot and their diagnosis revealed the ball from the thirty-two caliber revolver lodged in the inner layer of the pericardium of the heart. From the depth of this human hopelessness, with all the evidence of the triumph of the last enemy clearly apparent upon the body, Christian Science awakened me to a new sense of life which brought with it an almost instantaneous restoration to health. With the return of consciousness came the glow of warmth, driving out the chill of death.

It is noteworthy here to mention a point introduced in my primary class at the Massachusetts Metaphysical College relative to President Garfield's long period of languishing between life and death. The student asked why Garfield was not healed through the prayer of Christian Scientists who had volunteered their best when the dying president had been given up. By way of answering, Mrs. Eddy cited my case of healing to illustrate her point. She said, "We have with us in this class a man who was far more dangerously wounded than postmortem evidence showed Garfield to have been, and yet this man was healed in Christian Science." Mrs. Eddy then expatiated on the weight of universal belief for or against a case, saying, "Garfield, as President, was at the mercy of pitiless publicity, whereas the man who is with us was too inconspicuous to have been known beyond his neighbor-friends, and even they, as well as every relative, were kept from the bedside of the stricken struggler."

It is apropos of this subject to record here the substance of an inspiring conversation I once had with Mrs. Eddy along the lines of true healing or spiritual awakening, which in whatever degree realized prophesies the ultimate triumph of Life over death. During the conversation Mrs. Eddy questioned deeply into my experience. Her sweetly appreciative comment of it, I reverently record: "You have had a wonderful experience. You were thrown violently out of the house and picked yourself up outside; go not back into the house."

A spontaneous lesson

A very natural experience came to me one day which elucidated the true meaning of the Master's startling claim, "I and my Father are one" [John 10:30]—a scientific declaration of the oneness or unity of son and Father. Mrs. Eddy had called me to her, as she in directing affairs was wont to do, and before touching upon any point of the day's outline, she most graciously complimented and sweetly thanked me for the good work I had done.

I at once thanked her for her special word of loving appreciation, saying, "But, Mother, it was not I who did it; the credit belongs to God." Quick as lightning Mrs. Eddy gently rebuked my false modesty with her usual heavenly decisiveness: "Yes, dear, but God is never seen apart from man, and when I speak of God, I mean also His reflection, for I cannot separate them; they are one, and that one is God and man. I know and see God only in His reflection."

Our Leader's humble start as author

Even after she had written her inspired volume *Science and Health*, Mrs. Eddy continued for some time to do her own housework. And so it was in dusting cap and with broom in hand that a famous author, in search of the author of *Science and Health*, found her as she responded to his friendly knock. Mrs. Eddy related this historic incident of her early life with a view of awakening us to the fact that a true Christian Scientist begins patiently at the foot of the ladder which reaches from earth to heaven but does not remain there; inspiration indicates the need of legitimate progress and justifies its hope and expectation. Mrs. Eddy said of the experience that it was no disgrace for the author of *Science and Health* to be discovered wearing a dust cap and with broom in hand, but it would not have been in keeping with the inevitability of the law of progress for her to remain where her distinguished literary caller found her.

Increasingly spiritual Christmas celebrations

I am most grateful to have seen at Pleasant View Mrs. Eddy's natural footsteps from a glorious human sense of Christmas, most lovingly and practically celebrated with choice gifts, to that divine sense which she immortalized in her numerous writings for the inspiration of her followers. Mrs. Eddy's own notes to me so beautifully hint her divine leading out of the too-human sense of Christmas that I give [two of] them here. They, as a spiritual awakening, were Mrs. Eddy's gift to me on that memorable Christmas:

Joseph, dear:

Please purchase for Mother these
things, and put my card in each package
and sly it into their rooms for Christmas.

With love always,
Mother

Enclosed with this note to me was a list of the names of every member of her family and all helpers at the cottage, with Mrs. Eddy's own selection of the presents for each one.

The joy with which this great, godly woman entered into the Christmas spirit reminded me of the Master's words, "Except ye ... become as little children, ye shall not enter into the kingdom of heaven" [Matthew 18:3].

[But] before I could start for town to do her Christmas shopping, the following note came, lifting my thought above it all:

Dear Joseph:

I did not think of what I was putting
on you of materiality. I am sorry.

Let me change the program....
Give yourself a new *Science and Health*
when it appears; and give your thought
to God. Help me that way.

With love,
Mother

[Another year, 1899,] the following Christmas note gladdened my heart, not because of the check for one hundred dollars which Mrs. Eddy sent with it but because of her reassuring words:

My beloved Student:

> With gratitude and love for your kindness and faithful help the past year,

> I am lovingly your debtor, Mother,
> Mary Baker Eddy

Her reassuring words of "gratitude and love" have always meant much to me, but what is such an individual remembrance compared to the gift of her life to the world through Christian Science?

Mrs. Eddy's life of spiritual uplift is hinted in her exalted portrayal of "What Christmas Means to Me," in which [are these] final words:

> I love to observe Christmas in
> quietude, humility, benevolence, charity,
> letting good will towards man, eloquent
> silence, prayer, and praise express my
> conception of Truth's appearing.

> The splendor of this nativity of Christ
> reveals infinite meanings and gives
> manifold blessings. Material gifts and
> pastimes tend to obliterate the spiritual
> idea in consciousness, leaving one alone
> and without His glory. [*The First Church of
> Christ, Scientist, and Miscellany*, pp. 262–263]

An enriching encounter during a difficult trial

It would be quite impossible to write what I feel about the heart-rending situation that was forced upon Mrs. Eddy through the so-called "Next Friends," who had concocted a scheme whereby to prove Mrs. Eddy incompetent.[27] While the persecuting trial was upon her, Mrs. Eddy called me from my new Field work to take again my place among the workers at Pleasant View for a few weeks. The morning after my arrival, Mrs. Eddy called me into her study to instruct me in the work I was to take up. I found her serious to the point of sadness, under the weight of that maliciously instigated court proceeding.

During the conversation that ensued, Mrs. Eddy deprecated the wickedness that was, through human relationship, trying to discredit her in the eyes of the world in the hope of ending her living leadership as the pioneer Christian Scientist. Her only son,[28] not understanding the power of God in Christian Science to shield him from the evil influence of the personally ambitious, had become the open avenue for insidious workings against his mother. As she ruminated upon the miserable situation, she plaintively soliloquized, "For every mistake Mother has ever made, she has suffered, and suffered, and suffered." But, O, how her sweet face lighted up when tenderly, reassuringly I said to her, "Cheer up, Mother, for this is the last channel of flesh-relationship through which evil would presume to reach you."

In spite of her own immediate and great need, Mrs. Eddy found time to lovingly inquire about my activities in the Field. She was glad that I had prospered, glad to know of the building of a little church in my new Field of service. Of these she said, "I like those small beginnings. First, the right thought, then right words, and words proved by the hands." It was inspiring once more to hear her read to me as she did upon the first morning of my return. She read naturally, sweetly, and without glasses a large share of two chapters from the Bible. What I had learned in previous years of service was renewedly emphasized now upon my return—namely, that it is impossible unselfishly to give without also receiving. I had come to Pleasant View only to give, but I left feeling greatly enriched.

Precious exchanges

Out of motherly appreciation, Mrs. Eddy presented me with a very neat gold watch on the inner plate of which was engraved, "With Love, Mother." In thanking her I said quite earnestly, "It will remind me always to be on time." Mrs. Eddy smiled appreciatively and said, "Yes, dear, it will remind you that time is precious and belongs to God; and throughout time, it will say to you—'Watch!'"

One evening during the Primary class term, Mrs. Eddy gave a class reception [so] that we might all take her by the hand and at the same time get better acquainted with one another. The benedictive tone of that memorable evening was sounded for me during my few moments apart with my venerable teacher. As I took her hand, I said, "Mrs. Eddy, I have passed through very trying experiences before coming to this class, but *Science and Health* saved me." Her very earnest, reassuring, motherly response was, "Yes, dear, and it will save everyone who adheres to its inspired teaching and spiritually enlightening leading."

One Easter Sunday morning Mrs. Eddy called her household to her and gave us an Easter lesson to which I cannot hope to do justice from memory, but I want to hint the spirit of it and to share a few of the quickening points which I noted at the time. After elaborating upon the true meaning of Easter, she hinted the inevitability of spiritual radicalness in the progressive unfoldment of the new birth. She said:

> You must get rid of the "old man,"
> the old woman; you cannot make them
> better and keep them. You are not getting
> rid of the old man if you try to make him
> better. If you should succeed in making
> him better, he would stay with you. If you
> patch up the old and say it is good enough,
> you do not put it off, but keep it. If you
> try to make the old satisfactory, you are
> preparing to keep it, not to put it off.
>
> We have but one Mind, and to abide
> in this perfect freedom of individuality
> is the resurrection, is to have risen above
> material or lower demands. The resurrec-
> tive sense is positive; it is, "yea, yea and
> nay, nay." The resurrective sense does not
> listen compromisingly to error. It is *always*
> about its "Father's business," reflecting
> Principle. Jesus' whole life was resur-
> rective; that is, his life was a constant,
> conscious rising spiritually above sin,
> sickness, death. And his resurrection from
> the grave was to sense a type of divine

Love's final triumph over the human belief
that matter is substance or has power to
impose limitations [on] Mind or man.

Caring for Mrs. Eddy's animals and property

The coachman at Pleasant View was not a Christian
Scientist, but he believed himself to be a thorough
horseman. [One] horse had been lame a week or more when,
one day while out on her drive, Mrs. Eddy inquired of the
coachman, saying, "Henry, can you cure the horse?"

Henry answered promptly, "I think I can. There is a
certain liniment which I think will heal him."

Mrs. Eddy said, "How long a trial do you want?"

"About ten days," Henry replied.

"Very well," Mrs. Eddy said, "Make the most of your
time."

At the end of the ten days, the horse was still very lame.
Mrs. Eddy said to Henry, "The horse is still lame; have you
given your medicine a fair trial?" Henry frankly admitted
that he had.

Mrs. Eddy then said to him, "Will you now let Mr. Mann
have as fair a trial to treat the horse with the mental medicine of Christian Science?"

Henry replied that he would be glad to see the horse
healed in any way. Whereupon Mrs. Eddy called me to her
and said, "Joseph, please take up the horse that Henry has
failed to heal and demonstrate, in healing him, the power of
Mind-healing." In less than a week, the horse was perfectly
sound, to the rejoicing of all.

A windmill was operated at Pleasant View to add to the
supply of spring water for the little pond some distance

from the house and at the foot of the slope in the meadow. One unusually windy day, a very annoying squeak developed, which with every revolution of the wheel could easily be heard at the house. I knew it to be Mrs. Eddy's special hour of prayer for the world. Determined not to have her disturbed by this wicked noise, I cast about for a volunteer from among the men who would silence the discord. To my surprise I found the men afraid to go up that height with the mill in operation in so strong a wind. And so it happened that I, filled only with the desire to help Mother, took an oil can and smilingly, hand over hand, went up into the mill. I oiled the gearing, healing the squeak with [l]ove's lubricant, and thence to earth again to the joy of every observer. But little did I, or anyone dream, that Mrs. Eddy also had been an interested spectator.

The next day Mrs. Eddy preceded our usual business interview with the following sweet, motherly disclosure: "Mother admired your agility and fearlessness when yesterday, for her sake, you clambered up into the windmill to arrest the offender hiding there behind that threatening wind, but you will not do it again, will you, dear?"

I saw clearly as she spoke that it was no mere motherly favoritism which prompted Mrs. Eddy's loving consideration of me; but rather I saw the scientific reason behind it—namely that faithful service involved my awakening to a sense of my individual value to her beyond any mere hand service. Mrs. Eddy knew better than a commanding general knows that the malicious enemy trains its sharpshooters upon an exposed officer before it risks a shot at a private.

The same wise motherly concern was evidenced by

Eddy's Yale automobile with John Salchow at the wheel and Joseph Mann in the passenger seat

Mrs. Eddy when she learned that I had cleared the north roof of the house of all snow to prevent snowslides from frightening the horses as she entered or emerged from her carriage. But I assured Mrs. Eddy that I was quite awake to my danger and reassured her by telling her that, when I went up on the roof, I tied myself to the chimney with a strong rope. At this she laughed heartily and commended me for my ingenuity.

A true sense of home and service

Mrs. Eddy wanted me to employ what real grace I had in helping to save those who had come to serve at Pleasant View from the homesickness which tempted those who had not fully left a human home to find their real home in the Christ-mind. I am grateful to let her own letter speak for itself:

Pleasant View
Concord, N.H.
Nov. 21st

My dear Student:

I thank you for your faithful work on my book[;] it encourages me to know I am so near being done with this *careful* work on *Science and Health.* The best of it is the book will be so perfect a standard now in capital letters and all else. I consider you now in my employ as usual and there is always enough to be done.

Keep dear Mrs. _____ from being homesick. They all have it so much easier when away than when at the post besieged, they are apt to go away.

But they should be at this post of duty more than all others[,] and God will bless them for it more than for aught else. This I know to be true.

With [l]ove, Mother
M.B. Eddy

The world, from the standpoint of its carnal criterion, can never appreciate the righteousness of a spiritual leader. Jesus' enemies could hardly tell the truth about the humble Way-shower, who really lived in heaven even while he sojourned, for the good of the world, on earth. Of Jesus Mrs. Eddy writes in *Science and Health with Key to the Scriptures,*

"The world acknowledged not his righteousness, seeing it not; but earth received the harmony his glorified example introduced" [p. 54]. What Mrs. Eddy here says of Jesus is equally true of herself. She was really known only by those who had the good fortune either to live understandingly in her home or to see her in the light of the spiritual understanding of Christian Science. So my prayer is to write of Mrs. Eddy as a friend or as one who understands her sufficiently to tell the truth about her.

CLARA M. S. SHANNON *(1855–1930)*

*A native of England, Clara Shannon immigrated to
Montreal, Canada, with her family in 1873 and soon
began a singing career. In 1887, she was healed through
Christian Science of a severe physical ailment and took
Primary class instruction from Mary Baker Eddy the
following year. That same year, she began her healing
practice in Montreal and, after taking Normal class from
Eddy in 1889, began teaching Christian Science. Shannon
also established the Montreal Institute of Christian
Science[29] and helped organize the first branch church
there.*

*In 1892, Shannon began serving as a metaphysical
worker in Eddy's Pleasant View household. She served off
and on there, sometimes for long stretches, until 1903 and
then again briefly in 1907. Her longest period of service
was from September 1894 to January 1899. During that
period, in 1895, she was elected a First Member of The
Mother Church.[30]*

Shannon moved back to England in 1903 and established her healing practice there. From England, she traveled twice to Palestine, once in 1906 and again in 1910. Following her final term of service at Pleasant View in 1907, Shannon returned to England and, at Eddy's request, began teaching Christian Science in London, where she taught and healed until her passing.

In writing her reminiscence, Shannon describes herself as "one who is grateful to be able to testify to the truth about our beloved and revered Leader."

Golden Memories

CLARA M. S. SHANNON

This grand and glorious woman has been the means of revealing to the world God as Spirit, and the universe, including man, as wholly spiritual—His spiritual ideas and reflection. Oh, what a wonderful revelation, what a mission! Think of the enormous work which she achieved—what she had to work out of, to rise above, to conquer, in order to give mankind this spiritual [t]ruth of which the Master promised, "The truth shall make you free" [John 8:32]. [She is] the revelator of heaven and earth and man spiritual.

Mrs. Eddy's discernment as a child

When she was a tiny child, her sisters used to take her to school with them because she always wanted to go. During the time allotted for their lunch, they would sit her on a table and would say, "Mary, what are you going to do when you are grown up?" To which she would reply "I will 'ite a book."

When she was only a few years old, she used to sleep on a trundle bed. Sometimes her mother would go out in the evening after putting Baby to bed, and her father would sit in the parlor reading. Mary would call out, "Father, I know what you are doing; you are reading the newspaper." To which he would reply, "Hush, child, and go to sleep." Then she would say, "I'll read it to you," and she would tell him what he was reading although she could not pronounce the long words.

My reason for saying this is because of what we read in *Retrospection and Introspection* in "Voices Not Our Own," where she speaks of this time of her childhood and of the voices which she heard (see first edition, p. 16).[31] Also in a letter to Judge Septimus J. Hanna, published in his pamphlet "Christian Science History,"[32] she writes:

> I can discern in the human mind,
> thoughts, motives, and purpose; and neither
> mental arguments nor psychic power can
> affect this spiritual insight. It is as impos-
> sible to prevent this native perception as to
> open the door of a room and then prevent
> a man who is not blind from looking into
> the room and seeing all it contains. This
> mind-reading is first sight; it is the gift of
> God. And this phenomenon appeared in my
> childhood; it is associated with my earliest
> memories, and has increased with years.
> It has enabled me to heal in a marvelous
> manner, to be just in judgment, to learn
> the divine Mind,—and it cannot be abused:
> no evil can be done by reason of it. (p. 16)

She was certainly a very unusual child. One Sunday, after church service was over, Mrs. Baker took little Mary with her to call on the pastor's wife, who was very ill. She was thought to have a tumor. Although she and her husband had been married for fifteen years, they were childless, which was a grief to her because she loved children dearly. Mrs. Baker read the Bible and sang some hymns, in which the little girl joined, and it cheered and comforted their pastor's wife very much. After they left the house, Mary said, "Mother, I saw a dear little baby all cuddled up close and warm inside." So Mrs. Baker told her that there were no babies there. She said, "But, Mother, I did see it: a little baby all cuddled up inside." Afterwards, this seemed wonderful as, to the amazement of her friends, this lady gave birth to a son.

Certainly from earliest childhood, Mary Baker was full of grace and truth, and her vision transcended the usual mortal limitations in more ways than one.

Here is an anecdote that Mrs. Eddy told me as a lesson in economy, which was to teach me not to be wasteful. When they were children, in the winter evenings they used to shell corn for food for the chickens, etc. On one occasion little Mary was sitting by the fire, and as she shelled, a grain of corn fell off her lap. She pushed it with her little foot towards the burning log. Her mother said, "Mary, get down and pick up that corn." She answered, "Oh, Mother, it is only one grain." "Never mind," said her mother. "It will help to make a meal for a little chick." I have not forgotten that lesson.

Starting out as a young bride

On her wedding day in 1843, our Leader stopped at Concord for the night in order to visit her old home at Bow

An illustration of Eddy's childhood home in Bow, New Hampshire

on the next day. The young bride and bridegroom [George Glover] were journeying to the South by a sailing ship, and before [Mary left] home, her mother had given her a letter addressed to herself with injunctions that she read it with her husband when they were halfway through the sea voyage. Before this time, however, a severe storm arose, and the captain said that he did not think there was any hope of saving the ship. So she and her husband kneeled down in their cabin, praying to God to save them. She said, "I want to read my mother's letter. I know we are not halfway across yet, but this may be the only opportunity." She read the letter, a beautiful letter, such good advice, which was treasured. It was helpful to them then; she saw all its meaning and its love, and this helped her much. They continued in their prayer to God. In a short time the captain came below to say, "The wind has suddenly subsided, and we are safe." Coming on deck they found a peaceful sea, and the journey was continued in calm and peace and without any further misadventure.

The next important event in her life was the loss of her husband, and to her it seemed to be the loss of everything. She was very beautiful with long curls, which her husband used to admire greatly. After his burial she shut herself up in her room and gave orders to a maid to sit outside the door and not permit anyone to enter. She continued this for days, eating very little.

One day a friend of her husband, who was a Freemason, went to the door and forced the maid to allow him to enter. Within, he beheld that lovely, tear-stained face, her hair disheveled, her eyes red with weeping, saddened with grief, dimmed with sorrow. In vain he tried to console her and to waken her from her dream of loss and sorrow. Her grief was such that she refused to be comforted. At length he said, "What would your husband say to you if he came now and looked at you? What would he say to those curls? Are they as beautiful as you would like him to see? What would he say to this face? What would he say to you for this action and [for] yielding to your agony of grief?"

She said that wakened her; she got up saying that it was all right—he could go away, he had done his work. She arose, washed her face, recurled her hair, and made herself natural. Oh, what a sad experience and deep grief such loss was to that dear one. Then the Masons and friends helped her get ready to return to her parents, and as she has written about that, I will not repeat anything, as it can be read in her own words in *Retrospection* (p. 19, see also *The First Church of Christ, Scientist, and Miscellany*, pp. 312, 330, 333, and 351).

Friends of the family and the early years of motherhood

Some months after Mrs. Glover's return from the South, her son [George Glover II] was born. The babe seemed unhappy, crying, and sometimes screaming piteously, yet none could comfort him. Then one day, when he could not be comforted and was screaming very severely, a young man, a friend of her childhood, called to see her and the family. The babe was in her arms screaming. He asked her if she would allow him to hold her little one for a while, and this she was very glad for him to do. He took the babe out of the room, and she heard him talking to the child: "I know what you want: you want a father, you want your papa. I'm going to be your father, Little Man, I'll be your papa." Thus he talked to the little one for some time and the screams stopped. The babe went to sleep and never screamed again in such a manner. This seemed a very curious coincidence and his mother was most grateful. This young man was a dear friend whom the family had known from boyhood.[33]

When her little George was a tiny child in Tilton, New Hampshire, Mrs. Glover used to take him to church on Sundays, and they had to cross a bridge over a stream. One day in spring, when the water was high, she was taking him across it, and he seemed to be afraid, not wanting to go further. To her horror she saw that the bridge was giving way and [that] she must arouse him in order that they both might be saved from falling into the water. So she said, "If Georgie doesn't go on at once, Mama will throw him into the water," and at this the little fellow went on one step after the other, she behind him. Hardly had they crossed the bridge when it collapsed into the stream beneath. She sat on the grass, the little one in her arms, and thanked God in tears for their delivery.

About here I would like to tell of an occurrence which happened years after this. Our Leader speaks of the Rev. Richard S. Rust, D.D., who resided in Tilton and helped her when she was young. One day, at Pleasant View, she received a letter from Doctor Rust asking her if she would see him, as he was passing through Concord on his way to reside at some other place far away and did not expect to be near Concord again. So she answered saying how glad she would be to see him. Accordingly she prepared for that visit, and it was a great joy to me to see these two dear friends, how they greeted each other so affectionately, not having met for so many years. Each knew, or expected, that it would be the last visit on this side that they would have together. I can still hear his words, "Sister, shall we sing a hymn together?" and her reply, with such a sound of joy in her voice, "Yes, let us sing '[In] the Sweet By-and-By.'" In the back parlor (where Mother told me to sit so that if she needed anything, such as a book, checkbook, paper, or message to be given, she could call to me knowing that I was near at hand), I listened to those two voices praising God. I can never forget that song, sung by those two saints. Then they sang "He Leadeth Me" and "Tell Me the Old, Old Story." It made me weep to hear and to see that communion: it was a "Communion of Saints," and I was very grateful for that great privilege.

These are only memories of happenings, but they are very sacred to me and very precious. They tell their own story of purified hearts and consecrated lives.

Early demonstrations of the truth soon to be discovered

The history of [Mary Glover Patterson's][34] healing from a severe accident in the street when she slipped on the ice has been recorded, so I will not go into particulars about that. Mother told me that when she was lying unconscious on the bed, her old friend and pastor of the church of which she was a member, called to ask of her condition. Seeing her unconscious, he spoke to her, and that seemed to reach her thought and roused her to consciousness. It was Sunday morning and he was on his way to church. He told her this, and she said, "Come back." He said he would come back but that she [might] not be there. It seemed as though she would have passed away before his return, [but] to his amazement, she met him at the front door.

It was [after the pastor's first visit] that she turned to her Bible and read the texts that are mentioned in her own writings. She rose from her bed, dressed herself, and went downstairs. When the dear grandmother, the one she called "Grandma," saw her, she said "Oh! Has Christ come again to earth?" and our Leader said, "Grandma, he never left." Years afterwards I asked the grandson of this old lady about this experience, and he said he had often heard his grandmother speak of it. These are only memories of things Mother told me about quite independent of her writings.

While she was visiting Dr. Quimby, Mrs. Patterson cured a number of his patients, and in the hotel in which she was staying, a gentleman who was dying was brought off the train. His wife was taking him to his old home in Canada. A doctor who was in the train advised moving him immediately [as soon as] the train reached the next station and taking him to the hotel which was close by. Very soon after he reached it, he passed away.

Our Leader, who was in the hotel and heard about it, went to the bereaved wife's door and knocked. The lady opened the door, and our Leader tried to comfort her. She said, "Let us go and waken him." She went and stood beside him for a few minutes; then she told his wife that he was waking and she must be close by so that he could see her when he opened his eyes, which he shortly did. He said to his wife, "Oh, Martha, it was so strange to be at home and you not there," and he spoke about meeting his parents and others of the family who had died before. Our Leader remained there for three days, and during that time he continued to live. Another man who was severely injured and had broken limbs was also cured.

The call to write *Science and Health*

[When] I asked Mrs. Eddy why she wrote *Science and Health with Key to the Scriptures*, she told me that one day she was called to a lady who was dying of consumption and that there were three or four doctors there—fine men who had expended all their medical knowledge in trying to save this lady from death. When they found that there was no hope of her recovery, they decided to test "that woman," as they had heard of someone who had been cured by her. The husband of this lady sent for Mrs. Glover,[35] and when she entered the room, the patient was propped up with many pillows and could not speak. Our Leader saw that what she needed was an arousal and quickly pulled all the pillows away from behind her. As she fell backwards, the patient said, "Oh, you have killed me." Mrs. Eddy told her that she could get up and that she would help her dress. She was instantaneously healed and well. Mrs. Eddy asked the doctors to leave the room while she helped her put on her clothing, after which they rejoined the doctors and her husband in the sitting room.

One of the doctors, an old, experienced physician, witnessed this, and he said, "How did you do it? What did you do?" She said, "I can't tell you, it was God," and he said, "Why don't you write it in a book, publish it, and give it to the world?" When she returned home she opened her Bible, and her eyes fell on the words "Thus speaketh the Lord God of Israel, saying, Write thee all the words that I have spoken unto thee in a book" (Jeremiah 30:2), which showed her God's direction.

After the publication of *Science and Health*, a clergyman came to her one day and advised her to withdraw the book from publication as it would be a failure and nobody would buy it. If it was true, [he said], it was much in advance of its time. Her answer was, "Get a bucket, and if he could dip the ocean dry, he could expect Christian Science to fail." Oh, what a faith! What an example for us was that mind and life of hers.

Encounters with spiritualists

In these early days, Whittier the poet was ill and dying of a supposed incurable hereditary disease. The spiritualists had tried to cure him and had failed. Mrs. Eddy was called to help him, and he was healed at once.

There were two ladies (who were spiritualists and mediums) who were interested in the spiritualist paper called

The Banner of Light. These two ladies expressed their desire to meet Mrs. Eddy, as they said she was a greater medium and spiritualist than they. She agreed to meet them at Whittier's house. One of them said to her, "I can see you as a child with your mother in the house of a woman who was ill. I can hear you singing." Mrs. Eddy said, "Yes, that was right. What was the hymn?" The medium answered correctly. To test them, she immediately thought of someone who was the reverse in appearance to her mother. She said to this medium, "You say you saw my mother; can you describe her to me?" This lady said, "Oh, yes," and she began to describe the lady of whom Mrs. Eddy was thinking. In her description of this lady, she said she was tall, with dark hair and eyes, and very slender. "Now," said Mrs. Eddy, "I have proved that it is not spiritual; it is simply mind-reading. For my mother whom you were describing, you were only describing my mental picture of someone I know who is tall, with dark hair and eyes. Now I will describe to you my mother: she was short and stout; she had golden hair and beautiful blue eyes; and she was a blonde."

Poverty, persecution, and problems publishing *Science and Health*

In those days she had to face and overcome poverty as well as other errors. She told me that her income was only $8.00 a month. She was very fond of the delicious Bartlett pear, and with this she always ate brown bread unbuttered. When I asked her why she did not have butter, she told me that when she was poor, if she wanted a pear, she had to do without butter and that she had become accustomed to eat[ing] the bread without butter, so that now it tasted sweeter without the butter.

We have read about the persecutions which she surmounted and proved powerless to stop the growth of the Cause of Christian Science. She told me that for a time, while living in Lynn in her own house, when she went to Boston to see her publishers, she had to return home in the early afternoon, for she was followed by different men. (This was to frighten her.) During the night the doorbell was rung many times by men who came one after the other, and the policemen in the street kept watch on the house. This went on so much that for a time no one would live in the house with her. Then Dr. Eddy[36] said that the only thing he could see would be for her to marry him and thus give him the right to have a room in the house and to protect her. (In the third edition of *Science and Health*, we read of his trial and experiences during that time). Later on, God showed her the wisdom of taking such a step.

In speaking to me of the troubles she had with her publishers,[37] Mrs. Eddy told me how she met John Wilson. When in great anxiety about securing the right publisher, she and her husband, Dr. Eddy, were going into Boston one morning and were conversing about the publishing of *Science and Health*. On the way they met a gentleman whom Dr. Eddy knew, and he said, "Here is someone who may be able to help us—he is a publisher and an honest man." He introduced Mr. Wilson to Mrs. Eddy, and she told him of her trouble and of her desire to have her book published correctly. He said he would read the manuscript over and see what he could do to help her. The result was that *Science and Health* was published correctly.

I never saw greater and more sincere gratitude than she expressed in later years, and if you will look at the book named *In Quest of the Perfect Book* by William Dana Orcutt, part of a chapter there is entitled "Mary Baker Eddy."[38] I remember the day to which he refers when speaking about Mr. Wilson. When Mrs. Eddy heard of Mr. Wilson's difficulties, she gave Mr. Orcutt a check to hand to him.[39] After Mr. Orcutt left, and she was upstairs in her room, she said to Mr. Frye and me, "I want you to remember this: John Wilson must never want. We can see what has caused his financial trouble. We Christian Scientists owe him a debt of gratitude for what he has done with *Science and Health*, which cannot be overestimated, and he shall never want while I have a dollar." Such was her gratitude for his work with our beloved textbook. His need was met.

Church government through divine guidance

One day I wanted to have some proof of which I could speak concerning God's guidance of the Cause of Christian Science, and I had the following proof, which left no doubt whatever. One night the Directors of The Mother Church wished to have guidance as to the wisdom of taking certain steps in something concerning The Mother Church which was of great importance. Late that night some letters were brought from them telling Mrs. Eddy about the circumstance and asking advice. At that hour Mrs. Eddy had retired and was sleeping, so we thought it best to wait until the morning, or till she wakened, before bringing them to her. In a short time she wakened and rang her bell, asked if any letters had come for her from the Directors, and wanted to see them at once, as she said there was a great need of wisdom. After reading them, she told us what it was, and she said, "I don't know what is best to do, but Love will show me the way." She told me to get her block of paper and pencil and to write.

I sat on the carpet beside the hot-air register and wrote at her dictation. She said, "God *bids* me do so and so, but I don't see the reason why." Several times she corrected that manuscript, saying, "That does not make the meaning clear enough. I must put better words to express what God meant," and she dictated for hours, and as I finished writing each sheet, I passed it on to Mr. Frye for him to copy on the typewriter. At about 2 or 2:30 a.m., I said to her, "Mother, why don't you wait to write this till tomorrow?" She said "And what would become of our Cause if I waited? This will be on its way to Boston at half past five, ready for the Directors' meeting at eight o'clock." Then I replied that we read in the Bible that "The darkness and the light are both alike to thee, and there shall be no light there," and we both laughed heartily. And in the morning, at five-thirty, it was on its way and arrived in time for the meeting.

Later in the morning, after she had been for her walk on the veranda, she said to us, as she came into her room, "Love has shown me the reason why," and she explained to us the reason. Then she said very seriously, "I want you always to remember that Mother had to obey God before she knew the reason why." Afterwards, when the news of the result reached her, she had the proof that all was well and that she had acted rightly, and God's directions were carried out. That was a heavenly lesson in obedience to spiritual direction, and times without number there were *proofs* that the Cause of Christian Science is governed by God, divine Mind.

Lessons to the household and an interesting demonstration

From my diary, here is a lesson which Mother gave us on the sixth of April, 1896:

> Remember, evil has no power to harm good or those who make good their refuge and are doing right as far as they know how. If we go into evil, we are not in the refuge because "he hath set his love upon me, therefore will I deliver him." [Also,] "He hath made good his refuge, there shall no evil befall him," etc. [See Psalms 91:14, 10.]
>
> Evil has only power to destroy itself and evildoers; it can only hurt itself. It can't hurt those who do right; if it [comes] near where they are, it can't touch them or harm them or influence them, but it does destroy itself. (This was a lesson to Laura [Sargent], Mr. Frye, and myself).

On my going downstairs to breakfast one morning, I met Miss Morgan, [who] told me that the farmer (who served Mrs. Eddy with milk), when he came that morning, seemed to be very solemn and said his well was dry; there was no water in it. It was so bitterly cold that everything was frozen, and the well from which he obtained water for his cattle was empty. On the day before, he was obliged to go to a brook or river, which was frozen, some distance away. He had taken barrels in his wagon which he filled with ice and snow from the river and took home to melt so as to have water for his cows. This was very hard work, it took a long time, and he seemed much distressed. During that day

I mentioned his difficulties to Mother, telling her just what had happened. She smiled and said, "Oh, if he only knew." Then, after a moment's silence, [she added], "Love fills that well."

The next morning, when the farmer brought the milk, he was overjoyed and told Miss Morgan that a wonderful thing had occurred. That morning early when he had gone out to attend to the cattle, he found the well full of water, and in spite of the bitter, cold day with all the ice and snow around, the well was full of water. He said it must have been Mrs. Eddy's prayers that had done it all. She must have had something to do with it for it was a miracle. He had a great reverence for Mrs. Eddy although he was not a Scientist. That day, when we were at dinner, I told Mother what had happened and just what the man had said. Oh, the joy and sweetness, the illumination and love of her face is ever to be remembered. Her expressions of praise and gratitude to God were glorious, and she said, "Oh! Didn't I know."

More lessons for the household workers

In my diary on September 1, 1896, is a lesson. She said, "We stand face to face with God's law of Love, and bow before the Christ."

Through struggles, overcomings, hope deferred, etc., lose self as matter, gain [the] true sense of Spirit and idea. Rejoice in tribulation.

Another lesson on January 31, 1902: Mother told us to study daily the Sermon on the Mount. Pour in Spirit first; then as we ascend the mount, we are working out of the valley of darkness and doubt, of material belief and blindness, up into the pure, bright atmosphere of Spirit, of the realization of Life, Truth, and Love. This is the mount of transfiguration. Then we shall be like the blind man whom Jesus healed; some did not know him [after he was healed]. It is the Christ-life that is the result of the Christ-love that brings peace.

Another lesson from Mother dated April 1, 1902: This morning when Mother came in from the swing, she called Mr. Tomlinson, Mr. Frye, and me into her room and told us that she had been thinking of the way she first used to heal, how she never used any arguments, for she did not know how to argue to heal disease. It was like the little girl who said, "Dod Dod," and the sick were instantly healed. [Mrs. Eddy] never lost a case up to the time her husband was taken. She showed us how it is God who heals and not the student, and that we must have faith in God, in the allness of God, in the omnipotence of Truth, and know that God is *all*, and then we will see the healing done: "He spake, and it was done" [See Psalms 33:9].

She spoke of those of our dear ones who have passed on and showed how the good which they realize and reflect mingles or meets with the good which we realize, but we cannot commune with each other. She showed the necessity for us to have more faith in *God*—not to keep to the letter and mere argument, but to rise to the consciousness of Love—and "To flee as a bird to yon mountain" [see Psalms 11:1]. [She said] that if a little bird was going up the mountain, it would not step one step after another to reach the top, but it would *fly* upward and flee to the mountain. She had reached that place this morning.

Another lesson on April 13, 1902: Mother showed us that our thoughts, our whole consciousness must be single on the side of good, thrown on the one scale, so that the whole weight may be in the one scale [with] nothing to put into the other, [just] as to us now, God, Love, must be all. God demands this of us, and the demand will not be withdrawn till it has been obeyed. The I must go to the Father; the ego must go there because "I and my Father are one" [John 10:30], one Mind and no separation. There is no sin, sickness, nor death because "The law of the Spirit of life in Christ Jesus hath made me free from the law of sin and death" [Romans 8:2]. We can now overcome evil with good, which means that there is no evil, but "Thou shalt have no other gods before me" [Exodus 20:3]. We have but one Mind and must make that one real. We are there now—I and the Father are one.

Another lesson: If we are misjudged, persecuted, it is a sure sign that we are ascending the mount. This must inspire us to go forward, a steep and rugged hill. "I am with you" [see Matthew 28:20].

To correct one error means the correction of the entire problem.

Aim at one mark, and hold there till the result is gained; aiming at many different points leads to malpractice.

Have faith in God, knowing that the work is done. You have got to know a negative is not anything. You have got to proportionately know the allness of Good.

Another lesson: If we stay and work among the students (taught as we have been), listening to them and they to us, we are rotating round and round. They cannot teach us nor we them, for they know as much of the letter of Christian Science as we do. For us to progress, we must go alone and work out our own salvation, and then if we meet one to teach

Truth who has not learned before, we know more than that one and teach what we have learned of God through experience; this is progress. We have not got the momentum of long years to work out of, which we would have had, had we stayed where we were and gone on working in the old lines.

I was very much impressed by listening to our Leader's audible communion with God (which we call prayer). I heard her address God, "Precious Mother Love, darling Mother, show me thy way. Oh, show me thy way!" There seemed to be such a perfect communion with divine Love, as a child has with its mother. When referring to God, she nearly always called God Love and would say, "Love will show me."

I remember that the last lesson she gave to several of those who were there while I remained was when she was reading the Bible to us one morning in 1904. While reading some of the words of Jesus, she looked up and said, "Never let error escape you undetected. Never see it as something; always see it as nothing. What is your next step?" Not one of us could give her the correct answer. She then said, "Go and *prove* it nothing; evil will never be nothing until we can say there is no evil or belief in it, and God is all. Evil will never seem nothing to you until this has been accomplished." And when I was saying good-bye to her that morning, she spoke to me about teaching Christian Science in London, and she said, "You must teach the [t]ruth so long as error is taught and called Christian Science. Who can do this better than one whom I have taught for so many years?"

One very important and lasting lesson that taught me much [came] one day when an article had to be sent to a newspaper for insertion on the same day, and our Leader told me to take charge of her work. It seemed too big a demonstration for my understanding, and I said, "Oh, Mother! I haven't enough of the mind that was in Christ Jesus to make that demonstration." Her rebuke to me was one of the most blessed experiences of my life. She said to me, "Would a mother give a child a weight too heavy for it to carry? Would Love give you a task beyond your strength?" I do not forget the expression of her face; it revealed to me what was Truth, and I said, "No, Mother," and went to my room. After some time she called me and another (who had to see about some business outside) and showed us the way quite clearly. I went back to my room and was there some time, realizing the [t]ruth of God's spiritual idea. In a short time she rang her bell for me, and when I reached her she said, "It is all right; you have struck the tone," and the result was Truth manifested. What other in this century has stood the test and proven her leadership and Christian character as our Leader has, standing on Principle and manifesting the Christ?

Interesting comments and instructions

I remember one morning our Leader called Mr. Frye and me and said, "I want you to listen to what Love has shown me." She said, "In *Science and Health* we have the sentence, 'The senses of Spirit abide in the understanding, and they demonstrate Truth and Love.' Now listen to what God has taught me," and she repeated this: "The senses of Spirit abide in Love, and they demonstrate Truth and Life." She removed the word *understanding* and put *Love*, and removed *Love* from the end of the sentence and put *Life* in its place. You will find this in the present edition of *Science and Health*, which Scientists study now, on page 274, line 12. In the eighty-fourth edition, published in 1894, we find the old sentence, on page 170, line 17, and in *Science and Health* published in 1902,[40] we read on page 274, line 12, "The senses of Spirit abide in God."

Another time, while reading a newspaper article written against herself and Christian Science, [Mrs. Eddy] said to me, "How do we destroy a lie? Only by telling the truth." That showed her that in connection with herself and Christian Science, she must do something to have the truth told about both. The result of this was the first Publication Committee, who would reply to newspaper news which was false.[41] Later on, the Board of Lectureship would give the public the true interpretation of Christian Science and its Discoverer.

Another morning, in February 1902, while [she was] reading aloud from Jesus' words in the Gospel—she was reading the chapter in which we find the words, "Let thine eye be single, and thy whole body shall be full of light" [see Matthew 6:22]—I stopped her with the following question: "Mother, what does it mean to keep your eye single?" She replied, "It means having only one reality, and that is Spirit," and then she looked up and said, "Never forget this," and I never have. So many times it has been a great blessing to me.

There is one lesson that I would like to mention here on overcoming evil with good. In the early days, a gentleman (who had been seriously ill) whom I was helping with Christian Science treatment had received treatment for one week and was much better, but not completely well. I was alarmed at having a patient for so long as a week and wrote to ask my teacher to let me know of what sin I was guilty.

She telegraphed for me to come to her and listened to the story of my experience and of how the seeming error was handled. She then told me that man was already healed and that what was preventing both of us from realizing this was malicious mental malpractice against my Christian Science practice, and that I must stop treating for disease and just handle that. When I reached home the next morning and met him, he was well; this taught me much.

Watching and praying, day and night

There was a great need [to pray] for the Church and our Leader. Both were attacked by error, and as our Leader and those with her were in the front rank of the battle, it meant watching and praying without ceasing.

At that time there were only two of us [serving as metaphysical workers in the household], Mr. Frye and myself. What Scientists called working, our Leader called watching and praying. We had to take turns watching alternate hours, day and night, for months so long as it was needed.

In order to do this myself and be punctual in beginning my watch at a certain hour, I bought a new alarm clock and held it under my face and would lie down on the outside of the bed fully dressed. It seemed to me so difficult to be wide awake and thus capable of doing my duty. When the alarm bell rang a little before the time to commence my watch, I used to get up and walk about the room to be thoroughly aroused; then I would begin my turn at watching. When the hour came to an end, I was so thoroughly awake that I could not go to sleep for a long time, but it was a comfort to know that the work was accomplished.

Invitations to the Original Mother Church

When the Original, The First Church of Christ, Scientist, [or] The Mother Church, had been built and dedicated, the Rev. Mary Baker Eddy, our beloved Leader, received a scroll of gold from the members of her Church, on which was inscribed an invitation to her to come to Boston and receive as a gift The Mother Church which had just been completed (see *Pulpit and Press*, pp. 76–78).

On March 20, 1895, our Leader received from the Christian Science Board of Directors—Ira O. Knapp, William B. Johnson, Joseph Armstrong, and Stephen A. Chase—a letter and precious gift, a facsimile of the cornerstone of the church edifice made of granite with a golden box enclosed [in it], which [is] referred to in *Pulpit and Press* (see pp. 85–87).

To Calvin Frye and me, our Leader said that she would reject all earthly honors and adulation, that she did not forget that on one day Jesus went up to the temple riding on an ass and the people spread their garments and palm leaves before him on the way, and the next week he was crucified on Calvary.

She also said that when she saw the Church, which was her "own vine and fig tree" which Love had given her, she would visit it when no one knew she was coming.

She went there for the first time on April 1, 1895. When our Leader decided which day she would go, she wrote a letter to Mr. Joseph Armstrong, who was one of the Directors, telling him that some friends would visit the Church on April 1 and asking him to kindly arrange for someone to be there to open the Church door and conduct the friends around the Church. She did not mention who the friends were.

Mrs. Eddy's first visit to her Church

Mother lunched very early that day, and as soon as she was ready to start, we drove to [the] Concord railway station. When the train arrived, Mother, Mr. Frye, and [I] embarked for Boston in a private compartment of a Pullman car. It was a memorable journey, and when Boston station was reached, Mother told Mr. Frye to engage an ordinary cab to take her to The Mother Church. On reaching the Church, Mr. Frye helped her get out and rang the bell at the Church door. It was opened by Mr. Armstrong, who was so surprised to see who it was and gave our Leader a loving, affectionate, and hearty welcome, offered her his arm, and conducted her up the stairs. He showed her which was the door opening into the auditorium and went to fetch a key to the Mother's Room.

Mother then walked into the auditorium, and I followed and remained at the end of the Church near the door so that if she needed anything, there was someone at hand.

Our Leader walked up the left aisle of the Church facing the Reader's desk; she went very slowly and at times would stand still and look up and around; this she continued to do until she reached the Readers' platform and stopped at the steps leading up to it. There she knelt on the first step, and I well know how her grateful heart was going out in thanksgiving to divine Love for all the way that God had led her.

After some minutes she ascended the steps and stood behind the First Reader's desk for some moments, then behind the Second Reader's desk and looked up and around; then she descended the steps on the right-hand

PHOTO W. T. CLARK. COURTESY OF THE MARY BAKER EDDY LIBRARY

The Mother's Room in the Original Edifice. At Mrs. Eddy's request the room was permanently closed in 1908.

side of the Church and walked down the aisle, still looking around and up at each window.

She then came out of the auditorium and entered her room, the "Mother's Room," built by the Busy Bees.[42] She looked at the inscription over the door and [at the one] outside the door as she entered.[43] Then she examined all that comprised the Mother's Room. After that our Leader sent for those of her students who were near enough to be summoned at such short notice and gave them a glorious lesson in Christian Science.

[After] our Leader had talked to her students, who were so happy [to be] together, her supper time had come, and at six o'clock she had it there in the Mother's Room. We had brought it all ready from Pleasant View. Later she said she would like to see the Church lighted up.

Nearly everyone had returned home by that time, and

The Christian Science Board of Directors in 1895, from left: Ira Knapp, William Johnson, Joseph Armstrong, Stephen Chase

here I must pay tribute to the faithfulness and loving care of the Board of Directors, who remained in the Church watching there all night in the Directors' Room.

Our Leader went into the auditorium again and walked up the same aisle and again stood at the First Reader's desk. After our beloved Leader reached the First Reader's desk, she repeated aloud first one verse of the ninety-first Psalm, her first words being, "Because he hath set his love upon me, therefore will I deliver him: I will set him on high, because he hath known my name." After that she began at the first verse and repeated the psalm through to the end.

Then she went to the Second Reader's desk, and in such a pleading voice she repeated:

> Guide me, O Thou great Jehovah,
> Pilgrim through this barren land:
> I am weak, but Thou art mighty,

Hold me with Thy powerful hand.

Bread of heaven ...

Feed me till I want no more.[44]

Then there was silence, such a silence, and it seemed as if that dear voice was being echoed throughout that auditorium. None broke the sacred silence, and in memory I still hear that voice so clear and filled with love.

Then Mother crossed the Church and noticed Mr. Coleman weeping; he was sitting in the pew in front of me with his head bowed leaning on the pew in front of him. He was so overcome with joy and memories of the past and by what he had just seen and heard. Our Leader went into the pew and sat beside him, touched his shoulder, and said, "Why, brother, don't you remember in the days gone by when we went to the Hall to have our services there, how you and I had to pick up pieces of paper and bits of orange peel in order to make the room clean." Then she reminded him of several other things which happened in those days and, telling him how different it was at this time and how much we had to thank God for, encouraged him to look up with thanksgiving and rejoice.

It touched me very deeply when she spoke to us both of some of her experiences in the early days. Her conversation brought smiles to his face, and I arose and moved away to another part of the Church while they sat and conversed together, which I knew must be to him a holy benediction.

Again looking all around and speaking to the others who were present, she returned to her room where she spent the night. The next forenoon our Leader returned to Pleasant View.

I looked upon Mother's visit to the Church as its real

spiritual dedication and consecration to the Cause of Christian Science.

Daily duties bring spiritual gain

One great lesson Mrs. Eddy taught me was of "the mammon of unrighteousness" (see Luke 16:9–11), such as sweeping, dusting, and doing necessary things, and mothers having charge of homes and all the responsibility of their houses which rested on those who had to do their own work, provide for their children's clothing and education, and accomplish little things about the house to make it home. This is what we would call the mammon of unrighteousness, or material duties. If we would make good use of the discipline that fulfilling these duties brings to us, they would furnish us with experiences which would ultimate in spiritual gain, because being faithful in that which was least, we would be faithful in much and receive heavenly riches—stores of truth in spiritual understanding—which would be expressed in exactness, correctness, faithfulness, and perfection. "The maximum of good is the infinite God and His idea, the All-in-all" (*Science and Health*, p.103).

Then she said that God had taught her how to make a bonnet and told me this story, which happened before the time she taught Christian Science. She had promised to give a temperance lecture, and she did not have a dress or bonnet which she thought suitable to wear there, so she walked down Tremont Street and, looking at the shop windows, saw two bonnets which she liked and felt would suit her. She could afford to spend two dollars on a bonnet, and these were Paris models. So she went into the store to the millinery department. She spoke to two young ladies who were attendants there and asked them to show her some of the same shape as those in the window and to sell her some inexpensive material which she could use for making a bonnet as nearly like the models as possible. They entered into the spirit of the occasion with her and sold her a frame, tulle and ribbon, and a pretty flower, which she paid for and took away with her and made her bonnet herself. An intimate friend who met her afterwards admired her bonnet and told her so and said it looked like a twenty-five dollar model bonnet, and Mother told her that the materials cost her just two dollars and [that] God taught her how to make it.

Also with her dress, she took her old dress (which was too shabby), unpicked it, washed, ironed, turned, and re-made it, and put some narrow velvet on the outside of the bodice; you will see it on her in the picture with that little baby. God taught her to make that dress also, and she was well dressed for the occasion.

Mother told me how she happened to have that little baby in her arms. She went into a photographer's studio to ask about the price of photographs, and when she entered his reception room, she found a lady there holding a baby, which she was trying to pacify. The child was screaming, which made it impossible for him to be photographed, and our Leader noticed that every little while the baby looked at her and then screamed again. She said to his mother, "Won't you let me hold your baby for a little while; perhaps I could quiet him." And the baby put his arms up to meet hers. As soon as she took him, he put his thumb in his mouth, as you will see, and there is the picture of contentment. Then

PHOTO MORRIS ALLARD DAVIS. COURTESY OF THE MARY BAKER EDDY LIBRARY

Mary Baker Eddy holding the infant she quieted in a photography studio

the photographer, unknown to Mrs. Eddy, took a photograph of her and the child and afterwards sent her a copy, asking her to accept it, and said that it was such a beautiful picture, he could not help taking it.

Mrs. Eddy's healing work

I must relate another sacred experience of our dear Leader's healings. One day, when she had finished her lesson in the class of which I was a member, she asked me to wait after the other members had gone, and as she was standing in the classroom at 571 Columbus Avenue, a gentleman called to see her, bringing with him his sister, who greatly needed healing.

Mrs. Eddy met them at the door of the room and asked

him to wait downstairs while she talked to his sister. The belief was insanity, and she looked terrified. Our Leader told me her delusion was that a serpent was coiled around her body and was crushing her. I stood in amazement, watching Mrs. Eddy's face as she turned and looked at the woman who fell on the floor screaming, "It's crushing me—it's killing me!" Our Leader looked upwards, as if she had seen the face of an angel in her communion with God. In a moment she said to the woman, "Has it gone?" But there was no reply. Mrs. Eddy repeated her question, but the woman still seemed not to hear it. Then she spoke with authority and asked, "Has it *gone*?" The poor woman looked up, and her whole body was shaken and quivering as she answered, "Yes!" I watched the changes of expression that came over her face, from fear to *peace and joy*. And, oh, the love that was expressed in our Leader's face as she looked down on her, stretched out both arms, and lifted her up, saying, "Get up, darling!" Then our dear teacher put that needy one's head on her shoulder and patted her face as she lovingly talked the truth to her. Mrs. Eddy then went out of the room and talked to the brother, who took her home, and then she asked me to come and have supper with her and to sing to her. During the evening she turned to me and said, "You saw what happened to that lady today? Well! She will never be insane in this world again." And she has not been.

One day our Leader illustrated how it takes moral courage to do one's duty. She told of a gentleman who was in a street car in Boston and had his little daughter with him. The child wanted to sit on his knee and put her head on his shoulder and go to sleep, and he would not allow her to do that, insisting that she should stand and move about. His treatment of the child seemed so cruel that a Scientist who was sitting in the seat behind him spoke to him and asked what was the trouble. He explained to her that the child had, unknowingly, taken some poison, and he was on the way to a physician to give her an antidote; [he said] that if he allowed her to lie down and go to sleep, she might never waken again. Our Leader wanted to show me how we needed such arousals if our eyes were not open to detect the error which must be overcome, or [else] it would put us to sleep.

Mother told me that when she was first at Chickering Hall holding services and preaching, the caretaker one Sunday brought his daughter, who was ill with consumption and had a distressing cough. After the congregation left the building, she was sitting in one of the end seats, waiting

Chickering Hall in Boston, where Eddy preached and held services

for her father. As Mrs. Eddy went down the aisle to go out at the front door, she saw the little girl and noticed how ill she looked. She stopped and spoke to the child and said to her, "Don't you know, dear, that you haven't any lungs to cough with or to be consumed? You are God's child!" She talked the truth to her and told her what she was as God's idea and to know that she was well, and the child stopped coughing and was instantly healed. When her father came to take her home, he was amazed to find that she was well.

One day a man whom she had seen jump from a great height called to see her.[45] He had on dark goggles. She asked him if he were not afraid when he took that leap. He explained to her that if he were to become afraid the jump was too high, he would be killed. After [she had talked] to him in a most heavenly way for some time, one could see by the expression of his face how enlightened he was mentally. Then she began again and talked to him about his lack of fear, he still asserting that he had no fear when jumping [because] he knew he could do it. She said to him, "Why not apply the same rule to your eyes?" One, he told her, had been destroyed through an accident; the other was all right, but he wore the dark goggles to hide the bad eye. They were sitting in the library, and as she talked to him, I could see and feel that his fear was removed, and his thought was full of hope and joy, although he did not then realize the blessing he had received. A day or two afterwards, the cabman who drove him [from Mrs. Eddy's house] to the station reported that he had two perfect eyes when he reached the station. Afterwards, the man wrote to Mrs. Eddy telling her of the wonderful healing he had experienced and expressing his gratitude.

Trust in God during a time of trial

Christian Science is best learned from our Leader's works. (See *Science and Health*, pp. 147, 446, and 456.) When Mrs. Eddy was revising the fiftieth edition of *Science and Health* in 1891, she was living in a furnished house—62 North State Street, Concord, New Hampshire—while Pleasant View was being built. She was passing through deep waters at that time and wrote to ask me to call and see her on my way to Boston to her students' Association of the Massachusetts Metaphysical College. I went and was so grateful for the great privilege of that visit. In her letter she wrote that her hair had turned white and [that] I must not be surprised when I saw her. When she greeted me in the drawing room, I was very much moved, as I could see by her face what deep waters she was passing through. She said to me, "The cup is bitter, bitter!" Tears came to my eyes. She looked up and said, "But the Father makes it sweet!" and talked to me in a way I have never forgotten.

One thing that our Leader taught me was always to give God the glory, and whatever I undertook to do, I was to say, "With God's help I will do so and so," and to know that the good that I would do, I do, and the evil that I would not do, I could not be made to do. She also said that in years to come the loyal Christian Scientists would have to make clear to people that it was not Mrs. Eddy who did the healing, but Truth and Love. (She wrote [on page 495] in *Science and Health*, "God will heal the sick through man, whenever man is governed by God.") Our duty would be to overcome the belief in mortal mind of worshipping her personality.

A dramatic—and instructive—healing

I feel it is only right that I should relate one very wonderful and sacred experience with Mr. Frye. One day, while I was writing Mrs. Eddy's dictation, she sent me with a message to Mr. Frye, who was in his room. When I reached the door, which was open, I saw him lying on his back on the carpet, apparently lifeless. I returned to our Leader and told her about it, saying, "It seems as though he has fainted." She immediately rose and we both went to his room. She kneeled beside him and lifted his arm, which fell inert. Then she began to talk to him. I had been praying for him, but what she said to him was a revelation, to which I listened in wonder. Such heavenly words and tenderness, such expressions of love I have never heard, telling him the truth of man's relationship to God. After a while he opened his eyes, and as soon as Mother saw that he was becoming conscious, her voice changed, and most severely she rebuked the error that seemed to be attacking him. Her voice and manner were so different, according to the need, that I was deeply impressed.

Presently, she told him to rise on his feet and gave him her hand to help him to get up. Then she turned round and went out of the room down the passage where she had been sitting. Then she called out, "Calvin, come here!" And he followed her. She spoke to him for several minutes, striving to wake him up—at times thundering against the error. Then she said, "Now you can go back to your room." He went from the passage towards his room, but before he entered, she called him again and talked to him, and this was repeated several times.

I said, "Oh, Mother! Couldn't you let him sit down a few minutes?" She said, "No, if he sits down, he may not waken again. He must be aroused—we mustn't let him die—he is not quite awake yet!" She began to talk to him again and reminded him of the time when she rented a farm for one day not very far from Concord, when she, Martha [Morgan], and Mr. Frye together drove out and spent the day there, and she began to remind him of the experiences of that day. That reached him, and she said, "You haven't forgotten it, Calvin?" And he said, "No, Mother." And he laughed heartily. Then she talked more of the [t]ruth to him and told him he could go back to his room and his "watch."

She explained to me that when you speak the Truth to anyone, if the Truth you speak causes him to laugh, cry, or get angry, you have reached the thought that needed correction.

Mr. Frye was a changed man after that experience, to which we never referred. To me, such a demonstration was a glorious inspiration and lesson.

Unwavering love

When I read the [article] in *Miscellaneous Writings: 1883–1896* [called] "Love Your Enemies," a particular experience which our Leader had in 1899, and which I recorded, is recalled, by which I saw the carrying out of her teaching in that [article] exemplified in her life. One of her former students who had manifested great enmity against her and was persecuting her and falsifying her character was dealt with in the following manner. One morning, as our dear Leader sat writing letters, she called me and said, "To whom do you think I have just written?" From the look on her face, I said, "I suppose someone to whom no one else would write!" And then she said, "It is to So and So, and I have invited her to come and see me. I have given her two days from which to select the time most convenient to her and have asked her to telegraph and let me know the day." She read the letter through to me and told me to enclose a stamped telegraph form. I said, "Oh, Mother, how could you write to her when you know she is doing all she can to harm you and not hiding it but talking about it?" She said to me, "You must learn to love that woman!" I said, "Do you love her?" [She answered,] "Yes, and I am trying to bless her! If you and I do not love her, who can or will?"

To that letter Mrs. Eddy received no reply. When the second day named came, before going out for her drive, she put on her special best dress and ordered the carriage to be at the door to take her for her drive an hour earlier than usual, in order to be home early before her guest arrived. Before leaving, our Leader ordered another carriage to be sent to the station to meet her. Just as she was putting on her gloves before entering her carriage, she called me from my writing and said, "Will you promise me something?" I said, "Of course I will if it is something that I can do." She said, "If Mrs. _____ comes before I return, I want you to greet her kindly." I said, "Yes, Mother, I will!" Then she said, "Lovingly?" with a note of interrogation in her voice. My answer was, "I will try!" Then she said, "Just heavenly?" I answered, "I will go upstairs and ask God to help me to do that—to show me how." Lastly, she repeated, "Now remember what I say—kindly, lovingly, just heavenly!"

I went to my room and prayed very earnestly to divine Love to help me, for as it was right for [this woman] to feel that, it was right for me to manifest it. In a short time I felt such a desire that she should come and [was] willing to welcome her in the most heavenly way that I knew of because I knew what a blessing there was awaiting her through an interview with our Leader and [what] great good would result.

Our Leader returned from her drive an hour earlier than usual, and when she got out of her carriage, she said, "Has she come yet?" I said, "No, Mother." "Never mind," she said. "I will wait in the drawing room for her." In the meantime, the carriage had been sent a second and third time to meet three trains in succession. The last time it was too late and too dark for her to have come, [but] our Leader sat in the parlor waiting till then; after [that] she rose to return to her sitting room and said, "Oh! What a benediction of love she would have received! It would have saved and comforted her!" I too felt sorry for her to have lost such an opportunity and a great blessing. I learned a lesson of love such as I have never forgotten.

Dominion over the elements

At Pleasant View, dominion over weather, storm, etc., was just the same as over other seeming material conditions. After a prolonged drought, the inharmonious condition was met by our Leader's watching and praying, the effect being rain when there was not a cloud visible in the sky. At other times heavy, dark clouds appeared when there was no rain. Also Truth was demonstrated to quell storms.

During part of the year, cyclones were sometimes experienced at Concord, and one day Miss Morgan came to me and said that the clouds were gathering and there was going to be a dreadful storm, and she called me to look through the windows of her room, which was at the end of the house, looking towards the stables. Above, I saw dark clouds which seemed to be coming towards us very rapidly, and as Mother had told me whenever I saw a cyclone or storm coming up I must let her know, I went to her room immediately and told her. She rose and went to the veranda at the back of the house. By that time, the clouds had reached overhead. She then went into the front vestibule and looked on that side of the house. Then she returned to the veranda, and I heard her say, "The children in Boston!" I ran downstairs to the front door, opened it and went outside, looked up, and saw the clouds hanging over the house—very heavy, black clouds—and in the middle, right over the house, there was a rift. They were dividing; part were going one way and the other part in the opposite direction. This seemed to be such a strange phenomenon. I went in, closed the door, and went upstairs to Mother on the veranda and told her what I saw. I said, "The clouds are divided just overhead!" She said to me, "Clouds! What do you mean? *Are* there any clouds?" I said, "No, Mother!" She was looking up, and I could see by the expression on her face that she was not seeing clouds but was realizing the Truth.

I saw the black clouds turn to indigo, the indigo to light grey, and the light grey turn to white, fleecy clouds which dissolved, and there were no more. She said to me, "There are no clouds to hide God's face, and there is nothing that can come between the light and us—it is divine Love's weather." That was early in the evening; the wind had been blowing terrifically, and Mr. Frye and another gentleman were in the attic, trying to pull down a large, American flag. It was a "fete" day, and a gentleman had sent this flag as a gift to Mrs. Eddy. It was very large, and Mr. Frye and this friend were trying to pull it down, and the strength of the two men was not sufficient to pull down that flag, but suddenly the wind subsided and the flag yielded. The next morning, early, when the mail was delivered, the postman was amazed to see that nothing had been disturbed in the garden, as from a short distance down the road and in the town, there had been a great deal of damage.

Lessons on seeing and conquering error

Mother explained to us what the momentum of evil was, and her explanation of evil indulged in was indeed terrifying. She showed us that, if we neglected to do our duty and did what was wrong without detecting, correcting, and overcoming error, but continued repeating the same mistakes and justifying ourselves, the suffering which would result would be simple interest, which we would have to pay. Then, if Christian Scientists refused to see the error when it was shown and willfully or maliciously continued to repeat it, allowing their thoughts to be governed by hate, malice, jealousy, or any of these subtle conspirators, this would result in moral idiocy and would bring compound interest. Then the experience of hell would ensue. After this she wrote that letter to the church at Concord [which is published] in *Miscellany* on pages 159–163.

Another lesson that Mother gave us was on self-justification. She said:

> At any time, if we make a mistake and
> do not detect it as a mistake, and we are
> shown that it is a mistake and rebuked for
> it, [yet] we justify ourselves in what we have
> done, this is taking sides with error and

is a proof that we are being governed by
error. But if, when the error is uncovered to
us, we see our mistake, accept the rebuke,
and condemn that error in ourselves or
to someone else, then we are governed by
Truth, and rise, and have overcome the
error, and become more spiritually minded.
We have gained a step in Christian Science.

Another lesson she gave us was taken from [Ezekiel], where we read, "Take away my stony heart and give me a heart of flesh" [see 36:26]. She showed us that a stony heart was a heart hardened by materialism and lack of sympathy, lack of love and compassion. *That* was a stony heart, and we must look to God for deliverance and pray that He take away that heart and give us a heart of flesh, which is a tender, loving heart, unselfish, full of sympathy, lovingkindness, and compassion—that is a heart of love seeing one another's need and supplying it with love which is divine.

Mrs. Eddy invited her Students' Association to visit her at Pleasant View. Her rooms were filled with students and she gave them a glorious lesson. She saw how error was trying subtly, through mental suggestion, to reach the thoughts of her students and other Scientists, and she saw how necessary it was to open their eyes to what was being done, and one of the things she wanted to impress on them was the necessity to study *Science and Health* daily and thoroughly and to abide steadfastly in the [t]ruth in that book. She said that the enemies of Christian Science studied *Science and Health* and took certain portions of it to try to reverse them in the thoughts of the students. One suggestion was that in *Science and Health* we are taught that there is only one Mind and that man is governed by and reflects that Mind. This was studied by the malpractitioners, who argued to the Christian Scientists as follows:

"Are you Mind?" Answer, "No!"

"Are you matter?" "No!"

"Then what are you?" "Nothing, because you have not any mind!"

She told us that those arguments were intended to produce on the minds and characters of Christian Scientists, insanity, dementia, imbecility, and moral idiocy, and we must guard our thoughts and constantly affirm, "I have got a mind and that mind is divine." So long as our thoughts were on a spiritual basis and we were thinking spiritually, our thoughts could not be robbed or tampered with by error or mental suggestion.

The development of the *Church Manual*

The first time that Mrs. Eddy saw the need of a manual for The Mother Church was in connection with teaching, and she told me to write to Mrs. Adams and Mrs. Webster of Chicago. She wanted to see them to explain to them the need that she saw to preserve the teaching of Christian Science pure and unadulterated for future generations, and the wisest way she could see at that time was to have a manual on teaching Christian Science. They came, and she showed them the right thing to do was to have a committee of her old, loyal students, with themselves, and for them to compile a set of by-laws in connection with teaching. This was done. Afterwards, God showed Mother that it was wise to make by-laws to govern all church members as well as teachers, which ultimately developed into the present *Manual of The Mother Church*, which includes articles and By-Laws for teachers and teaching, as well as for church discipline.

I was very much impressed by the attitude she took in connection with discipline of church members when charges were made against them. In the *Church Manual* we find Article XI, Section 2, about Matthew 18:15–17, and Section 4 of the same article [says] that there is a preliminary requirement on the part of the one bringing the charge against another [to] have implicitly obeyed Section 4 of Article XI before bringing the charge to her notice.[46] This seemed to me to be so just, in the way Jesus would have acted.

At another time, when making some By-Laws which were needed, she said "This *Church Manual* is God's law as much so as the Ten Commandments and the Sermon on the Mount. It is God's law and will be acknowledged as law by law." And she smiled and looked up from her writing and said, "I mean by the laws of our state, even if it has to go to the higher courts." [And] in *Miscellany* on page 230, we read, "Notwithstanding the sacrilegious moth of time, eternity awaits our Church Manual, which will maintain its rank as in the past, amid ministries aggressive and active, and will stand when those have passed to rest."

LAURA C. NOURSE *(1845–1929)*

*Born in Wisconsin, Laura Nourse moved in childhood
with her family to New York. She was educated in the
Methodist church but did not become a member. Later,
while staying for health reasons at a Seventh-Day
Adventist sanatorium in Michigan, she became interested
in that faith but eventually drifted away from it. By the
1880s, she was living with family members in Queens,
New York, where a friend who had benefited from
Christian Science treatment encouraged Nourse to try it.
She did so and, having improved somewhat, took Primary
class instruction, though she found aspects of the teachings
hard to accept.*

*Over the course of the next year, Nourse grew more
comfortable with the theology of Christian Science, and
in 1886 she began healing others. Her first patient was
cured almost instantaneously, and later Nourse's own
health problems were fully healed. By 1887, she was listed
in* The Christian Science Journal *as a practitioner in*

Brooklyn, New York, and in 1888 she took Primary class from Mary Baker Eddy. Eventually, Nourse became a Christian Science teacher. She practiced Christian Science healing for several years in New York and Michigan before settling in Eau Claire, Wisconsin, where she taught her classes and held associations for many years. Nourse also wrote poems, one of which—"In Transitu"—was published in the Journal *and became the basis for two hymns in the* Christian Science Hymnal.[47]

Climbing the Mount of Revelation with Our Teacher

LAURA C. NOURSE

In November 1888 I entered, by invitation, a class taught by Mary Baker Eddy, Discoverer and Founder of Christian Science. The class was taught on Columbus Avenue. My idea of the place itself is very indistinct; I can only recall some events connected with the class teaching. It was the first class she had taught in seven lessons, and she said, "It was the most wonderful class she had ever taught." At the close of the seventh lesson, she said: "I can take you no farther. If you choose to remain and take the remaining five lessons (to which you are entitled) from my son, Dr. E. J. Foster Eddy, you can do so. *I* can take you no farther." As I remember it now, no one uttered a word, and no one remained. She had taken us up onto the mount of revelation, where we beheld the allness of God, and man in His image and likeness. We had been taught of God. There was no desire to be taught of man. "Lips were mute and materialism silent" before the wonderful vision [see *Science and Health with Key to the Scriptures*, p. 15]. We returned to our homes to ponder these things in our hearts.

Two or three incidents connected with the class teaching deeply impressed me. There were two clergymen in the class. I think it was about the third or fourth lesson, early in the session, when she asked one of them a question, and he said, "Mrs. Eddy, I do not know. I am in a mental and physical earthquake this morning, and I don't know what I do know." Sweetly and so gently came the answer: "Brother so-and-so, I know just how you feel about it. I have been right there myself—but now, see here," and she came right down to his mental plane and very gradually and gently took him up to her own. She taught us how to teach as the Master taught; how to love as he loved. No person taught in that class needed any further instruction from man. "Truth had been revealed. It only needed to be practiced" [see *Science and Health*, p. 174].

One more incident immediately concerned myself. Mrs. Eddy had discovered either that I did not know how to handle malicious animal magnetism or did not see the need of doing so. She asked me a question. I have never been able either to recall the question or my reply. She stopped her class work, and turning directly to me, said these words: "*You will handle it, or it will handle you.*" The words were burned into my consciousness, as with a hot iron, and were never forgotten. We all loved her, and, with myself, that love has grown and strengthened with the years.

She said one day, "Many times while I was writing that book *Science and Health*, have I laid down my pen at night and said, 'I hope some time to understand what I have written today.'" Her loyal students are still studying the book and hope sometime to be able to understand and grasp its infinite meanings. As St. Paul said, "Now we know in part. Then we shall know, even as also we are known" [see I Corinthians 13:12].

SEPTIMUS J. HANNA *(1844–1921)*

*Born into a family of farmers in Spring Mills,
Pennsylvania, Hanna was educated through a
combination of public schools, academy training, and
private tutoring. By the time he was 18, he had moved to
Illinois and the Civil War was underway. He enlisted and
served the final year of the war as captain of an Illinois
regiment. After the war, Hanna resumed his study of the
law and in 1866 became a junior member of the firm
Sapp, Lyman, & Hanna in Council Bluffs, Iowa. Soon
thereafter, he served as county judge for the area. In 1869,
Hanna married Camilla Turley and began work as city
attorney for Council Bluffs. For a period, he was also
deputy U.S. district attorney.*

*In 1872, Hanna moved his law practice to Chicago,
Illinois, but ill health caused him to relocate to Colorado
in 1879, where he eventually resumed his practice. From
1882 to 1886, he was registrar of the land office, a quasi-
judicial position tasked with settling multimillion dollar*

mining claims. When his wife was healed by reading
Science and Health with Key to the Scriptures,
*Hanna became interested in Christian Science and was
healed as well. He took Primary class instruction from
Rev. J. S. Norvell in December 1886.*

*While attending the National Christian Science
Association meeting in New York in 1890, Hanna was
asked to lead a society of Christian Scientists in Scranton,
Pennsylvania, so he and his wife moved there. He began
his healing practice and helped establish Scranton's first
branch church. By the following year, both of the Hannas
were listed in* The Christian Science Journal *as
practitioners in Scranton.*

*Hanna first met Mary Baker Eddy in 1891 and was
called by her to Boston to serve as Editor in 1892, a post
he maintained until 1902, with Camilla working as
Assistant Editor. During this time, Hanna filled a variety
of other positions as well, such as pastor (1894) and
then First Reader (1895–1902) of The Mother Church;
member of the Bible Lesson Committee (1895–1898);
President of The Mother Church (1896–1898); President
briefly and then Vice President (with Eddy as President)
of the Board of Education (1898–1910); and then
once again President of the Board of Education from
Eddy's passing in 1910 until his own passing. The same
year Hanna retired as Editor and First Reader, he was
appointed to the Board of Lectureship and spoke on
Christian Science all over the U.S., in the British Isles, and
in Canada until 1914. During this time, the Hannas lived*

in Colorado Springs, Colorado, until 1911 and from then on in Pasadena, California. In 1907, Hanna taught the Normal class at the Massachusetts Metaphysical College at Eddy's request and the following year began teaching Primary classes annually until his passing.[48]

Correspondence and Other Exchanges with Mary Baker Eddy

SEPTIMUS J. HANNA

When Mrs. Hanna took up Christian Science as a study, I looked on indifferently until I began to see that she was being helped by it, and then my curiosity was somewhat aroused, and I began to note its effect upon her. Mrs. Hanna became attracted to Science through the healing of some of her intimate friends living in Council Bluffs, Iowa, her former home, where her parents then resided. Having heard of the healing of her friends, she inquired of her mother what it was that was working these miracles. Soon after this her father sent her as a New Year's gift a copy of *Science and Health with Key to the Scriptures*, then published in a two-volume edition. When the books came, she was very busy with some special household duties and felt she had not time to read the books at once and suggested that I do so. One evening I took up the first volume and began to read it but soon laid it down with the remark that I could make nothing out of it.

In a short time she began to read it, and as was her habit when she read books in which she became intensely interested, she read late into the night, or rather into the wee small hours. As I have said, there was an almost instant change in her looks and manner. It was not long before she began to help me physically, and I made the remark to some of my friends that she was doing things that I knew she could not do before she began to read that book. Two or three months went by before I was interested enough to make another effort to read the book, but when I did so, I began to see in it [the] reasonable and logical presentation of God, man, and the universe for which I had hoped but had not before found. Yet I did not take up the serious study of the subject for about a year after this time.

My first visit with Mrs. Eddy

I saw Mrs. Eddy for the first time under the following circumstances: I was acting in the capacity of teacher and preacher at Scranton, Pennsylvania, where I began work in Christian Science in June 1890, this being also the first work I had done as a Scientist, excepting that I had spoken a few times to audiences in Denver, Colorado. At this time the Rev. L. P. Norcross was pastor of The Mother Church in Boston. Mrs. Eddy was residing in a place at Roslindale, a suburb of Boston, which had been purchased for her but which she did not like and did not long occupy. Mr. Norcross kindly arranged to have me call and see her in this home.

I had a delightful visit with her and was deeply impressed with her personality. I shall not undertake to describe this impression, but let it suffice to say that there was a dignity of demeanor about her that seemed to me unique and such as I had never witnessed in such a degree in anyone I had ever met. She appeared to me to be tall and stately although in reality she was of medium height. Her eyes appeared to be dark, almost black, whereas they were in reality a deep blue. Her conversation was confined largely to spiritual affairs and the Christian Science movement, and I saw that she was wholly devoted, in all her thought and purpose, to God and humanity. In the course of her remarks she asked me if I thought Christian Science was the second coming of Christ. I answered that, so far as I understood it, I sincerely believed it to be such.

Up to this time I had fully expected to return to Colorado and told her so, but she replied that she wished me to remain in the East as there was a work for me to do there. This, of course, changed my purpose, and I returned to Colorado only long enough to close up my business affairs. I was detained there about three months, [and then] I returned to Scranton and continued my work there until called to Boston to take the editorship of *The Christian Science Journal*.

An instructive letter

While in Scranton I received a number of kindly and encouraging letters from Mrs. Eddy. One of these I wish to copy into this sketch, and it needs a word of explanation. Mrs. Eddy sent to Mrs. Hanna and myself a copy of a photograph of herself which had just been taken. I understand this was the last photograph for which she sat, and I may say that I regard it as the best picture of her as she appeared in her later years that I have seen. As soon as the students at Scranton saw this photograph, a number of them wished copies of it. I wrote Mrs. Eddy of this wish, and this letter is [the] reply:

*Portrait of Mary
Baker Eddy taken
by S. A. Bowers
in 1891*

Concord, N.H.
March 23, '92

Rev. Mr. Hanna
My dear Student,

Many thanks for your pleasant, far
reaching thoughts. You will find the cross
is light—and sometimes heavy! Both conditions are the weight we, not God, give it.

Jesus said "my burden is light"—
again he fainted under it.

Mr. Bowers sells at about one half his
usual price until April. He will supply you.
All orders for my photographs at his office

are proper. I am pleased with the pleasure
your dear students find in looking at my
shadow, for it does reflect my mental mood.

One word of advice on your good work.
When teaching the Bible and *Science and
Health*—those who talk little if any between
the lines of the latter teach it. The effect
of my writings is often diluted and sometimes lost by attempting to explain them.
It is the seed which once sown springs up,
and if seemingly obscure at first, it makes
its way in the soil of thought, upward,
and though least understood it bears
the biggest results of all books. Like the
seed which when sown is least and the
biggest in bearing—that Jesus spake of.

My love to Mrs. Hanna.

Most truly,
M.B.G. Eddy

Two parts of this letter impressed me deeply—the reference to the cross, and especially this original passage: "You
will find the cross is light—and sometimes heavy. Both
conditions are the weight we, not God, give it. Jesus said
'My burden is light'—again he fainted under it." This was
a conception of the cross entirely new to me, and has been
of great help to me in bearing what has at times seemed to
be a cross almost beyond my ability to bear. The other part
of the letter is what she says of teaching. I have endeavored
to follow this admonition in my teaching, and I have had

painful evidence of the truth of what she says of attempts to explain her writings. The effects of wrong interpretation of her writings have been brought home to my attention in numerous instances and in many ways. Much poor work and an incalculable amount of injury to individuals and to our Cause have followed this wrong teaching. Nevertheless the power and grace of predominant good have sustained our Cause and will continue to do so.

Editing the *Journal* while being taught by our Leader

In the autumn of 1892, I was called to the editorship of *The Christian Science Journal*, Mrs. Hanna becoming my assistant. The subscription list of the *Journal* was then thirty-eight hundred, and there was a dearth of material with which to make up the first issue, which was the November 1892 number. We were hard put for articles, but I utilized some of my own productions previously written, and we managed to make up the required size.

After reading this number, Mrs. Eddy wrote me the following gracious and encouraging letter:

> Pleasant View
> Concord, N.H.
> Nov. 1, 1892

> God bless you[,] Judge Hanna! I have just read your part and am *satisfied* of the *C.S. Journal's* future success under such management. I would esteem it a privilege to present your names to the Mass. Met. College C.S.A.[49] for Honorary

members—the names of Judge and
Mrs. Hanna—at the next session of this
Association. May I do this? After you pass
through a course in Christian Science with
me for your teacher, you will then receive
the admission as others of its members.

In haste,
Most truly,
M.B.G. Eddy

Mrs. Hanna and I did not enter class with Mrs. Eddy until she taught her last class in 1898, but soon after we entered upon the editorial work, she began to call us to her and gave us private instruction, sometimes [with] her talks continuing for two or three hours. She did this several times in all—as I remember, seven; and then [she] publicly declared us to be her students. The privilege of being thus instructed was beyond estimate. She gave us not only general instruction but such specific direction as the circumstances of the time and the exigencies of our work demanded.

In a letter to us she said, "I have given you *two* lessons that I could not have given in a class, and they will not lose their effects in time nor in eternity." This we firmly believe and have thus far had much convincing proof of the truth of this prophecy.

My work as pastor and Reader for The Mother Church

In 1894 I was called to the pastorate of The Mother Church, continuing in this capacity until the change in the method and order of the church services occurred, when I became [the] Reader, conducting two services as such and reading discourses made up of alternate Biblical and correlative references from *Science and Health*. It was extremely interesting and instructive to find what a consistent and harmonious discourse could thus be prepared. Then came the order for two Readers and sermons compiled substantially as they are now.

I was not long in seeing, in some measure at least, the wisdom of this method of preaching the gospel. I might now write almost a volume on this subject but will limit my remarks to just one point, and that is the uniformity of Christian Science preaching wherever Christian Science services are held, and they are now held in nearly every part of the earth, and thus is the same gospel being preached in effect to all nations, in accordance with the teaching and prophecy of Christ Jesus. This single fact abundantly justifies the wisdom of our Leader in making this astonishing innovation in public Christian worship.

I continued to act as First Reader in The Mother Church until appointed to the Board of Lectureship in 1902. Mrs. Hanna and I also remained in the editorial work until then.

Mrs. Eddy's demeanor

February 5, [1893], we received a letter [written at Mrs. Eddy's request] inviting us to visit. It was at this time that I saw in [her] what I have never seen in any other person I have ever met. I will endeavor to describe this, but it will be a poor effort.

During a single conversation Mrs. Eddy would change her manner and countenance many times. Sometimes she would appear youthful and sprightly, almost to girlishness. This is what I would call her normal appearance, and she would present this appearance when talking about ordinary social or current events and affairs; the instant, however, she would begin talking about Christian Science or spiritual matters, her whole look and manner would change. Her features would seem to enlarge from their normal, delicate look to an almost masculine and stern appearance. She would gesticulate in a masculine and decided way, and at such times words and sentences would be uttered in the stately and majestic way she expressed her thoughts in writing. Her eyes would become larger than normal and would seem to be dark—almost black—as they appeared to me when I saw her at Roslindale; she would seem to be oblivious to the presence of others, looking away into space or into the future. Her whole demeanor would be that of one enraptured and illuminated. At such times I could only describe her as being on the mount of vision. As quickly as she [had] changed to this mood, she would resume her normal look and manner and become again the sprightly and charming hostess. I have seen her, soon after she came from the "mount," run upstairs for some article she wished to show us in as sprightly a way as would a girl of sixteen. As I have said, I never saw a person whose mental moods affected her features, look, and manner as did hers. This can be explained only by recognizing the supremacy of her spiritual nature over her physical in an extraordinary way.

Letters from Mrs. Eddy

During the time Mrs. Hanna and I were Editors of the periodicals, we, of course, received many letters from

Mrs. Eddy. They contained much instruction and sound admonition as well as caution. From one of these I extract as follows:

> Many thanks for receiving my plan. Your editorial on excluding the Scriptures is the thing I like and have touched upon in many a class of mine. My earliest, best impressions of Truth which could come at that date were received from reading the New Testament every morning at school.
>
> N. B. Watch the signs of the times, and if your pearl is too pearly for the pigs at present, put it up in its casket, and take the next other notion of your subject, and wait for the public growth, i.e., be more gentle in denunciation, propositional, and bait your readers till all are more ready to swallow your pearl.

Of like kind is the following:

> I have erased your verities because they are spoken *too soon*. Wait for growth. The textbooks contain it all—but so arranged as to require growth before it is spoken by those who have not grown to it. The letter *killeth*. It is the spirit, understanding, behind the words which maketh alive. I doubt not that your article is grand. But it is true that my students are killing to a fearful extent the spirit and effects of my writings by using them so glibly in theirs.

In a letter dated August 2, 1896, she wrote:

Do not attack hypnotism; do not take Scriptural authority for its identification. But allude to it briefly when you do speak of it, as you would a ghost story.... Mankind has been frightened into sickness, and encouraged in sin, by the pulpit making sin a reality and descanting on it. Let us be careful. I would not name hypnotism in your next issue, but later if you please, you can, so as to keep it uncovered and show its *imposition* as a healing means, or an honest claim.

August 14, 1897, she wrote:

Every time you have been to my knowledge tested by divine Love, in your faithful discharge of high offices, you have shown a loving charity and a most Christian spirit. And I do pray that I may not give you a single additional care or sigh.

Oh[,] may God spare me this occasion. I never feel that you do wrong[;] you cannot indulge a wrong thought with your *own* volition turned as it is to Truth and Love. But the temptations that beset all true Christians are either to feel too sharply the burdens borne or to try to lay them down.

Now beloved in Christ, you nor I can *suffer* for *doing good*. It is our *life*[,] our growth[,] our spiritual element, that is mightier than all the means of mortals to thwart this result—yes, infinitely beyond

them. Now just turn all your powers to find
peace and rest in the *Good you reflect* and
that *upholds* you.

Know this, that there the necromancers
fail[;] they cannot come nigh that secret
place. There you *are safe*[,] and because you
put your trust in Good, God *will* deliver
you[,] and you cannot fear but will *walk
where you look*, and be strong.

… Be calm, full of *trust* and *joy*, for the
blessings you have brought on us all by
your fidelity to God and man must[,] will[,]
return to you after due time.[50]

In the *Journals* for April and May 1894, I published an
article on the Ten Commandments, the purpose of which
was to interpret their meaning from the Christian Science
standpoint. I had given the commandments a good deal of
careful study, but did not feel warranted in publishing my
interpretation without submitting it to Mrs. Eddy. In those
days we were in the habit of submitting to her criticism articles of a scientifically definitional kind before putting them
in the *Journal*. (This article was republished in the *Journal*
for November 1898.)

In a letter dated May 10, 1894, Mrs. Eddy thus wrote of
said editorial:

Your editorial was excellent. Four years
ago, Mrs. Otterson was looking over my
New Testament and found I had marked
the verses of the Sermon on the Mount,
with their correspondences to the [T]en
[C]ommandments. She asked questions

and seemed to drink in, as no student
had done before, my meaning, or rather
Jesus' meaning, which I interpreted. I
told her I had written it in detail, but
had not the time to fix it for the press.
When to see you save me this trouble,
of wishing it done and not doing it, was
just glorious. Your thoughts so far as
expressed were quite in line with mine.

I received a letter from Mrs. Eddy dated December 18,
1894, establishing the new order of service in The Mother
Church, from which I quote:

I received last night a certain sound in
the direction I named to one of you sometime since, viz: that no sermons are to be
preached by mortals in The Mother Church
as pastors appointed or placed over this
[C]hurch; that the Bible and *Science and
Health* are to be the preachers. A general
Sunday School must be adopted, the proper
appointments and arrangements for which
I leave to the present pastor and First
Members of the Church in committee.[51]

Correspondence concerning
Christ and Christmas

The poem *Christ and Christmas* was published during
our editorial connection with the work. The correspondence we had with Mrs. Eddy in reference to it gave us, in
some degree, an inside view of her thought and purpose
in bringing it out. She saw soon after its publication that

her students were not receiving and understanding it as she intended they should. Some were going to extremes in their effort to interpret it, and others were not seeing its spiritual meaning at all. She therefore withdrew it for a time. Later she had it quietly catalogued with her other writings, no special attention being called to it. She never intended it to be shelved or overlooked and forgotten, but knew that in time it would do its work. Referring to this poem [in an article beginning on] page 371 of *Miscellaneous Writings: 1883–1896*, Mrs. Eddy says:

> This poem and its illustrations are
> as hopelessly original as is "Science and
> Health with Key to the Scriptures."
> When the latter was first issued, critics
> declared that it was incorrect, contradic-
> tory, unscientific, unchristian; but those
> human opinions had not one feather's
> weight in the scales of God. The fact
> remains, that the textbook of Christian
> Science is transforming the universe.
>
> "Christ and Christmas" voices Christian
> Science through song and object-lesson....
>
> Knowing that this book would
> produce a stir, I sought the judgment of
> sound critics familiar with the works
> of masters in France and Italy....
>
> It is most fitting that Christian
> Scientists memorize the nativity of Jesus.
> To him who brought a great light to
> all ages, and named his burdens light,
> homage is indeed due, — but is bankrupt.

> I never looked on my ideal of the face of
> the Nazarite Prophet; but the one illus-
> trating my poem approximates it.

In a letter dated December 9, 1893, Mrs. Eddy thus
wrote concerning this poem:

> The sweet poverty of matter that
> my illustrations depict, Mrs. Stetson's
> students call *caricatures*, and reading her
> mind behind scenes[,] she feels thus, too,
> although she will be loath to acknowledge
> this, and possibly it has not come to her
> conscious sense; but I recognize it in her
> mind.[52] This poem and its illustrations
> of C[hristian] S[cience] will be met by
> students who are not taught properly as
> "*Science and Health*" was met at first[,] by
> the world sneered at. But rest assured, I
> have put into my vineyard not only a wine
> press, but digged a ditch round it. I have
> got the expressions of distinguished artists
> and travellers all over Europe and Asia
> saying[,] "It is *new*, but a fine work of art."

The start of the *Christian Science Sentinel*

The following extract from a letter dated June 22, 1898,
is the first intimation I had that Mrs. Eddy contemplated
the establishment of a weekly Christian Science newspaper.
The brevity with which she treated important matters
relating to the movement is strikingly noticeable in this
extract: "I deeply appreciate your kindness on my behalf in
following up the newspaper mess. I beg pardon for detaining

issue of *Jour[nal]*. What can we do to meet this plot? Have a *weekly folio sheet*. I see no other way." This brief message set in motion the wave of purpose that brought forth the weekly *Christian Science Sentinel*, as it was finally named.

I did not feel equal to taking on the additional care and responsibility of a weekly periodical and so wrote Mrs. Eddy. I asked that someone else might be selected for that work. To this she replied:

> I thought you would see the *coil* of the serpent, and reserve yourself for the weekly newspaper. An editor is the hardest thing to manufacture in the world, even a poet not excepted. Your help must be worked up to their offices. We cannot wait for that now. Do you not see the wisdom of resigning your place as trustee, and then I will appoint? I would have done so in the first place, had I dreamed that it would require me to say who at last must, should, be editors.
>
> You and Mrs. H. must be at the head of the *C.S. Messenger*,[53] for no one else can take this place at present, till they work up to it. I have *not time* to teach them the wisdom that is required for it. Your experience gives you the advantage. I trust your dear heart to understand that Mother sees the necessity of what she writes at this time.

Her next reference to the weekly was in a letter dated September 8, 1898:

> The weekly must be a folio of the size
> that you can afford. The old is *put off.*
> The first of our organs has gone by, in its
> proportions. We are bigger now tha[n] then.

September 16, 1898, Mrs. Eddy wrote:

> Your highly interesting monthly and
> weekly issues are well sustained. They
> exhibit experienced and skillful workman-
> ship. The last little sheet opens a vast area
> of influence all on the right side. God bless
> you in this as in all thy undertakings.
> Every truth you promulgate, every good
> and ardent thought you entertain, though
> it expose you to the aim of evil, makes you
> healthier, wealthier, wiser[,] and longer-
> lived—the evidence of the senses to the
> contrary notwithstanding. Go on in this
> path, and your immortality is brought to
> light.[54]

The *Weekly* first appeared September 1, 1898, and the editorial [in the following week's issue] is not out of place in this sketch as it contains what the editor believed to be Mrs. Eddy's conception of the purpose and scope of the publication, and the letter above copied indicates her approval:

> The *Weekly* has made its first bow to the
> Field. We trust and believe it was received
> in the spirit in which it was sent forth—the
> spirit of love and helpfulness.
>
> The dedicatory poem of the Rev. Mary
> Baker Eddy is pregnant with meaning for
> the hour.[55]

Sincerely do we hope that "the eyes of them that see shall not be dim, and the ears of them that hear shall hearken."

Our great effort should be to have constantly seeing eyes and hearing ears. As the children of Israel and the disciples of olden time saw and heard, they were instructed and blessed. In so far as they failed to see and hear, they met the inevitable penalty of such failure, whether it took the severer form which came from wilful disobedience, or the milder form which came from ignorant or careless disobedience. As it was then, so is it now. So shall it continue to be "to the end."

January 19, 1899, Mrs. Eddy wrote: "*Sentinel* is the proper title for our weekly, the last name is nothing but a date and too weak for a paper of ours. Also let me prophecy [that] "Sentinel" and the motto with it describe the future of this newspaper. It will take that place and must *fill* it when numerous periodicals of our denomination are extant."

Comments on my work as a lecturer

One of the great achievements of Mrs. Eddy was the establishment of the Board of Lectureship. The results of the lecturer's work, even thus far, are beyond human estimate, and if this be true of the present, what shall we say of the great future yet in store along this line of endeavor?

Mrs. Eddy was kind enough to write me a number of letters giving her estimate of the lectures which I have prepared and delivered. In a letter to me dated

August 26, 1902, she says:

> I have read your lecture with deep
> interest. I see how it will do much good.
> Whoever opens the eyes of the children
> of men to see aright that Idea on earth
> that has best and clearest reflected by
> word or deed the divine Principle of
> man and the universe, will accomplish
> most for himself and mankind in the
> direction of all that is good and true.

In a letter dated August 29, 1902, she again refers to [this] lecture as follows: "Today for the first time I have caught time to read thoroughly your lecture. It is rich in [S]crip-tural scholarship—it is a clear-cut statement of profound truth so logical in premise and conclusion that it must be convincing to all right thinkers."

October 13, 1902, Mrs. Eddy wrote as follows:

Pleasant View
Concord N.H.
Oct. 13, '02

Judge and Mrs. Hanna,
Beloved Students:

> Your letter was refreshing. I can do you
> most good by pointing the path—showing
> the scenes behind the curtain. The united
> plan of the evil-doers is to cause the begin-
> ners either in lecturing or teaching or in our
> periodicals to keep Mrs. Eddy as she *is* out of
> sight, and to keep her as she *is not* constantly

before public. This kills two birds with one stone. It darkens the spiritual sense of students and misguides the public. Why[?] Because it misstates the idea of the divine Principle that you are trying to demonstrate and hides it from the sense of the people.

Your first lecture foiled this purpose, and has done, will do, *much* for you and our Cause. Hence the snare to make you prepare another *quickly*. Deliver your *first* and no matter how often; incorporate in all your other lectures the main points of what you wrote in the first lecture about the Leader of Christian Science. Keeping the truth of her real character before the public will help the students and do more than all else can for our Cause. Christianity in its purity was lost by *defaming* and *killing* its early defenders. Do not let this period repeat that mistake. The truth in regard to your Leader heals the sick and saves the sinner. The lie has just the opposite effect[,] and the evil *one* that leads all evil in this matter knows this more clearly than do the Christian Scientists in general.

I have not yet got your last lecture delivered in Chicago. Please forward it at once. God bless you! God keep your eyes open to the movements of evil so that your good be effectual and not diluted.

With love always, Mother
M.B. Eddy

My motive in what I have written is as unselfish as my daily, lonely, toilsome life.

Mother

In a letter dated September 16, 1903, Mrs. Eddy says:

Your letter and lecture are received. Accept my thanks. I enclose the supplied word 'spiritual' in the lecture for this reason: There is a tendency to teach that man is physically as well as spiritually God's son. This error loses the logic of Christian Science. The likeness of God, Spirit, is *spiritual,* and in no way allied to matter. Please keep the distinction clear, else it follows that sin, inseparable from the flesh or physical man, is a part of His image or likeness. *One* deflect in divine metaphysics breaks the link in Science, hence our statement of this Science must be consistent.

N. B. Your lecture is sound, grand, calculated to do much good.

In a letter dated August 4, 1904, Mrs. Eddy says:
I am made glad each time that I hear reports of your grand, persuasive, lawyer-like lectures. Press on. You can accomplish great *good*, and *cannot suffer* for your

labors of love. Our Cause is rushing on. Its chariot wheels are heard before the lips can speak its coming. Let us have on our wedding garments, for purity and peace now await our bridals.

Letters about teaching Christian Science

I have been connected with the Board of Education since its organization. I received many letters from Mrs. Eddy in connection with the Board. The following letter dated November 29, 1898, was addressed to Mr. Edward A. Kimball. [Editor's note: Eddy asked that the letter be sent to Hanna as well.] It read, in part:

> Pleasant View
> Concord, N.H.
> Nov. 29, 1898

My dear Student,

> The Board of Education must have by-laws and this is one of them: No student shall receive a certificate of qualification nor shall be accepted for examination who has not a fair education in English and especially the grammar of the old tongue and the branches requisite for good writing, speaking, and teaching Christian Science in *good English*. I am disgusted with the awful orthography, language, ignorance, [and] manners of some College students. Had I known of

this lack of learning[,] I would not have received them into a Normal class. So this must be a condition specified by the Board.

With love,
M.B. Eddy

March 10, 1902, Mrs. Eddy wrote, in part, as follows:

Judge Hanna,
Beloved Student:

The obstetrics is a snare. God gives spiritual and not sexual teaching. I was never quite satisfied to have it taught. The real Christian Scientist can deliver the mother in travail with the [t]ruth, the same as disease is healed. And the laws of our land will not protect a failure in the one case any more than the other. An M.D. teacher of obstetrics does not evade the fact that his student, the obstetrician[,] has no regular diploma.[56]

With love,
Mother

Guidance regarding testimony meetings and the *Manual*

The following letter set in motion the machinery that resulted in the present mid-week testimony meetings. The prophetic vision therein apparent has been wonderfully realized:

Pleasant View
Concord, N.H.
January 15, 1895

To be read at your next Friday evening meeting.

My dear Students:

Make broader bounds for blessing the
people. Have Friday evening meetings to benefit
the people. Learn to forget what you should
not remember, viz., self, and live for the good
you do. Conduct your meetings by repeating
and demonstrating practical Christian Science.
Tell what this Science does for yourself and
will do for others. Speak from the experience
of its Founder, noting her self-sacrifice as the
way in Christian Science. Be meek; let your
motto for this meeting be: *Who shall be least and
servant;* and Little children, love one another.

Affectionately yours,
Mary Baker Eddy

The following letter will suffice to indicate how the
Manual grew from its small beginnings into the formi-
dable book it now is:

Pleasant View
Concord, N.H.
July 1, 1895

Judge S. J. Hanna,
Mr. E. P. Bates,
Mr. W. B. Johnson,

My dear Students:

The [d]ivine teachings to me this morning I must send to you at once.

When I first named the *Church Manual*[,] I did not realize the scope of the title. My purpose included nothing more than a pamphlet containing the Church Rules and By-Laws and other matter that is already published in a Church circular. But you commenced a Manual proper. The idea pleased me, and I procured for you my vision of years bygone. This morning I am turned backward, and taught by God to let the dead bury the dead and have no resurrection until the last trumpet shall sound. By this I mean I have been led to see that now is not the time to recapitulate the Church history. The field is far from fit for this harvest. I was sensible the church history could not be given in full without doing much harm.

"Blessed are the peace makers." Where no tale-bearer is, the strife ceaseth. Have no more Sunday services after July 6th, till the first Sunday in September. The summary of my letter is: Neither write nor compile any more Church History. Just have a little preface, and a pamphlet giving Rules and By-Laws of the church, and what is already published in your circular. Drop your Manual.

What you have gathered into [manuscripts] of Church history is not lost, but a little treasurer [sic] laid away in your Church vault or iron safe, there to remain like the contents of the corner-stone, till God calls for it, which may never be.

My present impressions are that Christian Scientists are making material history and evil altogether too real. The Science teaches that those have no reality whatever.

As I have said before, tell Mr. Johnson to collect all the First Church of Christ, Scientist, Rules and By-Laws, and only those which belong to this [C]hurch and have been made under the new Charter, and your Church circular. Put them together in one package, and send them to me at once. Then I will do my part and return them to you for immediate publication.

With love, Mother,
Mary Baker Eddy

Background on the Lesson-Sermon

The Bible Lessons were originally prepared after the order of the International Series of Bible Lessons; that is to say, the subjects of this series were followed by our Bible Lesson Committee. Each Lesson was preceded by an Introductory prepared by the committee, bringing out the scientific or spiritual sense of the subject; this introduction being followed by the Bible text constituting the subject; and this text being followed by a Golden Text. After this followed three footsteps which were designed to develop the stages of spiritual progression contained in the Lesson. Following this came what are called expository notes made up of correlative selections from the Bible and *Science and Health*.

While Mrs. Hanna and I were members of this committee, the method was changed by direction of Mrs. Eddy, who selected the subjects for the year as they now stand. The committee gradually evolved uniform Lessons in length, and finally arranged the Lessons into six subdivisions as they are now prepared.[57]

After being a member of the committee about two years, I withdrew from it because of pressing duties in other departments. This work of preparing the Bible Lessons was so interesting and instructive that I reluctantly left it, but necessity demanded that I do so. There is no more important work than the building up of these great sermons, and the Field of Christian Scientists, as well as Christians throughout the world, owe to the faithful work of the Bible Lesson Committee an inestimable debt of gratitude. As I have before said, I regard this method of preaching the gospel to all nations as one of the grandest achievements in religious history.

The Church building and First Reader's residence

We were in Boston during the building of the first Mother Church edifice and had the privilege of aiding in this achievement, which was done so quietly and so quickly that it astonished not only Boston but the whole country. Writing of the laying of the cornerstone, Mrs. Eddy said:

May 20, 1894

My beloved Students,

I enclose the names of contributors to
be published in your *Jour[nal]* together with
other matter on [c]orner-[s]tone laying.
Note the *simplicity* of the ceremony[:] "His
voice was not heard in the [s]treet." Note
the registry by *my hand* of the names of the
Christian Science Board of Directors. Note
the names of the two dear young watchers
through the stormy 3 nights at the [c]orner-
[s]tone. Note the miracle of the fishes out
of whose mouths were taken so rapidly the
money which builds our church. *Laus De[o]*.

With love,
Mother
Mary Baker Eddy

In connection with this cornerstone, Mrs. Eddy wrote
her poem "Laus Deo" (see *Miscellaneous Writings*, p. 399), in
reference to which she wrote us the following letter:

Pleasant View
Concord, N.H.
Sept. 27, 1894

My beloved Students:

This is almost too good to credit.
But the *evidence* is *grand*; a man of
whom I can say, An Israelite indeed.
I thank *you*. My "Laus Deo" hymn

arrived today set to music. This is
apropo[s]. My love to dear Camilla.

With deep love,
Mother

The following letter to Mrs. Hanna indicates Mrs. Eddy's
wish that her Commonwealth Avenue house in Boston, No.
385, should become the temporary residence of the First
Readers in The Mother Church:

> Pleasant View
> Concord, N.H.
> July 12, 1894

My beloved Student:

You can scarcely know how my heart
thanks you for your tender care to walk
with me the narrow path and help me bear
my burdens. I can see in all these signs of
these times why God sent you and your
noble husband to me in an hour of need.
Truly God is *good*, and but for my sore
experience I would never have loved Him[,]
the *infinite* Good, as I hope that I do.

Dear one, the parting and pangs you
have so recently borne, and so bravely,
yea, Christianly, is a sweet usury to which
you are putting your God-given talents.
Keep on bearing the cross; it is the only
way to the crown. Rejoice that God finds
you ready and willing to follow, and

fulfill [g]ood in His appointed way.

Yes, you guessed my secret! I do want Judge Hanna and his wife in 385 Commonwealth Avenue, and none else will get this offer from me. But there is one circumstance I will name. Perhaps I shall cleanse and refurnish that house, wherein God has specially dwelt and sent forth His orders to mankind, for my winter home. This is an event not yet decided upon in my own mind.[58] I wait on God; my times are in His hands. He will do with me what seemeth to Him good. I do not see my way clearly yet what He would have me do. When I do see it, I will let you know. Now this almost ought not be spoken. But you and your husband should know it and *will not mention it*. With love to him, and to dear Camilla.

I am tenderly, truly thine,
Mary Baker Eddy

As is well known, all the First Readers in The Mother Church and their families have since that time occupied this residence during their term as Reader.

Thwarting malice

The attempts to blacken Mrs. Eddy's character were so repeated and so widespread that it required constant watchfulness to keep track of them. If history did not show how those who have endeavored to establish reforms

Mary Baker Eddy's home at 385 Commonwealth Avenue in Boston

in the world have been maligned, libeled, persecuted, and crucified, and if it were not true that even in these times of boasted enlightenment and Christianity, history is largely repeating itself, it would seem incredible that there should have occurred such wickedness as has been uncovered in connection with the plottings referred to.

It came within my province, among many similar instances, to assist in driving one of these attempts to its source and defeating its purpose. I received a letter from Mr. Frye informing me that a Mr. Goddard, a professor of philosophy in Clark University, at Worcester, Massachusetts, was endeavoring to collect evidence against Mrs. Eddy's character with a view to publishing a book. On receipt of this letter, I called Alfred Farlow and James A. Neal to my aid, and we called upon Mr. Goddard and had a long conversation with him. He frankly told us he had heard so much against Mrs. Eddy that he honestly supposed what he had heard was true, and without any evil intent but as a matter of psychological interest, he was contemplating the publication of a book of the kind mentioned. He said, however, that he had not up to that time been successful in verifying what he had heard of Mrs. Eddy. Before we left him, he expressed his belief that he had been misled in the matter and assured us that he would go no further with his proposed book. It will be understood why this gentleman was deceived when it is known that Worcester was for some years the home of the excommunicated student of Mrs. Eddy who was publishing abroad these scandalous falsehoods against Mrs. Eddy, and some of her attacks were published in the Worcester press.

Those who are in position to know of the inner life of Mrs. Eddy know that she walks constantly with God, looking to Him for guidance in her every step and relying upon Him alone for direction in the great religious movement of which she is the head. Deeply was the writer impressed while sitting with her at her dining table in

Concord not long since when, in childlike simplicity yet with deepest seriousness, she said, "I am learning more and more to take God with me into every detail of my life."

EDWARD E. NORWOOD *(1868–1940)*

*Born in Memphis, Tennessee, Edward Norwood grew up
in the Methodist church and had planned to be a minster,
but his studies, which included theological training at
Vanderbilt University, were interrupted by chronic illness,
from which he had suffered all his life. In his mid-twenties,
he became interested in Christian Science and was healed
within three weeks by reading* Science and Health
with Key to the Scriptures. *Following several months
of extensive study of the textbook, he joined The Mother
Church and was active in the establishment of the first
Christian Science branch church in Memphis. Before long,
he took Primary class instruction and was listed in* The
Christian Science Journal *as a practitioner.*

*Norwood took Normal class from Mrs. Eddy in 1898,
taught his first class in 1899, and married Rose Barnwell
in 1900. The couple lived briefly in Washington, D.C.,
before spending more than a year in Charleston, South
Carolina, where they both served as Readers in the*

branch church; in addition, he assisted with Committee on Publication work there. In 1902, the Norwoods moved back to Washington, D.C., where he served as First Reader of Second Church, Washington, D.C., and once again participated in Committee on Publication work. Along with his healing and teaching, Norwood wrote often for the Christian Science periodicals and played an important role in publishing the 1907 edition of Science and Health. *The couple's daughter, Mary Rose, was born in 1907.*

Blessed by Serving Our Leader and Her Cause

EDWARD E. NORWOOD

In the spring of 1893, I found Christian Science. My dear mother was condemned to die of an internal, incurable disease, and a friend told her of Christian Science and later brought a practitioner to call. Her clear, loving explanations of the Truth at once interested me. I began to read *Science and Health with Key to the Scriptures*, first to my mother and later for myself. I was amazed at it. Like a shining light (which it indeed was), the Truth led me on, and I literally could not read fast enough. The first year the book was read sixteen or eighteen hours a day. At the end of about three weeks, I realized that I was entirely healed, and this joyful experience was wonderful. [59] And with the healing came a most gracious spiritual uplift, which to a greater or lesser degree has remained.

The new heavens and earth were appearing to my enraptured gaze, and I still cherish the memories of those first months. In less than a month after beginning the reading, I had quite a number of healings. My first patient was my brother's bulldog, then my Jersey cow, and then our colored cook. Of course it was more love and faith than understanding, but some of the demonstrations made then were as quick and satisfactory as any since. For these early proofs of God's presence and power, I thank God!

Aided by correspondence with Mrs. Eddy

My dear mother was wonderfully helped during the first few weeks, and indeed, we fondly hoped she was entirely healed. I had written a very fervent, grateful letter to Mrs. Eddy, telling her of my mother being so wonderfully helped, and my own healing, and desired to do something to show my gratitude. The letter was addressed, "Rev. Mary Baker Eddy, thou who art highly favored among women!"— the salutation the angel gave Mary [see Luke 1:28].

My mother lingered during the summer and fall, and passed on November 3. Just two days before she left, I had a letter from Mrs. Eddy as follows:

> Pleasant View
> Concord, N.H.
> Oct. 25, '93

> Mr. E. Norwood
> Memphis, Tenn.

> Dear Sir:

> Your favor interests me. Nothing is more desirable than to learn of those in early life choosing the good part.

> The sketch of yourself was highly gratifying. It is quite common to hear of those

healed by reading Science and Health. Are
you thinking of making Christian Science
a study and practice? The spirit of love you
manifest inclines me to ask this.

Please write again and tell me how you
are getting along, and if you know Mrs.
Mims of Atlanta, Ga.

Very kindly,
Mary B. G. Eddy

The spiritual impetus that came with this letter carried
me through the trying experience of my mother's demise
and helped me to make a demonstration both over the
sense of grief and also over what human sense might call
the highest claim in mortal mind, namely the dying request
of a mother. My dear mother called me to her bedside the
day before she left and taking my hand said, "Son, you'll
give up this Christian Science for me, won't you?" Though
I knew but little, then, of the workings of error, I answered
not, but silently declared that Love protected and sustained
me and that error could not tempt me through *any* channel.
To show how well I was protected, my father and sister
stood near me, and neither heard one word of the request!
So I was spared any reproaches.

Some time before this, I had withdrawn from the
Methodist church and felt their prayers and appeals quite
forcibly—the mesmerism of old theology. In fact for some
time I was utterly miserable—[and] knew the cause—but
could not seem to meet it. At this time, in response to
Mrs. Eddy's invitation to "Please write again and let me

know how you are getting along," I wrote her and mentioned the mental darkness. I have not forgotten the wonderful freedom that came to me three days later when she read my letter and the claim was instantly healed. I rejoiced with joy unspeakable and thanked God.

Church work and class instruction

The little church [in Memphis, Tennessee,] was organized, and I was elected assistant pastor, and a year later, at the change of order of service, was made Second Reader. In the meantime, in the spring of 1895, I went to New York City and went through a class with Carol Norton, and again in the fall of 1897, went through another class with him. The following year, November 1898, both of us studied Christian Science in the wonderful class with Mrs. Eddy.

The invitation to the class was as follows:

> Pleasant View
> Concord, N.H.
> Nov. 15, 1898

Beloved Student:

I have a great blessing in store for you if you will be in Concord on Sunday Nov. 20th at Christian Science Hall [at] 4 p.m. Strictly confidential.

With love, mother
Mary Baker Eddy

I got my notice just in time to catch the very last train that would take me there, and it began to lose time the minute it left Memphis. *My*, but I worked to know the

[t]ruth, and got into New York City late and had to literally *run* across town to catch a Sunday morning train for Boston and Concord. Every mile of the trip was a demonstration, and many, many blessings [were] gained on the way. The morning stars were singing together as I passed through Boston at 5:00 o'clock Sunday morning, and a happy Southerner (albeit a tired one) took [the] train at North Station for Concord!

How well do I remember that blessed experience! The happy throng at the Eagle Hotel on Sunday morning, November 20; the beautiful service at Christian Science Hall in the morning, when our dear, old Brother Ezra M. Buswell was the First Reader; and the eager, expectant dear ones assembled at the Hall at four o'clock! The air was fairly vibrant with divine Love, and the consciousness of Good's presence and power most wonderfully clear. After all were seated, Mr. Kimball read the statement from Mrs. Eddy (as given in *The First Church of Christ, Scientist, and Miscellany*, pp. 243–244) and later the Fairest among Fifteen Hundred Million and Altogether Lovely came in (see Song of Solomon 5:10, 16).

Although I had seen her several times before, she looked more radiantly glorious than ever, and the glory of her countenance was unspeakable. She came in, attended by Miss Clara Shannon and Mr. Calvin Frye, and as we arose in respectful greeting, she stepped up to the platform with the agility of a child and the grace of a queen. She began by saying, "I am very glad to see you all, especially the dear ones whom I've never met before." She also said, in the beginning, "I have been waiting fifteen years to teach this class, and those whom God has appointed,

I have called to teach." This evidently was a special class of seventy (three were absent) that she had in mind, for the [Massachusetts Metaphysical] College had been closed but nine years before—or in 1889.

She taught from "Recapitulation" but quoted many times from other parts of *Science and Health* and *much* from the Bible. The first day of the class (it lasted two whole afternoons), the chief question was, "What is God?" The second day, the leading question was, "How would you heal the sick instantaneously?" Each one arose to answer, and each one of the sixty-seven present agreed [that] one great thing, among others, was to "realize the presence of Love." Mrs. Eddy listened very patiently. Then she said, "You have answered very well—very well, indeed. But you don't get quite close enough. Now let me tell you how I'd heal instantaneously." (We all listened very intently.) "It is not so much to realize the *presence* of Love—but *love! Love* enough, and you'll raise the dead! *I've done it!*" And it just looked like an angel from heaven sat there before us!

Just before that, Harold Frederick, the English novelist, had passed on in London under Christian Science treatment. Mrs. Eddy expressed her great regret, saying she would not have had it happen for all of her possessions. And immediately after, speaking of material so-called substance, she said, "I wouldn't give a button, *I wouldn't give a button,* for all the materiality there is, for I already have too much of earth and not enough of heaven."

She also spoke of man being coexistent with God and used this illustration: If one stands before a mirror, his reflection does not *grow* into full size. It is so, at once. So is man coexistent with good—the image of Mind.

The whole class was a remarkable demonstration of God's power and presence as manifested in one of His saints. She spoke so lovingly and tenderly of the children—the child-thought—and said, "When I pass them out driving, they make me the most graceful bows, for they know that I love them!"

All through the class the spiritual teachings of the Scriptures were emphasized, and she said, "Every word in the Bible is capable of spiritual interpretation." And she dwelt much upon God as divine *Mind*.

Moments of profound clarity

An experience I had during the class may be of interest, and I shall relate it. I had prayed earnestly to [God,] good, for a great unfoldment, a clearer and broader vision, and suddenly, during the second day's lesson it came. I do not seem to remember whether she quoted from *Retrospection and Introspection*, [beginning on] page 88: "Mind demonstrates omnipresence and omnipotence, but Mind revolves on a spiritual axis, and its power is displayed and its presence felt in eternal stillness and immovable Love. The divine potency of this spiritual mode of Mind, and the hindrance opposed to it by material motion, is proven beyond a doubt in the practice of Mind-healing." Whether she quoted it or not, it was very clear in my thought. Suddenly it did seem a veil was lifted or a window opened, and I could see, in one of those supreme moments (that never leaves one where it found him), the reality of things—the majestic oneness of the spiritual universe—its vast quietness—the infinite Mind—the eternal stillness, which is really primal energy. And as I looked, the symbols around me, the personalities, the class, all externals, seemed to fade, and a wondrous sense of reality appeared—and ah, my friends, it was awesome!

I understood somewhat what our Leader means by "the unlabored motion of Mind" [see *Science and Health*, p. 445]. And [I saw] that what mortal mind calls activity is lethargy, inaction, inertia, and is the seeming obstruction in the way of the operation of divine law. I realized, to some extent, the joy and activity of what is forever going on in Mind; all that hides it is the misty curtain of false belief, which lifts at intervals. I got such a glimpse of the Way—the road our great Leader trod—the first one since Jesus walked in it, and my heart yearned to go on! But anon the veil dropped down, and I was back again. Let me add that this last summer (1918), while standing beside a little stream in Maryland, I had a similar experience, and because the first was being caught up in Mrs. Eddy's concept of good and the last was more of demonstration, the latter experience has been clearer and remained longer.

Upon relating this once to Mr. Joseph Armstrong (then Publisher of Mrs. Eddy's books), he told me of a similar experience when, just before the class, Mrs. Eddy called him to Pleasant View to consult about [being] substitute First Reader (in Judge Hanna's absence). She told him about the coming class and what she hoped it would do for the world. He said as she talked, the wonderful vista opened, and for a few moments *he* saw what *she* saw, and he said, "I never dreamed of such a heaven on earth." And this was the mental state in which that God-blest woman abode more or less all the time!

A follow-up to class

Well, after the class, I returned home, and my work was on a higher basis [with] better healing, and I began to teach students.

Some time after the class, I received the following explanation of the trinity with a note from Mr. McKenzie, as below:

> THE TRINITY
> Father, is man's divine Principle, Love.
> Son, is God's man—His image, or
> spiritual idea.
> Holy Ghost, is Divine Science, the
> Messiah or Comforter.
> Jesus in the flesh was the prophet or
> wayshower to Life, Truth, Love, and out of
> the flesh Jesus was the Christ, the spiritual
> idea or image and likeness of God.[60]

MARY BAKER EDDY

The accompanying note from Mr. McKenzie:

> Concord, N.H.
> Jan. 3, 1899

> Beloved in Christ:

> By request of our beloved Mother and
> Teacher[,] the enclosed jewel of truth, lumi-
> nous with love, is sent to enrich with light
> the members of her last class.

> Your fellow worker,
> Wm. P. McKenzie

Restlessness stilled

For a time I had a strong desire to leave Memphis and wrote Mrs. Eddy about it. In reply she wrote:

> Pleasant View
> Concord, N.H.
> Dec. 24, '98
>
> Mr. Edward E. Norwood, C.S.B.
> My beloved Student,
>
> Why do you anticipate being removed from your field and the Readership in church?
>
> Do you desire to change your location? I know of no reason why you should change your place. When any strong impression comes to you in such lines[,] "try the spirits" before you submit. Mentally treat yourself that nothing can govern your actions or come to your thought that is not from the [d]ivine Mind. Be strong there.
>
> So many sinister suggestions come to mind, watch! And each day commit yourself to the care of our one Parent, trust Him, turn to Him in all your ways for light to direct your footsteps and wisdom to enable you to separate the tares from the wheat—so that you can judge well between the human or the evil "suggestion" and the good or [d]ivine impulse.
>
> With love to Mrs. King,[61]
>
> Yours tenderly truly,
> M.B. Eddy

It will be observed that while she did not *advise*, yet the way was clear, and I remained there for over a year, and then the way was so clearly opened, there was no doubt as to the wisdom of my going.

A need for unity in the Washington, D.C., Field

As I understood the question, there was a great need [in Washington, D.C.] for unity of the two churches, and we steadily worked for it. This was opposed by a minority in Second Church, who were quite strong in their opposition. They argued that as Mrs. Eddy had sent me to be First Reader and the term was for *three* years, it would not be wise or obedient to disrupt the church until the time expired. This was finally agreed to, but the work of harmonizing the two branches went on, and just before my term was ended, I wrote Mrs. Eddy, rehearsing the facts and asking if she had any counsel in the matter. The following letter was her reply:

Pleasant View
Concord, N.H.
July 15, 1905

Mr. Edward Everett Norwood, C.S.B.
Beloved Student:

Your request for my permission to unite the two churches in Washington, D.C.[,] I hereby give you; but this does not settle the question because I have no right to do so. I hope that you all will see clearly your duty in the case and do it in the interest of Christian Science.

Lovingly yours,
Mary Baker Eddy

A meeting of Second Church was held, and the minority seemed so violently opposed, they offered no hope of unity, even though First Church, which had over three times as many members, offered to disorganize, elect new Readers, [and] adopt new bylaws, if Second Church would lovingly come in. So the majority (lacking just two votes of the necessary two thirds to disorganize) lovingly took letters of withdrawal and joined First Church as individuals. I had the satisfaction later (by word of mouth of Mr. Joseph Armstrong) that Mrs. Eddy highly approved this action, and later she lovingly counseled Second Church to unite, which of course was done. Thereafter the church prospered, and in the course of time, as a legitimate and needful unfoldment, at this date (1918) there are three strong congregations here in Washington.

Defending our Leader

In the summer of 1904, a publishing house of New York issued a sumptuous and elaborate volume (the edition deluxe costing $1,000 each) called *The Book of Presidents*. It was devoted to the biographies, etc., of our presidents and also of other prominent Americans, and [it] contained accounts of four women, one being Mrs. Eddy. I was commissioned by our Leader to arrange for the Christian Science manuscript to be in it and, in course of the work, had to interview Hon. Charles H. Grovenor, Representative in Congress from Ohio, who was in charge of the publishing of the book. Through a misunderstanding, he seemed quite resentful of Mrs. Eddy, and we had an argument, which seemed for a time about to culminate in a fistfight. It became necessary for me to defend our Leader most vigorously and to remind

Mr. Grovenor that he was talking to a Southern gentleman who was used to being treated as such and expected to be on this occasion. He very quickly cooled and apologized. It became necessary to write the incident to Mrs. Eddy's secretary, whereupon she wrote me the following letter, enclosing a twenty-dollar gold-piece:

> Pleasant View
> Concord, N.H.
> September 18, 1904

> Mr. Edward E. Norwood, C.S.B.
> Beloved Student –

> Please accept this symbol of my thanks to you for obedience to [the] Golden Rule and great kindness to me.

> Sincerely yours,
> Mary Baker Eddy

Assisting with the publishing work

Some time in October 1906, Mr. Joseph Armstrong, Publisher, rang me up from the Arlington Hotel to come over to see him. He then informed me that Mrs. Eddy had selected me ("as a good Christian Scientist," she said) to have charge of the making of the plates of a revision of *Science and Health*. Of course I gladly assented to the work and selected Mr. William S. Campbell (First Reader of First Church, [Washington, D.C.]), a former newspaper man of the West and then an expert proofreader in [the] Government Printing Office, to assist in the work.

Mr. Armstrong and I called on Mr. Charles E. Stillings,

then the Public Printer, who referred us to Judd and Detwiler, the largest printing house in Washington. They took the contract at $1.08 a page, to which Mr. Armstrong agreed, placed the work in my hands, and went home. The six hundred pages of *Science and Health* mounted on larger sheets with margins, with changes in Mr. Lewis C. Strang's handwriting, were turned over to the printer as they needed it. This firm (of Judd and Detwiler) agreed to do the work in *two* weeks. Mr. Campbell and I would wait and wait, wondering at the delay in copy, and finally, after much mental work, discovered that Judd and Detwiler had "farmed out" the work to The Globe Printing Co., though pretending to do the work themselves! (I may say, in passing, that I dismissed all patients, locked my office door, and Mr. Campbell and I were there alone. We were on duty from 9:00 a.m. to 10:00 p.m. or later during six weeks. The work, of course, was profoundly confidential, and the printers were enjoined to secrecy also.)

As soon as we found out the work had been sublet, Mr. Campbell and I went over to The Globe Printing Co. and remained every day and evening until the work was finished. It was most trying, for the type was set by machine instead of by hand, and every mistake corrected necessitated resetting a line, and generally several other mistakes would appear. We had to correct some paragraphs as many as thirty times.

Changes to the "Fruitage" chapter

Three weeks went by, and one day a letter came from Mrs. Eddy by special messenger, Miss Mary Tomlinson, as follows:

Pleasant View
Concord, N.H.
Nov. 3, 1906

Mr. E. E. Norwood,
Beloved Student:

I hope that Mr. Armstrong has not interrupted the harmony of my business arrangement with you regarding the plates for the revised edition of *Science and Health*. Please read carefully all the [t]estimonials in the copy and select those which you consider the best and place the most attractive testimonials at the commencement of the chapter on "Fruitage."

The number of pages in this chapter can be accommodated to the [t]estimonials even if this should make my book exceed a little the 700 pages of the present edition.

N.B. The great point to attain was the *time* it should take to make the plates. Two weeks was agreed upon and now is it three weeks, and the need of my plates is *imperative now*. Please shorten this delay if possible.

Lovingly yours,
Mary Baker Eddy

The letter continued on the next page:

Pleasant View
Concord, N.H.

Another word to you

Mr. Norwood, C.S.D.
Beloved:

If there [are] not enough new [t]estimo-
nials of the new ones to make out the 700
pages of *Science and Health*[,] you can retain
some of the old testimonials that are now
in this book. Be sure to have 700 pages in
this edition[,] and if it over runs this a little
in the make up, no matter. But the original
number must not be lessened.

Lovingly and gratefully,
Your leader, and a Free Mason's widow,
Mary Baker G. Eddy
Give my love to Mrs. Norwood.

It was very trying to have our dear Leader disappointed, and we did all we could to hasten the work; but it
did seem that malicious animal magnetism was on hand
and active every minute. In the meantime a large number
of pages of *Sentinel* testimonies [were] sent to me, and I
was directed to select the best of them, revise them, prune
them, mentioning not more than two diseases, and giving
each a title. In fact, a new "Fruitage" was put in. This, itself,
was quite a job, but of course I was glad to do it. (This same
chapter remains intact at this time, November 1918.)

It may be of interest to note that during this time, my watch, a very good one, began to gain in time, until it was three hours a day. Regulating did it no good, so I let it go, and as soon as the work was finished, it resumed its normal condition. Mr. Armstrong told me he had the same experience in the building of The Mother Church, and the jeweler told him, "It is *you*, not the watch."

Confidentiality necessary in the publishing work

When the time came to send, first, the proofs and, later, the plates, to Concord, our dear Leader sent me a sacredly confidential letter, giving minute directions as to the manner of doing it. This letter was a most remarkable proof of her wonderful understanding of God—and of the illusion of mortal mind and its so-called activities. In the letter she said, "Let no one see this but your own dear self," and when I read it, I had such a glimpse of ineffable good and the supreme spiritual height that our God-crowned Leader had attained—it was transcendental! *God bless her!*

How well Mr. Campbell and I kept the secret was shown when I say that while Mrs. Campbell and Mrs. Norwood both knew (in a general way) that we were doing something for headquarters, Mrs. Norwood first knew of it when Mr. Strang informed her at Pleasant View late in November, and she told Mrs. Campbell upon her return to Washington.

The beautiful letter our dear Leader wrote me at the completion of the work follows:

Pleasant View
Concord, N.H.
Dec. 1, 1906

Mr. Norwood, C.S.B.
My beloved Student:

Words are weak to express my gratitude
for your strict demonstration and success in
conveyance. Also, your fidelity in all entrusted
to you. I was not mistaken in my man if I
were in some men.

My prayer is for all that learn through
suffering, and for all who learn by enjoying,
to enter into the rest of rightness; for every
experience human is met, compensated[,] or
punished by *divine Love*. Dear one, learn with
me to have but one God, to know of no other
Mind, for this will bring peace and spare us
the sorrow and agony that so-called mortal
mind has in store.

One [M]ind and loving others as we
would be loved is the panacea for all our
wrongs, trouble[,] and strife.

I hope sometime to reward you for your
dear heart and your helping hand in my
behalf.

Give my love to Mrs. Norwood.

Lovingly gratefully yours,
Mary Baker Eddy

Payment for the publishing work

Mr. Armstrong told me to send in a bill to Mrs. Eddy for my work, and I said, "I have none. I want to do it for love, for she has done so much for me." He replied, "Well, if you wish to send her a receipted bill, do so, but send it, and name your own terms." So I sent her a bill, marked "paid," for $150.00 for six weeks' work (at [the] same rate the staff at Pleasant View were paid). In a few days I received a letter from Mr. Calvin Frye as follows:

> Pleasant View
> Concord, N.H.
> Dec. 13, '06

> Dear Brother Norwood:

> Our beloved Leader sent to you yesterday by American Express a small box containing $100 in gold, and she desires to thank you for your receipted bill for services in connection with work done on *Science and Health.*

> Yours Fraternally,
> C. A. Frye

I saw how foolish to try to get ahead of Mrs. Eddy!

Our Leader's gift to the world

Mary Baker Eddy was the most remarkable woman in the history of the world. Her eyes were blue but, when animated, seemed dark brown. Her features were strong, nose and chin distinctively firm and characteristic; her height was about five feet six inches, but her person possessed and expressed a dignity and manner of gestures most graceful. Her majesty [was] indescribable. Her voice was most musical, and manner gentle and compassionate, yet withal positive and firm. As one on her staff many years told me, "You would not tell Mrs. Eddy more than once that a thing could not be done."

When Mary Baker Eddy was raised from her dying bed, she got a glimpse of the great fact that *God is All, the infinite and eternal Mind, and there is none beside Him*. Then she set out to learn and demonstrate the Principle and rule of it. Jesus showed that dying didn't kill us, and Mrs. Eddy showed that "being born" doesn't cause us to live. The "scientific statement of being" is the most wonderful paragraph in any language and will revolutionize human consciousness. The truth in that remarkable statement *is* man, for man is the true understanding of God. In other words, man isn't something that *knows* God. *Knowing* God is *being* man. We find God only as we find our real selfhood. And Mary Baker Eddy showed us how to do it. She came that we might have Life and Truth and Love, and joy and purity and humility, and honesty and substance and peace, and have them more abundantly.

The Christ, the spiritual idea, comes to the moral, that which believes in matter and is held by it, and cuts it off from the physical. The moral, thus freed, unfolds to the spiritual and is saved. And we don't die out, dream out, nor are [we] toted out on someone else's shoulders, but we must *live* out, *think* out, *love* out—and there's no discharge in that war!

Thank God for Mary Baker Eddy! She has set before me an open door, and no man can shut it [see Revelation 3:8], and going on therein, I find and walk in the path of Life, in whose presence is fullness of joy, at whose right hand there are pleasures forevermore [see Psalms 16:11].

Remarks our Leader shared with others

Christian Science being exact and demonstrable, its followers need to be careful, of course, not to give anything out as coming from its Leader that is not properly authenticated. The sayings and incidents which I quote and relate in the following pages were either told me by her or by others whom I know to be honest and clear. In that sense, therefore, it may be safe to assume they are authentic. So, read in this light, they may be a help to future generations. We know our dear Leader's words were always wise and meant much, even in the little things:

+ (Mr. Kimball told me this.) Once a new edition of the *Church Manual*, with new By-Laws was printed, but not published, as Mrs. Eddy directed it to be held until further notice. At last one Saturday it was put on sale, and that day he was at Pleasant View. He said he never saw such a thunderstorm and lightning in his life, and afterward it developed to be but local. He told me that Mrs. Eddy pointed out the window to the storm and said, "This is mortal mind's answer to my *Manual*."

+ She said, "Often I sent out an angel (a new By-Law), and it would come back bruised and bleeding, and I'd have to take it in and cherish it until the Field was ready for it."

+ Mrs. Eddy told a student that if he desired his neighbor's children to succeed and prosper at school and elsewhere, his own would also.

+ She said that when confronted by two or more courses to pursue, and a sense of doubt as to the wise course, *as a general rule*, the thing *least pleasant* is the one to do.

+ The first time she met one who afterward became her student, she said, "Thou art my son; this day have I begotten thee."

+ And another student, drinking a glass of lemonade, said, "This seems very good." Mrs. Eddy said, "It is good; enjoy it."

+ Talking to several students, she said, "You will heal instantaneously when you believe what you say." (How well this corresponds to what Jesus said, explaining [the disciples'] failure to heal: "Because of your unbelief" [Matthew 17:20].)

+ To another student, she wrote, "Just where mortal mind says, 'I can't,' you must know, 'I can'—for 'I can' is the Son of 'I am.'"

+ In a letter to a student, she defined *love* (verb) "as giving all, asking nothing in return, unselfish, impartial; the opposite of human love."

+ She said that human reasoning is as material as pain.

+ She was once asked if she was demonstrating over death. She replied, "I am trying to understand what Life is."

+ She once said, "We must know that the world is ready for Christian Science."

+ She once [described] Soul as "God's eternal recognition of Himself as All-in-all."

+ She said, "Some people are like wheelbarrows—they need to be pushed along."

+ She was lecturing in the early days and had a question box, reading and answering the questions as she took them out of the box. One was, "How is it that Mrs. Eddy, a professed follower of the lowly Nazarene, wears diamonds and velvet?" Mrs. Eddy smiled and replied, "I will say to the friend who asks this that this diamond cross at my throat was given me by a gentleman whose wife was raised from a dying bed; and this dress, which he calls velvet, is velveteen, cost $1.75 a yard, and has been made over three times!"

+ A child was brought to her with a cataract on each eye, blind. Mrs. Eddy began to talk to her of God, Truth and Love, when the child, animated by error, stamped her foot and said, "I hate you. I hate you. I could sit up all night to hate you!" Mrs. Eddy replied, "My darling, I love you. I love you, why I could sit up all night to love you!" and at once the cataracts fell out and the child saw.

✦ She said, "My students, as a rule, meet error
when it comes but do not always do their work
and prevent it [from] coming."

✦ She told a student but six months before
going away, "I feel I am just really beginning to
understand *Science and Health*."

✦ "Do not bring your troubles to me. I am not the
one to settle them. I will do what belongs to me
patiently and faithfully, but this is not my work.
Only yourselves can do this work and establish
love and peace in your own hearts and dwell
together in harmony as Christian Scientists. I
have shown you the way, walk ye in it."

✦ "But love is safe in divine Principle and never
safe out of it. God gives you the sweet peace
and wisdom of impersonal love, and there is no
other."

✦ "The weather expresses our concept of it and can
be handled as any claim if you do not hold it as
something apart from you, governed by some
other power or almanac. God governs all. This is
the way Jesus stilled the tempest."

ANNA B. WHITE BAKER *(1849–1931)*

*Little is known about what led Anna B. White Baker and
her husband, Dr. Alfred E. Baker, to take Primary class
instruction with Flavia Knapp in 1896. Anna had been
raised a Quaker, and Alfred was a homeopathic physician at
the time of their marriage, but both left behind these modes
of thought, devoting themselves to the study and practice
of Christian Science. Both were members of Mary Baker
Eddy's last class in 1898, and soon after, both answered
her call to serve. In 1899 Eddy asked Alfred to go into the
healing practice in Concord, New Hampshire, so the couple
moved there. By 1900, both of the Bakers were listed in* The
Christian Science Journal *as practitioners in Concord.
Anna also served in Eddy's household off and on until 1902.*

*Anna Baker's reminiscence begins with this author's note:
"The material in this book is authentic. It has been compiled
from a journal kept during long residence in Mrs. Eddy's
home, from notes verified by her, or from references taken
verbatim."*

Happy Memories of Mary Baker Eddy

ANNA B. WHITE BAKER

My first introduction to Mary Baker Eddy was in that inspiring "Class of Seventy" in the year 1898. It was held in Christian Science Hall in her home city, Concord, New Hampshire. I remember well my impression of her. She was seated on the platform silently waiting for the class to assemble.[62] I thought she was very beautiful. Her eyes were large and luminous, her hair was silvery gray, and she was plainly but becomingly dressed in light silk with a white shawl over her shoulders. She had a queenly presence, and her extreme dignity made her seem unapproachable. Her first question—"What would you do in order to heal the most difficult case?"—put to each member of the class made me feel as if I were positively without thought or speech. But as the answers came, her face grew interested, kind, and motherly. I felt love lifting me into a comforting nearness to her, and I was ready to answer when my turn came.

It was the privilege of my husband and myself not only

Christian Science Hall in Concord, New Hampshire

to be members of this class but to enjoy a very intimate acquaintance with Mrs. Eddy afterwards. Our work in healing had received a great stimulus from her instruction, and we desired to serve more earnestly the Cause to which our Leader was giving her entire time and labor. It was nevertheless a great surprise to receive from her, three

COURTESY OF THE MARY BAKER EDDY COLLECTION

The interior of Christian Science Hall in Concord, New Hampshire

months later, a personal letter saying, "I send you a call, loving, full of hope to come and help us in Macedonia."

Our move to Concord, New Hampshire

This was an opportunity the importance of which I was not then fully aware. To have known Mrs. Eddy at that time in her life when she was very alert and busy in her great work, when she seemed at the acme of her spiritual unfoldment, was a privilege that becomes ever more precious. We answered the call at once, and February 1899 found us established in Christian Science Hall in Concord, New Hampshire.

It was located near the business section of the city

at the corner of State and School Streets, but a short distance from the state house and other public buildings. A wide lawn at one side made an attractive setting. It had been remodeled from an old colonial dwelling and was a gift from Mrs. Eddy to the Christian Scientists of Concord. The entire second story front was made into one room suitable for holding services and had a seating capacity of three hundred. The first story was used for a Reading Room, a practitioner's office, a private room for Mrs. Eddy, and a suite of rooms for a small family. An old-time feature of the place was a commodious stable which adjoined the house. The Hall was torn down afterwards in order to erect the present Christian Science [branch] church.

It was rare that a day passed without some spoken or written communication from Mrs. Eddy or a greeting as her carriage passed the Hall. The fact that a student had come there who had been a medical practitioner[63] and had accepted Christian Science, believing it to be the true method of healing disease, established a decided interest in the work. Consequently, when cases given up by other physicians were healed by Christian Science, the services at the Hall began to be better attended. In place of but forty original members, there were soon one hundred, and in the following three years, the membership grew to be two hundred and fifty. From this time Mrs. Eddy's representatives in Concord were treated with appreciation and true courtesy, and she herself was not only regarded with great esteem but acknowledged as a prominent citizen to whom Concord was glad to give every consideration and possible assistance.

An aptly named home

Pleasant View was a very appropriate name for the residence of Mrs. Eddy. It was situated a mile from the state house, outside the city proper, and was set well back from the street. From the windows were interesting glimpses of lawns and flower gardens, a miniature lake, orchard, rolling meadows, and the distant hills.

She received us on our first visit in the library and, after a pleasant conversation, took us to see some gifts which were in the parlor. One of these was a beautiful gray rug made entirely of feathers. She talked of other objects of interest and then led us to a stand in the center of the room, upon which was a large scroll of gold. The names of the donors were engraved upon it, and while it was unique, it seemed an inappropriate and senseless gift to present to one whose thought and work were with the things of the Spirit. My silence evidently betrayed my thought, for she closed the case saying, "You do not like it. It is too much of earth and nothing of heaven."

We returned to the library which was plain and quiet in tone. It was furnished in excellent taste and, as we afterwards learned, was the room in which Mrs. Eddy enjoyed entertaining her guests. She talked to us for an hour. We were deeply impressed with her spiritual thought and mental alertness, and realized that she needed able and willing workers to aid her.

She always sat with her back to the view and, when asked why she did so, said, "I could not do my work if I saw those hills; they recall so much to me."

This room was furnished in oak and contained only

what was needed for her convenience. It opened into her small bedroom, which had in it the things she lived with for many years, plain and comfortable, without ostentation of any kind. A small stand by the bedside had on it her Bible and *Science and Health with Key to the Scriptures*.

An old-fashioned flower garden full of bloom in season was a delightful feature of the place. Mrs. Eddy never wanted flowers in her study. I wondered at this, when the other parts of the house were so attractive with them, and one day asked her why it was. "Because they fade," she said, "and I want to think only of life."

Unflagging commitment to Truth

Mrs. Eddy's mission was revealed because of her own miraculous healing. Through devout meditation upon the work that Jesus did in those far-off centuries, she became convinced that the commands given then to the disciples were to be heeded here and now: "Verily, verily, I say unto you, He that believeth on me, the works that I do shall he do also; and greater works than these shall he do; because I go unto my Father" (John 14:12).

A great deal of criticism resulted from [her] early attempts to heal in Christian Science. But nothing deterred the Leader of this new movement, our beloved Mary Baker Eddy. She traveled thorny paths with unflinching courage and bore bravely the prejudice of both family and friends. Many patients given up to die were healed by her, thus justifying her faith. In the silent hours alone, she heard the voice of God bidding her press on. Her faithfulness, devotion, and courage have been rewarded, and a multitude of followers bear witness to the truth which she revealed.

It was inevitable that Mrs. Eddy's teaching should have aroused prejudice, but a personal interview with her usually changed this feeling into one of respect or admiration.

A member of a Jewish [temple] once came to Concord to seek an audience for the purpose of convincing her of an error in her doctrine, believing that having accomplished this, there would be no essential difference between her faith and that of the Jews. An interview was granted, and when he called upon us afterward, he appeared sad, dejected, and disappointed.

"Did you not see Mrs. Eddy and talk to her?" I asked.

"I saw her, but I could not talk to her," he replied, "I only listened. I never met such a woman. She is very wonderful."

He had lost his desire to convince her that *she* was making even one error. He realized, as do all who have had similar experiences, that her convictions were born of deep religious research and spiritual intuition.

She quickly turned to the Bible for the verification of her thought. Her familiarity with both the Old and the New Testaments enabled her to speak with authority and without hesitation. A lesson was seldom given without verifying her instruction from Scripture. It seemed impossible even to approach the height that she had attained, but the clarity of her teaching gave us great courage to press on and not weary.

Although she was sometimes tired of unjust censure, she nevertheless kept her vigil with God and grew patient and forgiving, realizing that not one would be left out of His kingdom.

The Cause of Christian Science has been established entirely upon healing. No effort of any opposition can destroy the fact that this healing has been done, that the truth which was preached in Galilee was for all time. Mrs. Eddy's faith has been proven by her works. The religion which she named Christian Science is today known throughout the world, and even little children bear witness to its truth.

She was very wise in all such circumstances. When asked to define any phase of her religion, she was glad to do so and to make plain that the healing of both sin and disease through spiritual understanding is its basis.

Our dear Leader bore the burden of much that was often wearisome, and even a little thing that was proof of good judgment in a student cheered her. We recall moments when a very sad face appealed to us for a word that bespoke courage, the assurance that her students were striving in all ways to help her and that her work was truly blessing the world.

Good humor, high expectations, and healing

One day she sent especially for me to come to the carriage, and as I spoke to her, I saw that she wore a costume of gray silk made very simply, with a bonnet to match her dress.

"How exquisite you look," I said.

She laughed and replied, "This is my Quaker costume and I am wearing it for you."

Afterwards when I was with her at Pleasant View, she told me how she had heard my criticism of very gay attire she once wore in public. It had made such an impression that she enjoyed a little fun at my expense.

Her quick discernment of a problem required response

from those who were helping her. If she received it and accomplished her purpose she was happy, and all was well. If it was otherwise, hope and courage failed her, sometimes. Her lamp was kept trimmed and burning, and she demanded that a student should keep awake without surveillance from her. She was severe with any unnecessary lack in those of whom she expected much, and it was proof of her love that she was so. No excuse or apology could be offered. If unable to meet the emergency, there was at once a rebuke.

But with a student in whom she saw possibilities, she was withal patient and waited for the awakening of the spirit, her heart full of rejoicing when it came. The stern attitude would change immediately, and she was again bright and happy. Looking back into those years, one could readily discern her longing to make every day count as gain. Her demands had to be met, and she had neither time nor desire to tarry with inefficiency. Therefore it was often the case that a student was not retained at Pleasant View. It was a peculiar and difficult position, but those who were able to serve have had a rich reward.

Her thought went out to the afflicted, not in pity but rather with the love that healed. One day while watching the approach of a storm, she saw a man on crutches enter her gate. She sent word to give him shelter—and food if he was hungry. He was fed and directed to the carriage house to wait until the storm was over. Months afterward, when some of the family were driving to the city, the carriage was stopped by a workman who was breaking stone on the road. He asked if they could recall having seen him before. They could not, and he told them that he was the man whom they had once sheltered from a storm. While waiting, he had fallen asleep and did not wake until the storm was over. Then he said, "I rose and walked without my crutches and have never needed them since."

He did not understand it. Mrs. Eddy recalled the incident and acknowledged that she had "prayed" for him.

Communing with God and demonstrating His truth

When Mrs. Eddy had something to tell us which she said, "God has just told me," she rose into an attitude of thought that was truly sublime. We listened with an intense desire to understand and remember every word. At such times she seemed to be lifted above all that was human into the atmosphere of a divine consciousness. In this realization of the truth of being, she wrote *Science and Health*, and those who have read and comprehended the spirit of the book must acknowledge that a holy influence inspired her thought. Only as we comprehend how spiritual she was, can we interpret the truth of all that she has written and given to the world.

"I love to talk with God," she once said, "and He is taking me on so fast that I am almost afraid to look behind for fear the students are so far away that I cannot see them."

This religious temperament born in her made her such a student of Scripture that it became her life. Only for a moment would she turn aside and tarry with worldly things.

Devout in her nature and believing that the sorrows and ills of humanity could be healed by the realization that man has a spiritual birthright, Mrs. Eddy gave herself up to a consecrated obedience to the Master's command to his disciples to go into all the world to preach the kingdom of God and to heal the sick.

It was clearly evident to her that the message was for this age. She became the loving disciple, and we have records of her marvelous healing from the beginning of her work. Some saw her heal instantaneously, when the invalid was unconscious and seemed [to be] passing away. We have heard her tell of very remarkable healings for which she said, "I made no charge, although I was in need of many comforts."

It mattered not that a storm of criticism began to thrust itself upon her. She was convinced that the truth of that early century was "God with us" today, and [she] labored on through trials, intrigue, and condemnation, never hesitating and not heeding the desertion of family and friends. God was truly with her, and she has proven this in the results that bear witness to her faithfulness and obedience to the law of Spirit.

If anyone believed that she had supernatural power, she immediately sought to dispel such an impression. Her interpretation of Scripture was clearly explained to the students, and they were taught that individual growth in the understanding of life as it really is, is the only way to gain the ability to heal spiritually.

Not only hundreds but thousands everywhere throughout the world acknowledge themselves today better Christians because they have learned to live saner, more consistent lives through following the practical application of Christianity as taught by Mrs. Eddy. They do not appear as a superstitious people. They wear no badges to proclaim

An illustration of the summer house at Pleasant View

their faith but go about their work rejoicing in greater peace and freedom. Materiality is no longer the dominant influence, and Life, Truth, and Love are more and more clearly understood.

Mrs. Eddy is held in reverent love by all who have known her and accepted her instruction. They realize that she has pointed the way to Life eternal. Quiet and unpretentious as was her life, she has made for herself an enduring monument in the gratitude of her followers. The work which she established will continue through all the ages if her students are faithful to the trust she has bequeathed them.

Mrs. Eddy's daily routine

The days at Pleasant View were very busy ones. There was no time for idle thinking or listless waiting. The entire household was awake and alert in the early morning. Mrs. Eddy was herself the first to greet the day, for at five o'clock, even on dark winter mornings, she was accustomed to read from both the Bible and *Science and Health* and to make a note of thoughts which came to her then.

At six-thirty she breakfasted alone upon a dish of porridge and an orange, and at eight o'clock was in her study ready for work. Frequently a student was called for a pleasant greeting, and some work assigned; then the mail was sorted, and soon she was busy and absorbed, and no one intruded unless called.

At ten o'clock or a little later, she put everything aside and went to the veranda in the rear of the house, where she remained until the approach of the dinner hour at noon. In the cold of winter she was wrapped in a warm cloak and furs with a quilted hood which almost hid her face, and usually for two hours [she] enjoyed the fresh air, either walking or sitting in her chair-swing. The hours spent there were never idle. A pencil and tablet were always at hand, and barring all intrusion, she was able to solve important problems and, as she frequently said, "Get into closer communion with God."

It was considered an offense to interrupt her during these times, and I recall with what regret it was necessary for us to take to her one morning an important message that required an immediate answer. Her rebuke was expected, but when she heard [the message], we were rewarded with her gratitude. "God sent you," she said, "and you have saved the Cause."

At these morning hours she seemed to be lifted above all troubled thought of shadows that sometimes clouded her days and to receive renewed assurance that she was divinely blessed in the spiritual healing accomplished through her teaching.

She was ready punctually at twelve o'clock for dinner, and she expected it to be served on time. Twice when the meal was late, she refused to be present at the table. It was her silent rebuke, and never to my knowledge did this happen again.

At one o'clock the carriage was at the door for her accustomed drive. She liked to remain out for two hours unless the weather was extremely disagreeable. On pleasant days she enjoyed the country, which was very picturesque about Concord. At other times she preferred the ride through the city, where she saw the children. Many of them knew her, and their smiling faces made her heart glad. She rode in a closed carriage, but the windows afforded ample view of the world outside. When her mind was not absorbed with some important work, she enjoyed her rides so much that she returned greatly refreshed.

Unless Mrs. Eddy had an appointment to meet someone

after her drive, she went at once to the study and occupied herself with such work as was always waiting for her. The afternoon mail usually brought matters of business demanding attention. Not until after supper at six o'clock did she put aside the duties of the day. Then she gave herself up to enjoying an hour of reading. The Christian Science periodicals were read first—and sometimes criticized.

Mrs. Eddy deplored lack of culture at every point. I once told her that I had been severely censured for sending my daughter to college because she would have so much to overcome.

"Is that your thought?" I asked.

"No," she said with emphasis, "I wish every student I have had a college education. I want them to be able to talk intelligently with educated thinking people everywhere."

She was a subscriber to the *Literary Digest* and read it regularly, thus keeping herself generally informed of important world conditions. She once asked a student if she always read the Christian Science periodicals. When this student replied that she received more benefit from reading the textbook [*Science and Health*], Mrs. Eddy said, "I want you to read them and do so with a critical thought. I do not mean to openly criticize them, but the educated thought that silently corrects is helping to improve them, and it is your duty to do this."

At eight o'clock in those days, Mrs. Eddy retired for the night, not always to sleep but to endeavor to do so. If the day had been a troubled one, she was too apt to pass a restless night. But she knew that no night existed in divine Mind, and she found her rest and strength in the firm conviction that God supplied every need.

We seldom found her other than bright and cheerful in the morning, ready for the day's demands, eager to add another chapter that would win for her a "Well done, thou good and faithful servant" [Matthew 25:21].

Safeguarding *Science and Health*

In a little time of leisure one day, Mrs. Eddy told me this interesting bit of history concerning her book *Science and Health*. She had two Quaker friends, Charles and Abigail Winslow, who had been very kind and helpful to her and who lived in Lynn. When she finished writing *Science and Health*, she took it first to them for criticism and advice. They read it, and Charles advised against having it published, believing it would injure the high social standing she had won in the love and esteem of the people.

"'Well, there it is,' I said to them. 'It is written. I was impelled to write just what I have said, and it is either of God or the devil. Now which is it?'

"Charles said, 'Well, I believe, Mary, it is of the devil.'

"But Abigail replied, 'Don't be too hasty in thy decision, Charles. How can thee prove that it is not of God? Thee had better wait and see.'"

This same friend, Charles Winslow, a wealthy wool merchant, saved her book from being stolen by a printer in Boston to whom Mrs. Eddy had taken the manuscript. Becoming suspicious because of the delay, she asked for its return and was refused. She tried several times to get it but was always given excuses, which led her to think it was being kept fraudulently. Finally she went to Charles Winslow for advice. At once he said, "I am going to Boston today, Mary. Come with me, we will get thy book."

On reaching the place, he told her to go in and demand the book and that he would follow and wait apart from her. After hearing excuses and refusals upon the part of the printer to return the manuscript, Charles stepped forward, presented his card, and looking at his watch said, "I will give thee just thirty minutes to get that manuscript here to us."

Before the time was up, they had it in their possession.

Sacrifices for the Cause

When Mrs. Eddy first began to interest people in Science, she gave lectures, which were attended by persons of different religious faiths and by some of no faith. In her audience were doctors, lawyers, and ministers. Both men and women of culture went to hear her. They were deeply interested but were not in accord with establishing an organization for spiritual healing. She explained, "I had to make an appeal to the more humble people before I could get anyone willing to work with me. These were willing to accept my book and my instruction and to follow *me*. The others wished to improve upon my book, and so we parted."

Let us give all honor to those early devoted workers. Through their unselfish devotion to the work, and their obedience to their teacher, the Church of Christ, Scientist, has been established. Its foundation rests upon the healing of both sin and disease and is secure only as this continues. If this should fail, the whole structure will crumble and fall. It can continue only as love and unity of thought govern its people, and fear, criticism, and condemnation are destroyed.

When troubled one day over something, Mrs. Eddy said sadly to me, "If my students only loved each other, these things would not occur."

The great purpose to establish her Church and to promulgate the Christian Science movement was paramount in Mrs. Eddy's thought. She never impressed us with a desire to have money for money's sake or cared about wealth in any sordid way. We seldom talked of it, but she said to me one day, "My family refused to aid me in what they thought was fanatical, and often I went hungry in order to save money for my work. In those days I wore a dress with forty patches on it." [Then she] quietly added, "But no one saw them. I took very tiny stitches and was happy. I knew God would deliver me if I was obedient to Him. My sister promised me a house with servants and horses of my own if I would give up 'such peculiar work.' I chose to obey God, and He has given me these things, and greater than these."

There was no love of display in her home, in her thought, or in anything she did, but one felt that order and thrift prevailed both in household affairs and in the management of the estate. Her wishes were always considered and complied with.

Although costly garments were occasionally sent her by students who wanted to assist in providing her wardrobe, she accepted and wore only those which suited her taste. She was devoted to a black silk dress which was worn until it needed much repairing. Raising her arm one day, she laughingly showed me a hole at the elbow but refused to give it up because it was "so comfortable."

No expense, however, was spared to further the Cause of Christian Science. Here, money was needed, and she demanded that it be used whenever necessary to obtain a desired result. She told me how surprised she once was when a Director hesitated to comply with her request to make a necessary alteration in *Science and Health*, saying, "That will necessitate changing the plate and be very expensive."

"I am sure he will never forget the lesson I gave him," [she said]. "It astonished me that a question of cost should be a consideration where a spiritual value was concerned."

When her officials advised dropping the price of *Science and Health* to one dollar because works on Mental Science[64] were beginning to be sold at that price, she said, "No, put it up to three dollars; then it will be purchased because thought to be of greater value."

Compensation for Christian Science healers

When it was necessary that her students should devote themselves exclusively to healing, Mrs. Eddy realized that they needed to be compensated for their time, and a charge of five dollars was agreed upon for treatment lasting not more than a week. This was adhered to for many years. Later she reconsidered it and advised making the same charge as that made by a physician whose practice was in the locality where the patient lived. This change was not an easy problem to determine. One practitioner said, "Dr. _____ would charge five hundred dollars to amputate a limb. What must be the fee of the Christian Science practitioner who is called in and saves the limb?"

There was just such a case in point. The practitioners in that particular city therefore agreed to charge one dollar for each day's work and felt that it would meet with Mrs. Eddy's approval.

In talking at another time in regard to healing, she said, "Give your patient the best treatment you can; then leave the case to God. Never keep a patient in your thought."

Points of interest in correspondence

In reading over some letters from Mrs. Eddy, I find occasional statements which can be separated from those of a purely private nature, which I therefore feel at liberty to give:

> Truth does negat[e] error. Love does overcome hate.
>
> Know that God, good, teaches you how to pray, and if you ask aright and believe, you do receive.
>
> Never in mental practice hold a person in your thought. It always needs great wisdom to do this. The safe way is to treat for mortal mind and not for any personality when arguing mentally.

Referring to a student, she writes thus:

> He must cease to mesmerize himself; then he can conquer the malicious mesmerism. He must master the demands of the senses, or they will master him, and this is not done by finding pleasure but pain in sense materiality, except Science conquers all that is false without suffering.

A letter came from over the sea one day, asking me to do something to stop the false reports which were being circulated about my husband. I was at Pleasant View, and knowing that he was ignorant of the letter, I went to Mrs. Eddy with the problem. I speak of this because of her treatment of it. She rose from her chair and emphatically declared that it was false and a fraudulent effort to rob her of his help and take from him his good name as a loyal student.

"If he was not doing the good work he is, he would not be attacked," she said emphatically. "Do you not know that the greatest number of clubs are always found under the tree that bears the best fruit?"

Then she sat down and for a long time was silent.

Exposing spiritualism

We had an interesting account of some of Mrs. Eddy's experiences [with] spiritualism today. [S]he told us of going to a séance with [two friends who] knew her opposition to spiritualism. Mrs. Eddy [told them] it could all be explained and had nothing to do with another world or with those who had departed from this life.

"To prove my assertion," she said, "I mentally recalled an experience of long ago, and the medium narrated it to us just as it had occurred, precisely as the mental picture of it came back to me."

"Then she asked me if she was correct. 'Yes,' I said, 'Just as it happened.'"

"'Do you doubt, then?' my friends asked."

"'Yes. I do. Spiritualism is either mind reading or sleight of hand and can always be proven as such. Now I can do the same thing, as I will show you.' The medium had a scar on her face, and I told them I would tell them the history of that scar. The occasion of it was at once brought to the mind of the woman, and I read her thought correctly. 'It is mind reading,' I said, 'and has nothing to do with departed spirits.'"

Mrs. Eddy told us that from the time she was a little girl she could always read another's mind. "From this has grown the report that I am a medium," she said. "I know I am not. I have only a gift which has nothing supernatural about it. The editor of *The Banner of Light* was present at this interview and said to me, 'You have something that we shall yet hear of.'"

Mrs. Eddy has taught that God is Spirit, and man made in His likeness is spiritual, but not Spirit, God.

Moments of advice and instruction

Today our Leader gave us a valuable talk on metaphysics. I wish every student had been there to hear it. Part was in regard to the great care that we should take never to interfere in any way with the lives of others by mentally intruding upon their thoughts to direct or advise them, and that we are never excusable for mentally addressing another unless it be to rescue him from danger of which he is not aware. "This is legitimate," she said, "just as it would be to save a person in the street from an accident when he was unconscious of danger or disabled from rescuing himself."

It is a great grief to her that her teaching is sometimes misunderstood and misused, or her writings misinterpreted by any who are attempting to follow her. But very hopefully she said, "God will direct them, and we must not interfere with His way, His plan for His children; we must know this and trust Him to lead them where they should go."

She impressed upon us the great necessity of rising to the understanding that will enable us to see the hidden error and make a whole healing so that there will be no relapse. She told us that, in her own practice, she never had a case relapse until a student visited a patient she was treating and said to her, "You will have a return of the old claim," and the malpractice produced the fear that caused relapse.

She frequently has said, "I never used arguments in my healing. I knew God's work was done, but when my students could not get up to this point, then I helped them to work by using the argument that destroyed fear and disease and [that] maintained the allness of God as Life, Truth, Love."

When she sees the importance of arousing a student so that no instruction [is] lost, she is the strong Leader of a great Cause, and what she is saying to one is said as if all must hear and heed it. Her voice, which before was low and almost merry in some tale of bygone years, is now strong and very earnest as she emphasizes the great necessity to be awake, to see the need of the hour, and to know what God is demanding of us. "Do not dream of God, but see that you are serving Him," [she once said].

Today a student from the West called unexpectedly to see her. She was tired and did not feel like talking. Looking up with a mischievous expression, she said, "Go tell him I cannot see anyone—I am sick." But in a moment she laughingly said, "That was Mary," and rising, went at once to the library, where she remained for an hour, returning refreshed and happy. Always when the human sense talked, she would say, "That was Mary."

Yesterday she told me very emphatically what I should do in a certain matter and said,

"Now, *will* you do this?"

"I will try," I replied.

She quickly objected and said, "Never say 'try.' That admits doubt. Emphatically say, 'I will.' You cannot bring out a demonstration with the admission of a doubt that you will succeed."

Today Mrs. Eddy learned of the death of her sister-in-law, Mary Baker, the wife of her brother Samuel. I went into her study when I knew about it and found her alone, tears in her eyes, overcome for the moment with the human sense of loss. "She is the last of my family," she said, "and I am now alone. Sister Mary would never believe that death is not a reality. I could not make her think my way. Now she *knows* she has not *died*. She has realized Life."

A lesson on spirituality

Mrs. Eddy gave me a lesson on spirituality today. I remarked that I was not spiritual and did not feel that I could attain to any very spiritual height.

"You must not say that again," she said, "and never have such a thought. What is spirituality? Do you not love to be true and to live honestly?"

"Yes, I do," I replied.

"Do you not love God and desire to strive for the unfolding of that in yourself which is like Him? You are honest, conscientious, diligent in your work; all of these are qualities of a spiritual nature."

I said that I had never been a Bible student nor a devotee of any church, but had lived from childhood under the quiet, kind, and gentle influence of the Quaker discipline.

"Because you love good, you love God," she said, "and therefore you must never say you are not spiritual."

I saw clearly in our conversation that in proportion as we are governed by materiality, indulging it instead of overcoming and refusing to be influenced by its suggestions, are we lacking in that which is spiritual. She substantiated my thought by alluding to the way in which many people indulge the sense of appetite, and said, "That is not indicative of spirituality."

Advice for parents

In conversation today Mrs. Eddy told us not to thrust Christian Science on the children, saying that if it influenced home or school, they would unfold naturally in its atmosphere. Otherwise, if forced to listen, to read, and [to] live by the rules of any religion, children naturally rebelled and turned from it.

Mrs. Eddy told us of a mother's distress because she could not get her daughter to be interested in Christian Science. It was evident to her that the mother was trying to persuade her daughter to become interested, and she said, "You are taking the wrong tactics, and of course she will object and will hate Christian Science."

"She hates Mrs. Eddy," the mother replied.

"It is the way you talk to her about me and your continual quoting me," Mrs. Eddy said she told her, and then requested that she bring the daughter to Pleasant View. She told us that after greeting them, she turned to the daughter and said, "'What was the score in the football game yesterday?' Immediately the girl's face lighted up. Then, we chatted together of the things that interested her, and I said not a word about Christian Science. I admonished the mother not to talk Science to her but to learn to live with her in her young life; then she would unfold naturally and mother and daughter be united."

This incident shows that Mrs. Eddy did not approve of the mistaken zeal that would thrust Christian Science unsought upon anyone [and thought] that to do so [would] injure the Cause and subject it to unjust criticism.

Her attitude towards those not of her faith was one of deference and polite consideration. Mrs. Eddy was very natural herself and wanted her students to be, both in appearance and in conduct. She said, "My students asked me in the early days if I wished them to wear a particular costume. I answered emphatically, 'No. Do not look peculiar. Appear your best.' I was misunderstood in this and have since had to condemn extravagance in dress."

Important lessons and comments

A very inspiring hour was given me today. Mrs. Eddy answered some questions that I had been puzzling over in regard to consciousness. I write her own words: "Consciousness is the centralizing power with respect to all ideas, just as the problem is the centralizing power for the numbers. It is the capacity to know God—in and through His idea, man—and all spiritual ideas, their qualities, idealities, and activities; that is, the capacity to know infinite Mind and its infinite manifestation."

I have copied on a flyleaf of *Science and Health* the following from her conversations:

> Body is the relationship of functional activities to make manifest ideas.
>
> Numbers of a problem are never diseased, but they represent the problem, and a misconception of the problem may relate them falsely, or call forth wrong numbers. So the body is never diseased, it represents the functions; but a misconception of the functions can make a body show forth a false belief.

Volition is the capacity to conceive,
define, and put into operation the ideas of
[i]nfinite Mind.

The following are other gems of instruction received
from time to time:

No one is loyal to Truth, to himself, to
his God, or is worthy of heaven, who has not
faith, pluck, and patience enough to endure,
without fainting, apparent defeat and
delayed rewards.

Students do not pray enough. They
should go by themselves at least three times
a day to pray. Their prayers should consist of
much giving thanks, more realization of the
perfect as well as the denial of error. There is
too much denial of error and too little realization of the perfect.

We must talk more closely to God. Bring
Him nearer to us more like the old style of
praying. We must feel and know that God
is what we live in—like the atmosphere
and the sunlight. [God] is all about us. We
must rest more in God. When treating a
patient, do as well as you can, and let God
do the healing.... Give up more to God. Ask
for daily bread, enough for today. A child
with its mother does not ask all the time
for tomorrow and next week if it will have

food and clothing, but runs along happy and trusts its mother's care. So we must do. Have trust in the one Father-Mother God, and without fear. The true thought brings the error to the surface, and if we fear not, it will pass off. Put physical ailments in the mental. Know they are the result of fear, anger, envy, or some wrong thinking, and do not fear the physical. Just ask for more light, more goodness.

There is no such thing as impersonal healing. There is always a person in it. There may be indirect healing.

When Jesus made concession to sense and was baptized, he immediately went into the wilderness and suffered out of it, although God was just as willing he should be baptized as He was that he should go into the wilderness because he could not learn the lesson in any other way.

While we are in the flesh, we will hate evil and love good.

The will of God is spiritual understanding.

Love will not fight, but stands, and standing, wins.

Age is the open door to eternal youth.

Oh, how much we lose by taking up the cross—lose self and win Love, lose the pleasure of meeting often our friends, and win the love of friendship.

Grant, O my God, that neither the joy nor the sorrow of this period shall have visited my heart in vain. Make me wise and strong to the performance of immediate duties, and ripen me by what means Thou seest best for the performance of those that lie beyond.

A Watch Prayer

All is love, peace, harmony,
Heaven is right here,
Truth reigns,
There is no strife.
Peace, be still!
Truth has destroyed the error,
Love has destroyed all hate,
All is peace, love, joy.

Gifts of gratitude

It was natural that gratitude should be expressed to Mrs. Eddy by those who had suffered long and hopelessly and had been healed in Christian Science. Often this was shown through touching letters, sometimes by a gift.

I found her one morning sitting by her desk looking at a box which she had just opened. It contained five cakes of Pears soap and was sent from the Philippines.

"What does it mean?" she said, her face full of interest and curiosity.

Taking up one of them, she found under it a bright new ten dollar gold piece, and under each one the same, fifty dollars in all, concealed by the soap. With it [was] a card saying, "With love and gratitude from a soldier, paid with the first money received from the government for my services."

Her eyes filled with tears, but they were tears of joy that she had given spiritual blessings to this boy and that, so far away and alone, he wanted to acknowledge his appreciation and love.

Another time came a gift of some exquisite handmade lace, one piece of which had her initials, M.B.E., woven daintily in it. Folded in the lace was a letter from the donor, a woman ninety years of age who had been blind and was healed by Christian Science. She had done this beautiful and very delicate work after her healing and sent it as a token of gratitude.

Sometimes gifts were sent by prisoners to whom the Christian Science services had brought comfort and help. One morning she gave me a little woven mat, one of a set made for her by a prisoner. As she handed it to me, she said with much earnestness, "Will you *treasure* it, and *not give it away?*" The expression of her face comes before me each time I look at it, so appreciative was she of the thought which prompted this gift.

I was called to the study one evening to see a handsome white cloak which she was trying on. It was richly embroidered and lined with violet satin, a garment such as a queen might wear on some royal occasion. Though very beautiful, it surprised me that anyone who knew of the quiet, consecrated life she lived should think it suitable for Mary Baker Eddy.

While others in the room were emphasizing its loveliness, she was evidently impressed by my silence and said to me, "What do you think of it?"

"It is very beautiful," I replied.

Then again addressing me, she asked, "What shall I do with it?"

"I should return it by the first express in the morning," I replied.

She took it off quickly and said to her secretary, *"Do just that,* Calvin."

She was instantly free from the burden.

Not long after, she read me a letter from the husband of the student who had sent the cloak, thanking her for having returned it. He was not a Christian Scientist and had been prejudiced against Mrs. Eddy until this occurrence, which had entirely changed his thought.

Examples of healing

The gifts that gladdened her heart were the reports of healing sent her. Over these she greatly rejoiced. We like to recall the glad expression of her face when we told her of the healing of a man who was severely burned. He was a cook in a restaurant in Concord, and some boiling fat had spattered over one side of his face. A Christian Scientist, who happened to be there, brought him quickly to our office. Although in great suffering, he was relieved of all pain in a very short time. He knew nothing of Christian Science and was very grateful for the quick relief given without any medical application. The following day he returned and reported that he had not had a moment of suffering after he left the office. In his broken English, he expressed gratitude and also keen interest in what had healed him.

Another instance was that of a workman at Pleasant View who had torn his eyelid but was healed very quickly. When this was reported to Mrs. Eddy, it gave her much joy.

"These," she said, "are cases of true healing." Such testimonies, and they were many, upheld her declaration of the healing power of Truth in this day as in that long ago when Jesus healed the multitudes.

The importance of naturalness

Once a student who had an appointment to see her arrived before the dinner hour was over. Mrs. Eddy greeted her in the library and asked if she had been to dinner.

"Oh, no, I could not think of food," she replied, "when I am to have such a feast of the spirit."

"I was disgusted," Mrs. Eddy said, "and told her to go to the dining room and eat a good, hearty dinner, and then she would be ready to hear and understand what I had to say."

She disliked affectation or mannerisms. It was this perfect naturalness about Mrs. Eddy that drew me to her and made me have all the more confidence in her teaching because I could appreciate her sincerity in the simple details of everyday living.

Everything she taught was expressed in a clear and simple way. Her instruction was concise and adaptable. It was founded upon the truth in Scripture as she interpreted it. If a problem puzzled her, she was apt to open the Bible and find there the counsel she needed. It was not unusual to hear her say, "God told me this today." It was as if she lived a life with God apart from the world.

Interpreting a dream

One spring day in 1902, Mrs. Eddy invited my husband and me to come and visit her and, after talking of many things, told us of a dream she recently had. She was out on the sea in a storm and the vessel was wrecked. It was sinking. She looked in terror for her three companions, three students, and saw them on a raft. She exclaimed, "How can they be saved! They will not be able to hold on." No vessel was in sight. Then she said, "I thought not of myself, but only of them, these three beloved students, and while fear was manifesting itself greatly, suddenly I felt a solidity under me—a support. It was not the merciless water any longer. It had suddenly become solid. I was being saved and knew they would be. I was no longer afraid but realized that divine Love was protecting me and would save all who were with me."

She then explained what the Scripture means when it says, "There was no more sea" [Revelation 21:1]:

> We are on the waves of error in solution
> when we know not the truth of being. We are
> afraid, we know that we may not stem the
> tide. This is mortal sense. This sense over-
> come by spiritual knowledge destroys the
> fear of error and our inability to meet it; and
> the understanding of God and Life changes
> our condition of thought, fills us with truth,
> and realizing the presence of God, "There
> is no more sea"—no more error in solution,
> no more error, just conscious [M]ind, which

overcomes all that is not [M]ind, and establishes the foundation, which is the rock of Christ.

Comments on Scripture

During the summer of 1902, when I was again with her, she called me to see a gift from abroad. It was a copy of the Wycliffe New Testament sent to her by some students in London. It bore the date 1380 and was said to be the earliest translation. A marker had been placed at Luke 1:78 and 79, which read as follows (copied verbatim):

> And thou child shalt be called the
> prophet of the Highest, for thou shalt go
> before the face of the Lord to make ready
> his ways, for to bring Science and Health
> (to give knowledge and salvation) to His
> people, unto remission of their sins, by the
> entrails of (through the tender) mercy of
> our God, in the which the springing up
> from on high (whereby the dayspring) hath
> visited us (for) to give light to them that
> sit in darkness, in the shadow of death,
> for to dress (to guide) our feet into the way
> of peace. So help (therefore) the child was
> comforted in spirit and was in the desert till
> the day of his shining (appearing) to Israel.

When she had finished reading this to me, she said:

> See there; was anything more like a
> repetition of my life! For six weeks I fasted,

eating nothing but bread and sometimes a
pear because I had no money, and waited to
hear what God had to say; then I wrote my
book. When I showed it to my friends, they
said, "Do not publish it." I took it afterwards to the literati, and they said, "If you
publish it, you will be pronounced insane."
I called it *Science and Health* and knew that it
was to bring health and peace to the world
through the remission of sin.

Independence Day remarks

Sitting in her swing in the bay window on the Fourth of
July, 1902, Mrs. Eddy called me to her and said [several] interesting things which I wrote down immediately afterward:

> Thinking of our flag, this comes to
> me, that the motto emblazoned on the
> escutcheon of Christian Science is, "Ye shall
> know the truth, and the truth shall make
> you free" [John 8:32], free from the domina-
> tion of evil. We are governed by God, He is
> our only governor. We are not governed by
> evil. Now in this lies your freedom.
>
> The independence of the Christian
> Scientist can be won only by turning away
> from seeking independence in mortal
> mind, for matter is but the substratum of
> mortal mind.
>
> My forefathers landed on Plymouth
> Rock in search of religious liberty, and I

have steered the ship of Christian Science, standing at the helm and at the rudder and doing most of the work, and I have landed on the Rock of Truth.

We must fight for our freedom. It will not do to sit down and dream or sleep, and expect to win, but we must fight and strive. We must strive, for Jesus said, "I say unto you, 'Strive to enter in at the strait gate'" (see Luke 13:24).

We think that we struggle and struggle, and when we get tired, we stop, thinking that we have struggled enough; but we must go on and get where we can say, "Not my will, but thine, be done" (Luke 22:42). "For many … will seek to enter in, and shall not be able" (Luke 13:24).

Facing evil fearlessly

Our Leader called us in at eight-thirty this evening and gave us a lesson, the summary of which is as follows:

We should overcome evil with good; we should not be aggressive with the world in our mental work, else we would have to meet and master that aggressive thought turned on us. It would not know what our effort was but would resist it, and be worse.

When I pray, conditions are better because I meet them with more of the spirit, and the uplifting thought heals.

We will find that our prayers do good to
the extent that we have overcome material
sense, or the flesh.

When we work on reversal, we should
know that all that is needed is that we shall
rise higher in spiritual understanding,
because the more light, the less darkness.

Then after an earnest appeal that we should go and "tell
no man" (Matthew 8:4) lest we be hindered in our growth
by the effort of error to overthrow our work, she read from
the first chapter of St. John, verses 14 to 17 inclusive:

And the Word was made flesh, and dwelt
among us, (and we beheld his glory, the glory
as of the only begotten of the Father,) full of
grace and truth. John bare witness of him,
and cried, saying, This was he of whom I
spake, He that cometh after me is preferred
before me: for he was before me. And of his
fulness have all we received, and grace for
grace. For the law was given by Moses, but
grace and truth came by Jesus Christ.

Closing the book, she said, "Doesn't this declare that
what I have been telling you is the truth? Do not be frightened at evil. Know that what you declare is the truth, and
the devil, the opposite of truth, cannot drive you from your
position. *Stick right to it.*"

An important lesson on the body

Mrs. Eddy called me to her today and gave me quite a

long lesson on the difference between the right and wrong concept of the body. I wrote it down and afterward read it to her to be sure that I had it correct. She said:

> We should not say that life is *in* the body
> or manifested on the body. It is not Science.
> The body is always mortal mind, and [L]ife
> or Spirit cannot be in mortal mind. It is the
> oblique reflection of reflection, just as the
> image in the camera is the inverted reflec-
> tion. Man is the reflection of Mind, and
> body or mortal mind is the reflection of
> reflection, the reversal of the truth. Do not
> say "material sense of body"; body is mate-
> rial sense, and you cannot make two of it.
> When man has risen out of mortal mind
> into [M]ind, he will not have organs or know
> anything about functions or breath. As long
> as we hold on to this mixture, we shall have
> death. Man is wholly spiritual—this is the
> ultimate of Christian Science. Truth cannot
> be manifested in error. We must get rid of
> the error and think no more about it.

I said, "When I cross out a figure as error, I erase it from the problem, and it is no longer in my thought."

"That is exactly it," she replied. "So when you overcome the wrong sense of life, you are free, and life is manifest. You have overcome the flesh and proven that man is the reflection of [T]ruth."

I said, "We must not annihilate the body, must we?"

"I want to annihilate every particle of matter," she

answered, and referred me to page 191 in the revised edition of *Science and Health*, which I read to her.

She said further that her students all over the Field everywhere were determined to put individuality into matter.

Letters of advice

The revelation of Truth, which healed Mrs. Eddy when material remedies had failed, impelled her to follow the command which Jesus gave to his disciples to preach the gospel and heal the sick. With unfaltering faith that this command was for all time, she established the Cause of Christian Science, renouncing drugs and material remedies in healing disease. The work that she has accomplished stands as a proof that she interpreted and practiced the spiritual healing which restored to health the suffering multitudes of that early day.

So desirous was Mrs. Eddy of protecting herself from the slander and the jeering of ignorance, that her students were cautioned again and again to be wise in their statements concerning her. The following letter explains her attitude of thought, the great desire she had to be free to do her work without the scorn and prejudice through evil report which is ever ready to attack a righteous purpose. It should serve us all:

> Do not say to anyone, "You must love
> Mrs. Eddy to be well," or anything like
> this. It gives the enemy a plea to urge, "You
> make her as God." You can speak of the
> good I do and so incline the individual to
> the [t]ruth relative to me. Any other way
> hurts the Cause.

P.S. Darlings, have one God, turn no mind to me but His—know that I am but the reflection—do not stop at the window. Reflect Truth, Love—not turn to aught but the one Light that lighteth all. Remember that this is just what you teach[:] *One*[,] only *One*. Stick to your text and that helps me—helps all—for it is the Science of [b]eing.

With love,
M.B.E.[65]

[This is from another letter:]

Do not lose your sense of the true denomination and turn from Mind to matter for help any more in C[hristian] S[cience] than in mathematics[,] or you change Science for sense and so lose your Principle and cannot demonstrate it. *Stick to your text.*

M.B.G. Eddy

Instruction in healing

[These are] excerpts from a manuscript on treatment by Mrs. Eddy:

Keep your aim, stick to your text, and have faith in your understanding of the letter of Christian Science: for instance, [if] the claim is paralysis, your aim is, there

is no inaction, there is action. Your text
is, God is Almighty, and you know it, and
error is a lie and is powerless. Your faith
is, that God is All and you know in whom
you trust. This will win every time; this
is the way Jesus healed the man who was
healed of blindness after three trials; stick
to it, and know we want to, and can heal
in every case. We know the Truth, and we
must be more positive that we know it. We
are not hypnotists nor hypnotized.

It is easier in belief for the practitioner not to believe in disease than for
the sufferer. The only proof one has that
he does not believe in disease is that his
thought of the disease destroys it. "Be
not deceived, whatsoever a man soweth,
that shall he reap" [see Galatians 6:7].
If one sows a half belief, the case will
linger; if one sows a whole belief in the
understanding, the case will show it. The
error is to think one believes what one
does not, and understands what one does
not, and then to console one's self with
this self-deceived state of thought. We
have no possible proof that the state of
our thought is right unless the effect of
the state of thought produces the right
result on the patient. Human reason or
human imagination is as material as pain.
Reasoning or reverie is as erroneous when

treating the sick as a sensation of fever would be. The spiritual attitude and altitude gained is the measure of success in healing. Human love can be mistaken; if it is divine, it removes fear and heals quickly. If it is human and yet not at all impure, it does not heal. I name these deep points in metaphysics to show what [is] wheat and what are tares.

In 1904, previous to our moving from Brookline to Philadelphia, I was with Mrs. Eddy three days. She talked much of the need of better healing. In the last moments before I left her, as she held my hand in parting, she said so earnestly, "It is not more churches or more teaching that we need, but better healing. Unless my students do better healing, our Cause is lost."

"Why do you not stop the teaching?" I asked.

She replied, "The time has not come for that, but *our Cause rests on the healing.*"

MARY E. EATON *(1871–1938)*

*An only child, born in Chelsea, Massachusetts, Mary
Eaton was introduced to Christian Science by relatives.
She left her job in the Chelsea library after taking Primary
class instruction with Flavia Knapp and beginning to
work as a healer. One of Eaton's patients was her own
father, who had been seriously injured in a railway
accident that left his hands and legs useless. He also had
a "vicious disposition." After a year of Christian Science
treatment, his disposition improved and then his health.
Following another year of treatment, he was completely
healed and able to work again.[66]*

*Eaton was a member of Mrs. Eddy's 1898 Normal class
and became a First Member of The Mother Church
in 1901.[67] Eddy expressed her gratitude for Eaton
both privately and publicly. While working in Eddy's
household, Eaton received a pin—"a dove completely
set in pearls"—from Eddy, who told Eaton, "You have
brought me peace, my dear." And in the March 7, 1908,*

Christian Science Sentinel, *Eddy published "An Expression of Thanks" to her.*[68]

Soon after taking Normal class from Judge Septimus J. Hanna in 1907, Eaton began teaching Christian Science in Boston. In late 1918, she moved to Toronto, Canada, where she taught for several years before returning to Boston in the early 1920s. She worked there as a practitioner and teacher until 1930, when she moved to Seattle, Washington, where she taught for five years before settling in New Hampshire. This selection is compiled from three brief reminiscences Eaton wrote.

Invaluable Instruction

MARY E. EATON

The first time I saw Mrs. Mary Baker Eddy was May 26, 1895, when I heard her give an address in The Mother Church; in February 1896, I heard her give another wonderful address there. On June 5, 1899, I heard her last address ever given in Boston to five thousand members assembled [for] Annual Meeting in Tremont Temple.

In 1897 and 1903, with thousands of Christian Scientists, I visited Mrs. Mary Baker Eddy at Pleasant View, Concord, New Hampshire.

Mrs. Eddy's last class

In November 1898, Mrs. Mary Baker Eddy taught her last class; it was held at Christian Science

Illustration from a June 1899 Boston Herald *reporting on the Annual Meeting of members of The Mother Church held at Tremont Temple on June 5th*

Hall, in Concord, New Hampshire. She had not taught a class for nine years, and she called it the "Class of Seventy." There were sixty-seven present. It was my great joy to be a member of that class of two sessions, one being held on Sunday [afternoon] and one on Monday afternoon. There were judges, lawyers, physicians, ministers, and many students in this Normal class who had studied in a Primary class with Mrs. Eddy before. There were a few young people in the class who had studied with other teachers in a Primary class, and I was one of the youngest in the class. I had taken two Primary classes with Mrs. Flavia S. Knapp in 1895 and 1897.

Mrs. Eddy seemed very humble in teaching our class. I never saw such humility—she seemed to be listening for God's voice before speaking to us. The principal thoughts which I gained from her teaching were "Love is Life" and childlikeness.

Elderly men would weep when they answered her questions, and I think we all had a time of weeping, and then,

Telegram to Mary Eaton inviting her to the "Class of Seventy"

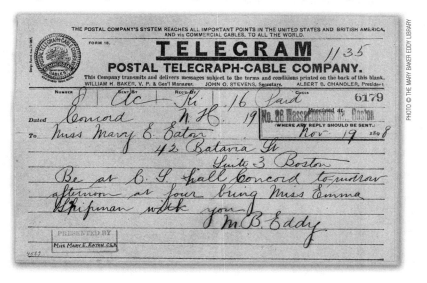

as Mrs. Eddy was very witty, she would tell us something funny to make us laugh.

Mrs. Eddy asked each one in the class, "What is God?" and "How do you heal instantaneously?"

Mrs. Eddy told us, "You shall run and not be weary— to run, to rise higher spiritually and not react, and not be weary but rest in divine Love and not relapse."

A focus on divine Love

Mrs. Eddy asked a clergyman, "What is the light that has to come to us in this age?" She told him his reply was intellectual [and asked], "Why did you not say 'Love?'"

Mrs. Eddy said, "When you love, you will heal instantaneously and raise the dead."

A student asked her the difference between human affection and divine Love, and she replied, "In human affection, you seek something to love, but in divine Love, you seek nothing, but everything"; and then she said in a commanding tone, *"Just love!"*

A student asked her how she would treat Christian Scientists who were not faithful to our Cause, and she replied, "Jesus said, 'I am not come to destroy, but to save'" [see Luke 9:56].

Mrs. Eddy said: "You can demonstrate wealth. If you stand before the mirror, your reflection is instantaneous, and just so, you reflect God in all your ways. All are yours, and ye are Christ's, and Christ is God's. As a man thinketh, so is he. Seek first God, and all these things shall be added" [see Matthew 6:33].

She asked a student, "Does man reflect the whole of God?" He replied, "Yes," and she approved of the answer.

Mrs. Eddy said: "Why make so much ado about nothing? Error is no more than a row of ciphers added from one wall to another, unless you place a unit with it and make something out of it. *Is there any unreality?*"

She took us up on the mount and revealed the Light as Love, and Love as Life.

Mrs. Eddy gave us her concept of God. She said, "It is like the father protecting and caring for his child; it is like the mother taking the little one in her arms and feeding it with the milk of the Word; it is like the tender shepherd caring for his flock, going out into the marshes after the lost lamb, calling, calling—listening for its little plaintive voice, taking it in His arms, carrying it home, and doing it over and over again."

Moments of instruction in Mrs. Eddy's home

In January, 1902, when in the home of Mrs. Eddy, she said to me: "You do not heal the sick; it is your faith that heals. In treating patients, do not repeat words over and over, as it has the effect of morphine, soothing syrup, or mesmerism. Christian Science treatment is prayer, but we do not plead with God to do what He has already done, but know His work is finished and man is His perfect idea. 'You shall know the truth, and the truth shall make you free'" [see John 8:32].

One day Mrs. Eddy asked me where I suffered physically when error attacked me, and she told me it was malpractice and healed me. Two years later, when she sent for me, she asked me if I had overcome that belief, and when I told her I had had no more pain, she said, "I knew it was nothing but mesmerism."

Mrs. Eddy asked me if I had much experience with malpractice, and I replied, "Yes." She said: "There is none. The way I meet it is by keeping the First Commandment. Know there is no evil mind to intercept God and you."

At the dinner table one day, I asked Mrs. Eddy why Christian Scientists were not more grateful to her, and she replied, "Because they have not grown to it. Two plants will be growing side by side—one will blossom, and the other won't."

She said, "Promptness is a virtue of my household, my household god."

I used the expression "passing out," and Mrs. Eddy said, "Passing on, dear; there is no life in matter to pass out, and do not put any into it, will you?" Then she said, "Excuse me for correcting you," and she buried her face in her hands and wept at the dinner table because I had thanked her for correcting me.

One day at the dinner table, Mrs. Eddy said to Mr. Calvin Frye, Mr. Irving Tomlinson, and me: "Christian Science is nothing personal with me; it is a revelation from God. There is but one Leader and that is God." Mr. Tomlinson said to her, "You cannot deny that you are a Leader in this age," and Mrs. Eddy replied, "I cannot deny that, but I can only be a Leader inasmuch as I allow God to lead me, whereas others allow self to lead." [Also] one day at the dinner table, Mrs. Eddy tried to impress us with loving more in giving treatments as she told us not to argue, but to love.

When I was in Mrs. Eddy's home, she asked me to realize that "there is no evil mind to make a law to prevent us from bearing others' burdens and so fulfilling the law of Christ, nor to produce an opposite effect, nor to prevent us from accomplishing that which we desire." She requested me to realize the meaning and not merely repeat the words.

After my visits to Mrs. Eddy, on returning home I would try to remember how she looked, but all I could remember was love.

LYDIA B. HALL *(1857–1935)*

*Lydia Hall grew up in Stoughton, Massachusetts. Her
father worked in a boot factory and a shoe shop. She
learned about Christian Science only a year before she
began working in Mary Baker Eddy's Pleasant View
home in 1898. She worked for nine months that first
time and again for nine months in 1901. Hall was
first listed as a practitioner in* The Christian Science
Journal *in 1900, under Whitman, Massachusetts, (in
Plymouth County). From mid-1901 through 1904, she
was listed under Brockton, Massachusetts. No further
listings appear after that.*

*From 1902 to 1905, Hall served in Eddy's household
as needed. After that, she lived, first with family and
then on her own, in different areas in and around
Boston. For part of that time, she worked as a
housekeeper. Little is known about Hall's introduction
to Christian Science or her study and practice of it,
but her eager acceptance of truth is evident in her*

reminiscence, which offers a glimpse into Eddy's approach to students as they progressed from feeding on the milk of the Word to its meat.

Sacred Service in Our Leader's Home

LYDIA B. HALL

I was called to Pleasant View in Concord, New Hampshire, in the year 1898 as cook for Mrs. Eddy. I had served at that capacity for several months when I was asked by our Leader to become her maid, taking the place of Clara Shannon. [After several months, however,] I took the place again as cook, remaining until I went home in 1899. After that, I was called from time to time as the need required for a longer or shorter period. My experience I treasure as the greatest privilege I ever had. As years go by, it becomes more and more sacred that I could have served our beloved Leader in my way.

I found in my work in any capacity [that] not only [was it] to be well done but the thought back of it must be in harmony with the divine Mind or it was not perfect. In my work as maid, I came in close contact with our Leader [and] saw and gained more than in any other position. The rebukes were pointed but with love. Each struggle enabled [you] to go higher in the understanding of God but lower in your own estimation. I never saw such a life of toil and self-sacrifice for the Cause and for humanity. She talked with me so much and told me so many wonderful things. I am so sorry I did not write them down, but I did not see the need of it when I had her near me every day.

Daily routines

Each morning it was my duty when she came into her study (after she sat down) to hand her the Bible or some of the books of the Bible. She would sit in silence [and] then open it for her message for the day. Sometimes she would read aloud. One morning she opened to the betrayal of Jesus. She was sad and said, "Who is to betray me?" At night she called me to her and said, "I know who it is—it is my son." This was long before the trial with her son. She always saw the enemy approaching in time to meet and conquer it. She said when everything seems to be going smoothly, that is the time to work as much as when you are having the struggle with the error.

She always went outdoors on the upper back piazza for two hours each day, winter or summer, to sit in her swing [and] to work for the world, to talk and commune with God. Sometimes she would say, "I cannot tell you what God told me today," [but] then again, she would. She would say to me, "Have more faith in God—talk with Him."

An hour before dinner she spent in prayer and the study of her book *Science and Health with Key to the Scriptures*. New thoughts would open up to her as she devoured the inspired book. At night she went to her swing in the front portico with windows open and worked and talked with God. She often called all her students together to tell them [what] came to her.

PHOTO BY CALVIN FRYE © THE MARY BAKER EDDY COLLECTION

The boat house and pond at Pleasant View, seen from the balcony

Lessons during the workday

At one time she asked me to do something for her. I said, "I will try, Mother." She said, "Never say, 'I will try,' for it leaves a loophole for error to get in, but say, 'I will.' That shuts the door on error." Another time she asked me to do something for her. I said, "I will do anything for you." She said, "Do it for God." [She was] always turning your thought from personality, [which] coincides with Revelation 22:8, 9.

I wish I might give more of what she has told me, but the spirit, the love, the uplifted sense of one who walked and talked with God will never leave me. I have served her but little to what she demanded of us. Now I see it as I did not then, but her blessing will follow us throughout eternity. How [can] anyone question for one instant that she was God's anointed, the greatest woman the world has ever known in every sense of the word? Following in the footsteps of Jesus the Way-shower, [she is] the only Discoverer and Founder of this new-old Truth that ever was since Jesus or ever will be throughout eternity, the only Leader who lives and works today and always for the [t]ruth which she gave birth to—Christian Science. There is but one Truth, one [W]ay, and all God's ideas will awake someday to see that this is the only [W]ay and turn at last toward home to their Father-Mother God.

CHARLES D. REYNOLDS *(1863–1950)*

*Charles Reynolds was born in, or near, Gettysburg,
Pennsylvania. His father was a farmer. After receiving his
early education in Gettysburg, Reynolds attended Johns
Hopkins University for three years and the University
of Pennsylvania for two; he graduated, however, from
the Theological School in Meadville, Pennsylvania.
Eventually, he was ordained as a Unitarian minister.
After preaching for a while in various New England
churches, Reynolds moved, for health reasons, to
Lancaster, New Hampshire, and preached there.*

*In 1897, Reynolds noticed a marked change for the better
in the demeanor of a parishioner and learned that her
improvement was due to Christian Science treatment. She
shared one of Mary Baker Eddy's books with him, and his
study of it resulted in complete healing. Approximately
three months later, he resigned as pastor and began his
full-time healing ministry.*[69]

Reynolds met one-on-one only twice with Eddy, but her requests and recommendations guided his career. Around 1900, she asked him to serve the Manchester, New Hampshire, church as First Reader, which he did, moving to Manchester from Lancaster. Later, Eddy recommended him for admission to the Massachusetts Metaphysical College, where he took Normal class from Edward Kimball in 1901, though Eddy herself signed his certificate. A year later, after substituting on the Bible Lesson Committee, Eddy made him a regular member. He served in this capacity for several years and was also the Committee on Publication for New Hampshire.

Reynolds married in 1904, and for about five years his wife, Grace, was also listed in The Christian Science Journal *as a practitioner in Manchester. In 1916, the couple and their three children relocated to California, where Reynolds set up his practice in Oakland and was an active member of the church there until he resigned his membership to help form First Church, Piedmont, California. Reynolds held his first class in 1917 in Piedmont, where the family lived until 1933. From that time on, Reynolds lived and practiced in San Francisco, California. His reminiscence is preceded by excerpts from the letter to the Board of Directors that accompanied his manuscript.*

Memorable Encounters with Mrs. Eddy

CHARLES D. REYNOLDS

Dear Friends:

My first meeting with Mrs. Eddy was November 8, 1900. The directness and openness of her conversation seemed very good to me. How were we progressing? She expected we were holding crowded services! The population, I remarked, is only 3,500 people. "I know," she said, "it is a small community. Too small! A man like you should be in a larger field. You know how to speak in public. We need men like that in our movement at this time, and you will be needed on the lecture platform."

"But," I hastened to remark, "I am glad to give up public speaking for the work of healing; I never enjoyed speaking."

"But it is needed," she replied.

Then she asked concerning my health and healing in Science. She was amused when I said that the doctors said they knew neither the cause nor the cure. "I am glad they confessed it," she added quickly.

Here she changed the conversation to the subject of animal magnetism—have I had experience in handling it, she asked. I related an instance of the overcoming of fear, which I gave as an illustration of the action of animal magnetism, and new as I was in Science at that time, I felt greatly relieved when she approved what I had said on the subject.

But by far the most interesting and instructive part in our talk was brought out by my question, [Is] Christian Science truly universal, the only Science? Discerning, without doubt, that I was in need of instruction, she took up earnestly and at some length the revelation of Christian Science as it came to her at first without understanding it. "I wrote," she said, "not knowing if what I had written was consistent and correct with the subject as a whole, but subsequent study and examination invariably proved that what I had written was correct. Electricians would ask me about electricity and chemists about chemistry, and I would answer them instantly and find afterwards that my answers were correct."

From this explanation I derived great benefit. I saw clearly that Christian Science came by revelation. That God spoke to Mrs. Eddy as truly as [He] did to Moses or Isaiah. She heard the same voice that Jesus declared—Christ. I saw, as I had not before, that Christian Science is God manifesting Himself and that He had found in Mrs. Eddy a channel that was transmitting His presence and power.

After Mrs. Eddy had finished speaking, then followed a deep silence. I seemed to have nothing to say, and as if recalling herself from a realm of pure thought, she said, "You must excuse me now." Extending her hand, I involuntarily used the title "Mother," and to my surprise my former prejudice against the use of that term had disappeared. I saw that up to that time I had entertained a false sense of its use. "Now," I said to her, "I feel that I can call you Mother."[70]

My impression of Mrs. Eddy might be summed up by saying that her view of men and issues was from an altitude

of thought and insight so high and pure
that she discerned their needs. In fact, she
knew more about us than we do ourselves;
[she was] one to be loved but never feared,
unless by our own unfaithfulness, fear
entered in.

　　With kindest regards to the members of
the Board, I am

Very Sincerely,
Charles D. Reynolds

My start in the ministry

Upon my graduation from a theological school at
Meadville, Pennsylvania, having thus prepared myself for
the ministry wherein I thought to lead a holy life and to
glorify God by preaching His Word, I was later to learn that
I had also to verify that Word by learning to heal the sick in
order to truly minister to the great needs of men.

I reported at Boston to the Unitarian headquarters, and
they sent me to Casco Bay, Maine, and also to several other
places to preach. None of them seemed to be satisfactory;
consequently I decided to find a church of my own, and a
place opened up for me in Boston. There I became ill, and the
doctor advised me to go to a higher altitude to recuperate;
following his advice I went to Lancaster, New Hampshire,
where a pulpit opened up for me in the Unitarian church.
In this place the churches convened to induct me into the
ministry. Mr. Collier, a well-known Unitarian minister,
conducted the ceremony.

My introduction to Christian Science

My health did not improve at this location as I had hoped. There was a group of ladies at this place reading Christian Science, and when one of them visited Portland, Maine, and [returned with] such a changed countenance and manner, I was so interested in the transformation that had taken place in her that I called upon her to hear what was the cause of the great change.

Upon hearing her story, I asked if Christian Scientists had any literature, and she offered me her only book, *Retrospection and Introspection*. I took the little book and was so eager to read it I could hardly wait to get home. I read almost day and night for several weeks, when the light broke through. Through the study of that book, I was healed.[71] About three months after this incident, I retired from the ministry and began to practice Christian Science. I could no longer preach in the orthodox manner, for now I knew my ministry included healing the sick as well as the sinful.

I then joined that group of Christian Scientists, and we formed a society, and about a year later it became a church (about 1900). By this time the news, the good news of my miraculous healing, had become quite broadcast, so much so that one day I received a letter from Mrs. Eddy, which read, "Dear Mr. Reynolds, do you sometimes go to Boston by way of Concord? If you do, would you be so kind as to stop over at Concord[?] I would like to see you." [It was] signed, Mary Baker Eddy.

My meetings with Mrs. Eddy

Can you imagine my surprise and joy? So immediately

I found ample reason to be going "by way of Concord." When I arrived there, I was met at the station by Mr. Calvin Frye with the black horses and the surrey and was taken to Pleasant View. Being seated in the parlor, I heard a rustle as of a silken garment descending the stairs, and a lady reminding me of my mother entered the room. I arose and Mrs. Eddy came forward smilingly, and cordially extending her hand, she said, "Mr. Reynolds, we are quite busy here today, but I will give you one hour." She sat down on a sofa. I was seated on a chair some distance away. She said, "Mr. Reynolds, will you not bring your chair over near me; it will make our meeting much more pleasant." Accordingly, I drew my chair up in front of her; she began to question me about my past and the work I had been doing at Lancaster. She asked me how I handled animal magnetism and how many members I had gotten together in my church at Lancaster.

While I was there, it being about Thanksgiving time, a most unusual and terrifying thunder and lightning storm came up and raged. Mrs. Eddy made no remarks at all about the seeming disturbance but went right along with her conversation. My first visit with her, instead of being one hour, turned out to be about four hours, thanks to the thunderstorm.

A few months after my first visit to Concord, I received another letter from Mrs. Eddy asking me to come again to see her. This time, she informed me that things were not going as well as they should at Manchester, New Hampshire. She asked me if I would become First Reader there if she appointed me. I replied, "If it is your wish, I will accept." After I was established in the church, she communicated with me, thus helping me in my work in building up one of the pioneer churches in the state of New Hampshire.

Knowing Mrs. Eddy through her works

When Mrs. Eddy spoke from the balcony at Pleasant View, it was a great occasion. Many of her students from far and near gathered to hear her, and I was one of those fortunate ones on that memorable event. My acquaintance with her has become fuller and richer through many years of study and practice of the truth revealed by her words and works.

What a great blessing has come to the world through the life of this woman of God. This age can scarcely fully appreciate her great gift to mankind—it is for eternity— but this age can catch a glimpse of its possibilities and power. We should expect when we turn to those precious textbooks, the Bible and *Science and Health*, to study them that they will pour out all we need, a new revelation of spiritual truths which feed us and supply our needs.

Ours is indeed a great privilege to be pioneer Scientists. We need to be faithful to our pursuit and practice of the truth; it brings God into our experiences. We need to become better acquainted with a God at hand, as a distant God is not a great refuge and strength.

Mrs. Eddy has revealed the way. She states in *The First Church of Christ, Scientist, and Miscellany*: "To begin rightly enables one to end rightly, and thus it is that one achieves the Science of Life, demonstrates health, holiness, and immortality" (p. 274).

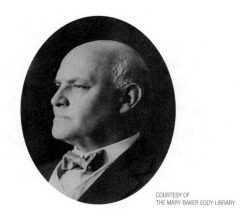

GEORGE H. KINTER *(CA. 1857–1922)*

The son of a farmer, auctioneer, and veterinary surgeon, George Kinter was born in Pennsylvania, where he grew up and eventually worked as a clerk for the Lackawanna Railroad. In 1880, he moved to Detroit, Michigan, and then in 1885 to Buffalo, New York. He married Elizabeth Lasher in 1886. Two years later, his mother-in-law, who was receiving Christian Science treatment at the time, visited the couple. Kinter began reading her copy of Science and Health with Key to the Scriptures *and was "slowly but surely and completely healed," he later explained, of a serious eye difficulty, chronic indigestion, and severe headaches. He took Primary class instruction from Annie V. C. Leavitt (one of Mrs. Eddy's students) in 1888 and two years later began devoting his full time to Christian Science healing. By 1891, both Kinter and his wife were listed in* The Christian Science Journal *as practitioners in Buffalo. And sometime in or around 1894, their niece Grace was born, whom they adopted.*

Kinter joined The Mother Church in April 1893 and was also active in his branch church, holding posts as clerk and Assistant Committee on Publication. In 1901, he took Normal class from Edward Kimball, who recommended him to Mary Baker Eddy. He served for one year in Eddy's household in 1903 as a secretary and metaphysical worker. Later, he served for shorter periods in 1905, 1907, 1909, and 1910.

By 1904, Kinter was advertising in the Journal *as both a practitioner and teacher. In 1906, he and his family relocated to Chicago, Illinois, where he healed and taught until they moved to Pasadena, California, in 1920.*

These excerpts come from two different parts of Kinter's reminiscences—one about the start of his work at Pleasant View in 1903 and one about Eddy's raising of Calvin Frye from the dead in 1905.

Our Leader as Healer

GEORGE H. KINTER

My first meeting with Mrs. Eddy was very significant to me. My personal introduction to her was by her lifelong friend and faithful student, Mrs. Pamelia J. Leonard, C.S.D., who regularly spent half of the year in Mrs. Eddy's home.

Mrs. Eddy received me most cordially and asked me many, many questions. In fact, she asked me about everything concerning myself and my family, excepting how old I was and whether we had children or not. She talked much and familiarly about the Cause—"Our Cause"—I noticed she spoke of it quite invariably.

Determining my fitness to serve

It occurs to me right here that some of the things which were said on this occasion might be [as] interesting as anything that I could write. I remember Mrs. Eddy asked me if I was as well and strong as I looked. How I was engaged, or rather whether I had any other occupation besides the practice, meaning by this the practice of Christian Science Mind-healing; whether I could come and stay a whole year without going home for any vacation; [and] whether I understood the terms prescribed in "our Mother Church *Manual*" for such service, adding that I could not carry on any other [work] while with her, not absent patients, nor work for my local church, nor even work for my own folks, because all my time would be required for the exactions of the work there.

When I told her I did understand the regulations with respect to the pay of those who were to serve in her home but that I did not see how I could get along with but two paydays in the year, she made answer, "Well, then, you shall have yours every month. Will that do?" "Yes, thank you."

That question settled, she proceeded to ask whether I could stand it to stay right in the house and be on call all the time; whether I had any chronic beliefs of sickness not as yet mastered; whether I loved this Cause more than anything else in the world, etc., etc., etc.

She then told me she thought I would do and proposed that I get some money for traveling expenses from Mr. Frye, go home and acquaint Mrs. Kinter with the plan, and ask her whether she [was] willing to lend me to the Leader for a whole year and whether she could see how she could run the house at home and take care of the practice without me. "But," added Mrs. Eddy, "she must have a voice in this plan."

I was to expect a telegram to come back at any time within the next week.

An unexpected change in plans

I remember that as I could not get a train home any earlier, I attended the Thanksgiving services at the Concord

Architect's drawing of First Church, Concord, New Hampshire

Church. I left Concord that afternoon for Boston, and on my arrival there secured Pullman car accommodations for home on a train leaving the same evening, which incident has a meaning of more than passing moment when I relate [that] before that train started for the west, there were several of the official staff busy trying to find me, as they ultimately did and informed me that I was wanted in Concord by the very first train, but none of them told me *what* I was wanted for.

Assuring myself that their instruction for my interception issued from Pleasant View, I canceled my sleeping car space, returned my railroad ticket, and hied me back to New Hampshire.

Upon presenting myself at Pleasant View [the] next

morning, I was complimented "for a quick readjustment of my traveling arrangements" and informed by the lady that she again had read Mrs. Kinter's letter to the effect [that] *"If 'Mother' needed me*, or *wanted* me for anything," she and Grace had decided they could get along without me, our dear Leader here adding, "a few more such Christian Scientists as that would make me far happier. May I keep this letter? I know that I am warranted in expecting that she will be happy to let you stay right on now because I need you at once."

"Telegraph for your clothes and get ready for your work. I wish we could have her here, too, yes, both of you."

"But tell me," she said, "who is Grace, referred to in this dear letter of Mrs. Kinter's?"

"Why, Grace is our niece, my deceased brother's child. She has been with us for a couple of years, and we expect to keep and educate her. She is practically our daughter, although not legally adopted, at least not as yet, although we have proposed this."

Then Mrs. Eddy said some of the sweetest of all the sweet things I ever heard her say. It was something like this:

> Well, you see, I did not know you had
> any children—and much as I need two
> such people as you and Mrs. Kinter, I must
> not and will not do anything to divide the
> family. It is bad enough to take one out of
> the home for an indefinite period, as I am
> doing, but to bring Mrs. Kinter here, too,
> would distinctly break up your home, and
> I cannot do this. I will get along somehow

if they let me have you, and I am sure now
that that letter which Mrs. Kinter wrote
you, before she knew what my telegram
might mean, is of the character of an inspiration. I shall not soon forget such kindness. But I do wish we could arrange it.

Still, this house is no place for a little
girl. Why, she would seldom see you, and
there is too much that is like solemnity here
for a child, who needs the bright things
of life. True, Grace would be at school all
day, but, you see, our evenings are oft our
busiest times.

How true! How true!

I submit that the kindly thoughtful attitude of
Mrs. Eddy's mind, her regard for others, and her consideration for others' comfort and happiness has here a fine,
practical illustration in fact, well worth emulation by us all
in all our dealings with each other as Christian Scientists
and with people generally. The general adoption of her
philosophy in this respect would make and keep the world
young. It approaches the sublime in human experience.

Mrs. Eddy's concern for my comfort

"Your principal duties at first," said Mrs. Eddy, "will be
to assist Mr. Frye; he has too much to do, and I will want
you, among other things, to look after my mail. You will
receive, open, read, and assort it, bringing to me only such
letters and telegrams as I should see, and this will require
you to be very wise."

"Have you a warm bathrobe? Well, until your trunk comes from home, go to town and buy one and let me pay for it, because I may want you at night, and you will not have time to dress. Moreover, my room is too cold if you are not warmly clad—I have my windows opened."

"Do you sleep in a warm or cool room? I always have my room cool with all the heat turned off at night. Your number will be five. When I ring five, come to me. You ought to have some sort of woolen socks, too."

At this I ventured to ask, "When shall I go to town to get the bathrobe?" [She answered:]

Why, you will not have time to go; just send for what you want at any time by my coachman, August Mann. He does all the errands for the entire household, but be sure to let Mr. Frye know what it costs, so that he may reimburse you for the expenditure, and get anything else you need or want at my expense.

I am sorry for the shabby room I have to put you into, but it is the last, and therefore the best one I have to offer you; but some day I am going to build me a new house, with twenty rooms upstairs, and then you shall have your pick. If you want any different furniture, get it and make yourself comfortable.

We have breakfast at 7:00 a.m., dinner at 12:00 noon, and our supper at six o'clock in the evening. Will that suit you? Do you drink coffee and tea? Because if you do, you won't get any here. We don't have either. We drink cocoa shells—it is a real nice drink and our faithful cook serves it good and hot.

Now you may go to your room. I want to write Mrs. Kinter. She has made it easy for me to keep you here, and I want to write her my thanks. I wish you would write her, too, how pleased I am with her letter. My, how it relieves me to have such friends.

Raising the dead

By way of further testifying to Mrs. Eddy's masterly demonstration of her Science, I will here relate, in such minutia of detail as will leave no room for question or doubt, one of the most tremendous proofs of the availability of Christian Science Mind-healing I have ever known. The fact that I was an eyewitness and in some minor respect a participant renders the incident of signal importance.

Late one winter night of January or February in the year 1905, Mrs. Eddy rang three (3), Mr. Frye's call, and presently repeated it; as it was a matter of frequent occurrence for any of us to be repeatedly called by her, although we all heard each of the calls, we never paid attention to these bells unless our own number was sounded.

Finally, she rang three a third time, and then my own number, five (5), sounded through the halls with such rapidity as to take me quickly to her chamber. Going there, I passed through Mr. Frye's room and noticed him in a sitting posture, apparently asleep—which, of course, surprised me for I also noted in my hasty trip that his bed, although it was turned down, had not been occupied.

On reaching Mrs. Eddy's own room I found her half sitting in her bed and much agitated. Knowing that I would have come through Mr. Frye's room, she asked me, "George, *where* is Calvin?" I answered, "He is in his room."

"Well, can it be possible that he is in bed and sleeping so soundly as not to hear my call. I have rung three times for him with no response. Such a thing has never happened before in all the 25 years he has been with me. Are you not mistaken?"

"Oh no, he is not in bed; he is sitting there in his arm chair. I will go and speak to him."

"Well, do go and come back as quickly as you can."

I went and found what appeared to me a decided case of coma. Then, very soon, she rang my own call again.

I hastened to her, and dreading to communicate what I feared, I told her he surely was sitting in his chair by his desk and evidently sleeping very soundly, for although I shook him sharply, he did not waken.

She bade me go again, arouse him, and tell him to come to her at once. I went, of course, only to have my fears confirmed. Mr. Frye had passed on—he had no pulse, he was stone cold—and [was] rigid. His closed eyes were fixedly set, and there were none of the common evidences of life.

Mrs. Eddy, weary with waiting for my return, rang for Mrs. Laura Sargent, who responded with her characteristic alacrity. She, also taking the shortest cut through Mr. Frye's room, as I had, gave me a chance to prepare her, which I did in a stage whisper.

Very soon Mrs. Eddy was out of bed and clad in her nightdress, in spite of our protests. [She] came quickly to Mr. Frye's room, where I was busy trying in vain to arouse him with my best understanding of Christian Science. But it should be noted that I had invited defeat by conceding that death had intervened. Plainly I had allowed fear to get hold of me. Everything seemed to contribute to this fear, and each added moment added to the fury of mental storm that beat around me. I was tempted greatly to exaggerate the responsibility devolving upon me. I was also hysterically apprehensive as to the discomfort that might come across to dear Mrs. Eddy in connection with such an experience as this taking place in her house.

I had never met but one of Mr. Frye's relatives, a brother, and I had occasion to believe that he did not fully endorse his brother's course in making such an absolute sacrifice of himself for the Cause and for its Leader. A thousand other anxieties hastily raced through my mind, and of course, my treatment for my good friend Frye showed no results.

But when our Leader arrived, all this was changed; she began at once to treat him, making such bold, audible declarations as to cause me to shrink back lest my now awakened sense of the gravity of the situation might prove abortive of her heroic endeavors. In my endeavor to step aside, in order to let her come that much nearer to the patient, I became consciously aware that our great, dear friend was so sparsely clad [that] I put my arm around her and essayed to urge her to return to her bed, but it was as though I had not spoken to her, so intent was she upon accomplishing the demonstration that she literally paid no attention to us. We were now both trying to persuade her. Finally, or presently, we desisted in these efforts and dear Mrs. Sargent rang for the maid, who went to Mrs. Eddy's chamber and brought a double blanket which we wrapped around her, and then Mrs. Sargent, on her knees, put stockings and night slippers on her feet, but all this caused not the slightest cessation of her work. Mrs. Eddy continuously denied the error and declared the [t]ruth with such vehemence and eloquence for a full hour, as I never have heard on any other occasion, even in that house.

In belief my back ached as I supported her, for she remained standing in a half-stooping position in front of her patient, there being just room enough for his chair between the window and his high roll-top desk. Her efforts were intensive to the highest degree. I remember quite well many of her utterances and actions. She said, for example:

> Calvin, wake up and be the man God
> made! You are not dead and you know
> it! How often you have proved there is no
> death! Calvin, all is Life! Life!! Undying
> Life. Say, God is my Life. Say it after me!
> Say it so that I shall know you realize it!
> Say it in a whisper, if need be, but make
> the declaration for yourself. Declare—I
> can help myself. I know there is no animal
> magnetism. I am not the victim of mali-
> cious animal magnetism. I have proved a
> thousand times that my knowledge of good
> in Christian Science is paramount to every
> attempt of error to put me out through
> malicious mental practice. I am victorious
> over evil thought and action, for I know

that God is All-in-all, all-powerful, all-loving, and always present.

Callie dear, are you, yourself, repeating what I am saying to you—and for you? Are you? Do you hear me? Do you understand me? Mother loves you for all your years of faithful service, but our dear God loves you infinitely better, and you cannot, you need not, die tonight! You are not dead, Calvin Frye. Rouse yourself. Shake off this nightmare of false, human belief and of fear. Don't let error mesmerize you into a state of believing Satan's lies about man made in God's image and likeness! Your lifework is not done. I need you. Our great, blessed Cause needs you.

Life is as deathless as God Himself for Life is God, and you are His spiritual offspring. Calvin, there is no death, for the Christian Christ Jesus has abolished death, and this treatment is not reversed by error.

Intermittently she chafed his hands, slapped his face sharply, and shook him briskly until, at last, after the lapse of an hour, he moved slightly and then spoke, at first in slow, low, guttural tones and spasmodically but, at length, coherently, until finally we could hear him say such things as "Don't call me back" and "Let me go, I am so tired," etc. etc.

To each of [these comments], Mrs. Eddy responded:

Oh, yes. We shall persist in calling you back, for you have not been away. You have only been dreaming and now that you have awakened out of that dreamy sleep, you are not tired. You love life, Calvin, and its activities too well to fall asleep. Thank the dear God, who is Mind, is omnipresent good, you do not concede any claim of the material senses. You don't have to and knowing the [t]ruth as you have practiced it, lo, these many, many years, you know that divine Love is the liberator, and you are freed from the thralldom of hypnotism, alive unto God, your Saviour from sin, sickness, and death.

Now then, give God thanks for He hath redeemed you. You are strong and well.

Another half hour was spent substantially as I have shown, in which period Mr. Frye conferred with us all quite intelligently. We took, almost carried, Mrs. Eddy back to her bed, and her dear women helpers lovingly tucked her in, making sure that she was good and warm before they followed her injunctions to all of us to go to our beds now and go to sleep because we would have a busy day tomorrow.

Her good night to Mr. Frye was characteristic of her and had in it a touch of wholesome, good humor. She said to him, "Now, Calvin, don't let the devil catch you napping again, for it takes a lot of valuable time sometimes to outwit him."

Before retiring, I proffered Calvin any assistance needed, but he declined with thanks and went to bed as usual. In less than half an hour more, the house was as quiet as heaven.

Next morning, Mrs. Eddy's bell rang us as usual for her breakfast, and on going downstairs, we who knew of the unusual night work learned that Mr. Frye was down early and had already had his breakfast at 8:00. Mrs. Eddy had us all ("the workers") in her sitting room, and the work for that day was outlined for us without the slightest reference to the experiences of the previous night. At noon Mr. Frye was in his accustomed place at the head of the table and served dinner. Several of the household would doubtless be surprised to read this account, for I never heard them speak of the occurrence.

Mind had triumphed over false material sense, and I am [as] profoundly grateful for the experiencee as I am to narrate it, mayhap for generations as yet unborn.

MINNIE A. SCOTT *(1871–1955)*

*Of Scottish descent, Minnie McCalden was born in
Ireland. The youngest daughter of a Presbyterian
minister, she came to the United States at the age of 17
and was active in Protestant church work in Boston as
a young woman. McCalden married Clarence W. Scott
in September 1892, and they both became interested in
Christian Science around the time of the dedication of the
Original Mother Church in January 1895. In May of that
year, while at a service in The Mother Church, she was
healed of grief over her mother's passing.*

*For a full year before the couple learned of Christian
Science, Scott suffered from the effects of a fall and the
recurrence of several ailments that had earlier plagued
her. These problems were quickly healed, however, when
she grasped that God's allness left no room for evil.
Referring to this healing, she said, "Christian Science
saved me from [the] necessity of an operation and freed
me from the use of several painful and unpleasant*

remedies." Soon afterward, she began healing others, and beginning in 1911, she was listed as a practitioner in The Christian Science Journal *for more than four decades.*

Scott worked in Mary Baker Eddy's household for three years, first at Pleasant View and then at Chestnut Hill. After July 1909, she no longer resided in Eddy's home but would help when needed. Reflecting on her years of service, Scott wrote, "To have come so closely in touch with [Mrs. Eddy's] compassionate love for everyone, her ready forgiveness, her daily practical application of Christ's Sermon on the Mount, I count among my richest blessings." Scott concludes her reminiscence with the following words: "These incidents are lovingly, gratefully, and truthfully recorded for posterity."

Serving Mrs. Eddy— An Invaluable Experience

MINNIE A. SCOTT

It is with joy that I recall my first glimpse of the Discoverer and Founder of Christian Science and the sense of God as infinite Love that flooded my consciousness that morning. I had just become interested in Christian Science.

On Sunday, May 26, 1895, I attended The Mother Church service and felt an air of expectancy and peace which was explained when Mrs. Eddy came down the aisle about the middle of the service and gave a wonderful address about God as Love and the great need [for] more love in the world. This address is recorded [beginning] on page 106 of *Miscellaneous Writings: 1883–1896*. Aside from what she said about love and [that] "Three cardinal points must be gained before poor humanity is regenerated and Christian Science is demonstrated: (1) A proper sense of sin; (2) repentance; (3) the understanding of good," [the address] was new to me when I read it in the first edition of that book.

After the healing that came to me that Sunday morning of grief over my mother's passing and uncertainty about the future, I never doubted the fact that Mrs. Eddy was the God-inspired revelator of Truth to the age. I saw Mrs. Eddy again several times when students were invited to Concord, and I heard her speak [in 1899] in Tremont Temple when she gave the sweet message found on pages 131–133 of *The First Church of Christ, Scientist, and Miscellany* that again brought peace and assurance of God's love, presence, and power available every moment.

One memorable incident still fragrant in consciousness was on a day I went to Concord, New Hampshire, with my husband and two friends who had not been there before. Either we were a little early or Mrs. Eddy was a little late in starting on her drive, but we got there just as her carriage was leaving the door and stopped as far back from the gate as we could, but when Mrs. Eddy passed, she bowed to us all and, looking into my eyes, gave me a carnation she held in her hand. The act was so natural, so childlike and gracious, that I did not think of her as a great person but as a loving mother encouraging a timid child.

The call to serve

When the Extension to The Mother Church was almost finished in 1906, I was asked if I would go to Pleasant View. The call came at 10 p.m. to come to Pleasant View and see Mrs. Eddy a little after 5 p.m. the very next day. My train was late, and the time had passed when I reached the house but was asked to see her the next morning.

When Mrs. Eddy called me to the library, after asking me how long I had been a student, etc., she said, "Now here you are at the fountainhead, and there is an opportunity for you to prove your gratitude by service." She then went on to tell me how she thought I might help her.[72] I falteringly told her that I was glad to serve but was wholly incompetent in that capacity because I had never made much effort in that direction. She stopped me by saying, "Your Leader had to learn those things when she established her home in Lynn," and smilingly added, "The Scotch have native abilities." Then earnestly and with loving eyes, she said, "My dear, you have only to lean on God as a little child, and divine Mind will teach you all you need to know every moment. Love will direct your footsteps and lighten your labors. This I know to be true."

I took up the work lovingly and am grateful to attest that as I did lean on God as a little child, I was able to prove true what she had told me. I remained with her consecutively until July 1909—with the exception of one week in April 1908—which was over three years. At Pleasant View I saw her every day, and often she talked with me alone or with others.

Periods of struggle

An incident occurred just before the *New York World* launched its bitter attack. [One] day Mrs. Eddy asked John Salchow, who was special policeman[73] on her grounds, to follow her carriage on his bicycle, which he did each day for nearly two weeks. Her secretary (Mr. Strang) was strong in his disapproval of this step—a manifestation of fear shown to the public. Then, just as suddenly, Mrs. Eddy told John he need not come, and the very next day the paper mentioned disclosed the situation that for two weeks men had been in

Concord watching an opportunity to hold up Mrs. Eddy's carriage and drag out what they called the "dummy" inside.

This incident showed that her action was the wisdom from above protecting her from the plot of mortal mind, and she obediently followed the heavenly voice to take the human footstep of the appearance of a bodyguard, the only thing mortals could understand.

During the attack of the *New York World* and the "Next Friends" lawsuit, she was patient, courageous, and joyful.[74] She never missed a day from her only recreation—her daily drive. [One] day when she returned, she no doubt felt the atmosphere of her home was intense—I can only speak for myself that the injustice of the whole affair seemed oppressive—and she called us all to her study and said, "We are never worse for persecution but better because we turn more unreservedly to God; now we all must lift our thought to God and pray like this—O divine Love, give me higher, holier, purer motives, self-abnegation, inspiration, and spiritual love."

Teaching by word and example

On Easter morning 1907, Mrs. Eddy called us to her study and gave us an inspiring talk on the resurrection. Among other things she said, "When a patient came to me to be healed, I did not think of patching up a sick body. I eschewed"—she said, with a wave of her hands—"that picture of man and saw him as God's idea." Mr. Kinter said, "That is what you mean where you say in *Science and Health with Key to the Scriptures* [that] Jesus saw the perfect man, etc." [see pp. 476–477], and she said, "Exactly." Then with the admonition to "lift your thought to God," she sent us back to our work.

She gave us several copies of "Evil Is Not Power" (a pamphlet) at different times, especially after telling me to meet the belief of mesmerism in regard to household affairs.[75]

Mrs. Eddy was always turning the thoughts of her followers away from her personality to seek and understand God. At the time of the dedication of the Extension, she asked her followers not to make any special visit to her home or allow the belief to grow that we worshipped her, but a few days afterwards she came home from her drive in tears because at every corner she encountered a group of people watching for a glimpse of her. She asked us to make a black curtain and put it in her carriage on a drawstring, which we hoped she would never need to use, but, alas, she did use it the next day. She had barely settled in her study after her drive when a note was delivered at the house by messenger. She called us all to hear it—the writer was conscience stricken to think that her curiosity had shut out the sunlight for one instant from the one who had done so much to bring the light of divine Love to others. No self-exoneration or excuse was offered, only deep humility and the desire to do better. Mrs. Eddy expressed her joy at this awakening and said the effort was repaid if one only had learned the lesson to turn from person to Principle.

Mrs. Eddy's thought was ever awake to heal and bless mankind. In the midst of her busy life on a hot summer day, she would remind us to send a cooling drink to the workers on her grounds, and because she recognized the gifts of nature as the supply of divine Love meeting human needs, there was always good weather when her crops were harvested. The neighbors soon learned to take advantage of her demonstration and harvest their crops at the same time.

Pleasant View grounds covered in snow

The move to Chestnut Hill

It was a memorable journey from Concord, New Hampshire, to Chestnut Hill that winter day [when Mrs. Eddy moved her residence], and the days that followed were busy ones indeed. Mrs. Eddy had found her [new] study too large—she did not realize how large her dimensions would make it—so she planned the changes that were made soon after, to have a stairway there and a file room off her bedroom.

The house was so much larger and the helpers more in number that I did not see Mrs. Eddy as often as before, but I still could see her at her desk in her room each day as my duties brought me to her door.

At a time when a disgruntled woman was anxious to see Mrs. Eddy, she called me to her study and asked me what I would do in such a case. "Would you just know that divine

Love was my protection?" she asked. I answered I would surely know that, but I would also take special care that the windows and doors on the first floor were kept fastened. She said, "My dear, you have answered me with the spirit and the letter. Now I know I can trust you."

She was always interested when those outside of the movement expressed a kindly thought toward Christian Science or some right understanding of her and her work. [One] day at Chestnut Hill, she called us all to her study and read to us, from a newspaper that had been brought to her, an editorial welcoming a Christian Science service in that town and giving a synopsis of Mrs. Eddy's life. After reading about herself, she said, "Here she is nearly ninety years old and reading this to you without her glasses." She could see the humorous side of things very quickly, and we often left her with a happy laugh.

Countering undue curiosity with love

The summer that she was so busy with the work of launching *The Christian Science Monitor* to have it appear as a Thanksgiving number, she was being annoyed by the caretakers in the next house who were watching her movements by the use of opera glasses from the windows, or the young girl who stood close to the gate, where the carriage had to go slowly, to stare at her.

At the same time, as we always find it when error screams at us, Love was pouring in its balm in expressions of gratitude for help received. One of these was a crate of peaches from students. An attractive basket was arranged and placed on Mrs. Eddy's desk to greet her on her return from her drive. On that particular day, the girl had been quite offensive in her attitude, and the man who drove the horses for Mrs. Eddy came in very much incensed and wishing to punish that girl. Just at that moment Mrs. Eddy called for him and sent him with her attractive basket of peaches and her card expressing love to the girl he wanted to punish.

The girl was overcome by this gracious act and was healed of her undue curiosity. The man had a lesson in forgiveness, and we all were blessed by Mrs. Eddy's method of overcoming ignorance and hate.

I took up the work at Chestnut Hill and stayed until July 1909, making in all over three years of intimate knowledge of Mrs. Eddy's daily life, and can attest to the fact

Chestnut Hill household workers in 1909, from left: Alice Peck (seated), Archibald McLellan, Elizabeth Kelly, Irving Tomlinson (seated), Nellie Eveleth, Katharine Retterer, Adam Dickey, Jonathan Irving, Frances Thatcher, Adelaide Still, Margaret Macdonald, Minnie Scott, Adolph Stevenson

that—[as] in the line from a hymn—"she lived the precepts that she taught" [see *Christian Science Hymnal,* No. 386].

The last time I saw her, she was at her desk in her study as usual and smiled as she saw me put some things back on her bureau.

I might continue to write of the many lessons learned from my experience in Mrs. Eddy's home, but it would simply add to the volume of gratitude from the many who appreciated the privilege of serving the one who had done so much for the world by bringing to our apprehension and understanding the practical working of the law of God, ever-operative and available. When bidding Mrs. Eddy goodbye in July 1909, I said to her, "I wish I could remember every word you have said to me." She said to me, "My dear, it will all come to you just when you need it, and you will find as you go on that your experience here with me will prove invaluable to you." I am grateful to record that I found this also to be true.

ADAM H. DICKEY *(1864–1925)*

*Canadian by birth, Adam Dickey moved with his family
to Kansas City, Missouri, during his teen years. From
1884 to 1899, he worked in his father's business, W.S.
Dickey Clay Manufacturing in Kansas City. Dickey
married Lillian M. Selden in 1887 and became interested
in Christian Science when she was healed in 1893. He
joined The Mother Church the following year, and both he
and his wife took Primary class instruction with Henrietta
Graybill in 1896. Dickey was healed of the use of tobacco
during this class and for the next fifteen years studied
Mary Baker Eddy's writings intensively.*

*In 1898, Dickey traveled with his wife to Mexico on
business for Dickey Manufacturing. While there, they
met a city official who was suffering from jaundice. The
Dickeys introduced him to Christian Science and prayed
through the night for healing. Soon, the man was cured.
Upon his return to Kansas City, Dickey resigned from
the family business and went into the healing practice.*

By March 1900, both of the Dickeys were listed as practitioners in The Christian Science Journal, *and both that year and the next, Adam Dickey took Normal class. The 1901 class was taught by Edward Kimball, one of Mary Baker Eddy's students. Dickey began teaching students of his own in 1901, the same year he became First Reader at First Church, Kansas City.*

Dickey served as Eddy's secretary in her Chestnut Hill home from February 1908 to December 1910, becoming one of her most trusted workers.[76] He was named a Trustee of Eddy's estate by her Deed of Trust in 1909 and again by her will in 1913; he remained a Trustee until his passing in 1925. Dickey also served on the Christian Science Board of Directors from 1910 until his passing in 1925. He taught classes in Boston most of that time and was Treasurer of The Mother Church from 1912 until 1917.

Dickey's well-known article "God's Law of Adjustment" was published in 1916, inspired in part by these remarks Eddy made to him: "Today divine Mind adjusts me to my work and adjusts my work to me. Under the law of adjustment, God's law, my work must be successful. Through steadfast declaration, work and worker, buyer and seller, are brought together[,] . . . and God's perfect law is brought into manifestation." Dickey strove for many years to understand and demonstrate the truth of these remarks before writing about them.

Memoirs of Mary Baker Eddy

I was born in Toronto, Canada, in the year 1864, the second son in a family of nine children, six boys and three girls. My father's name was Nathaniel Dickey, and he was a native of the town of Lisburn, Ireland, a devout and consecrated Christian of the early days. My father came to the United States in the year 1848 and afterward went to Toronto, Canada, where he engaged in the iron foundry business. I never knew a better man than my father. His life was one of uprightness and purity, and he was admired and respected by all who knew him.

My mother was a descendant of George Soule, who came over in the *Mayflower*. Her mother, Sarah Ann Soule, married Robert Simpson, a young Englishman, who settled in Ontario, Canada. My mother was scrupulously honest and frank. The Bible was an open book in our household, and the custom of family prayer and Bible reading, established in early years, remained with our family until the children were grown and had left home. I have always had a fondness for the Bible, and while still very young, attached myself to the Methodist Church, continuing active in young people's meetings and class work until I came into Christian Science.

My promise to Mrs. Eddy

It was the custom of our Leader to lie down for an hour each afternoon and rest. Sometimes she would fall asleep and upon awakening would seem mentally refreshed after her labors of the day. Many times when important matters were under consideration, she would, on awakening from these short naps, come to a quick determination as to the right method to pursue in whatever she had in hand.

On Tuesday, August 25, 1908, my bell rang, calling me to Mrs. Eddy's apartment. When I entered her study, she was lying on the lounge where she usually took her rest. Requesting Mrs. Sargent, Mr. Frye, and a third student to leave the room, she beckoned me to approach. She extended her hand to me, took mine in both of hers, and asked in a deep, earnest voice, "Mr. Dickey, I want you to promise me something, will you?"

I said, "Yes, Mother, I certainly will."

"Well," she continued, "if I should ever leave here—do you know what I mean by that?"

"Yes, Mother."

"If I should ever leave here," she repeated, "will you promise me that you will write a history of what has transpired in your experiences with me, and say that I was mentally murdered?"[77]

I answered, "Yes, Mother, I will."

"Now, Mr. Dickey, do not let anything interfere with

your keeping this promise. Will you swear to me before God that you will not fail to carry out my wish?"

I raised my right hand and said, "Mother, I swear before God that I will do what you request of me—namely, write a history of what I have seen and heard from your lips concerning your life."

"That will do, dear. I know now that you will not fail me."

Her whole demeanor was one of solemn intensity, and there was an eagerness in her voice and manner such as I seldom saw.

I returned to my room and pondered deeply over what she had said. In a few minutes one of the workers and Mrs. Sargent brought me a sealed envelope. In it was a penciled note reiterating the statement that she had made in our conversation of a short time before.

I knew that Mrs. Eddy had an aversion to having her private life spread before the public. I knew also that on several occasions the proposition had been made to her by others to write a history of her life and experiences, all of which she firmly declined to consider. Her reply to proposals of this kind was, "The time has not yet come for my history to be written. The person to whom this important work should be entrusted is not here yet, and I will not give my consent to its being done at this time." This was the nature of the reply she invariably made whenever some of her loving students proposed to her that her life history should be written.

In the request she had just made of me, I felt that Mrs. Eddy did not intend me to write a detailed history of her life, but I know she wanted the incidents and the circumstances of which I was a witness to be given to the world. I have hesitated to begin the narration of these incidents but have always been determined in my own mind that it should be done and have felt that, when the time came, I should have no difficulty in proceeding.

Sixteen years have come and gone since this promise was made. A great many changes have taken place in our movement, but the Cause has still gone on and flourished in spite of the attacks made upon it. Because of the extremely personal nature of what I shall be compelled to write, I still have a strong reluctance to record my memories, although I know this hesitancy is not my own thought but comes from without. The recollection of my solemn promise impels me to take up this work now at this late date and turn back to the record[78] I made while in our Leader's home of the events that are set forth. I am making use of nothing that is not authentic, and although I am unable to include more than a part of what I had written down, I am confident that there is sufficient to carry out the obligation which our Leader placed upon me.

A Leader on the frontline

People were not invited to Mrs. Eddy's house for their own improvement. They were invited there to work, and what she required of them was not that they should work for themselves but that they should work for her and for the Cause of Christian Science. Therefore, experience taught her that it was wiser and better at the outset to decline to receive people who were liable in any way to an attack from mortal mind than to accept such individuals and have them struggling with a belief of illness after they had arrived at her home.

Everyone who was in Mrs. Eddy's home was there because of his ability to work and to perform the tasks that were set for him. Many people seemed to be inspired with a belief that there could be no pleasanter occupation in the world than to work for Mrs. Eddy. They failed to realize that what Mrs. Eddy wanted and actually required of those about her was the mental support which she found necessary to receive from students in order that she might be uninterrupted in her work for her Cause and for mankind. Mrs. Eddy was at the head of a great movement, a Church that had grown up under divine direction and was designed, eventually, to destroy all evil and bring to suffering humanity a remedy for every form of sickness and sin. The same form of evil that attacked the work of Jesus and cried out, "What have we to do with thee, thou Jesus of Nazareth? art thou come to destroy us?" (Mark 1:24), was by no means lacking in connection with Mrs. Eddy's experience.

She was in a position somewhat similar to that of the general of a large army who is fighting for its existence. The attacks of the enemy would be made, if possible, on the leader of the defending army. Usually in such cases the commanding officer occupies a safe point of vantage far in the rear of his fighting troops from which he can issue orders and send forth his commands, unmolested and unthreatened by the attacking forces. In times gone by, the general of an army was required to be in the front of the battle leading his men, but in such events he was invariably surrounded by an able bodyguard sufficient to protect him from every possible attack. The members of this bodyguard were not weaklings, nor soldiers who had been disabled and had not regained their full strength. He was surrounded by the very flower of the army. The best fighters and most capable workers were at his elbow constantly.

Mrs. Eddy was in much the same position in the leadership of this movement. She could occupy no convenient retreat from which to direct the movements of her slender battalions. She must be in the front rank in the thick of battle every day, and she needed to be surrounded by the best workers she could find, who virtually acted as a bodyguard and a protection for her in order that she might be able to give her undivided attention to the work necessary to properly safeguard her church. Thus it was that every person who went to Mrs. Eddy's home had to be tried and tested before he assumed his duties.

I had always imagined that Mrs. Eddy lived quietly, as any other elderly woman would live, surrounded by comforts and luxuries and by those friends whom she wished to invite to share her home with her. I had no idea that she was constantly besieged by all the forces of evil and that she had to be in the frontline of battle, day and night, throughout all the years of her leadership.

My opportunity to serve

On January 29, 1908, I received a special delivery registered letter from the Board of Directors of The Mother Church which read as follows:

January 26, 1908

Mr. Adam H. Dickey, C.S.B.
The New York
12th & Paseo
Kansas City, Mo.

Dear Brother:

The Directors hereby extend to you
a loving call to serve our beloved Leader,
the Rev. Mary Baker Eddy, according to
the terms of the By-Law Article XXII,
Sect. 10, of the *Church Manual.*[79]

If you will come sooner than the ten
days, it will be very much appreciated.

As soon as you can after receiving
this letter, will you please telegraph me
at what time you will be in Boston? And
upon your arrival, call me by telephone at
Back Bay 1470 between the hours of 8:00
and 12:00 [p].m. and 1:00 and 5:00 p.m.
and at Back Bay 1506 at other times.

Very sincerely yours,
William B. Johnson
Secretary

Immediately I replied that I would leave Kansas City for
Boston the following Monday. On Monday, February [3],
1908, I left Kansas City bound for Boston with high expectations of the wonderful experiences which lay before me. I
arrived in Chicago the following morning. There, I had some
time to spare, and having been unable to purchase a copy
of the latest *Manual* in Kansas City before leaving, I visited
the Reading Room, a magnificently furnished apartment
on the top floor of a building on South Michigan Avenue. I
did not make myself known to the librarian, but observing
a consignment of new *Manuals* which had just arrived, I

purchased one and turned to Article XXII, Section [10]. Somewhat to my surprise, I saw that the wording had been changed so that the person accepting the call, instead of remaining with Mrs. Eddy for one year, unless she requested otherwise, the By-Law read, should remain for three years.[80]

This furnished me with much food for thought, but having put my hand to the plow, I could not turn back. Besides, the thought of being chosen to serve the Leader of the Christian Science movement for one year or a dozen seemed such a precious opportunity to me that even the prospect of being absent from my home for three years could offer no possible deterrent to me on this momentous trip.

I had much time to ponder the situation as the train carried me eastward. Mrs. Eddy, I had seen but once, on July 4, [1897], when she invited the members of The Mother Church to visit her at Pleasant View in Concord, New Hampshire,[81] and now I was to see her again and perhaps enter her household and serve her in some capacity, I did not know what. My thoughts were buoyant and hopeful, and I felt that no greater blessing could fall to me than to receive such a call.

Arriving at Chestnut Hill

The country was covered with snow, which fell during all the trip. Trains were delayed and traffic generally interfered with because of the constant snowfall. Instead of reaching Boston at three o'clock in the afternoon, the train pulled into the station at eleven in the evening.

In accordance with instructions in the letter from Mr. William B. Johnson, secretary of the Board of Directors, I called him by telephone at his home. He directed me to a hotel, said he would call for me at 6:30 the next morning, and asked if I could be ready. At the appointed hour I was on hand, although it was still dark. Mr. Johnson had inquired at what hour the first street car left for Chestnut Hill, and we boarded it as it passed the hotel. At Lake Street on Commonwealth Avenue, a horse and sleigh from a nearby livery stable met us, and we were drawn through heaps of snow until we arrived at Mrs. Eddy's front door. Mr. Johnson alighted with me and we were admitted to the home. The family was at breakfast when we arrived. Mr. Frye, who sat at the head of the table and assumed the position of host, invited Mr. Johnson to breakfast with us, but he declined and returned immediately to his home.

After meeting Mr. Frye, I was introduced to Mrs. Laura Sargent, whom I already knew, and to three other members of the household, including the gentleman [John Lathrop] who was serving temporarily as secretary to Mrs. Eddy. After breakfast he told me many things about Mrs. Eddy's household that were new and interesting to me. In fact, he was the only one who ventured to talk to me concerning my sudden entrance into the household and what I might expect as a result. I learned afterward the reason for the reticence that was assumed by the other members of the household. I was a comparative stranger, little known to any of them. They knew I had been sent for on Mrs. Eddy's call. They also were aware that I would have to pass the customary examination, through which everyone passed who was brought to Mrs. Eddy's home with the expectation of serving her. None of them knew whether I would remain after the interview long enough to unpack my valise or whether I would remain for three years. Many of the people who came to our

Leader's home scarcely crossed the threshold, while others were interviewed by Mrs. Eddy and remained perhaps a day or two, and when she saw their services were not to be desired, they were allowed to depart and return home.

During this first breakfast, conversation turned on my trip eastward, and I learned that I had been expected to arrive the day before, Mrs. Eddy having been caused some concern over the delay. They asked me in rather a pointed way if we had encountered much snow on the trip. I explained that the whole country was covered with a blanket of snow, which was responsible for my delay. Mr. Frye at once said, "We must tell Mother about that." I wondered at the time what there was in that little discussion that could interest Mrs. Eddy. I afterward learned that she had an aversion to heavy snowfalls and that they were the damaging results of error and ought not to be tolerated. It seems that this particular snowfall had been the cause of considerable damage, and the workers in her household felt that they might be excused for their failure to control the snow if Mrs. Eddy were informed that the storm was almost countrywide and not confined to New England.

Early impressions of the other workers

I had never seen Mr. Frye before, except as he occupied the seat beside the coachman as Mrs. Eddy took her daily drive in Concord on the occasion of my last visit there. He was a short, stout man with pale and thoughtful countenance, indicating that he was accustomed to an indoor rather than an outdoor life. He was quiet, even to taciturnity—extremely non-communicative—and with an abruptness in his short answers that might have given the impression to a stranger that he was impatient with his questioner. I soon found, however, that this was not the case but that, at the time of my arrival, he had been serving our Leader for a period of perhaps twenty-five years, and long association with her had taught him to mind his own business, and he expected others to do the same. There was another side to Mr. Frye's character, also, and at times he was quite genial and friendly in his relations with the other members of the household. He possessed a keen sense of humor, and he was a man who liked his little joke quite as well as did others of a more mirthful disposition.

Mrs. Sargent I had met when she was the custodian of the room that had been furnished by the children for our Leader in The Mother Church.[82] My wife and I visited this room in [1897], and it was Mrs. Sargent who showed us through the apartment. Her engaging manner and pleasant disposition made such a deep impression upon us then that we always thought of her as particularly amiable and loving. I found her devoted to Mrs. Eddy. She seemed to have but one thought and that was to serve, and the members of Mrs. Eddy's household who recall her will always think of her as the loving and devoted Laura Sargent.

Another of the workers I had never met before, and I found her [Sarah J. Clark] a wholesome, loving Christian Scientist who had been in our Leader's household for nearly a year. She remained but a short time after my arrival, returning to her home city, [Toledo, Ohio], where she had been long engaged as a teacher and practitioner. She will always be lovingly remembered by those who knew her best.

The student who was serving as secretary I already knew, having heard him read in one of the Churches of Christ,

Scientist, in New York City. He was there temporarily filling the place of secretary, which had just been vacated by my predecessor, and I found that he was awaiting my arrival in order that he might return to his work in New York.

I was taken to the room which was to be mine, directly over the library at the front of the house and on the same floor with the rooms occupied by our Leader. I found it equipped as an office as well as a bedroom. There were house telephones connecting with every room in the house except those occupied by Mrs. Eddy. The room was large, light, airy, and well furnished. My guide soon seated himself with me at the desk and began to give me an outline of what my duties were to be. This was the first intimation I had that there was a possibility that I might serve Mrs. Eddy in a secretarial capacity. There were numerous letters on the desk from various places, all of which had been opened by the secretary *pro tem*. He told me many interesting things regarding our Leader's daily routine—the hour when she arose, when she breakfasted, when she received and read her mail, as well as many other of her daily tasks which were performed at a set hour. I have always felt grateful for this friend. He was the first and only one, other than Mrs. Eddy herself, to give me any satisfactory explanation as to why I was there and why others were there also. He gave me a short sketch of the people in the house and also gave me bits of information that proved valuable to me afterward.

Remaining for a little over two weeks, this student then returned to his home in New York, and shortly afterward his place was taken by another worker [William R. Rathvon] who came at our Leader's request and was accepted as a member of her household.

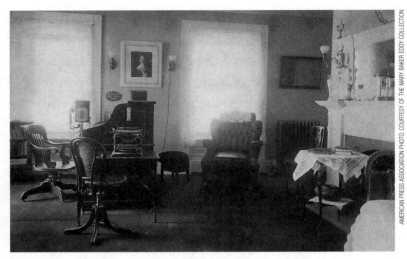

Adam Dickey's office and bedroom at Chestnut Hill

Calvin Frye's importance to the household

I was informed of Mr. Frye's association with Mrs. Eddy and was told that he had been in her employ for about twenty-five years. Mr. Frye originally worked in one of the shoe shops of Lynn, Massachusetts, where he operated a machine of some description.[83] He was a man of meager education but through reading and observation had cultivated a high degree of understanding. He was religious and devout by nature and was identified with a church in Lynn when he became interested in Christian Science. This occurred shortly after the passing on of his wife, and upon learning something of the teachings of Christian Science, he went through a class with Mrs. Eddy in the year 1881 and manifested a deep interest in her work. His devotion to the Cause of Christian Science attracted the attention of our Leader, and being at the time without any secretarial help, she turned to Mr. Frye to perform many little services for her, which he did with such eagerness and thoroughness that she eventually employed him as a sort of factotum, and he finally became a member of her household.

He assisted her in arranging and calling her classes; he tended the furnace and, in fact, did everything he could in the way of service to relieve our Leader from thought-taking or annoyances in connection with her great work. When she moved to Concord, New Hampshire, he went with her and always accompanied her on her daily drives, so that Calvin Frye came to be a household necessity with Mrs. Eddy. She told me that she found him scrupulously honest and trustworthy, and eventually she turned over to him the keeping of her accounts. He was her bookkeeper and cashier, as well as her secretary.[84] At the time of my entry into Mrs. Eddy's household, Mr. Frye sat at the head of the table and was virtually the host, so that when my informant whispered to me, "If I were you, I would cultivate Frye," it spoke volumes and showed me that because of his intense devotion and service to Mrs. Eddy, he was one of the most valued members of her household.

My first meeting with Mrs. Eddy

The morning mail had just arrived, and one of my first discoveries was that everything in the way of mail, packages, and things to be receipted came into the house via the secretary's office. I was almost startled to see the acting secretary pick up a letter opener and begin opening Mrs. Eddy's mail. He then explained that he was doing this under Mrs. Eddy's direction and that if I were to continue as her secretary, she would give me similar instructions.

About this time a knock came at the door, and Mr. Frye informed me that Mrs. Eddy wished to see me. I think my heart gave a few extra flutters, for this was to me the supreme moment in my Christian Science career. I arose and followed him. He led me along the upstairs hall from the front of the house diagonally across to a large room at the left and rear which was occupied by Mrs. Eddy as a study. Mr. Frye entered this room and I followed him. Mrs. Eddy was seated in a large chair beside her desk, and as we entered, she rose and extended her hand in greeting. After introducing me, Mr. Frye left the room.

Mrs. Eddy motioned me to a chair, and we had our first conversation. She was a woman of rather below medium height, slender, and having the appearance of a person between eighty and ninety years of age. Her complexion was clear and her eyes were bright. She talked with a most beautifully modulated voice. At times, when she was saying some unusually impressive thing, it took on qualities deep and orotund. It seemed like one of the best trained voices I had ever heard. Her hair was gray and becomingly arranged, and one thing that impressed me deeply was the daintiness and neatness of her attire. She wore the well-known diamond cross at her throat and a large marquise ring, set with diamonds, that she seemed to think a great deal of. Her dress was of heavy silk and cut and made without regard to the modes and fashions of that day. She wore a ruching[85] about her neck, which I afterward learned was replaced every morning. She seldom appeared in the same dress on successive days and seemed to have a complete and inexhaustible wardrobe. In short, I soon discovered that Mrs. Eddy was fond of dress and that she believed in daintiness, neatness, and order in connection with all her wearing apparel. Her hands were small and her fingernails were well manicured, a task which she imposed upon herself every morning.

After I was seated, she asked me many questions, among which were, what my age was, my birthplace, my schooling, and under what circumstances I had come into Christian Science. She asked who my teacher was, what my success had been in healing, and many other interrogatories which bore no particular significance to me at that time but which I afterward learned she felt were important. She seemed pleased to know that I had not come into Christian Science in search of health and was also interested to hear that I was one of nine children, all of whom were still living, [along] with the father and mother, who had attained to a healthy old age. She was impressed with the fact that we rarely if ever had need for a physician in our family and that the fear of sickness and disease had been almost unknown.

She then gave me a brief outline of some of the duties she would expect of me and asked me if I would like to come and live in her household, become a member of it, and enter her service as a mental worker.[86] I told her I would be most happy if she would employ me in any capacity whatever. After a few more words, she excused me and I left her study.

Learning of our Leader's needs

Upon reaching my own room, I sat down and was meditating on what had occurred when I heard the sharp ringing of a bell four times in quick succession. Presently, Mr. Frye appeared at my door and said, "Mr. Dickey, that is your signal to come to Mrs. Eddy's room. Whenever you hear four bells, it means for you to respond at once to her call." I immediately went to her and she again spoke to me—this time a little more intimately about her personal affairs. She explained that, as the Leader of a great movement, she had naturally acquired many enemies and that she was having considerable to meet by way of aggressive mental suggestion intended to injure or affect her physically. This seemed a very startling disclosure at that time, but nevertheless I accepted it. After receiving some directions as to how I should work for our Leader, I again returned to my room and pondered over the things she had said to me.

The followers of a great leader usually feel, as they have a right to, that they are well acquainted with and thoroughly understand the person whom they are following. This, however, was not true in the case of Mrs. Eddy. Very few people really knew her at all intimately, with the exception of perhaps two or three of those who spent a great deal of time with her, and even then she was often heard to say that those who had been with her the longest seemed to know her the least. It was generally believed among Mrs. Eddy's followers that she stood erect physically and mentally at all times and simply spoke the word to error and it would entirely disappear. There were occasions when she did rise to this height, but there were also times when she seemed to bend beneath the heavy load that mortal mind had placed upon her, and it was then that she really yearned for human aid and sympathy. She seemed to feel that she was more or less alone in her sphere of work and that those by whom she was surrounded did not really understand her or sympathize with her in the way in which she truly wished. Mrs. Eddy was not what might be called a worldly wise woman, and yet whenever a question of any kind arose that required a decision from the standpoint of wisdom, she was always able to appeal to the divine Mind and get her answer.

My brief stint as coachman

After dinner, Mr. Frye came into my room and said that Mrs. Eddy was greatly disappointed in not being able to take her drive. "Why can't she take her drive?" I asked. "There is nobody to drive her." [Mrs. Eddy's coachman had passed on "some time during the night with a claim of heart failure."] "Can't you?" I questioned. "No," he replied, "I never have driven a horse attached to a sleigh, and Mother is not willing for me to undertake it." "Would she like me to drive?" "Can you do it?" asked Mr. Frye. "Yes," I said, "I have been accustomed to horses all my life." When he informed Mrs. Eddy, she sent for me at once and questioned me about my ability to drive horses. I assured her that I was quite capable of performing this service for her and would be overjoyed to do it. This was my first experience in acting as coachman for Mrs. Eddy, but I was inwardly pleased to know that such a slight service meant so much to her. I drove the sleigh each day until a new coachman was installed [less than a week later].

In commenting upon the passing on of her coachman, she opened *Science and Health with Key to the Scriptures* and turned to page 187, line 13, and at the same time she said to me, "Mr. Dickey, when I turn to this book, I am like a mechanic who turns to his tools and picks up the one he wants. This reference on page 187 has a direct bearing on the case.[87] When it occurred, I knew where it came from, for it presented itself clearly to me in thought." After a short discussion of the subtle claims of malicious mental malpractice, she dictated what now appears in *Science and Health* [at the end of] page 442.[88]

Called together for a lesson

It was Mrs. Eddy's custom to arise promptly at six o'clock every morning. She rang the bell for her maid [M. Adelaide Still] at that hour, and one touch of the bell always called her. One could almost set his watch by the regularity with which this bell was rung. Mrs. Eddy did not breakfast with the family. Her meals were taken in her own apartment, and her light breakfast was served by her maid at seven o'clock, which was also the hour for the family breakfast.

The system of bells in Mrs. Eddy's house was a great institution. I think it must have been improvised by Mr. Frye, and at first thought one would be inclined to believe that a much better device might have been arranged. On longer acquaintance, however, it was found that this crude system of bell ringing was about the only one that could be effectively put into operation. A single cord with a button was located at a convenient place on Mrs. Eddy's desk, and the bells were connected in series; that is to say, when one touch was given to the button, one bell rang in the maid's room, in the upper hall, in the lower hall, and in the kitchen. This was done so that in whatever part of the house the maid may have been at the time the bell was rung, it would not escape her attention. Each worker had a definite ring, three, four, or five, or whatever the number might be, and if any worker left the home, his successor inherited the same number of bells. When Mrs. Eddy desired to call all of her workers together at one time, she usually gave the bell ten or fifteen taps, which always resulted in the quick appearance of her mental workers.

The first morning I experienced this wholesale calling

was a few days after my arrival when I heard the bells ringing apparently all over the house. I was still wondering what the commotion was about when Mr. Frye shoved his head through my door and said, "That means everybody." I responded with alacrity and found that others had arrived before me because of my ignorance as to what this sudden call meant.

Mrs. Eddy opened the Bible and read to us James 1, verses 21–25.[89] Then she gave us all a talk on being "doers of the word, and not hearers only," deceiving ourselves. She dwelt especially on the passage referring to a man beholding his natural face in a glass and straightway forgetting what manner of man he was. This brought out a new meaning to me that affected the whole passage, and I saw the right idea of man as never before. Our difficulty seems to be that we look at the reflection mortal mind sends back and accept this as our true being, forgetting that man is spiritual and not material. She said to us, "You are not doing your work as you should, and I shall not instruct you further until you have demonstrated something more of what has been taught. It would be a poor teacher that would take students up into the higher branches of mathematics before they had proved addition, subtraction, multiplication, and division. Therefore, until you demonstrate in better fashion what you have already been taught, I shall teach you no more." This is one of the gentle means of persuasion our Leader so often employed in endeavoring to get us to do better work.

The need for metaphysical defense

The reader here should understand that the people employed in Mrs. Eddy's home were there for but one purpose, and that was to serve their Leader and to protect her against malicious attacks of mortal mind in her endeavors to give to the world the religion of Christian Science. At this point I can almost hear some critical reader say, "What nonsense! Who is trying maliciously to attack Mrs. Eddy?" Remember the people's reply to Jesus, "Thou hast a devil: who goeth about to kill thee?" [John 7:20] Many times she struggled with some physical argument that had to be met before she could proceed with her regular work of directing the movement. Not only was it incumbent on her to keep a clear thought of the demands made upon her in her direction and control of The Mother Church and its branches, but she also had to keep her head above the malicious and intentionally directed attacks made upon her personally, having for their purpose and sole object the interruption of her work and the attempt, if possible, to destroy her life.

On the following morning she spoke to me about the determination we should exercise in doing our mental work. She said, "Never fear a lie. Declare against it with the consciousness of its nothingness. Throw your whole weight into the right scale. This is the only way to destroy evil." She then picked up a lead pencil from her desk, and grasping it in the middle with her thumb and forefinger, she balanced it there like a pair of scales. Then she touched the point with one of her fingers and pressed it down, forcing the other end of the pencil up, and said, "You can see that whatever you put in one end of the scale always throws the other end up. Now remember this, and never admit anything that will weigh against ourselves. When we admit a lie we put the weight into the wrong scale and this operates against ourselves."

United in our desire to serve

I was beginning now to become better acquainted with my duties and with what was expected of Mrs. Eddy's workers at Chestnut Hill. The household consisted at this time of about twelve members besides Mrs. Eddy. Included among the twelve were two gentlemen and two ladies; Mrs. Eddy's personal maid; another who, with her own hands, prepared our Leader's meals; the house man, who was Mrs. Eddy's trusted servant; the night watchman; the housekeeper; and the coachman, who took care of the stables. All of these dear people had left their homes and had come as associate workers in our Leader's house to serve her and the Cause of Christian Science.

Occasionally changes took place in the personnel of the household, it becoming necessary for one cause or another to bring in new workers and allow the older ones to return to their homes. At times the number of those present went as high as sixteen or eighteen so that there was quite a house full of people.

The main object in the thought of every one was to do what he could to serve Mrs. Eddy. She was endeavoring to live and carry on the work which God had given her to do, and when things went well with her, there was a spirit of cheerfulness and activity throughout the household that seemed to be reflected in the conduct of each individual member; but when Mrs. Eddy seemed to be laboring under the oft-repeated attacks of evil, the members of her household kept busily at work.

The most important work in connection with our Leader's home was that done by the mental workers, who

were there because of their experiences in the Field as practitioners and of their ability to handle the claims of evil as
they presented themselves. This work was done under the
direct supervision of our Leader, and through her secretary
she informed the other workers just what phases of error
she felt should be given special attention. Her secretary, at
her request, prepared what was denominated a "watch."
This consisted of typewritten sheets of paper containing
in numerical order the names or description of the phases
of error that Mrs. Eddy wished them to handle. She was
being constantly assailed by mental malpractice, and it was
necessary for someone to take up this work and aid her in
freeing herself from these different attacks. She seemed
to be the only one who was able to discern the course that
error was pursuing. Sometimes she learned this through
suffering, but she always knew it and would by means of
these "watches" notify the workers what their mental work
should be.

Each mental worker in the home occupied his own
room, which was large, airy, and comfortably furnished,
with a private bath connected. The injunction "Never
forsake your post" [see *Retrospection and Introspection*, p. 85]
was one that was strictly obeyed by every mental worker in
our Leader's home. Each was always to be found in his own
room, and when a change was proposed in the line of mental
work to be taken up, Mrs. Eddy would give her secretary
the language of the "watch," or perhaps it would be sent to
his room by Mr. Frye, Mrs. Sargent, or Mrs. Eddy's maid,
whichever one happened to be convenient when the inspiration reached our Leader. Carbon copies were made of these
"watches," and one was taken directly to the room of each

worker as a guide to him in his mental work. The subjects covered by these "watches" were endless in their variety.

Challenges in Church governance

Many times, while our Leader was working on the problems connected with the government of her Church, the physical effects of the discord she wished to overcome seemed to manifest themselves in her body, and often she was prostrated with suffering, apparently caused by the chemicalization of the conditions of thought she was endeavoring to meet which seemed to culminate in her own thought.

Some of the most important By-Laws of The Mother Church formulated themselves in the thought of our Leader while she was under a claim of suffering, which continued until the By-Law was ready to be passed upon by the Directors. Then the suffering disappeared, and everything went on harmoniously without a single trace of what our Leader had passed through. These experiences occurred when she [wrote] the By-Laws doing away with the Communion service in The Mother Church and also on the occasion when she disbanded the Executive Members of The Mother Church.[90] She suffered greatly in both these instances, but the moment she arrived at a decision and framed the By-Laws which treated with these two conditions, her relief was instantaneous, and she arose immediately, healed.

There is no question that the By-Law abolishing the Communion Service of The Mother Church came under this category. Our Leader had been suffering intensely for several days before this By-Law came out, and even while she dictated to me the words included in it, she was lying on the lounge in her study wrestling with a malicious attack of unusual severity. I took the proposed By-Law, as she dictated it, to my desk, and after transcribing it, I returned with it immediately to her room and was overjoyed to find her seated at her desk, wreathed in smiles, and pursuing her regular work with her usual vigor. I saw that something out of the ordinary had taken place, and afterward I learned from Mr. Frye that on many occasions when our Leader instituted improvements for her Church government, her action had been accompanied by severe manifestations such as appeared in the present instance, and yet not one word of complaint passed her lips. She was willing to take the suffering if she could only succeed in obeying the voice of God.

This caused me to ponder much, and I recalled the quotation from Isaiah (53:4, 5) [which] says: "Surely he hath borne our griefs, and carried our sorrows: yet we did esteem him stricken, smitten of God, and afflicted. But he was wounded for our transgressions, he was bruised for our iniquities: the chastisement of our peace was upon him; and with his stripes we are healed."

Calvin Frye told me that these experiences always came to Mrs. Eddy in this way and that whenever any great revelation came to her concerning that which seemed necessary for the welfare of our Cause, these struggles appeared in her body. This corroborates what she told me about feeling the needs of the movement in her body.

On one of these occasions, when her suffering seemed severe, she called us all into the room and quoted a passage from Shakespeare's *Macbeth* [act 5, scene 3]:

Canst thou not minister to a mind diseased,
Pluck from the memory a rooted sorrow,
Raze out the written troubles of the brain,
And with some sweet oblivious antidote
Cleanse the stuffed bosom of that perilous
    stuff
Which weighs upon the heart?"

It was at this time that she said to us, "You don't any of you realize what is going on. This is a dark hour for the Cause, and you do not seem to be awake to it." She said, "I am now working on a plane that would mean instantaneous death to any of you."

Expectations concerning the weather

One thing in particular that our Leader requested her workers to care for was the weather, and this was done in addition to the work of a committee in Boston appointed for that special purpose. During some of the severe New England winters when a greater amount of snow than usual was falling, our Leader would instruct her workers that they must put a stop to what seemed to be the steadily increasing fall of snow, which she looked upon as a manifestation of error. She had an aversion to an excessive fall of snow. She considered it as an agent of destruction, an interference with the natural and normal trend of business. We are quick to recognize the fact that an unusually heavy fall of snow in any community is a disastrous thing. It clogs the wheels of commerce, interferes with traffic, interrupts the regular routine of business affairs, and breaks in upon the harmony and continuity of man's peaceful existence.

Millions of dollars are spent annually in many places to remove the effects of heavy snowfalls, and so this was one of the points that was covered by Mrs. Eddy's mental workers. One of the "watches" issued January 15, 1910, requested her mental workers to "make a law that there shall be no more snow this season."[91]

When our Leader first came to live at Chestnut Hill in the spring and summer of 1908, thunderstorms and electric disturbances seemed to be unusually prevalent. This was another form of error which our Leader disliked very much. A gentle rainfall was a delight to her, but a destructive electrical storm she abhorred. She evidently looked upon it as a manifestation of evil and a destructive agency of mortal mind. Mrs. Sargent was the one to whom was especially assigned the work of watching the weather and bringing it into accord with normal conditions. For the three years during our Leader's stay in Chestnut Hill, and for several years thereafter, the recollection of the writer is that there were fewer and fewer thunderstorms until they almost ceased to be.

Upon one occasion after she had given her workers some instructions regarding the weather, and after we had all repaired to our several rooms to continue, a succession of taps on her bell called us all back into her sitting room, where, as was our custom, we arranged ourselves in front of her chair very much as the old-fashioned class in school arranged itself in front of the schoolmaster. Pointing with her finger to the first one in the class, which happened to be myself, she said, "Mr. Dickey, can a Christian Scientist control the weather?" "Yes, Mother." To the next person, "Can a Christian Scientist control the weather?" "Yes,

Mother." To the next, "Can a Christian Scientist control the weather?" "Yes, Mother." This question was put to each member of the class with the same reply. After we had all repeated our answers, an expression of rejection, not to say scorn, came upon her face, and she said with emphasis, "They can't and they don't."

This brought a look of surprise to the face of each member of the class, for we had just been instructed, as we thought, how to take care of the weather. She repeated the statement, "They can't," but immediately she added, "but God can and does." She continued:

> Now, I want you to see the point I am making. A Christian Scientist has no business attempting to control or govern the weather any more than he has a right to attempt to control or govern sickness, but he does know, and must know, that God governs the weather and no other influence can be brought to bear upon it. When we destroy mortal mind's belief that it is a creator and that it produces all sorts of weather, good as well as bad, we shall then realize God's perfect weather and be the recipients of His bounty in that respect.
>
> God's weather is always right. A certain amount of rain and sunshine is natural and normal, and we have no right to interfere with the stately operations of divine wisdom in regulating meteorological conditions. Now I called you back

because I felt you did not get my former
instructions correctly, and I want you to
remember that the weather belongs to
God, and when we destroy the operations
of mortal mind and leave the question of
regulating the weather to God, we shall
have weather conditions as they should be.

Every Christian Scientist will see the force of our Leader's
instruction in this respect. Mortal mind's attempts to take
out of the hands of the creator of the universe His dispen-
sation of weather should be met and overcome through the
realization of what really constitutes God's government
regarding the weather.

I have heard our Leader describe in a number of
instances how she has dissipated a thundercloud by simply
looking upon it and bringing to bear upon mortal mind's
concept of this manifestation of discord what God really
has prepared for us, and she illustrated this by a wave of
her hand indicating the total disappearance of the thundercloud and its accompanying threat.

Defending headquarters

As time went on, the serious nature of our work at
Chestnut Hill dawned upon my thought. I saw that we were
there filling one of the most important positions that could
be assigned to humankind.

The Leader and Founder of a great movement was
casting her thought over the welfare of the whole world.
Christian Science, if it means anything, is designed to
save the world from the penalties of its own sins and

shortcomings, as exhibited in sickness, sin, and death. Its purpose is to destroy and annihilate the claims of evil of every sort. Then it is not surprising that evil, which has a belief of intelligence, would retaliate by training its guns on the citadel of Christian Science and attempt to destroy that which is surely and effectually ridding the world of evil and all kindred beliefs. To have an assignment, then, as a protector and bodyguard of the Leader of this movement, and be permitted to share in the defense of its Discoverer and Founder, is an assignment of no small moment. Many times our Leader was attacked through mental influences of the most sinister and wicked nature.

In olden times the occupants of a fortress were attacked from without by means of bombardment of missiles of all sorts. There were intrigue, treachery, conspiracies, and plans brought into execution that had for their object the downfall of the citadel which was being attacked. The commandant of the fortress was aware of these methods of attack, and it was no difficult thing to provide against the onslaught of the enemy by reinforcing the battered walls and throwing up a shield of defense against the visible material missiles that were hurled against them, but in these days of cultivated thought, when the power of a mental assault is recognized, when mortal mind has changed its basis of attack from material missiles to mental shafts, they cannot be turned back by material walls. The defense of the headquarters of the Christian Science movement must be conducted in a vastly different way from that of the old-fashioned fortress. The educated and liberated mortal thought of today is employing its weapons of mental warfare surely and effectually, as it did the more grossly material weapons of former years, unless the Christian Scientist builds a strong defense. From the time Mrs. Eddy first began to preach and teach Christian Science, every conceivable form of weapon was turned against her in the hope that her work could be stopped and that evil would be left to its own devices in its attempts to control mankind.

When the stones were first hurled through the windows of her lecture room and onto the platform where she stood, she realized that she was fighting an uphill fight and that she had enlisted in a warfare the purpose of which was the destruction of the highest forms of evil.[92] In the later years of her leadership, there was no cessation or even diminution of these mental attacks upon her, but they continued with ever-increasing volume in the attempt to destroy her life and obliterate her work. It was for this reason that Mrs. Eddy called effectual workers around her. For this reason also they were sought out, examined, and questioned in regard to their ability to prove the teachings of Christian Science, and then [those who were qualified were] brought to Chestnut Hill to form a bodyguard or a defense for our Leader in the continuation of her work.

The transition to Chestnut Hill

Mrs. Eddy had lived for so long in her comparatively small home in Concord, New Hampshire, that the transition from this rather diminutive residence to the large, commodious home in Chestnut Hill introduced a sudden change in her daily routine that at times made it a bit awkward for her. It is true that the plan of the house at Chestnut Hill bore a striking resemblance to the one she had just vacated in Concord so far as the location of the rooms was concerned, but everything seemed so gigantic and extensive to our Leader that these circumstances troubled her not a little. She, therefore, decided to have some alterations made, and an architect from the west was sent for to effect the needed changes.

Her study at Concord was a room perhaps fourteen by sixteen feet, while the corresponding room in her Chestnut Hill house was at least twenty feet by twenty. Mrs. Eddy's desk and chair were located in the circular bay window, and the door, by means of which workers entered the room, was in the corner diagonally opposite. In complaining about the size of the rooms, our Leader humorously said that, when she called a student to come to her, she could not wait while he walked across such a great expanse of carpet from the door to where she sat, and something must be done to conserve her time. Happily, through the architect's skill, the changes were easily designed, and Mrs. Eddy moved her suite to the third floor while the necessary alterations were being made in her own apartment. The changes consisted in reducing the size of her study, in cutting down the dimensions of her bedroom, and in taking enough from the latter and adding it to Mr. Frye's room so that he might have a bedroom and a sitting room instead of one large room.

Orderliness, neatness, and dispatch were among the leading characteristics of our Leader, and to discommode herself by moving to the third floor, where the ceilings and the walls of the room conformed to the slant of the roof, meant no little change in her environment. [But] the carpenters, plumbers, gas fitters, electricians, painters, paper hangers, and iron workers all did their work smoothly and well so that the whole change was effected expeditiously and with a degree of harmony that is seldom seen in alteration work of this character.

I had always heard that it was difficult for Mrs. Eddy to find people who would carry out her orders implicitly, and when I entered her employ, one of the obligations I placed upon myself was to obey her absolutely, without question, no matter what she might ask me to do. It did not take Mrs. Eddy long to discover this quality of obedience in my thought, and she at once evidenced a pleasure in having me do things for her so that when she moved into her new room and settled it, I was privileged to stand at her hand and place everything where she wished it.

One of the last pictures placed in the room was a remarkably well-executed one entitled *The Return from the Crucifixion.* It represented the return of the women from the cross. It showed the beloved disciple ascending the steps of his home, sustaining the drooping form of the mother of Jesus, whom the latter had entrusted to John's care. The faces of the group shown in the picture, with the exception of Jesus' mother, were anxiously turned toward a hill beyond the walls of Jerusalem, where silhouetted against the sky appeared the three crosses, which stood as mute witnesses of the dreadful day's experience. After leaving Mrs. Eddy's study, I was recalled in a few minutes, and pointing with one hand to the picture just described and placing the other on her breast, she said in a voice deep and earnest in its subdued tones, "Mr. Dickey, I think you had better remove that picture. It suggests too much for me. Won't you kindly put another in its place?" This I did and removed the offending picture to the hall on the second floor outside of her room where it remains to this day.

Cultivating orderliness and punctuality

It was the custom of the workers in the house, when it became necessary to sweep and dust Mrs. Eddy's rooms, to perform this service while she was out on her daily drive so that when she returned all evidences of the cleaning operation would be removed. Experience taught them that unless everything [was] returned to its proper place, there would be a reprimand forthcoming from our Leader, and this occurred so frequently that the attendants were troubled in their efforts to get everything back exactly as they found it. In order, then, that no mistakes should be made and that they might not yield to the argument of error that they could not please Mrs. Eddy, a tiny brass tack was driven into the floor through the carpet, marking the place where each piece of furniture belonged, and always when she returned she would find everything just as she had left it. When once this habit of orderliness was formed by the house workers, they found their tasks lighter and everything made easier by reason of the fact that the furniture could quickly be put back in its rightful place, and no time [was] consumed in guessing or wondering if things looked just right. They also discovered that Mrs. Eddy was always right in her complaints about the misplaced furniture, for after they adopted the placing of brass tacks, no more objections came from her.

This may seem like a small matter for Mrs. Eddy to complain of, but when we study the situation and see that her room represented to her a condition of thought, it at once becomes explicable. This illustrated the fact that, even in such a simple thing as sweeping a room and rearranging the furniture, the following of a definite rule of Principle makes everything easier.

Orderliness and promptness grew to be a habit with the members of Mrs. Eddy's household. There was a clock in every room. Each member of the household had his own timepiece, and it was expected to be always in perfect running order. In Mrs. Eddy's sitting room there were three clocks. In her bedroom there were two, one of which was an old-fashioned alarm clock which she had fastened to the foot of her bed. This was done so that in the night, by simply turning on the light, she would know instantly what hour it was. On a table beside her bed, she kept a tablet of paper and a pencil, and many times thoughts that came to her in the night were written down for preservation. This obviated the necessity of her doing what she did when the

Mealtime at Chestnut Hill, from left: Calvin Frye, Adam Dickey, Lillian Dickey, Irving Tomlinson, Elizabeth Kelly, William Rathvon, Ella Rathvon

title of her textbook, *Science and Health*, came to her.[93]

Breakfast for the household was served promptly at seven o'clock every morning, and no one needed to be called or sent for. No announcement was made that breakfast was served. The fact is that at seven o'clock the members of the household walked into the dining room, and promptly at seven o'clock the associate worker placed breakfast on the table. At noon the same general order prevailed, and every one presented himself promptly in the dining room at twelve o'clock. No gong was sounded, no dinner bell, no summons of anyone. They were all there at the right time. This was also the case in the evening, so that everything at Chestnut Hill moved with the promptness and regularity of clock-work. There was no confusion, no friction, no lost time. Indeed, the question of meals and mealtime occupied very little space in the thought of the members of Mrs. Eddy's household. They grew into the habit of being in their place at the proper time. No matter what the obligation or duty was which had to be performed, if it could be arranged so as to be done in regular order, it was so arranged, and in this way tasks were lightened and duties were made a pleasure by having a regular hour at which to perform everything.

Appreciating beauty in thoughts and things

Notwithstanding the fact that our Leader's time was greatly taken up with the most exacting and arduous labors for her Cause, she nevertheless seemed to have ample time to devote to the appearance of her house, both inside and out. She noticed that one of the trees on her place did not appear to thrive, but was drooping and showing every evidence of dying. She learned that the superintendent of her grounds proposed to cut the tree down and remove it. Immediately she sent word to him to do nothing of the kind but to do what he could for the tree in his way, while she took the question up according to Christian Science. In a remarkably short time, the tree began to grow and thrive, and today it occupies a place on her grounds.

Mrs. Eddy never let down on anything. She kept everything up to the highest point of perfection—her appearance, her hair, her fingernails, her house, her horses and carriage—in fact, none of the evidences of age or neglect were ever allowed to show themselves. She admired pretty things and beautiful things as one may infer from a [telegram] to the St. Louis church, in which she points out that it is not evil to enjoy good things but that it is evil to be a slave to pleasure.[94] A short while before she left us, she ordered a new carriage, while the old one seemed to me in perfectly good condition. She seemed to realize thoroughly that things are thoughts and that the most beautiful things express the clearest and most advanced thought. It was a law with Mrs. Eddy that everything had its rightful place and must always be in that place.

Mrs. Eddy's daily drives

After her removal from Concord to Chestnut Hill, our Leader set the time of taking her daily drive at one o'clock. At this hour her carriage always drove to the side entrance, where she was accustomed to enter the vehicle. One thing was not definitely set, and this was the duration of her drive. She seldom remained out longer than half an hour and returned as the demands upon her time appealed to her. It was a long drive from her home to The

Mother Church, and only once during her residence at Chestnut Hill did she take the time to drive to Falmouth and St. Paul Streets, and then she did not alight but had her first view of The Mother Church [Extension] from her carriage.[95]

A daily drive with Mrs. Eddy was not a pleasure nor in any sense a recreation. She did it because she felt obligated to do so in order to refute the constant charges that she was dead or incapacitated. She knew that as long as she appeared in her carriage every day, it would satisfy mortal mind and meet the charge that she had already departed and was no longer with us. There were times when it was a very severe task to take this drive. Indeed, as time went on, this obligation grew more irksome to her, and on many occasions she [rode] when she did not seem physically able to do so, but she did it nevertheless and always succeeded in meeting the attacks upon her so that she returned master of the situation.

On one occasion, just prior to her leaving the house for her drive, my bell rang and I responded immediately to find her seated in a chair dressed for her drive, painfully drawing on her gloves. She said to me, "Mr. Dickey, I want you to know that it does me good to go on this drive." Instantly she felt my questioning thought, and she replied, "I do not mean that the physical going for a drive does me good, but the enemy have made a law that it hurts me to go on this drive, and they are trying to enforce it, while I want you to take the opposite stand with God and know that every act I perform in His service does me good. I do not take this drive for recreation but because I want to establish my dominion over mortal mind's antagonistic beliefs."[96]

I at once saw the point she was making and replied to her with encouraging statements of [t]ruth from her own book, and in a few moments every trace of the attack had disappeared and she was herself again, ready to take her departure. Before doing so, however, she said this:

> Mr. Dickey, I want you to see what we have done. We have routed the enemy and broken the belief that it injured me to go on this drive. Now take this lesson to yourself, and whenever anything happens to you of an unfortunate nature, do not admit anything on the wrong side, but instantly declare that the experience does you good. Even if you should fall down and break your leg, get up and say, "I am the better for this experience." This is the [t]ruth as God would declare it, for every attempt of evil, when surmounted and destroyed, helps the one who is attacked, and your quick and right declaration to the effect that, instead of harming you, it has done you good, breaks the claim of evil, and you become a law to yourself that evil cannot harm you.

Generosity and a sense of humor

A more generous person than Mrs. Eddy, I never knew. Our Leader loved to share what she had with others. When people sent her beautiful flowers, it was a rare thing for them to remain on her desk very long. Her thought seemed to be that in passing these gifts along she was making them do double service and distributing the love and joy that their presence brought.

To the students who were close to her, she frequently made gifts of money or some valuable article of jewelry, rings, pins, and so on. It just seemed to be her nature to want to give, and it was an inclination that she did not attempt to curb. Many times her monetary gifts were quite substantial. This characteristic of giving followed Mrs. Eddy from early years. She told me that when she was a child, she used to give away her playthings to poor children, and sometimes even her dresses, until her mother had to threaten her saying that she would have to punish her if she did not stop giving away her belongings.

When the little book of poems, in the white and gold with the wild rose design, first appeared, it was privately printed by our Leader, and the copies were sent to Chestnut Hill. These were received as usual at the secretary's office, and I immediately carried in one of the books for our Leader to see. At once she asked me to read something from it. I opened to the poem called "Constancy" and read it.[97] When I had finished reading, I looked up and saw that tears were streaming down her cheeks. "Mr. Dickey," she said feelingly, "that was written after I lost my husband." Then she autographed the first copy, numbering it "1," and gave it to me.

Not only in little things but also in more important directions, Mrs. Eddy showed her generosity. She was a constant contributor, through Mr. Frye, to various charitable institutions, and the callers at her home asking for such contributions were very numerous. Sometimes her generosity was imposed upon. At one time Mrs. Eddy received an invitation from the promoters of the Lincoln memorial in Washington to join as a founder.[98] The invitation solicited a subscription to the cost of the Memorial and stated that contributions were being made by the most prominent citizens of our country. It was beautifully engraved, and when I took it to Mrs. Eddy, she asked me what I thought about it all. I said, "Mother, I think people should be constructing a memorial to you and your work instead of your contributing to anything of this kind for somebody else." "Yes, Mr. Dickey," she replied, "but these things are needed in the world today, and it is natural for the citizens of the United States to recognize the greatness and grandeur of Abraham Lincoln's character. I shall send them a check for one hundred dollars." And she did so. That is the way she followed my advice.

From what has previously been said, the reader must not think that there was never anything but work of a strenuous kind at Chestnut Hill. There were days, and even weeks, when the clouds seemed to lift and the workers in the home had time for self-advancement and even for some little recreation. Mrs. Eddy was naturally of a bright and vivacious disposition. She had a wonderfully keen sense of humor and never failed to see that side of an incident. Even while she was stimulating and admonishing her workers to better efforts, sometimes the serious look on their faces would bring forth a smile on her part. Even in the midst of the most serious admonition, she would with difficulty restrain a smile, and I could see by the twitching of her lips that she saw the funny side of the situation and was amused within herself at the protestations and promises of better work on the part of her students.

Following God's lead

One of the chief characteristics displayed by Mrs. Eddy was her accuracy in everything she undertook. She left nothing unfinished or uncertain but carried everything out with most painstaking exactness. She was unusually careful in her choice of words and would many times hold a letter for hours, refusing to allow it to go out until she had found the exact word to express her meaning. Sometimes two or three different dictionaries would be consulted, and then after the letter had been changed several times, she would recall it and make still another change. On these occasions, which were numerous, she would apologize to her secretary and say, "Mr. Dickey, won't you forgive me if I ask you to bring that letter to me again?" I always assured her that I was perfectly delighted to make every change she suggested, for I always saw the improvement in what she was giving out. It was no task for me to write a letter for her, and the mere circumstance of coming into her room in response to her bell was always a joy to me. Frequently she would quote that well-known phrase attributed to Michelangelo, "Trifles make perfection, but perfection is no trifle."[99]

Shortly after the completion of The Mother Church Extension, the Directors obtained Mrs. Eddy's permission to place a marble statue of a woman kneeling in an attitude of prayer on a pedestal above the organ in The Mother Church. When the statue was completed, the Directors wrote Mrs. Eddy to that effect, stating that they would like to have her final permission to have the statue placed in position. In reply to this letter, she wrote declining to give her consent. When it was explained to her that the statue had been ordered with her permission, and that the Directors felt under obligation to take it, this brought forth from her a very decisive letter which ended the incident, and the statue never appeared.[100]

While the letter was being prepared she made several changes in it, each one being an improvement on the former phrasing. After the letter had been finished, and even signed by her, she called me back again, and said, "Mr. Dickey, I must apologize to you for calling you so frequently and troubling you so much, but won't you kindly bring that letter back to me?" I responded quickly and eagerly. Taking the letter, she glanced over it, drew her pencil through a word and replaced it with another. "There," she said with a triumphant smile, "that is exactly what I want to say." I took the letter from her to rewrite it, but before I could turn around, she reached forward and took it from my fingers, and placing it on her tablet she wrote the following words across the top of the letter: "Remember that the so-called human mind is expected to increase in wisdom until it disappears and Divine Mind is seen to be the only Mind."

"There," she said, "you may have that."

Mrs. Eddy realized that what was disturbing the Directors was the fact that she had changed her mind about something that they had considered quite important, but it seems that the changing of her mind was a privilege that our Leader reserved for herself, and she exercised it without any regard whatever for what had gone before or what had been said. She declared, "Is a leader any less a leader because she changes her mind?"

Then she said to me, "Mr. Dickey, people say I am changeable—that I change my mind frequently." Then she added this in a most significant way:

> I do change my mind frequently, but
> when I do, it is always God that changes me.
> Sometimes I will be headed in one direc-
> tion, like a weather vane, and will stay that
> way for several days. The next time you see
> me, I will have turned completely around
> and am going the other way, but in the
> meantime God has given me additional
> light and has led me to make the change.
> There have been times in working out a
> problem when I have not known just what
> step to take, and finding it necessary to
> make a move of some sort, I have taken a
> step as nearly as I could in the right direc-
> tion. Perhaps I would find out shortly that
> it was wrong, but this step gave me a new
> point of view that I would not have had,
> had I not taken it as I did. I would not
> condemn myself, therefore, for what seemed
> to be a mistake but would include it as
> part of the working out of the problem.

This thought, as expressed by our Leader, reminds me of an incident that took place sometime afterward. The Committee on Publication for The Mother Church[101] was preparing a very elaborate statement showing the differ-ence between Christian Science and a phase of Christian psychology, so-called. He sent his article to Mrs. Eddy for her approval. It passed through my hands, and I took it to her, stating that the author wished to issue this in printed form for extensive circulation. Without a moment's hesitation, she said, "No, that is not the thing for him to do. Tell him that I say to publish his article in one of the well-known daily newspapers and then await the result." I returned with her message to the Committee, and he remarked in a very loving way that he thought Mrs. Eddy had not seen the situation from his point of view and again expressed the hope that she would give her consent to his printing the article as he at first planned.

When I brought his proposal to her again, she was most emphatic in her rejection of it. She said, "Mr. Dickey, he is trying to accomplish too much by one bound." Then she said to me, "Did you ever take such a long step that you fell to the ground?" I said, "Yes, Mother, I have." Then she asked, "Would it not have been better if you had taken two steps and retained your equilibrium?" "It most certainly would," I replied. "Now," she continued, "this student is trying to do something at one step, which is not right, and I want him to do it as I first suggested. Please tell him again to publish this in a daily paper with a large circulation, and then leave it in the hands of God. He may never have to take another step." Again I communicated with the Committee, and he gladly accepted our Leader's proposal. The outcome was that the whole thing was settled as she predicted, and nothing more was heard on the subject.

Accuracy demanded in stating truth

In reference to Mrs. Eddy's exactness in her statements of Science, and her requirement that those about her should be exact in their statements also, I recall that she put a high value on the verbal utterances of a practitioner and usually preferred that the mental workers should make their statements audibly. If there was any flaw in their work, she could instantly detect it and set the student on the right track. A carelessly worded treatment bespeaks a careless or indifferent thought, and any form of carelessness or inexactness of thought or expression was quickly corrected by our Leader. On one occasion when she was in need of encouragement, I said to her, "Mother, you cannot have a return of an old belief." Up came the warning hand: "Don't put it that way," she said. "At one time I had a belief of excellent health, and your declaration, if carried out, would prevent me from expressing that belief of health, and that is what I am striving for." So I promised her I would never again be so careless. What I should have said was "diseased belief"—that error and mental malpractice could not cause the return of a diseased belief—or "You cannot be made to suffer from a law of malpractice declaring that you shall have a return of an old belief of sickness."

Upon another occasion, when our Leader was having trouble with her throat, she called me in to help her. At once I saw that the belief was that there was a gathering of phlegm in her throat, and I began to declare that mortal mind could not create and that there was no such thing as phlegm in her throat. She stopped me at once and said, "Do not say that; there is a natural and normal secretion of phlegm in the throat, and if we declare against that, we are likely to interfere with the natural function of the glands of the throat." Then I changed the statement and said, "There is and there can be no such thing as an abnormal secretion of phlegm in your throat." This she approved.

I remember that on one occasion when a student in Mrs. Eddy's house was corrected because of an unscientific statement she [had] made, Mrs. Eddy called her severely to account for her work in the presence of a number of others who were at that time under Mrs. Eddy's instruction. The student [Laura Sargent] began to cry and said, "I don't like you to talk to me like that; I want you to love me." Mrs. Eddy replied, "I do love you and that is the reason why I am talking to you in this way. If I did not love you, I would not take the time to correct you. It is because I want to have you be right and do right that I am correcting you."

Others' proposed changes to *Science and Health*

By reason of the fact that much of what our Leader has written conflicts with the general thought of mankind, many people wrote letters to Mrs. Eddy suggesting that she change her books in various places and improve them by adopting the suggestions of her correspondents. Here again, our Leader's determination to be guided by divine wisdom alone showed itself. One of her marked characteristics was that she rarely allowed anybody to criticize any of her writings or call attention to what he considered an inappropriate expression. There were occasions, however, when Mrs. Eddy did make changes in *Science and Health* at the suggestion of others, but these were the exception and not the rule.

One of the many proposals which came to her was a letter from her publisher, Mr. Allison V. Stewart, advising Mrs. Eddy that a correspondent had called his attention to her use of the word *hecatombs*, where she speaks of "hecatombs of gushing theories" on page 367 of *Science and Health*. I confirmed Mr.

Stewart's definition of the word by consulting the dictionary, where it defined *hecatomb* as "a sacrifice of the slaughter of one hundred cattle or oxen at the same time." It seemed at that time to me that this criticism was well founded, and when Mrs. Eddy received her mail on that day, I included this letter, which had in it a recommendation that our Leader use some other word, but the moment I presented it to her, her visage changed and instantly she said, "No, Mr. Dickey, I will make no alteration in that word. People do not always understand my sense of humor. This statement is used in a sense of ridicule. The word conveys exactly the sense I wish to present—namely, that a great slaughter of gushing theories, stereotyped borrowed speeches, and the doling of arguments are but so many parodies on legitimate Christian Science." Afterward, in further investigating the meaning of this word, I found that a well-known dictionary defines it as "a great slaughter." It was then quite clear to me that our Leader's version was upheld and that no change should be made in the word.

A Christian Science healer, who was formerly a practicing physician, wrote me a letter in which he stated that Mrs. Eddy had not employed the right use of the word *cicatrized* on page 162 of *Science and Health*, where she formerly stated "cicatrized joints have been made supple." He said *ankylosed* was the proper word and, no doubt, this is what our Leader meant. I showed the letter to her, and she demurred at making the change, but after a careful inspection of the dictionary, she allowed the change to be made.[102] She explained to me that she had used the word *cicatrized* purely from memory without investigating its real meaning, and she expressed gratitude for having had this called to her attention.

A letter received from a lady in England called attention to a statement made by Mrs. Eddy in *Miscellaneous Writings: 1883–1896* in reply to an English critic (see pp. 294–297). She referred to him as a "beer-bulged, surly censor," and my correspondent thought it was unkind for Mrs. Eddy to use the [term] *beer-bulged*, as it seemed to her like employing an epithet, when Christian Scientists should express nothing but love. Mrs. Eddy did not like the tone of the letter, nor the suggestion contained therein, but nevertheless the criticism did appeal to our Leader, and she revised the article, leaving out the [term] in question.

A painstaking revision process

Mrs. Eddy used to make slight changes from time to time in *Science and Health*. She was a constant student of her own writings, and after reading a passage, if it seemed to her that it could be illuminated or made plainer by some slight alteration, she would make it. These alterations, like everything else that emanated from Mrs. Eddy's pen, were most carefully handled, and great pains were taken to see that everything was just as she expressed it.

During the first part of my stay with her, these changes were handled by Mr. Frye, but later on they passed through my hands. Our Leader would first make the change in lead pencil in her book; then a letter was prepared to Mr. Stewart, her publisher, requesting that the change be made. This letter was signed by Mrs. Eddy, as her publisher would under no circumstances make any alteration in her books except in response to a direct request from her. The proposed change was then sent to the printer and a proof sheet made, which was in turn sent to our Leader for her approval. After this was obtained, the order was put through for a change in the plates, and when this was done, Mrs. Eddy was notified that the final arrangements were completed, and then the editions containing the change were issued. I am giving this detail in order that the reader may know how much care was exercised whenever a change was to be made in *Science and Health*.

Upon one occasion our Leader called me to her study, and I found that she and Laura Sargent were discussing an alteration in *Science and Health* that Mrs. Eddy had just proposed. They both seemed quite pleased with the change and asked me what I thought of it. I said at once that I thought it clarified the meaning of the text. The change was made at the top of page 503 in the chapter "Genesis." Our Leader had with her pencil erased the word *unfolding* in [the first] line and substituted the word *reflection*, and instead of the word *reflected* in the third line, she used the word *unfolding*, making the text read, "This creation consists of the reflection of spiritual ideas and their identities, which are embraced in the infinite Mind and forever unfolding."

After expressing my pleasure at the contemplated change, I left the room and afterwards looked for this alteration in subsequent editions of the book, but for some reason, unknown to me, the change never appeared. This particular work was not at that time under my care, and it may be that our Leader decided later to leave the text as it stood, but whatever was done I am sure was with her sanction and approval.

No lesser degree of care was exercised in all articles prepared by Mrs. Eddy for publication. There were many letters received by her from students in the Field, which she read with a great deal of pleasure. I found that, in her isolated position, she came in very little contact with the outside Field, and only through the avenue opened by these letters to our Leader, did she come in touch with the individual workers. These letters, usually expressing the gratitude of someone who had been healed or rescued from a critical situation in which mortal mind had placed the writer, were always read by Mrs. Eddy with pleasure and interest. If she wanted a letter published, she turned the page over and wrote "Eddy" across the back. Sometimes she would write, "Publish this," but these letters were always carefully scrutinized by her, and whenever she wrote her name across the back or across the letter, it indicated that the editor was at liberty to use it in his make-up of the *Sentinel*.

Preserving anonymity

One morning after she had called the class[103] into her room, she opened *Science and Health* at random to page 221 and began to read at [the first] line.[104] In a moment she paused, looked up at the class smilingly, and said, "Perhaps you will be interested to know that I am the woman who adopted that system." This was quite a surprise to us all. But she very quickly passed the incident by and made no further remarks in explanation of it. I learned afterward that in her first edition of *Science and Health*, referring to this same illustration, she used the editorial "we," thereby indicating that she herself was the person referred to. In subsequent editions, however, she spoke of "knowing a woman who when quite a child," and so forth. A short while after the above [class] took place, she called me into her room and proceeded to change the text of *Science and Health* so that instead of "I knew a woman who when quite a child," and so on, it read, "I knew a person who when quite a child," and so forth. All through this page, 221, and the following page, she changed the pronoun so that in each instance it referred to the person. Then with a very knowing smile, she handed me these changes and asked me to send them to her publisher and have them executed in *Science and Health*. I saw clearly at once why she made the change; it was because she thought in telling five or six persons that she was the individual referred to, she had to a greater or less extent liberated this information in human thought and that it might become knowledge that it was she herself who was referred to. This did not suit her, and she at once made the changes on these two pages so as to turn the thought of mortal mind away from herself.

Finding the right words

On one occasion Mrs. Eddy called me into her room, and I found her considering a change in the title of her book *Science and Health*. Instead of having it *Science and Health with Key to the Scriptures*, she proposed making it read *Science and Health, Key to the Scriptures*. She asked me what I thought of the idea and if I understood the import of it. I told her that I did indeed and that I thought it would be a splendid change as it would at once convey to people the thought that her whole book was the "key" which unlocked the Scriptures, and not [only] chapters 15, 16, and 17, as would appear from the inscription "Key to the Scriptures" found on page 499.

Mrs. Eddy was quite pleased with the idea and spoke favorably of it. She talked it over with her publisher and explained that she would like to make this change in the title of her book, provided it did not conflict in any way with her copyrights. Mr. Stewart, her publisher at that time, made inquiry from Mrs. Eddy's Boston lawyers, and the word came back that they would not advise her to do this as it might materially affect the copyrights of her book. Thus our Leader abandoned one of the inspired thoughts that came to her and would have enlarged considerably the thought of all Christian Scientists regarding her book *Science and Health*. I shall always look on the whole book as "Key to the Scriptures," as I am sure she desired that Christian Scientists should do.

On one occasion she was looking through the *Christian Science Hymnal,* where her poem "The Mother's Evening Prayer" is set to music. She made a change in the words "mother finds her home and far-off rest" by erasing *far-off* and inserting the word *heavenly*, as it now reads. She asked me what I thought of the change. I told her that to me it conveyed a much better thought. I said that "her home and far-off rest" carried the impression that she had a long and toilsome way ahead of her. She said, "That is just the thing I want to get rid of."

At one time there went out by mistake to the Field the impression that the first edition of *Science and Health* had been called in. In opening the mail one morning, I came upon a copy sent in by a woman responding to what she supposed was a call for the book and enclosing a beautiful note. I carried both the package and the note in to Mrs. Eddy. She took the book in her hands, opened it, read a few lines, turned the leaves fondly, read again for a little, and as she did so, I could see that past experiences were filling her thought. If ever you have seen a mother take down from a shelf or cupboard the first little shoes her baby wore and fondly touch them with love in her eyes, you can imagine how Mrs. Eddy appeared when she looked at that book. At length she closed it slowly, gently, and, placing it in my hand again, said with deepest feeling and tears in her eyes, "Take it, and put it away, Mr. Dickey—no one will ever know what it has cost me to write that book."

Twilight conversations

If our Leader had any favorite hour in the day, I think it was after the evening meal, at twilight, when she loved to sit quietly in her room and gaze from her window at the lengthening shadows. She invited me to come in at this hour whenever my work permitted me to do so, and on these occasions she always extended a greeting hand and asked me to sit down beside her. Often she told me many things of interest in her life. We had bright electric lights installed on the gateposts where her driveway entered the street, and she would sometimes make remarks about the vehicles that passed her residence. It might seem that these were idle thoughts for the Leader of a great movement and that such commonplace things as the traffic that passed her door could be of no possible interest to the Discoverer and Founder of Christian Science, but when we consider that Mrs. Eddy virtually lived in three rooms and seldom, if ever, gave any thought to the simple activities of the world about her, she might be excused for indulging in such trifles. She used to sit in her chair beside her desk, with her own room darkened so that she could better see what was going on outside. At her elbow on her desk was a tiny clock with a small electric light in front of it so that, when she pushed a button, the dial would be illuminated and she could tell the hour. Our Leader retired early, and it was seldom that she was not in bed by nine o'clock. The watchers were ready to take up their work at that time, and the one who covered from nine to eleven usually sat in her study outside of her bedroom door.

Rousing a lifeless worker

One evening, shortly after Mrs. Eddy had retired, Mrs. Sargent came to my door in great trepidation, informing me that she had found Calvin Frye unconscious on the lounge in his room and that she had been unable to arouse him. I hurriedly accompanied her and found Mr. Frye stretched on the lounge in a most uncomfortable attitude, speechless and eyes closed, apparently breathless and with no pulse or indication of life whatever. We continued our efforts to arouse him but with no success. We called to him, shook him, and used every means at our command. Finally another worker came in and united his efforts with ours, but we could gain no response of any kind in our efforts to call Mr. Frye back. We hesitated about letting our Leader know of his condition, but we saw that inasmuch as we were making no headway, we must inform her of the circumstances.

This was done by Mrs. Sargent. Mrs. Eddy was in bed, but she hurriedly rang her bell for her maid and started to arise and dress herself when she was seized with a sudden determination and, dropping back into bed, she said, "I cannot wait to dress. Bring him to me." Mrs. Sargent said, "But, Mother, he is unconscious. We cannot rouse him." She said, "Bring him to me at once." On receiving this instruction, the one who had come to our aid lifted the senseless form of Calvin Frye and placed him in a low rocking chair. Then we dragged him around through the hall, through Mrs. Eddy's study, into her bedroom. She sat up in bed with a shawl or some kind of a robe over her shoulders, and we drew Mr. Frye right up to her side where she could both touch and speak to him. It was an interesting moment. The workers stood around the small room and watched the proceedings. Our Leader reached out her hand and placed it upon Mr. Frye's shoulder and addressed him in a loud voice: "Calvin, Calvin, wake up. It is Mother who is calling you. Wake up, Calvin, this Cause needs you, Mother needs you, and you must not leave. Calvin, Calvin, wake up. Disappoint your enemies. You shall not go. I need you here. Disappoint your enemies, Calvin, and awake."

All this time Mr. Frye's head was hanging limp on his shoulder. I had hold of the back of the rocking chair in which we had placed him to steady him. I placed my hand on his head to lift it up. Mrs. Eddy instantly stopped me and said, "Do not touch him. Leave him entirely to me." Again, she repeated her calls to him to arouse himself and remain with her. It was now something like half an hour since Calvin had first been found, and while those who were looking on at our Leader's efforts to arouse him had not the slightest doubt that she would succeed in awakening him, yet the time seemed to pass without any appreciable response to her work. This did not discourage her. She redoubled her efforts and fairly shouted to Mr. Frye her commands that he awake. In a moment he raised his head and drew a long, deep breath. After this his respiration became regular, and he was restored to consciousness. The first words he uttered were, "I don't want to stay. I want to go." Mrs. Eddy paused in her efforts and, turning her gaze to the workers around the room, said, "Just listen to that." She again turned to Mr. Frye and in her commanding tones insisted that he awake and remain here.

Never shall I forget the picture that was before us in that small bedroom, the light shining on the half-scared faces of the workers, and our Leader's intense determination to keep Mr. Frye with her. I had heard of similar occasions when rumors had reached the workers in the Field that at different times our Leader had restored prominent students to life after experiences of this kind, but of this incident I was an eyewitness, and from the very first my attention was not diverted for one second from what was going on. I am simply relating this event exactly as it occurred.

It had been rumored that Mrs. Eddy's power of healing was lost, but those who were present on this occasion have a different story to tell. Our Leader rose to the occasion like a giant, and in commanding tones she demanded that her servant should live, and he responded. When Mr. Frye became fully conscious, she turned him over to one of the workers who remained with him through the night. The next morning he was about his accustomed duties. Not one in the house that I know of said anything to Mr. Frye concerning his experience. We do not know whether he realized how far he had gone or whether, indeed, he knew of the work that had been done for him. No questions were asked him as we felt it would not be well to recite the experience to him, but the fact remains that Calvin Frye had passed through what mortal mind calls "death," and the grave had been cheated of its victim by our Leader's quick and effective work.

Leading by divine direction

Frequently our Leader was called upon to make a decision of great importance at a moment's notice that would perhaps affect the future of her Cause for years. She seemed rarely to weigh in her thought what the consequence of her action might be. Her sole desire was to get the [d]ivine leading and follow that unhesitatingly. Often the reasons for which our Leader took action in certain directions were not clear to the workers about her. It would seem as if the reason advanced by her was a poor one and not worthy of the action she was taking. This, of course, was mortal mind's analysis of her work, and if she were acting from a spiritual impulse, it is not at all surprising that her reasons would not appeal to the judgment of onlookers. It always turned out, however, that her action was right, regardless of the reason assigned, which convinced those who were familiar with her work that her judgment was unerring in every detail and that in following the direction of divine wisdom, she never made a mistake. Often I heard her say with great impressiveness that in over forty years of church leadership, she had not made a mistake, a record that is most truly remarkable.

Mrs. Eddy's ideas of church government differed greatly from those of the general run of mankind. She knew that her Church, established as it was under divine direction, would incur the hatred and opposition of every known form of religion which has been evolved according to the wisdom of man. In order to be perpetuated, her Church must necessarily follow divine inspiration and not be the product of legal enactments or worldly wise evolutions. She told me that every government, every organization, every institution of whatever kind or nature, to be successful, must have one responsible head.

This is why she placed herself at the head of her own Church—because mortal mind could not be trusted to conduct it. This is why she did away with First Members, and later Executive Members,[105] for to place enactments of holy inspiration in the hands of groups of individuals was to incur the possibility of the divine idea being lost sight of and human wisdom taking its place. This is also why she reduced the authority of the conduct of The Mother Church into the narrowest possible compass. Indeed, she told me with pathos and earnestness that if she could find one individual who was spiritually equipped, she would immediately place him at the head of her church government. Asking me to take a pencil, she slowly dictated the following as I wrote it down: "I prayed God day and night to show me how to form my Church and how to go on with it. I understand that He showed me, just as I understand He showed me Christian Science, and no human being ever showed me Christian Science. Then I have no right or desire to change what God has directed me to do, and it remains for the Church to obey it. What has prospered this Church for thirty years will continue to keep it."

It was her child, her offspring; and her constant concern, day and night, was what was to become of this Cause. Those of her followers who were present in her home can testify to her anxious thought in this direction. On several occasions, when she was trying to get her followers to see the import of this and what it meant, she would say, with a gesture of despair, "What is to become of this Cause?" And again, when troubled about the future of the Cause, she would say, "If error can do this to me, what is it going to do to you?" She saw the possibility of future attacks of mortal mind upon her beloved Church, and her constant anxiety was for its preservation and future unfoldment.

She told me that she had constantly watched the growth of this Church as would a parent the development of its offspring. She said that in all things while she was the Leader of the Christian Science movement, she actually felt the needs of the movement in her body just as the mother of a young infant would feel the needs of the infant and supply them. Instantly, detecting that I did not receive the full import of what she was telling me, she explained herself by saying that the mother of a young babe always knew by the condition of her breast when her child needed nourishment, and she said that she also felt the same way in regard to the needs of the Christian Science movement. The needs of her Church were frequently met through the enactment of some By-Law, which, though it startled the Christian Science Field, yet it seemed to be the imperative demand of wisdom made upon our Leader. At times these decisions were arrived at after long nights of prayer and struggle.

[One time], when she was wrestling with what seemed to be a physical disturbance, I was trying to help her and in talking over the situation with her, I said, "Mother, you can't be made to feel the effect of mortal mind thought and mortal mind cannot make you feel its argument." At the time she was lying down with closed eyes, but as soon as I made the statement that "mortal mind cannot make you feel its argument," she looked up and, raising her hand in warning, said, "Don't say that, Mr. Dickey." Then she went on in her loving and quiet way to explain that when she was able to feel what mortal mind had in thought, it enabled her to do that thing which was most helpful to the Cause of Christian Science. This, I think, exemplified the loving, self-sacrificing thought of our Leader. She was willing to endure the sufferings mortal mind imposed upon her, for thereby she was enabled to take some action that would be helpful to her Cause. How much we all owe to this dear soul, who thus offered herself as a perpetual sacrifice for the good of humanity, we may never know.

Striving to defend our Leader

At this time there were four mental workers in the house in addition to Mr. Frye, and the hours of the night were divided into four separate watches. The first watch was from 9:00 to 11:00 p.m.; the next, from 11:00 to 1:00 a.m.; the next, from 1:00 to 3:00 and then, from 3:00 until 5:00 in the morning. These watches were assigned to different mental workers, and their task was to counteract the malicious evil influence of mortal mind directed against our Leader and her establishment during their two hours. When a watch was kept, or in other words, when the mental worker was successful in freeing our Leader from attacks during that time, she always knew it, and the one keeping his watch was commended the next day. If the watch was not kept, and they were far more frequently not kept than kept, a corresponding rebuke was administered to the one who [had] failed. This may look like strenuous work, but be it remembered that no one in that household worked half so hard as our Leader did, and we were there to do this work and rejoiced when it was accomplished. It was a constant battle for our Leader even to live in order that she might devote her time and energies to the conduct and welfare of the great Cause which had grown up as a result of her foundational work.

On many occasions all the workers were called in and admonished because of their seeming inability to meet the prevailing conditions. It was our Leader's custom, when she went to her study in the morning, to first open the Bible and read whatever appeared on the page before her. This was apparently done at random, and yet she seemed directed in this work so that the reference on most occasions was particularly fitting to the subject under discussion. One passage especially seemed to thrust itself forward on these occasions. It was Matthew 24, verse 43: "But know this, that if the goodman of the house had known in what watch the thief would come, he would have watched, and would not have suffered his house to be broken up."

One morning after she read this passage to us, our Leader said, "We must watch and pray. Prayer means desire. We can have words without the desire, but that is not prayer. Prayer must have no selfishness in it. Hanging pictures and arranging furniture for another's pleasure is unselfishness, and to the degree that it is unselfish, it is like God. To be able to dress and adorn oneself beautifully is selfishness. To do it for another is unselfishness." Then she quoted lines 30 to 31 on page 192 of *Science and Health*: "Whatever holds human thought in line with unselfed love, receives directly the divine power."

The importance of watching

At [another] time, when we were all called into her room, she [spoke of those who didn't last as her employees]:

This matter of students coming here
for a few days and then going away and
proclaiming what wonderful things they
have learned is a menace to the Cause.
When they learn anything, they stay here.
They are not sent away. When they are sent
away and give out the idea that they know
so much, they are overreaching themselves
and deceiving others. Where all students
have failed is in not knowing how to handle
animal magnetism. If we don't break
the belief that mesmerism has power, we
are still the victims of mesmerism, and
it is handling us. Now then, the main
point is to keep your watch. Keep your
watch. Jesus said, "Could ye not watch
with me one hour?"(Matthew 26:40)

Then again she quoted, "If the goodman of the house had
known in what watch the thief would come, he would have
watched."

"If you can defeat the mesmerist in this, you can defeat
him in all things," she continued. "He boasts that he can
make a law for you, six months ahead, and then work to cover
every hour in the night. You must break their supposed laws
that they can produce suffering asleep or awake." After a
long talk and many illustrations and admonitions, we were
dismissed. We were all recalled in a few moments and asked,
"Now, what is the great necessity I have been impressing on
you?" I replied, "Demonstration." Others said something
else. She said, "No, you are all wrong. You have missed the

importance of the lesson I have just given you. I felt it and called you back to show you your ignorance. The lesson is this—keep your watch." Then we were dismissed. Shortly we were called back again, and she said, "What I have to meet, you will all have to meet, now or again. Therefore, know that the mesmerist cannot afflict either you or me with erroneous beliefs." We all solemnly promised to "keep our watch." Our Leader responded, "Amen."

During the course of the talk, she said:

> If you will keep your watch, I shall be a well woman. If you stay here until you learn to handle animal magnetism, I will make healers out of you. I had to do it, and did it for forty years, and you must do it. You must rise to the point where you can destroy the belief in mesmerism, or you will have no Cause. It tried to overcome me for forty years, and I withstood it all. Now it has gotten to the point where the students must take up this work and meet animal magnetism. I cannot do it for you. You must do it for yourselves, and unless it is done, the Cause will perish, and we will go along another 1900 years with the world sunk into the blackest night. Now will you rouse yourselves? You have all the power of God with you to conquer this lie of mesmerism. The workers in the Field are not healing because they are not meeting animal magnetism which says they cannot heal.

Then she turned to each one and said, "Will you keep your watch?" They all answered, "Yes." She turned to me and said, "Mr. Dickey, will you keep your watch?" I said, "Yes, Mother, I will." She leaned forward in her chair and took my hand in hers, and I knew from the pressure, as well as the look she gave, she knew I would keep my watch. In explanation she said, "To keep your watch doesn't only mean to be awake at that hour and be working mentally. It means to do the work and succeed in breaking the mesmerism for the two hours assigned. If you don't succeed, you haven't kept your watch."

At another time she said, "There is a new form of sin or malpractice that has been revealed to me that nobody has ever discovered before, and that is that evil is trying to produce sudden death in sleep. The serpent typifies evil, and the moccasin snake will lie right beside a person who is awake and never touch him, but as soon as he falls asleep, he will attack."

I have been trying to record many of our Leader's words as nearly verbatim as possible, but I am unable to record more than a small portion of her sayings. The one thing she has impressed on her students is that they must handle animal magnetism and defeat the mental murderer and mental assassin who are working to defeat this Cause.

A lifetime of watching and praying

When Mary Baker was still a very young child, perhaps not over eight years of age, she was a close and devoted student of the Bible. Her mother used to read to her the story of Daniel and how he prayed three times a day with his window open toward Jerusalem. This made such an impression upon the child that she also decided to pray every day to God—not only three times but seven times. She knelt before God and poured out her little soul to Him in prayer, and in order to be free and uninterrupted in this devotional work, she would leave the house and retire to the woodshed, where she could be alone, and there she knelt and prayed seven times, daily. In order that she might not fail in fulfilling her obligation, she kept a small piece of chalk and marked on the side of the shed each time so that she might not miss even one of the seven prayers she had obligated herself to make.

As Mrs. Eddy related this incident to me, her whole face lightened with a joyous expression, and she said, "Just think of that little tot praying seven times a day and making a record of each prayer so that she would not miss one! Did ever you see or hear of such a thing!" I assured her that I had not, and as I talked with her about it and expressed my pleasure in hearing of the incident, I said, "That is very characteristic of the devotion that many of us have seen you display in your work as Leader of the Christian Science movement." She replied, "Yes, I have always been devoted to what I had in hand and considered that everything I did to forward this movement was an obligation to God that had to be sincerely kept."

M. ADELAIDE STILL *(1873–1964)*

*A native of England, Adelaide Still grew up in a working
class family. She stopped attending school in her early
teen years and entered domestic service. At age 15, she
joined the Congregational church, where she learned
about Christian Science from the teacher of her Bible
class. Still bought* Science and Health with Key to
the Scriptures *in 1900 and took Primary class with E.
Blanche Ward the following year. In 1906, Still moved
to the United States. After approximately a year as a
nursemaid for a Christian Science family, she began
serving in Mary Baker Eddy's household in 1907—initially
as a housekeeper and then as Eddy's personal maid.*

*After Eddy passed on in 1910, Still stayed on as a
caretaker of the Chestnut Hill home and a companion to
Laura Sargent, who lived there until her passing in 1915.
Still found her association with Sargent instructive and
uplifting, as this comment in 1940 demonstrates:*

I helped Mrs. Sargent by looking up references, typing up notes, etc., while she was preparing to teach the Normal class in 1913, and had a very happy time doing it. . . . I think I gained almost as much as the students who were in the class. Next to the privilege of serving our beloved Leader, I consider that of my close association with Laura Sargent, and I am very grateful for the years in our Leader's home both before and after her passing.

Still left the Chestnut Hill home in 1918 and worked for a while in the Treasurer's Office of The Mother Church. Many of her residences from this point on were quite close to The Mother Church. In 1960, while living on Norway Street, she wrote, "My window looks out on the Church Park and it is beautiful. I am grateful for it."

My Years in Mrs. Eddy's Home

M. ADELAIDE STILL

To understand Mrs. Eddy's life and experiences, it seems necessary to take into consideration something of the different states of consciousness that she seemed to manifest. Many students think that because she reached the mountaintop where she could receive the revelation of Divine Science, she must have remained there most of the time, just speaking the word and all error melt[ing] before her. A study of her writings shows this to be a misapprehension. She repeatedly tells of the struggles she had in teaching and establishing and founding the Cause. She told us that she found herself on the mount of revelation where all was good [and] there was no evil to her consciousness, but she did not know how she got there. In order that the revelation should be proved practical in redeeming mankind, she had to come down from this mount and seek the way to demonstrate it daily. Her discovery did not work out her problem for her; she had to take every step in proving the Science for herself, as well as blazing the trail for those following in her footsteps.

Through her intense longing to know God, through the spirituality of her thought, had come her first healing. Then, through her consecration in studying the Scriptures and searching diligently for Truth, she found the underlying law governing the healing and learned how to turn her thought away from material sense—how to enter the "Holy of Holies" and to claim and prove the omnipotence and omnipresence of divine Love, both for herself and others. This true consciousness enabled her to become the Leader, and through absolute reliance on God, she manifested the marvelous wisdom and foresight in establishing the Cause [that] has protected and guided it hitherto and will continue to protect and guide it through all the ages in proportion to the consecration and obedience of Christian Scientists to Mrs. Eddy's teachings. Through this state of consciousness, she rebuked and awakened her students both in the home and in the Field, stirred them to greater spiritual activity, and often showed a wonderful prescience and wisdom.

Mrs. Eddy's ongoing spiritual growth

This does not mean that there was no human self to "be evangelized" (*Science and Health with Key to the Scriptures*, p. 254). Just as with the rest of the human race, many of the traits, opinions, likes, and dislikes that she manifested were the results of early environment, education, and experience. She told us that as a little child she could not sleep until she had put her shoes straight, and if her mother got a plait in her dress when she was ironing it, she (Mary) would go away and cry about it. Her early training also gave her a great sense of economy. She told us that one day her brothers and sisters were popping corn and dropped a few grains on the hearth. After they had gone, her mother called her and said, "Mary, you pick those up; there is enough there to keep a little chicken alive."

Sometime, the human will be wiped out by the divine, and only the perfect will remain, but until we are ready for this, it seems necessary to give something of the human, if only to encourage us to press on in the battle. If Mrs. Eddy had not found that "the currents of human nature rush in against the right course" (*Miscellaneous Writings: 1883–1896*, p. 212), could she have given us the multiplied instructions contained in her books? Had she not learned through experience that "the human struggles against the divine, up to a point of discovery," could she have shown the weary ones how to overcome animal magnetism and to prove "the impotence of evil, and the omnipotence of good" (*Miscellaneous Writings*, p. 121)?

St. Paul says, "But we have this treasure in earthen vessels, that the excellency of the power may be of God, and not of us" (II Cor. 4:7).

In *Miscellaneous Writings*, Mrs. Eddy says, "In every age, the pioneer reformer must pass through a baptism of fire" (p. 213).[106] And on page 12 of *Christian Science versus Pantheism* she says, "The altitude of Christianity openeth, … a door … that he who entereth it may run and not weary, and walk, not wait by the roadside, — yea, pass gently on without the alterative agonies whereby the way-seeker gains and points the path."

That Mrs. Eddy should have stayed with us for so many years after her discovery, that she should have accomplished such a great work as establishing and founding the Cause of Christian Science—manifesting so much wisdom in organizing and building up the Church and in giving its By-Laws for the guidance and protection of its members—is a marvel for which we can never be grateful enough, and which should prove an inspiration to each and every one of her followers. In *Miscellaneous Writings* on page 253, she says, "Do the children of this period dream of the spiritual Mother's sore travail, through the long night, that has opened their eyes to the light of Christian Science?"

In reading these reminiscences, it is well to remember that they record only the last three years of her pilgrimage on this plane [and] that she had passed through many battle-scarred years, which seemed to take their toll of her physical strength so that she required more tenderness and care than in the earlier years. I have tried to give a true account of the things I have recorded as preserved in my own writings and from my recollections, but while many incidents are indelibly impressed on my consciousness, dates and exact wordings may be open to question because of the length of time that has elapsed since their occurrence, although wherever possible I have verified them from the periodicals and have taken every possible care to be accurate.

My young adult years

When I was in my thirteenth year, my father became ill, and as he did not improve, [he] was forced to give up his work a year later when we moved to Bristol, Gloucestershire. It had been my desire to become a schoolteacher, but it was not possible for me to continue my studies, and as there were three younger children, I was compelled to take a position in domestic service. My first reference from the village schoolmaster stated [that] I had "received a most careful home training;" however, I was not fond of housework, and I am afraid I was often a sad trial to some of my employers.

When I was fifteen, circumstances led me into a High Church family, and because I was seeking the truth about God, I yielded to their persuasions and was baptized and confirmed in the Church of England. This was a great trial to my parents, who tried to dissuade me and prayed for me continually. The struggle forced me to reach out to God for a solution of the problem and finally brought a condition of humility, and I yielded, gave up the ritualism, and a few months later applied for membership in the Congregational church at Stapleton Road, Bristol, which my father favored and which he had attended as a young man. Not long after this he passed on, and his passing brought so much trouble, poverty, and unhappiness to the family that I could not understand how God could allow it.

I passed through a number of years of doubt and darkness trying to find God but was never satisfied. In 1898 I went to London to live and then decided to renew my membership in the Congregational church and try to find the truth without bothering about creeds or doctrines. In 1900 our Sunday School teacher introduced Christian Science to the Bible class that my sister and I attended. I was very much interested, and in November of that year, I bought the textbook. In May 1901, I became a member of First Church of Christ, Scientist, London, and in July of the same year studied with Mrs. E. Blanche Ward, C.S.B., by whom I was then employed. In April 1906, the way opened for me to come to the United States. I landed in Boston on May 6, just a month before the dedication of the Extension of The Mother Church.

My first interview with Mrs. Eddy

Mrs. Daisette S. McKenzie was one of the channels through which I came to this country and obtained employment here. At the time she was a member of the Business Committee (see the *Manual of The Mother Church*, Article XXIV, Section 9), part of whose duties was to find helpers for Mrs. Eddy's household.

In the early part of 1907, the Committee, comprised of Mrs. McKenzie, Mr. James Neal, Mr. Thomas Hatten, and Mr. Calvin Hill, was looking for a personal maid for Mrs. Eddy and had two or three interviews with me to see if I would be eligible. Arrangements were made for an interview with our Leader, and I went with Mrs. McKenzie to Pleasant View. Strict secrecy was enjoined upon me. My impression is that this was in February, but of this I am not sure; the ground was covered with snow and the Merrimack River frozen as we passed it on the train. We drove in a sleigh from the station to Pleasant View and arrived there in time for me to see Mrs. Eddy immediately after she came in from her drive. This was the time when she usually saw visitors or prospective employees, although in these later years she did not interview those who were not to come into frequent contact with her.

She was sitting in the tower corner of her study when I was shown in. Mr. Frye placed a chair for me and told me to "speak up." I was there for a few moments only and evidently was not then ready to enter her service. I had tried to do my mental work and to quiet my thought, but to sense there was still much excitement underneath, and the few questions Mrs. Eddy asked me were not what I was prepared to answer. The first one was, "Is there good sleighing in Massachusetts?" She had just come in from a sleigh ride, and it was a perfectly natural question for her to ask, but I knew nothing about sleighing conditions and do not remember what answer I gave. She then said, "How long have you been a practitioner?" I told her I was not a practitioner. She finally said, "Well, I'm sure you are doing good work where you are," and the interview was ended. A few days later I received a letter from a member of the Committee saying that Mr. Frye had written that I was to put the whole thing out of my thought. [Then] the following May someone was needed to help the housekeeper there. Mr. Frye was asked if they should send me, and he replied, "Yes, send her along."

Joining the staff as a housekeeper

The morning that I left Boston for Concord, I spent a little time with Mrs. McKenzie, and as we went down in the elevator from her apartment, I could see that she was thinking deeply, evidently seeking for the right thought to prepare me for the new experience before me. Just before we parted, she said, "Remember, half the world is condemning Mrs. Eddy and the other half is deifying her, and the workers there stand between the two." This came back to me many times after I was in the home and was confronted with some of the problems that came up there. A few days before this, Mr. McKenzie had said to me that it was remarkable that I should have been brought all those miles across the ocean to serve our Leader.

Soon after my arrival at Pleasant View, the question came up as to what I should be called. My first name, Minnie, was used by my family, but this was the name of Mrs. Eddy's cook, who had been with her for a number of years, so I had to choose another. I thought my second name, Adelaide, would be considered too long, so I told them they could call me "Ada," and so it was until 1909, when Mrs. Eddy was going to autograph a copy of *Rudimental Divine Science* for me and I asked her to write my own name in it. She wrote the name, "Minnie A. Still," as I had written it for her, but as she handed me the book, she said, "Why did you let them call you 'Ada'? I'm going to call you by your right name. Which would you rather be called, 'Minnie' or 'Adelaide'?" I told her that I should like "Adelaide," so she called Mrs. Sargent and Mrs. Rathvon and told them to call me "Adelaide." She did not always remember the change, but when she did, I enjoyed hearing her; she had a very pretty way of saying it.

Daily routines in a crowded household

My duties were to do the table work,[107] wash dishes, and help with the cleaning. Those were the days before vacuum cleaners [had been] invented, so we used to tear up damp newspapers into rather small pieces and scatter them on the carpets to catch the dust as it arose from the sweeping.

Everything that love could think of was done to spare Mrs. Eddy any disturbance or change from the usual routine, so her study was cleaned while she was out for her drive, which at that time lasted forty minutes. Three of us would be ready, waiting outside her study door, each with a pail of damp paper, a broom, and a duster, and the moment she left the room, we would go in, each taking a corner to clean. We never failed to have the room in order when she got back. Sometime after the move to Chestnut Hill, the time of her drive was shortened to twenty minutes, but the workers still managed to get her room cleaned and in order by the time she returned, and it was very seldom that she knew which day it was done. However, on a few occasions the desk or chair would not be in quite the right position, so someone, I think it was Mr. Dickey, suggested that we put brass-headed nails in the floor behind the desk and chair to mark their position. The shortness of time for cleaning made it expedient to do all that was possible to avoid mistakes.

Mrs. Eddy retained the customs of her New England training, so her rules for meals in her household were [to serve] breakfast at seven, dinner at twelve, and supper at six. She had given up having her meals in the dining room sometime before I went there, her dinner and supper being served on a tray in her study. For many years her breakfast, consisting of cornmeal mush and milk, was served in her bedroom at six o'clock punctually, but the last year or two she allowed me to bring it an hour later [and] changed breakfast to [just] a glass of milk, fresh from the cow.

Every available space at Pleasant View had to be utilized to accommodate Mrs. Eddy's growing family of helpers. Spaces in the attic under the rafters were partitioned off for bedrooms, and still there was not enough room, so the cottage, where Mr. August Mann and his family lived and which contained more rooms than they needed, was used [for] overflow. At times someone would come to Concord from Boston almost every day, and it was not unusual for Mr. McLellan or other officials who came on business of

Princess and Dolly at the stable door at Chestnut Hill

the Church to sleep on cots in the parlors or library if they had to stay the night.

The carriage horses at that time were named Princess and Dolly. There was a notice in the stables at Pleasant View saying, "Always speak to the horses before entering the stalls," and I was told that it was placed there at Mrs. Eddy's request. Mrs. Eddy's thoughtfulness was shown in many small ways such as this, as well as in larger ones. She made it a rule for the secretary to bring up the hods of coal for the cook; it was also his duty to carry Mrs. Eddy's dinner tray up the stairs because the long skirts of those days made it difficult for the women not to step on them.

I learned that the mental workers were called "the watch" or "the watchers" and that it was their duty to take turns day and night working impersonally for the protection of the home and the Leader, and to handle specific questions or problems that might come up for the house or the Cause. At this time the "Next Friends" suit was in progress, and they were working on that.[108] One morning Mrs. Eddy called for the household workers (not "the watch") and talked to them. I was not permitted to go in with the others, but Mrs. Minnie Scott told me Mrs. Eddy said, "During forty years I have had many trials, and when this came up, I was not disturbed. If the world calls me a fool, that does not make me one. The senses say that we dwell in matter, but you know, and I know, that we dwell in Mind."

An unexpected encounter with Mrs. Eddy

Among other things, I was told how exact Mrs. Eddy was and how she often rebuked severely when anything was not right. My first thought was, "I'm glad I didn't become her maid." Then, as a sense of love and gratitude filled my consciousness, I thought, "If she has struggles, she needs loving help more than she would if she always walked over the waves of error, and I'm willing to do anything that God wants me to do."

It was Mrs. Eddy's custom to come downstairs between nine and ten o'clock and to walk through the lower rooms, sometimes calling the housekeeper to rearrange or change the furniture or curtains, but it was not often that she went into the kitchen. We tried not to enter the rooms or disturb her in any way while she was downstairs, but a few mornings after the experience narrated in the last paragraph, I needed to go to the dining room to put away the breakfast dishes, so I said to Anna, the housekeeper, "Do you think Mrs. Eddy is down? It is a little early for her." She said, "No, and you have to put your dishes away anyhow." There were two swinging doors between the kitchen and dining room with a small vestibule between them, and as I opened the one from the kitchen, Mrs. Eddy opened the one from the dining room. She stepped forward, and placing her hand on my arm, looked into my face very searchingly. She then said "Good morning" to me, stepped forward and shook hands with August Mann, who was taking orders for the day's marketing, stepped back, again placed her hand on my arm, and stood there while she spoke to each one in the kitchen. She then went to the library and rang for Mrs. Laura E. Sargent and asked her who it was she saw in the kitchen. Mrs. Sargent told her I had come to help Anna. Mrs. Eddy asked, "Is she a good helper?" and Mrs. Sargent told her that I was.

A few days after she had found me in the kitchen, her maid reminded her that she had served almost the full time required by the *Manual* and that she would like to return to her family. Therefore, when Mrs. Eddy came downstairs that morning, she said, "Who was that whom I saw in the kitchen?" Mrs. McKee gave her my name, and she responded, "You send her to me." When I went to her in the library, she asked who my teacher was and if I came to Science for physical healing. I told her, "No, but because I was hungry to learn the truth about God." She said, "That's right, dear, that is the best motive." The week before there had been a severe storm [that] shook the house so that it seemed as though the wind might take it off its foundations. Mrs. Eddy asked, "Did you see the storm?" When I answered, "Yes, Mrs. Eddy," she said, "You know that it was divine Love that saved us, don't you?" She then said, "Will you be my maid?" I replied, "I should like to, Mrs. Eddy, but I have never done work of that kind." She said, "I know it, dear, but I'll teach you. Now you go back to your work and say nothing to anyone about it, and when I'm ready, I'll send for you." She did not ask me a single question about my material qualifications. As I was leaving the room, she said, "I have been asking God to send me the right one, and I believe that He has." This was a great comfort in later days when things sometimes seemed difficult and error tried to talk to me.

My start as Mrs. Eddy's maid

Two days later, on July 14, 1907, Mrs. Eddy sent for me and said, "I want you to start now." Mrs. McKee stayed on for a day or two to instruct me in my duties. There were many little things to remember, so those who had preceded me had made a list of them, and I found this a great help as I was very anxious to save Mrs. Eddy any unnecessary trouble. The first item on the list was to go to the kitchen, fix her breakfast tray, and take it and a pitcher of hot water to her at six o'clock. I might mention here that the house had only one bathroom, but there was an extra lavatory. However, as was customary at that date, each room was fitted with a washstand and a set of ware; each member of the household had to get his own hot water.

While Mrs. Eddy was eating her breakfast, I got her clothes ready for her to put on, asked which dress she wished to wear, etc. While she was dressing, I dusted her study, keeping on the alert lest she call me, as she frequently did. She dressed her own hair, except for the last touches, and manicured her own nails with a small penknife she kept in her pocket for that purpose. Everything, no matter how small, had its place and was always kept in it. Anything out of place or not quite straight was a sign to her that animal magnetism was governing us and merited, and usually received, a rebuke. When her hair was fixed, I buttoned her shoes and put on her collar—a high-necked one with a jabot attached and fastened at the back with bar pins. Then I would offer her several pieces of jewelry to choose from. Very often she wore a gold chain with a heart shaped locket with a diamond in the center, which was given to her by Calvin A. Frye, and she often spoke of his long, faithful service to her. She told me that her husband Mr. Asa Eddy first interviewed Calvin Frye and employed him to serve her. On special occasions she wore either her diamond cross or crown. She said that this cross was given to her by a patient she had healed, and she always wore a ring which she treasured for the same reason—that it was given in gratitude for healing which came through her treatment in the earlier days.

Calvin Frye's gift to Mrs. Eddy after he had served 22 years

Listening to our Leader's lessons

As soon as Mrs. Eddy was dressed, she went to her chair in the study and opened first her Bible and then her *Science and Health* and read whatever verse or paragraph her eyes first rested upon. She usually read these aloud to [whoever] was in the room with her, sometimes calling the mental workers and giving them a lesson from them. She told me always to be there when she gave these lessons, but the others came in and stood around her, while I stayed in the background. She sometimes asked me afterwards if I [had] heard what she said. When I told her "Yes" and thanked her, she would say, "That's right, dear, you always be here when I teach my class."

The first mornings I made a few notes, which I will give here:

> July 15, 1907. Opened to Romans 14:22: "Hast thou faith? have it to thyself before God. Happy is he that condemneth not himself in that thing which he alloweth." Mrs. Eddy said, "We should allow nothing which we cannot justify. He who sees sin and condemns it not will suffer for it. Can we work out a problem correctly if one figure is not in accord with the principle of mathematics? Can I enter the kingdom of heaven if I allow one sin? Will not that destroy the whole problem?"

Some days later, a student was out gathering flowers at a time when Mrs. Eddy needed him. When he came in, she called all the students together and gave them a lesson from which I made the following notes: "Art thou a Christian Scientist? Then prove it in principle, practice, and demonstration. Is it easy to tell another his fault? Having a good time is not fighting the devil. Having a good time and dwelling in the pleasures of the senses will not bring you into heaven."

After reading the selections and explaining them, she would sit in her chair thinking and praying until nine-thirty, when she went downstairs, as I have previously stated. She had a system of bell calls. If she wanted me, she rang once; twice for Mrs. Sargent; three times for Mr. Frye; and four for the secretary, etc. To call the "watchers," she kept touching the bell—"splurging," she called it—until they came. There was a bell on each floor and one in the kitchen, so no matter where we were, we could hear our call and went as quickly as possible. At eleven or eleven-thirty, she read her morning mail, which the secretary had placed on the desk for her. Her instructions were to bring to her attention only such letters as were necessary or of special interest. From these she selected those she wished to have published in the [*Christian Science*] *Sentinel*.

It was not unusual for her to call the students and give them instruction as to their work on the "watch." She would dictate instructions for the "watchers" to anyone in the room with her and tell her to take them to one of the secretaries and ask him to type a copy for each member of the "watch." Sometimes the instructions were not changed for two or three days; sometimes, several times a day according to the need. Or as I have stated, she often gave the instructions orally.

Mrs. Eddy's evening hours

At six o'clock she had her supper. I have been asked many times if Mrs. Eddy ate meat and have answered that she did not each much at the time I was there, but she did not take a stand against it. She did not drink tea or coffee and did not expect the students in the house to drink it, but if there were workmen who were non-Scientists on the place, she would send word to the cook to make them some coffee, especially if the weather was cold. She ate simple food, never seeming to tire of homemade ice cream and custard pudding, which were served twice a day; also she had a cup of soup both for dinner and supper, cream of tomato being her favorite for some years. Sometimes a little meat for dinner such as liver or squab; for supper, fish hash, creamed toast, or cereal.

She took the time after supper for a little social relaxation. Mr. Frye would sit with her while Mrs. Sargent and I had our supper. She liked to sit in the twilight but had a little clock which had a tiny battery attached. Mr. Frye made a small shade, using a key ring as a base, so that the light was thrown on the face of the clock and she could watch the time. After we came to Chestnut Hill, the students in the house had powerful lights placed on the lamp posts at the gate so she could watch the traffic go by. When I returned from supper, I often found Mr. Frye chatting with her about events or news of the day. At Chestnut Hill Mr. Dickey sometimes took turns with Mr. Frye in sitting with her. She was usually in bed by nine-thirty. Always her *Science and Health* and a pad and pencil were placed on the marble-topped table at the head of her bed, and occasionally she would call us all in after she had retired and give instructions for handling certain phases of error or some special problem which needed solving. Mr. Frye told me that nearly all of *Unity of Good* was dictated between the hours of four and six on cold winter mornings, when he had to wrap a comforter round him to keep from freezing.

Nothing was too unimportant to be done rightly, nor any error small enough to be overlooked. She sometimes quoted this saying attributed to Michelangelo: "Trifles make perfection, but perfection is no trifle." She would not allow us to excuse error. When I tried to give some reason for a mistake, she said, "That's it; talk with the devil." Once, when someone told her she had done her best, she said, "If you had done your best, it would have been right."

Handling threatening weather

On several occasions I saw Mrs. Eddy dispel a storm. The first time was on August 3, 1907, in the late afternoon. The sky was overcast, and it was very dark. Mrs. Eddy sat in her chair in the tower corner of her study, watching the clouds with a smile and a rapt expression on her face. She seemed to be seeing beyond the storm and her present surroundings, and I do not think that she was conscious of my presence. In a few moments the clouds broke and flecked, and the storm was dissolved into its native nothingness. About half an hour later, I took her supper tray to her, and she said to me, "Ada, did you see the sky?" I replied, "Yes, Mrs. Eddy." Then she said, "It (meaning the cloud) never was; God's face was never clouded." This agrees with what another student recorded as having been said by Mrs. Eddy; namely, "When I wanted to dispel a storm, I did not say, 'There is no thunder and no lightning,' but I said, 'God's face is there, and I do see it.'"

Dr. [Lyman] Powell speaks of her calling the students in and asking them if a Christian Scientist could control the weather. I was there but in the background as usual. She asked the question of each one separately, and each one replied, "Yes, Mother." She said, "They *cannot*, but God can." These are the instructions she gave on one occasion for handling the weather:

No surplus electricity.

No destructive winds.

No tornadoes.

No cyclones.

"He sendeth His rain upon the just, and upon the unjust" [see Matthew 5:45]. God makes the weather; mortal mind does not.

Facing a court-appointed examiner

Sometime in August the alienists[109] who were appointed by the judge in the "Next Friends" suit came to examine her. The same malicious element of mortal mind which crucified Jesus and persecuted the early Christians had decreed that our beloved Leader, the Discoverer and Founder of Christian Science, in belief a lady of eighty-six years, should face the ordeal of proving her sanity and that she was capable of taking care of the money which she herself had earned and which had come to her as the result of years of self-sacrificing labor and love in behalf of mankind.

She received them in her study, in her favorite corner with windows all around her, and as we looked at her on that hot summer afternoon, there was no sign of fear expressed; her face was clear, calm, confident, and bright, and I was sure that the moment the opposing lawyer saw her sitting there, he knew he had not a chance of winning his case. The door was wide open during the interview so that the students in the hall could see and hear what was being said. She called me in once or twice to find something for her.

The alienists began by asking her how she discovered Christian Science. She told them about her study of and experiments in homeopathy, but before she got to the principal part of her narrative, they interrupted her to ask questions about investments—whether she preferred stocks or bonds, etc. She answered them intelligently and wisely, and they, being satisfied with her answers, rose to go. She then asked them if they would like to see her "singing machine," which at that time was a comparatively new invention. As soon as they had left the room, she remembered that she had not finished telling them about her discovery of Christian Science, so she told me to ask them to please return to her study. When they complied with her request, she asked them to be seated, and they could not do otherwise than listen to the rest of her story.

On the day that the petitioners left Concord, Mrs. Eddy said to me as I was dressing her for her drive, "What do you think of my two sons, leaving Concord without even coming to see me? How little they love their mother."[110]

Moving to Chestnut Hill

Not long after the withdrawal of the lawsuit, Mrs. Eddy called the "watchers" and told them that she was thinking of moving and would like to be near Boston; I think she expressed a preference for Brookline. Someone was instructed to get photographs and particulars of houses for sale, and we were all told to tell no one about it. Pictures were shown to her of different places, and at last the estate at Chestnut Hill was decided upon. The house was too small for Mrs. Eddy's household, and work was started in

November to enlarge it. Whenever she decided to make any move, Mrs. Eddy wanted it carried through as quickly and as secretly as possible. This was probably to give error less opportunity of circumventing it. Therefore instructions were given to those in charge of the work to proceed as rapidly as possible, and she inquired frequently as to the progress that was being made.

About the first of the year, Mrs. Eddy was told that the house might be ready by the end of January, but as the time drew near, it seemed to those doing the work that this was almost impossible; the plaster had not dried enough for the paper to stay on the walls, and there were many other difficulties to be overcome. Mrs. Eddy kept asking each day how much longer it would be before she could move, and she finally said that she would move on Sunday, January 26, or not at all.

At first, she had not seemed certain whether she wanted to move most of the furnishings or leave them at Pleasant View so that she might return in the summer if she wished. Packers were engaged to pack the more valuable pictures and bric-a-brac; when that was done, we asked her if she wanted the books from the library to go, and she said, "Yes." We kept repeating such questions until practically all but the furniture was ready for removal.

The more personal articles, the table linen and flat silver, were taken to the new house by those who came from Boston on business. Mr. McLellan was then Chairman of the Board of Directors, as well as Editor in Chief of the periodicals. Mr. Calvin Hill was the buyer for the house, and Mr. William B. Johnson was the Clerk of the Church at that time. It was easy for these gentlemen to take a full trunk with them to

Calvin Frye at the front gate of Pleasant View

Boston and bring an empty one back without arousing any suspicion. Thus the secret was kept, and apparently no one suspected that Mrs. Eddy was planning to make the move. Even the relatives of the workers in the home did not know anything about the change until they read it in the Monday papers, the day after we went to Chestnut Hill.

On Sunday, January 26, Mrs. Eddy started as if for her drive at the usual time. Then hacks came up one after the other until all the household were on their way. Mrs. Eddy's carriage went round a longer way so that when she reached the station, we were all on the special train which had been engaged for her, and as soon as she was seated, we started on our journey.

When we arrived at the Chestnut Hill Station, there [were] a carriage and horses (I am under the impression that Princess and Dolly and the carriage had been sent ahead) waiting for Mrs. Eddy, and taxis or hacks for the rest of us so that we were at the door when she arrived.

The day before, reporters from a Boston paper had visited the house and discovered that it was practically ready for occupancy. Discarded Concord papers, which had been used in packing, gave them a clue, and they easily guessed the identity of the owner. Naturally they were anxious to take advantage of the "scoop" and publish the story in the Sunday paper. This publicity was what Mrs. Eddy had tried so carefully to guard against. Mr. McLellan and Mr. Alfred Farlow did all they could to prevent the publication. I was told they stayed at the offices of the editors until two o'clock in the morning and had to promise that if the story was not published, this particular paper should have reporters present at the time of Mrs. Eddy's arrival. Also, I believe the story of her departure was telephoned from Concord after the train left, so a group of men were waiting when she reached the door. Mrs. Eddy at once sensed the situation and said to John Salchow, who was near her carriage, "Can you get me out of this, John?" He said, "Yes, Mother," and picking her up in his arms, carried her up the stairs and sat her in her chair in the study, thus preventing her from being annoyed by an interview right after the journey. The cook had prepared supper for Mrs. Eddy before leaving Concord, so it had only to be warmed, and by the time she went to bed, I had everything in her bureau drawers, etc., in the same order in which they were at Pleasant View.

Adjustments to Chestnut Hill

My one thought was for Mrs. Eddy's comfort, and consequently my first impressions of the new house are hazy. I remember that it seemed very large after the Concord home and that it was terribly hot everywhere. There was a blaze of light from the top of the house to the bottom, and the rooms were filled with flowers to welcome our Leader.

The main part of the house had been remodeled on the same plan as Pleasant View with the tower corner in her study, but some of the Boston students or officials thought that her rooms should be more in accord with her position, so they had asked her if they might make them a little larger than the ones she had been occupying. She gave her consent to this, but when she arrived, she found that her study and bedroom were almost double the size of those she had just left. She had not been consulted about the wallpaper, and instead of a light color, such as she liked, there was a dark paper with a large flowered pattern on it—very handsome but not what she would have chosen. Altogether, the rooms did not seem cozy and homelike, and were a great disappointment to her. At first she scolded those around her for not telling her what was being done, but when we assured her that we knew nothing about it, she sat still, and after a while, as she looked around her, she said, *"Oh, splendid misery, splendid misery."*[111] What made the rooms seem even larger was that the furniture of her old rooms had been duplicated, but no more had been added. When she came into the study the next morning, she looked around her and said, "A *great barn* of a *place*." Then, sitting in her chair, she found that the windows were too high for her to see the drive and the road. This was another trial.

After a few days she asked if there wasn't a suite of rooms where she could go while these rooms were made over. Mr. Frye and the others talked it over, and it was decided that the dressmaker's rooms on the third floor would give her the most privacy, so she was told about them. Then she called the architect, Mr. Beman,[112] told him what she wanted done, and asked if she could have a small elevator put in to connect directly with her rooms. He at first told her that it could not be done without cutting through the beams of the house. She insisted that it could be done, and after further consideration of the plans of the house, he told her that there was just one place where it could go. She said, "There, I *knew* it."

The alterations were made as speedily as possible. That part of the house was partitioned off, and the men worked in three shifts of eight hours each. The study windows were lowered ten inches, and space was taken from the study for the elevator and a stairway to the third floor.

Companionship needed after the move

There is no doubt that a belief of homesickness tried to tempt Mrs. Eddy during the first months after she left Pleasant View. She missed the old scenes, the view, and the familiar houses which she had looked out on for so many years.

She now required me to spend all my time with her during the day and very soon asked Laura Sargent to do the same, although occasionally Mrs. Ella Hoag, and later Mrs. Ella Rathvon, relieved her; but after this, we never left

Illustration of a carriage circling a reservoir near Chestnut Hill

her alone. If one left the room, the other always remained. Even when she had callers, she would tell me to stay in her bedroom with the door open between, and as the visitor left by one door, I would enter by the other. The only exception to this rule was when Mr. Dickey brought her mail to her at two o'clock. Mrs. Sargent and I were free then, unless she rang for me to find something for her and told me to remain. This was sometimes a trial to Mr. Dickey or Mr. McLellan, as they liked me out of the way when business was being transacted.

She grew to love her rooms and her drives around the reservoirs very much. She made it a practice to go into the sitting room at least once a day, and someone would play and sing for her, usually Mrs. Ella Rathvon after she came. On Sundays, and sometimes on other days, Mrs. Eddy would call the students together to join in the singing, and occasionally she would give us a talk on Science. Mr. Rathvon would sometimes keep time with his foot while we were singing, and she would call my attention to it with a smile of amusement. She loved many of the old hymns and songs, some of her favorites being "I Love to Tell the Story," "Wonderful Words of Life," "I'm a Pilgrim, and I'm a Stranger," "Galilee, Sweet Galilee," "The Old Oaken Bucket," and "Comin' Through the Rye," etc. She changed the words in two lines of "Guide Me, Oh Thou Great Jehovah," from "I am *weak*, and Thou art mighty" to "I am *Thine*, and Thou art mighty," and from "Feed me *till I want no more*" to "Feed me *now, and evermore*." Once, when we had been singing "I'm a Pilgrim, and I'm a Stranger," she looked up at me with a smile and said, "I'm not a pilgrim, I'm not a stranger. I can tarry, I can tarry, all the day." One day Mrs. Rathvon had to go to the dentist, so Mrs. Sargent offered to play and sing for her. Mrs. Eddy looked surprised, and said, "Why, I did not know that you *could* play." After a few hymns, Mrs. Sargent looked round and Mrs. Eddy was fast asleep in her chair with a smile on her face. There was a Victrola record of the twenty-third Psalm and the Lord's Prayer, which she liked to hear, and when they were finished, she sometimes said, "Thank you, Mister Man," [referring to the Victrola].

The coachman's passing

Now, let us go back to the first weeks at Chestnut Hill. Mr. August Mann had been left in charge of the Concord estate, so Mrs. Eddy had a new coachman named Burt. (I do not remember his first name.) We had been there only a week or two when one day, as Mrs. Eddy was nearly ready for her drive, I looked out as usual to see if the carriage was at the door. It was not, so I called Mr. Frye. He made investigations and found that no one had seen Burt that day. There were several workmen on the place and one of these had fed the horses, but no one had thought of looking up the coachman, who lived in a cottage on the estate. Some of the students went to the cottage and climbed through the window; they found him lying in bed as if he were peacefully asleep, but he had passed on. His wife was the mental worker for their family, and she had gone to Vermont to arrange about having the furniture brought to their new home. The students worked for a time and then called the medical examiner. He pronounced it heart failure. Mrs. Eddy did not go out that day, but Mr. Dickey, who had been there only a short time, drove her for the next few days until another coachman could be found. Mrs. Eddy called us several times during the next day or two and gave us lessons on this occurrence. One thing she told us was that there was a snake in the East that would not attack while the person was awake. At this time she wrote the statement "Christian Scientists, be a law to yourselves that mental malpractice cannot harm you either when asleep or when awake," and she gave instructions that it should be put in the textbook (*Science and Health*, p. 442). The article "Take Notice," on page 236 of *The First Church of Christ, Scientist, and Miscellany*, confirms this.

Writing and revising

Mrs. Sargent told me that she once asked Mrs. Eddy why she employed Mr. Wiggin to edit and criticize *Science and Health*. She replied that she wanted to see its effect on one who was not a Christian Scientist—wanted to get it where he would pass it. Laura also told me that when he was reading the proof sheets of *Science and Health*, he kept sending back to Mrs. Eddy the pages about Jacob (308 and 309). Each time she would quietly sit down and make some minor changes. At last Mr. Wiggin sent back the proof sheets with "Jacob much better now" written across the back.

I have been told that Mrs. Eddy once wrote [this] to Judge Hanna:

> I have erased your verities because they are spoken *too soon*. Wait for growth. The textbooks contain it all—but so arranged as to require growth before it is spoken by those who have not grown to it....
>
> Wait patiently on the Lord as I wait on students."[113]

Once Mrs. Sargent asked, "Mother, how did you do the wonderful healing when you first discovered Science?" Mrs. Eddy thought for a moment and said, "I just got out of God's way." Mrs. Sargent also told me that one evening Mrs. Eddy called her and said, "See what I've written, Laura." Then she read to her "The Mother's Evening Prayer" [see *Miscellaneous Writings*, p. 389] and told her that it had come to her during the past half hour. Very few changes were made in it.

Mrs. Eddy made revisions in her books right up to the last; most of them were comparatively unimportant in the last years. She would pick up a book from her desk, and if an improvement in a sentence suggested itself to her, she would pencil it in the book, then call Mr. Frye, and tell him to send it to the publisher. Whenever a revision was made, the copy she was using was changed for the new edition as soon as it came out. When the "Next Friends" suit was on, she inserted the words "Materia Medica, Anatomy, Physiology, Hypnotism, and Envy are the next friends of Man," [but] finally erased [them] altogether.

I was very much impressed with the time and care which she gave to anything intended for publication. She would call one of us and dictate the words as they came to her; then she would take the paper and ponder it, correct it, and re-correct it until often it was lined and interlined from beginning to end so that she sometimes had to re-dictate it from the corrected copy. After it was typewritten, she would go over it again, and it was likely to have more corrections when the proof reached her. Thus she spared neither time nor labor in the endeavor to prevent anything from going out that could be misunderstood or misinterpreted. Every word and even the punctuation were carefully and prayerfully pondered before it was actually published. It was my duty to destroy the discarded copies, and I was often tempted to keep one or more of them, but I yielded to this desire on only one occasion.

Malicious evil would not leave Mrs. Eddy alone with her work. She had been settled in Massachusetts but a few months when the papers began to report that she was ill or had passed on. In May 1908, she dictated a letter to me intended for the *New York Herald* (see *Miscellany*, p. 275). After she had finished the letter, it was quite different from the first draft, and when I was burning the discarded copies, I found the following which was in my handwriting: "The

Christian Science student's affection, fidelity, and devotion are born in the furnace and blossom in wisdom won by experience. This is the price and reward of taking one's treasure out of material vessels."

After she passed on, I found, pasted in the back of her *Science and Health*, a piece of paper with the following on it: "Whenever there seems to be a need or lack in your experience, this simply indicates the scientific fact that this seeming need is already supplied by God's gracious abundance. Then give thanks with your whole heart because you have learned in Christian Science that God's supply is on hand." Most of this was in my writing, but Mrs. Eddy had written in the last few words and signed it.[114] In the copy of *Miscellaneous Writings* which she was using before she passed on, these words were written in Mrs. Sargent's writing: "O learn to know that you can lose nothing that is real." (This was written in the margin on page 341 opposite "O learn to lose with God!")[115] Laura would never have written this in Mrs. Eddy's book unless she had given her instructions to do so.

Day-to-day interactions

Mrs. Eddy always enjoyed conversing with those whose work or education lay in a line of thought above the ordinary. Her face would be animated, and her eyes would shine and flash with pleasure, especially when she had carried her point or had asked some question which her visitor could not answer. As I have stated, I was usually in the next room, and quite often she called me to find a book or something for her. I remember one day when her cousin Henry Baker called. Mrs. Eddy asked him some questions about Mind and matter. He was not a Scientist and could not answer her; he tried but got all balled up. He scratched his head and looked rather confused. Mrs. Eddy then said something humorous which made him laugh. She kept this up for a little while; he left, chuckling to himself as if he had enjoyed it. However, when I went to Mrs. Eddy's side, she looked up at me with a twinkle in her eyes and said, "I've given Henry a dose of Truth that he will not get rid of for a long time."

I think that what I have written will show that Mrs. Eddy was very childlike in many ways and that she made us feel at ease when we were reflecting good and doing our work in a way which showed we were alert and handling the error which would have made us hinder her work. But if she saw that error was handling us, she could "thunder His law to the sinner, and sharply lighten on the cloud of the intoxicated senses" (*Miscellaneous Writings*, p. 277). She would tell me sometimes, "You are dead and buried, and plucked up by the roots this morning" (see Jude 1:12). Any working Scientist will understand that [this] is at times true of any mortal. Sometimes the suggestion would be strong that I wanted to get away. Unless this was met, my work would suffer, and Mrs. Eddy would say, "If you don't do better, I shall have to send you away." That would awaken me, and I would go work to meet the error. At other times, after a rebuke, I have gone into her study and found that she had forgotten all about it, and she would say, "What are you crying for, Adelaide?"

We were there to help Mrs. Eddy, and we did not talk to her of our own affairs. If we seemed to be struggling with a belief of sickness, we tried our best to hide it and to overcome it ourselves. One day Laura Sargent seemed to be quite ill, and Mrs. Eddy noticed it and rebuked it. When Laura left the room, she was no better, apparently, but later in the day found that she was healed and returned to her work.

When I was first with her, and it seemed difficult to remember all the little things necessary, she called me to her and said, "Ada, *know*, 'Divine Love thinks my thoughts and I cannot forget.'" At another time she said, "*Know*, 'Divine Love is all, and because it is all, I cannot be robbed of my love nor be made to forget.'"

An important By-Law and the start of the *Monitor*

At the time of the Communion service in The Mother Church in June 1908 (see *Miscellany*, pp. 140–142), Mrs. Eddy seemed very restless and unsettled on that Sunday; she kept calling us. At last she turned to Laura Sargent and said, "What is it, Laura? I have always suffered for what was not right with my church." Mrs. Sargent could not answer her. Mrs. Eddy turned away, and we knew from her attitude that she was praying and meditating. I think it was the next day that she wrote the By-Law abolishing the Communion service. She called Mr. Frye and told him to send it to the Directors. Quite often it took Calvin some time to see the reason for Mrs. Eddy's moves, and he said in this instance, "Oh, Mother, I wouldn't do that, if I were you." She said, "Calvin, *you do as I tell you.*" After he left the room, he remarked to Laura and me, "She'll ruin her Church." Mrs. Eddy went out for her drive, and while she was out, Mrs. Sargent picked up a copy of the *Message to The Mother*

Church for 1902, and her eyes rested on this paragraph: "Are earth's pleasures, its ties and its treasures, taken away from you? It is divine Love that doeth it, and sayeth, 'Ye have need of all these things.' A danger besets thy path? — a spiritual behest, in reversion, awaits you" (p. 19). When Mrs. Eddy came in, Mrs. Sargent said to her, "See what I opened to, Mother." Mrs. Eddy replied, "*There, see that,* call Calvin here." When he came in, she said to him, "Calvin, see that." He made no further protests to her, but he was not convinced of the wisdom of the move.

Early in the summer she began thinking and praying about a daily paper, although for a time she said nothing about it. She had written the name "The Christian Science Monitor" on a scrap of paper and laid it on her desk for some weeks before she gave the word to start it. I have a faint recollection of her telling Mr. McLellan in July to have it started, but she later cancelled the instruction. She was evidently waiting for the command to come from God. Then one day—in August, I think—she told Mr. McLellan to start a daily newspaper at once, and call it *The Christian Science Monitor.* She then sent a letter to the Trustees of the Publishing Society confirming this. Mr. McLellan explained to her a little of what it would involve to start an international daily paper: that there was not room in the Publishing House and that it would require correspondents all over the world, etc. She then asked how long it would take. He consulted with the other Directors and the Trustees, and the next time he came, he told her that the shortest time would be three months. After that, she inquired each time she saw him as to the progress being made, and as the end of the three months drew near, she counted the days. At last she was told that the first copy would be ready the day before Thanksgiving.

She took an interest in every detail; samples of paper and type were brought to her, and a sample copy was made for her inspection. She demanded a better quality of paper. It was she who chose the motto, "First the blade, then the ear, then the full grain in the ear," and told them where to place it. When the first complete copy was handed her, she clapped her hands and appeared to be overjoyed. At last her dream of years was realized—a Christian Science daily newspaper. It has been said that about the time she seriously began to consider the publishing of this paper, someone wrote to her suggesting that she do this and outlining, to some extent, the makeup and policy of such a newspaper. This may be true, but her writings prove that the idea had been with her for years, that she had dreamed of it, prayed, and meditated over it; and it was her demonstration which brought it forth.

Mrs. Eddy's study of her own works

Mrs. Eddy often read her books critically and revised them; at other times she read them for comfort and help, and would sometimes speak of them as though she were not the author. One day I went into her room and found her reading *Rudimental Divine Science*. She turned to me and said, "Why, this is wonderful, Ada. Have you got one of these?" I had given mine away a few days before, so I told her that I did not own a copy just then. She said, "You ask Calvin for one, and bring it here to me." I did this, and she wrote my name and the date in it, and "Affectionately, Mary B. G. Eddy."

Mrs. Sargent often quoted from the Bible or [Mrs. Eddy's

own] books when Mrs. Eddy seemed to need comfort or support, and sometimes she would say, "That is wonderful, Laura, where did you find it?" One or two quotations from *Unity of Good* stand out in my thought as being frequently quoted:

+ "The scientific man and his Maker are here; and you would be none other than this man, if you would subordinate the fleshly perceptions to the spiritual sense and source of being" (p. 46).

+ "The sweet and sacred sense of the permanence of man's unity with his Maker can illumine our present being with a continual presence and power of good, opening wide the portal from death into Life; and when this Life shall appear 'we shall be like Him,' and we shall go to the Father, not through death, but through Life; not through error, but through Truth" (p. 41).

And sometimes when the waiting seemed long, [this verse was read]: "For we are saved by hope: but hope that is seen is not hope: for what a man seeth, why doth he yet hope for? But if we hope for that we see not, then do we with patience wait for it" (Romans 8:24, 25). Also Romans 5:3–5, [which includes this statement]: "tribulation worketh patience." There were many others, but these have remained in consciousness, while the others have faded out. Mrs. Eddy quoted more than once, smilingly, "Good time comin', almost here, long, long time on de way."

No formulas or sets of references were used in Mrs. Eddy's household. Sometimes she would give me something to read in *Science and Health*, but it would be only for that special occasion and not to be used habitually. Occasionally she would tell me to go to my room and "take yourself up" for half an hour.

Interesting exchanges and an example of obedience

Mrs. Eddy was very grateful for faithful, loving service, and on more than one occasion she said, "God will bless you, dear ones, for your loving service to me." One day when Laura and I had done some small thing for her, she said, "Who will take care of you dear ones when you get old?"

She would not allow [people] to say they would "try" to do anything it was right for them to do. One day when she asked me to do something of which I was not quite sure, I said, "I'll try, Mrs. Eddy." She said, "Try, *try; do it!*" I used to have a habit of saying "I'm sorry" without very much depth of feeling when anything went wrong. One day, when I had said it two or three times in succession, she looked up at me with a twinkle in her eye and said, "How many times does that make?"

Laura Sargent told me that one evening, as they were sitting at the supper table, Mrs. Eddy was eating a piece of pie when she said, "If I should pass away while sitting in this chair, I should wake up right in the chair, and the piece of pie would be here." Mrs. Sargent asked, "Should we be with you, Mother?" She answered, "I haven't proved that yet."

In the spring or early summer of 1909, it was again reported that [Mrs. Eddy] was either incapacitated or had passed on. When they came in from the drive one day, Mrs. Sargent told me that a car with reporters from *The*

Boston Traveller had followed the carriage. Mr. Bowman, the coachman, was trying to avoid them [when] Mrs. Eddy asked, "What do they want, Calvin?" He replied, "They want your picture, Mother." She said, "Well, let them have it." The carriage stopped, and Mrs. Eddy leaned forward for them to take the picture. Afterwards the reporters sent enough copies so that each member of the household could have one.

When a strong impulse or intuition came to Mrs. Eddy, she hastened to obey, even though she did not always know the reason. She has said to us, "God has told me to do this, and I must do it." Mrs. Sargent told me that at the time of the change of trusteeship of the land for the Original Mother Church, Mrs. Eddy wakened one morning and, calling Calvin Frye, told him to get Henry Baker there as quickly as possible. When she reached her study, he had just arrived. He said, "Good morning, Cousin Mary, what did you want of me?" She said, "I don't know, Henry, but God told me to send for you." He laughed and asked, "Well, how are you getting on with your Church?" Mrs. Eddy replied, "Fine, I have the deed in my pocket, and it is to be registered today." He asked, "May I see it?" After he read it, he told her there was a clause in it that would have caused a situation worse than before, and it would have been more difficult to get it adjusted after it was registered.[116]

Adam Dickey's continued service

Mr. Dickey has told how, when he agreed to enter Mrs. Eddy's service, he had thought it would be for one year. On the way to Boston, he purchased a *Manual* and found that the By-Law had been changed to read, "for three years consecutively." As the year drew towards a close, he talked with Mrs. Eddy about it and told her he had made preparations for leaving his work for one year only and that Mrs. Dickey was unwilling to have him remain away longer. Mrs. Eddy shrank from another change and talked with him repeatedly to get him to stay the three years. At last he told her that if she would let him go back to Kansas City for two weeks so that he could hold his association and talk with Mrs. Dickey, he thought he could make her see that it was the right thing to do. He explained that when Mrs. Dickey saw that God demanded a thing, she was willing to make any sacrifice to be obedient. Mrs. Eddy consented to this proposal, and at the end of two weeks he returned, bringing Mrs. Dickey to Brookline with him, but not to the house. Later she was invited by Mrs. Eddy to spend some weeks in the home, but afterwards she returned to the hotel.

Towards the end of 1910, when the three years would have come to an end in a few months, Mrs. Eddy again began begging him to stay on indefinitely. She said she could not stand the ordeal of breaking in a new secretary at that time and that when the country was at war, a soldier was required to give up his freedom and

COURTESY OF THE MARY BAKER EDDY LIBRARY

Mrs. Eddy's grandsons at Chestnut Hill, from left: George W. Glover III and Andrew J. Glover

his family and to serve for the duration of the war. She said she was on the battlefront continually, and Scientists should be as willing to sacrifice and serve in the mental battle for religious freedom as a soldier would be for his country. After several of these persuasive talks, Mr. Dickey promised that he would stay on indefinitely. Mrs. Eddy then gave him the certificate of C.S.D. for his three years' service.[117] Mrs. Dickey also wrote a note to Mrs. Eddy saying how glad she was to give her husband to her for further service. Either then or when she promised the first time, Mrs. Eddy expressed her gratitude by giving Mrs. Dickey an amethyst pin with a gold setting. She sent for several pins and let Mrs. Dickey make her own selection.

A visit with her grandsons

On July 16 (I think it was 1909 or 1910),[118] Mrs. Eddy's grandsons, who were staying in Brookline for a short time, visited her. George was a good-looking young man with auburn hair, if I remember rightly, and Mrs. Eddy told him that he was very much like his grandfather, Major Glover. Andrew, the younger, was a tall, rather awkward-looking lad of about seventeen. Mrs. Sargent and I were in the room during the interview. Mrs. Eddy talked with them, and after a few moments asked them if they would like to stay with her for a little while. Andrew seemed to be the spokesman, and he answered, "Oh, no, we've got a store; we must get back." George did not have much to say but just sat and smiled at her and answered only when a question was addressed directly to him. Mrs. Eddy gave each of them a copy of *Science and Health* in which she inscribed the name and date and "From your loving grandmother, Mary

Baker Eddy." She seemed to be very much pleased that they had come to see her. When they got outside, reporters were waiting with a camera and took a photograph of them with the garden wall as a background. A day or two later, they sent Mrs. Eddy a copy of it, and she had it framed and always kept it in her room. She also had a picture on the what-not of her granddaughter, Evelyn. She treasured this picture and had written on the back of it, "My darling granddaughter, passed on."[119]

Occasions for watchfulness and pleasure

In the summer or fall of 1908, Mrs. Augusta E. Stetson was planning a larger and more magnificent church to be built on Riverside Drive, New York City, and began to solicit subscriptions for it.[120] It was apparent to many that the motives back of this move were not right, and Mrs. Eddy was told about the proposed plans. She sent for Mrs. Stetson and, upon her arrival in Boston, sent her an invitation to accompany her on her drive. While they were out, Mrs. Eddy persuaded her to give up the project. About this time Mrs. Eddy dictated the article, "Consistency" to Mr. [Archibald] McLellan and asked him if he would publish it under

ESTES STUDIO PHOTO, COURTESY OF THE MARY BAKER EDDY COLLECTION

Evelyn Tilton Glover,
Mrs. Eddy's granddaughter

his own name.[121] He replied that he would. She then said, "Can you do this?" He replied, "I can."

Some visiting Scientists who were being taken through the house had a sixteen-month-old baby with them. If I remember correctly, his father was the Committee on Publication for Montana. The little fellow was unusually bright and active for his age and absolutely fearless. Mrs. Martha Wilcox took him in to Mrs. Eddy. She held out her arms to him, and he immediately went to her; he could say a few words and tried to talk to her. She was delighted with him and looked around for something to give him. There was a small silver stamp holder on her desk, and she gave it to him. Most persons coming to see her were thinking of what benefit they or theirs would receive from the Leader. When we returned this baby to his mother, she said, "I knew he would do Mrs. Eddy good." At the time this amused us, but it may have been one reason why Mrs. Eddy appreciated the child so wholeheartedly, for she was quick to realize when someone was trying to draw from her mentally and had no patience with it. She constantly instructed us to keep our thoughts away from her.

It is not my intention to give the impression that we were so continually on duty that there was no recreation for us. At one time we took up the study of astronomy and used to go on the roof at night to find the constellations. Mr. Dickey told Mrs. Eddy about Halley's comet when the papers were talking about it, and she instructed him to get a telescope so that we might look for it. Somebody started a grammar class for those who wished to improve their English. Also, in the evenings I would often read aloud to Miss Nellie Eveleth while she was sewing, and quite often others would listen with her. The workers whose duties did not bring them into frequent contact with Mrs. Eddy attended church regularly, but the rest of us were content to stay home and serve our Leader. We used to go out on the grounds; some of the "watchers" played ball in the afternoon when the weather permitted while others went motoring while she was on her drive, starting immediately after the early dinner.

Sometimes she would say to us, "Laura," or "Adelaide," whichever she was addressing, "You may go to church this morning, if you wish." We would invariably answer, "Thank you, Mother, but we would rather stay here," sometimes adding, "We have our divine service in serving you." Her face would light up and she would say, "Thank you, dear." Several times she asked me, "You will stay with me as long as I am on this plane, won't you, Ada?" I did not expect her to pass on and could not see my way to promise this outright, but I would reply, "I'll stay as long as God wants me to, Mother." This always pleased her.

About once in six months she would call in the household workers (not the "watch") and read or talk with them. On one occasion, when she had read from the Bible, she said, "There, what do you think of me, nearly ninety years old and reading without glasses." (She had glasses but oftener read without them than with them.)

On rare occasions she would draw one or the other to her and kiss us, and occasionally when we had her comfortably settled, we kissed her forehead. Sometimes she smiled; sometimes she would say smilingly, "What are you kissing—matter?"

Generosity and tenderness for
workers and watchers

Although Mrs. Eddy had the New England sense of economy and would allow no waste or extravagance, she was also very generous. The following will give a hint of her generosity. In the fall of 1909, the Trustees of her property sent her a note telling her she had a large surplus of money on hand which she could use as she wished. She immediately called me to her and asked what salary I was getting. I told her, and she said, "You're a pretty good girl. I'm going to pay you the same as the mental workers; Laura, you tell Calvin to pay her the same as the others." She also told Laura to buy herself a new hat and to tell Calvin to pay for it. There were many times that she said to me, "That's a pretty waist you have on, Adelaide; you tell my dressmaker to buy you one, and I'll pay for it." At times she told Calvin to keep a supply of gold coins in her desk so that she might give them away. In the early days at Pleasant View, so I was told, everything for the household was very carefully budgeted, and the housekeeper was allowed only a certain sum for the table, but as Mrs. Eddy's income increased, this restriction was removed, and on several occasions in the last years, I heard her tell Mr. Dickey that if there was anything he wanted, to tell the housekeeper to get it for him.

At Christmastime 1909, one of the workers, I think it was Mrs. Scott,[122] suggested that we, the household helpers, should write a letter to Mrs. Eddy expressing to her our love, loyalty, and appreciation and wishing her a happy Christmas. Mrs. Scott wrote the letter and we all signed it, and it was put on her desk for her. The message on page 263 of *Miscellany* was the response to this. After we read it, it was sent to the Publishing Society for publication, but the editors sent each of us a facsimile copy of it. On New Year's Day I was among those in the room when she wrote "Extempore" (see *Miscellany*, p. 354). I am under the impression that she then called the household helpers together, as well as the "watch," and read it to them.

One night in April 1910, error seemed to strike at Mrs. Sargent quite severely. Miss Eveleth and I stayed with her until midnight, when she seemed somewhat better, but when morning came, she said she was not equal to her work, and it seemed best for her to take a little time off to recuperate. Mrs. Eddy missed her very much and kept asking when she was coming back. She asked me what the trouble was with Laura, and I told her that she was just tired out and needed a rest. Mrs. Eddy immediately took a pad and wrote the article "A Paean of Praise" (see *Miscellany*, pp. 355–356) and gave instructions for it to be printed in the next issue of the *Sentinel*. She also wrote a note to Laura, and when she received an answer stating she would return in a few days, she was very happy. Laura came back a day earlier than she had promised and surprised Mrs. Eddy.

That afternoon after Mrs. Eddy had attended to her mail, she expressed a desire to go into her sitting room for a while. She had been seated only a moment when Mr. Dickey came in and told her he had something for her—something she would like. She looked up at him and asked, "Is it Laura?" He nodded, and she clapped her hands and said, "Oh, good!" Mrs. Sargent came in and knelt down in front of her, and Mrs. Eddy took her face in her hands and kissed her, first on one cheek and then on the other. She could not make enough of her.

Mrs. Eddy's final year

I have no recollection of any important steps taken in 1910. During [the previous] three years, she not only abolished the Communion service but made other significant changes, i.e., abolished the General Teachers' Association, did away with the Executive Members, and closed the Mother's Room in the Original [Mother] Church to visitors. All these moves made it easier for the Cause to be carried on harmoniously after she had passed from our sight, and there is no doubt that she was governed by divine wisdom in making these changes.

During this year she seemed to be drawing more and more away from personality. She was just as much interested in the Cause, [however]; in fact, it did not matter what threatened or what happened, her first thought was, "How will it affect the Cause?" But when students passed on, she did not seem inclined to write tributes or take any personal notice of such events. Her last official act was to make Mr. Dickey a Director in Mr. Ira Knapp's place.[123]

Sometime during the last months, a few of the students, realizing that Mrs. Eddy was not so strong physically as she had been, consulted an official of the Church and suggested to her that she should change those By-Laws requiring her signature. She talked with them two or three times about it, and one afternoon after they left the room, she called Calvin Frye and said to him, "Calvin, you know what they want me to do, don't you?" He replied, "Yes, Mother." She asked, "Would you do it?" He replied, "I'd keep it in my own hands, if I were you; it's giving them too much power." She said, "You are right."

She then called the "watchers" and told them of her decision, and that was the end of it.

During the last week in November Mrs. Eddy seemed to be suffering from a belief of congestion and cold, but it did not appear to be serious, so we did not feel anxious about her. One of the students was working for her, and the "watchers" were working impersonally as usual. On the Sunday before she passed on, after our usual little service of songs with her, she said something to the effect that after this she would not meet there with us very often.

On Thursday, December 1, when I went into her room at seven in the morning, Mr. Frye said, "Don't wake Mother yet, Adelaide, she did not get to sleep until four o'clock." Later she wakened, dressed, and came out to her study, and when the time came, she went for her drive. Some may ask why we did not persuade her to stay home since she seemed to be having a struggle. I don't remember that we tried to dissuade her from going on that particular day, but we had on a few occasions said to her, "Don't you think it might be wise for you to stay home today, Mother?" But she had indicated that she did not wish us to interfere. She had been watched so much that she felt someone would be ready to report it if she did not go and would say she had passed on or was ill. Laura accompanied her on the drive, and she told me that Mrs. Eddy seemed to be thinking deeply and that she said, as though she were thinking aloud, "Oh, if the students had only done what I had told them, I should have lived and carried the Cause."

When she came in, she seemed to collapse. We took off her wraps and got her on the couch as quickly as possible, and all the "watchers" came and sat in her room. She was not unconscious, but it was evident that error was making a pretty strong claim. After a little while, she rallied and asked for a pad and pencil, and when they were handed to her, she wrote the words, as recorded, "God is my life." She ate her supper as usual.

The next morning she did not dress but insisted on leaving her bed and going to the study where she lay on the couch. Later she insisted on dressing her hair. The next morning, Saturday, she stayed in bed, but she was alert and sent messages to the "watch." In the afternoon she sat up in bed and was evidently working for herself. When she got through, she was much better and said, "Drop the argument. Just leave me with divine Love; that is all I need." She was very happy, and we all thought the demonstration was practically made. However, later she became unconscious for a little while, but the [t]ruth was declared for her, and she came out of that. When she settled for the night, I left her.

She had not been left alone for two or three nights before this; the mental workers had been taking turns, two of them watching for two hours, when another two would come on duty. Mr. Dickey and Mrs. Sargent were with her when I left. About ten fifteen they thought she asked for me and rang my bell. I went to her and said, "Did you want me, Mother?" She said, "No, dear." Mrs. Sargent said, "Her hands are cold; I wonder if her feet are." I felt of them and started to put a comforter on her, but she said, "Don't, dear." I wanted to stay, but Laura and Mr. Dickey both persuaded me to get some rest, saying that I should probably be needed again through the night and that I would be on duty all the next day.

The next morning when I went to our Leader as usual at seven o'clock, Mr. Frye was sitting outside her bedroom door, and he said, "Mother has gone, Adelaide." Mrs. Sargent told me later that about fifteen minutes after I left the room the night before, Mrs. Eddy asked for water and sat up and drank it. A little later Mr. Dickey, who was on the other side of the bed, asked if she was breathing. Mrs. Sargent leaned over her, and she said Mrs. Eddy drew one more breath, and that was all. There had been no struggle and no last words; she just quietly went to sleep. This was at 10:45 p.m. I was told that the rest of the "watchers" were called down, and Mr. McLellan and one or two other officials of the Church were sent for. They all faithfully held to the [t]ruth but could not awaken her.

The days following Mrs. Eddy's passing

The next morning the medical examiner came. After the symptoms were described to him and he had made an examination of the body, he pronounced the trouble as pneumonia. Miss Eveleth and I were in the room while the attendant (a woman) prepared the body for burial. Ushers and officials of the Church were stationed around the house and grounds to guard against strangers or reporters. We had all done our mental work to the best of our understanding, and there was no sense of death in the house.

An account of the services was printed in the *Monitor* at the time and reprinted in the *Journal* for January 1911. I shall not try to describe them beyond saying that the members of the household were seated in the upstairs hall, while the relatives of Mrs. Eddy were in the room where the casket lay, and those who came by invitation were in the hall and the other rooms downstairs. Judge [Clifford P.] Smith, First Reader of The Mother Church, read the service. These selections were read:

Bible	*Science and Health*	
Ps. 91: 4, 9–11, 14–16	410: 4–19	265: 23–30
John 13: 34, 35	57: 23–30	598: 23–30
John 14: 15–27	574: 27–30	516: 9–23
	66: 6–16, 30–1 (next page)	

This was followed by silent prayer and the repetition of the Lord's Prayer. "The Mother's Evening Prayer" was then read by Mrs. Carol Hoyt Powers, the Second Reader of The Mother Church.[124]

All the members of the household followed the casket to the cemetery. When we reached the receiving vault, Judge Smith read the twenty-third Psalm and [then] the last verse in Jude as a benediction. The casket was placed in the receiving vault until the mausoleum could be built on the beautiful spot chosen by the Directors.

After we returned to the house, Mr. Dickey, speaking for the Directors, told Mrs. Laura E. Sargent that she was appointed to take charge of the house; that I was to stay with her; and that Lulu Phillips, the cook, would retain her position. He said that the services of the others, with the exception of John Salchow, who would remain at the lodge, would no longer be required. A watchman was engaged to stay in the house at night.

Our Leaders' sojourn in the wilderness

"The woman fled into the wilderness." (Rev. 12:6)

"WILDERNESS. Loneliness; doubt;
darkness. Spontaneity of thought and
idea; the vestibule in which a material sense of things disappears, and
spiritual sense unfolds the great facts of
existence." (*Science and Health*, p. 597)

To those who cling to an idealized human concept of
Mrs. Eddy, her experiences in the wilderness seem inex-
plicable, but many students who have been through deep
waters themselves and who have come up against the determined resistance of mortal mind to Truth are ready to
understand somewhat of her experiences, and to them they
are a source of encouragement and strength.

It is easy to criticize or condemn, but who knows or
understands even a little of what it cost our beloved Leader
to come down from the mount of revelation to investigate and uncover malicious animal magnetism and show
us how to meet it? While there [on the mount], she healed
everything that her thought touched, but after a time she
saw that she would have to probe the false claim of evil to
the bottom before it could be intelligently handled and
destroyed. In speaking of this experience, she told us that
she walked the floor for three days and nights with perspi-
ration pouring from her. In *Miscellaneous Writings*, Mrs. Eddy
says, "I shall not forget the cost of investigating, for this age,
the methods and power of error" (p. 222).

To come down from this mount to find a way of
teaching others who were not ready to rise to her plane
of thought how to prove the Truth for themselves, beginning with their feeble understanding and perception, was

truly a task of great magnitude. Having given them her explanation of the Scriptures, Mrs. Eddy then apparently allowed them to use their own methods to some extent and watched the results. When she saw that manipulation and rubbing prevented the healing, she demanded that her pupils should rise higher and employ only mental and spiritual means. Some were not ready to take this step and turned against her and the [t]ruth she taught. This opened her eyes to mental malpractice, and she saw that she would have to probe the modes and methods of malicious animal magnetism and uncover them to the world.

In the early editions of *Science and Health*, she speaks of the shock of finding a student malpracticing. She told the students in the house that from this time on mortal mind poured out upon her all the malice, hatred, and torment that was possible.

In an extract published in the *Journal* and taken from a letter written to First Church, Eau Claire, Wisconsin, July 15, 1899, she speaks of herself as "the woman in the wilderness." The definition of *wilderness* in *Science and Health* explains many of her experiences. My record of the last years would not be complete did I not relate a few of them.

I was in the room when she asked Mr. Dickey to promise to tell the world something of the mental malpractice which was directed against her. I do not remember her exact words to him, but it was evident that she wished some record made so that those who had grown to it might understand a little of what it had cost her to stand and establish the Cause. In *Miscellany* she says, "At this period my demonstration of Christian Science cannot be fully understood, theoretically; therefore it is best explained by its fruits, and by the life of our Lord as depicted in the chapter Atonement and Eucharist, in 'Science and Health with Key to the Scriptures'" (p. 136). Also, on page 34 of No and Yes she writes, "Physical torture affords but a slight illustration of the pangs which come to one upon whom the world of sense falls with its leaden weight in the endeavor to crush out of a career its divine destiny."

There were days when everything would go along happily and harmoniously, but there were many struggles with the so-called powers of darkness; yet when the demand came to do something for the Cause, she turned her thought unfalteringly to God, never doubting, never fearing, until the answer came to her and the divine command was carried out. No one who saw her at those times could ever doubt that she was inspired when she wrote or made any move for the Church. She has said to us, "God has told me to do this, and I must do it."

Mrs. Eddy was continually reaching out for some student in the Field with sufficient understanding and spirituality to be equipped for the work in her household. If she came cross some article or testimony in the periodicals which appeared to indicate a high spiritual altitude on the part of the writer or practitioner, she would have [him or her] sent for; but it was not often that one was found with the necessary equipment and ability to stand.

One time during the first weeks at Chestnut Hill, I had an experience [that] may help to show how error sometimes worked. It seemed as if nothing I did was right, and I seemed to be struggling both mentally and physically. Mrs. Eddy was not happy about my work, and I knew she was trying to find someone to fill my place. One day when, as I waited in the hall with the sunshade while the robes were being put around her in the carriage, Mr. Archibald McLellan came along and spoke to me. He probably sensed the need and questioned me purposely. After one or two questions, he said, "How long is Mrs. Eddy out?" "Twenty minutes," I replied. He then inquired what I did during this time, and I told him it was my dinner time. He said, "It isn't very long, is it?" and I said, "No, but I wouldn't care what I did if I could only please her." He replied, very quietly, "Well, you can; you can." He must have known the truth about the situation, for when Mrs. Eddy returned from her drive, she was happy and greeted me in her usual loving way, and that was the last of the error. Later I learned that a letter had reached her making a misstatement about my former church affiliations. Error had worked in this way to make her send me away. No doubt she learned the truth later, as the Business Committee had all my records.

Lest someone may think I have exaggerated Mrs. Eddy's trials, I should like to relate the following story which was told to me by Mrs. Minnie Scott, who was at the time a member of the household. It may serve to give an inkling of what our Leader had to contend with. Mrs. Scott had a niece about twelve years old. One day this child was playing with a neighbor's little girl. She asked Grace what Sunday School she attended. Grace replied, "The Christian Science Sunday School." Immediately a look of hatred came on the child's face, and she spat on the ground and said, "Mrs. Eddy's got to die." Grace did not answer, and she reiterated, "Mrs. Eddy's got to die; everybody's got to die. We've got twenty bishops praying day and night for Mrs. Eddy to die." Grace's mother was sitting at the window watching and was astonished to see the change in the child's face and the hatred of Christian Science and its Founder which must have been instilled in her thought.

In earlier editions of *Science and Health*, there used to be this statement: "The [m]aximum of [g]ood is always met by the maximum of suppositional evil."[125] Mrs. Eddy later saw the wisdom of changing this, but it helps to explain her experience.

Honoring our Leader

The writer knows of no better way of ending than by quoting [words] written by Laura E. Sargent in 1913. After speaking of Mrs. Eddy's work, she said:

> It was the spirit of Love in the blessed life
> of Mrs. Eddy which enabled her to discern
> and faithfully voice God's message to this age.
> Beyond the belief that her passing footsteps
> have taken her into the next degree of life's
> preparatory experience, the advancing thought
> still watches, works, and waits for the divine
> ultimatum, the prophecy of Christ Jesus fulfilled
> in the spiritual reign of Life, Truth, and Love on
> earth, the fatherhood and motherhood of God
> manifested in the universal brotherhood of man.

> For the accomplishment of this divine purpose,
> our beloved Leader worked and prayed, and from
> the "signs following" we see that her labor was
> not in vain .... The ascending consciousness,
> transfigured with the realization that life is, was,
> and ever shall be, is released from the trammel

*Newspaper illustrations of The Original Mother Church during the
June 1899 Communion service conducted by Septimus J. Hanna
(First Reader) and Eldora I. Gragg (Second Reader)*

of a false belief in death and finds wings for a
heavenward flight, whose infinite compass of
fetterless joy and power no human will can impede
or defy. The earth resounds with the echo of
that ascending thought whose range of glorified
vision is ever broadening into higher expression.

WILLIAM R. RATHVON (1854–1939)

William Rathvon was born in Lancaster, Pennsylvania, where he grew up and was baptized and confirmed in the Lutheran church. In 1863, just before turning nine, he stood fifteen feet away from President Abraham Lincoln as he delivered his Gettysburg Address. Decades later, in 1938, Rathvon recorded his memories of that day at the Boston studios of radio station WRUL.

An alumnus of Franklin and Marshall College, Rathvon married his first wife, Lillie K. Stauffer, in 1877; the couple then moved to Kansas. In 1880, their son, Martin, was born and Lillie passed on. Rathvon moved to Colorado, first to a mining camp and then to Denver. He married Lillie's sister, Ella Stauffer, in April 1883. The couple raised Martin, who named his first daughter Ella.

During the late 1880s and early 1890s, Rathvon was successful in business, but he lost his wealth in the Panic of 1893. Soon after this, while in Chicago, the couple learned

*of Christian Science, and within three months Ella was
healed of an organic trouble for which surgery had been
advised. Both Rathvons took Primary class instruction
from Mary M. W. Adams in Chicago before returning to
Colorado.*

*They lived first in Florence, Colorado, where they
introduced Christian Science, working as healers until
they moved to Boulder in 1902. William also worked
in the oil industry in both locations, dividing his time
between business and healing. The couple took another
Primary class in 1903, this time from Edward A. Kimball.
After taking Normal class from Septimus J. Hanna in
1907, William taught his first class in Colorado in 1908.
Following a brief interruption to his teaching while in
Mary Baker Eddy's household, he taught for nearly two
decades in Colorado and later in Boston.*

*William began serving in Eddy's home in November
1908. The following spring, Ella moved to the Boston
area, and that fall, she, too, began working in Eddy's
home. Both served until Eddy's passing. In January
1911, the couple moved back to Denver and resumed
their healing work. Almost immediately, William was
appointed to the Christian Science Board of Lectureship
and began traveling extensively, speaking throughout the
United States and in Europe, Asia, and Australia. Ella
often traveled with him. In 1918, William served for a
few months as Treasurer of The Mother Church and then
was appointed to the Christian Science Board of Directors,
where he served until his passing.*

*By 1920, the couple was living full time in Boston, and
their young granddaughter was with them. Ella passed
on in 1923. Two years later, William married Lora
Carney Woodbury, who, following William's passing,
finished compiling his reminiscences, which he had begun
assembling almost a decade earlier.*

Treasured Time at Chestnut Hill

WILLIAM R. RATHVON

I t has fallen to my lot to have known the author of *Science and Health with Key to the Scriptures* intimately in the last few years of her earthly activity. One November day in 1908, Mrs. Eddy called me to her side from my home in Colorado, and there I remained until that once happy household at Chestnut Hill was left joyless and desolate by her going. I was privileged to share her daily counsels for more than two years, and from the time of my first half hour's heart-to-heart talk with her, down to the afternoon when, standing at her side, I saw her marvelous hands shape her last written words, "God is my life," I have never wavered in my belief that she has been the chosen evangel of Truth, entrusted with those good tidings of great joy that have been [a]waiting man's readiness since the days when Jesus trod the dusty fields of Syria and sailed the blue waters of Galilee.

The establishment of a great religious organization whose twelve hundred growing branches belt the globe;

the installation of a simple form of service which fills those churches twice each week with throngs of worshippers who are drawn neither by music, eloquence, nor sensational entertainment; the building up of efficient agencies and institutions for the dissemination and protection of a radically new system of ethics; and the launching of a great metropolitan daily in the interests of clean journalism whose success has set a new mark in the newspaper world—these things or any of them would give eminence to the life-work of the most ambitious of men. To a modest woman, Mary Baker Eddy, belongs the credit of them all.

But these achievements, grand as they are, weighed little with her compared with the fruits of her consecrated endeavors to bring more and more of peace on earth and good will to men, and to guide us to a clearer and more practical understanding of the Fatherhood of God and the brotherhood of man. The applause of men, like their abuse and condemnation, were brushed aside as cobwebs when she was once assured of the approval of God.

I could by the hour recite to you incidents of Mrs. Eddy's wisdom and sagacity, of her strength and determination, of her wit and humor, of her love for little children and her delight in the beautiful, of the inexpressible charm of her manner and the eloquence of her voice, but it is not of these things that she would have me speak.

It was her desire—almost daily expressed—that her followers should disregard her personality and address their thought to the things of God, which she has disclosed to them. She would have us study her books and not her personality. She would have us know her by what she wrote and not by how she looked. Years ago she instructed her students to follow her only as she followed Christ (see *Message to The Mother Church for 1901*, p. 34), and though she was a rare Leader, she was an ideal follower of all that was truly good.

When my pen gets started working about our Leader, it is not easily stopped. The two years of my life when her home was my home, I had unlimited opportunity to know her as one knows and loves his own mother.

Our start in Christian Science

I became very successful in business, but my wealth, mostly in silver mines, was wiped away in the Panic of '93, and we were left practically penniless. While sojourning temporarily in Chicago, through association with friends of former years we learned of Christian Science, and without resistance it entered our lives, ever to remain.

Before leaving Chicago we were taught by Mrs. Mary W. Adams, an early student of Mrs. Eddy's, and the following year (1894) left for Colorado to begin pioneer work in Christian Science in the little town of Florence, the center of the oil district. After eight years we moved to Boulder, Colorado, a university town where Christian Science had just obtained a foothold. I was at that time actively engaged in the production and refining of oil, had an important position with a large company, and was dividing my time between the duties of my business and my Christian Science affairs. My business and practitioner's offices adjoined so that I spent the mornings at business and afternoons at my Science work. From Boulder in 1903, we were called to go through the Primary class in the Massachusetts Metaphysical College, taught by Edward

A. Kimball, and in 1907 I was called to go through the Normal class taught that year by Judge Septimus J. Hanna.

Willing to serve as needed

About this time, Mrs. Ida G. Stewart, a fellow student with us in Mrs. Adams's class, was in Denver as representative of the Board of Directors of The Mother Church, in search of suitable material to serve our Leader. In our interview with her, we were asked if we would leave everything and go to our Leader if called. "Can we come together" was our first question, as we had never been separated for more than a day or so in our many years of married life. The answer was "No," so we asked for time to demonstrate our decision. Next morning we notified her, "We are ready to come at any time, in any way, singly or together."

Shortly after this Mrs. Rathvon was called and left for Boston immediately. Her interview with the Directors was entirely satisfactory, but for some reason which we could not then understand but which I could later conjecture from my knowledge of how things were managed, she was told that Mrs. Eddy would not need her this time, so she packed up and took the train for Colorado, completing a round trip halfway across the continent that had been fruitless so far as we could then see.

Months then elapsed without any word from headquarters when one July day in 1908 came a telegram summoning us to Boston. After our arrival in Boston on July 21, I was interviewed by the Board of Directors preparatory to going to Chestnut Hill for inspection. I find an old memorandum dated July 21, 1908, describing my first encounter with the powers that be, which I shall here insert:

July 21, 1908

Ella and I were sitting here in Room 325 of the Lenox after breakfast this morning when the phone tinkled and I heard Mr. Stewart's voice, as expected. "Can you meet with the Directors at 9:30 this morning? It was then just nine, and the ensuing fifteen minutes were used in working mentally to clear the way.

On the strike of 9:30, I pushed the janitor's bell to the left of the main entrance of the church and was admitted by a plain, motherly looking woman (caretaker, I presume) to whom I made known my errand. After being interrogated by another woman or two, I was shown into the Directors' office, where were seated at the table Mr. Knapp, with long, white beard such as Abraham wore, and with him Mr. Johnson, Clerk of the Church, with white band tie and Prince Albert coat, somewhat suggestive of the country clergyman in manner and look. Soon came together Messrs. McLellan and Stewart, well-dressed and well-looking. I was given a seat near the head of the table where sat Mr. McLellan.

"Tell us how you came to Christian Science" was the first question asked me. I covered everything in as few words as I could, from the time "Doc Adams" first broached

Christian Science to me down to the present.
Others asked me a few questions, but
my case seemed well understood before I
appeared, thanks to Ella's full recital at her
previous interview with them. The trial, my
willingness to drop everything, my former
church connections, our work in Florence
and in Boulder were in turn inquired into.

That was Tuesday afternoon, and here it is
Thursday noon, lacking a little, and the word
has not yet come. Ella and I have been within
earshot of the phone almost continuously, but
it has been silent as a clapperless bell. Ella was
kept listening from Monday until Saturday
late before it tinkled for her, and then only
to say that she could go, the "present need
being supplied." She still thinks I will be
summoned and has the notion that her not
returning directly to Boulder is somewhat
displeasing to the "powers that be," and she
is therefore all ready to start homeward via
Asbury Park early tomorrow.

False starts on the road to service

The next day, Friday, I was told how to get to Chestnut
Hill, where our Leader was expecting me in the afternoon,
and at this date twenty-two years afterwards, I recall my
impressions as though they were of yesterday. John Salchow
met me at the Reservoir with the surrey and drove me to the
home. Going up the wide approach, as we passed one of the
Jersey cows browsing, this verse from the Scriptures came to

mind: "I would rather be a doorkeeper in the house of the Lord, than to dwell in the tents of wickedness" (see Psalms 84:10), but it turned out I did not have to do either.

I was shown into the library and sat by the window until Mr. Dickey made his appearance and we chatted a little, though he did not in any way indicate that he knew what was to follow in a few minutes. He then asked me if I would like to see Mr. Frye, and shortly Calvin appeared and I got my first glimpse of the little man who had so much to do in managing the temporal affairs of our Leader.

Our interview was brief and memorable. After a friendly greeting, saying that he had heard Mr. Dickey speak of me before, he said, "Mother thought that if you were still in business, it would be better for you to wait a while longer." After a few minutes of general talk, he retired and I bade goodbye to Mr. Dickey and made my way back to the cars and my hotel. At night I left for Colorado as my dear wife had done before under similar circumstances.

Early in September Ella was summoned again to Boston. Mr. Calvin Hill drove her out to Chestnut Hill, where she was taken to Mrs. Eddy's room for an interview lasting about twenty minutes, when it was decided that she was to return home again. Then came another call for me in November, and I was on my way to Boston again.

Referring to some old letters written home at the time, I find some extracts that are pertinent. One tells of my arrival again at the Lenox and my calling up Mr. McLellan:

November 19, 1908

After profuse and friendly inquiries about my wife, Mr. McLellan said, "Let me

see, I will have to let you know later what
your next move will be. I will call you sometime this evening and let you know when
I can see you tomorrow." After a few more
words of greeting, we hung up and parted.
The whole proceeding reminded me so
vividly of another not long ago, even to the
waiting to hear the sharp rattle of the little
bells, as I am now doing, that I cannot help
but feel that the sequel may be the same
also. But it does seem odd to rush a fellow
across the continent as tight as steam can
make it and then set him down to suck his
thumbs for hours after he gets here. Well,
perhaps it is good discipline. If it does not
teach one to labor, it certainly does to wait.

My turn to serve

The next morning Mr. McLellan called early, and
arrangements were made for my going out to Chestnut
Hill. Referring again to my home-written letters:

Friday, November 20, 1908, 10 a.m.

I am to take a Newton Boulevard car,
get off at Lake Street, which I believe is the
terminus. Then a White Steamer will come
along which will be numbered 07M—the
chauffeur will have a green coat so I will
know him. He will get me over there by
two o'clock, at which hour the interview is
fixed. Mr. McLellan asked how my business

affairs were fixed, and I explained that I
have arranged so that I can be away long
enough to determine whether the trial
results in my filling the bill or otherwise.
If it looks like a longer stay, then I can
make my arrangements accordingly. He
said, "That's all right, for the stay may last
for years, and it may begin at two o'clock
today." I said I had a trunk, which seemed
to please him. I told him I was not looking
forward to the opportunity with any degree
of eagerness but was entirely willing to serve
wherever I had work to do that was mine to
do. He said, "Those that are eager are not
the ones that are wanted."

The next letter I wrote home bears the same date of
Friday, November 20, 1908, but was written at 7 p.m. I shall
again quote:

I have just come from the supper table
where I was given the seat of honor opposite Mr. Frye. Mrs. Sargent and Miss Peck
of Butte, Montana, [were] on one side, and
Mr. Tomlinson and Mr. Dickey on the
other. Then we sat and chatted a while in
the library before coming up to our several
rooms. Mr. Dickey had four bells ring, so
he left Mr. Tomlinson and me by ourselves,
the ladies having gone their ways before
and Mr. Frye vanishing as soon as he had
pushed the bell three times announcing the

meal at an end. At table all were very kind
to me and talked much about Colorado in
general and Boulder in particular—and oil.
They seem so interested in whatever has to
do with things outside, probably because
they have had to take it secondhand so
long. For supper we had salmon, beef loaf,
hot rolls, jam, figs and dates, and a salty,
hard, crisp cracker they called "educators"
that reminded me of pretzels.

My room is on the third floor; just across
the hall is Rev. Tomlinson's; further down,
Miss Peck's; and the rest of the third floor
rooms I am not acquainted with. Below is
Mr. Frye's room and near it Mr. Dickey's.
Later Mr. Dickey showed me to my room,
which I will tell you about tomorrow, and
explained somewhat of what I would be
expected to do. Contrary to expectations,
there is not so much clerical work as mental.

Love and a laugh during my interview with Mrs. Eddy

On the evening of my first day at Chestnut Hill, Mrs.
Sargent took me upstairs and introduced me to our Leader.
Her appearance was about what I expected from what had
been told me. She appeared as frail as a bird but also as
buoyant and capable—as though she could fly or soar to
whatever height she might desire. But no description could
have prepared me for the effect her very presence exerted—a
tangible yet undefined influence I felt at the time which could

best be expressed by the one word *love*. This impression was confirmed and substantiated during the two years to follow.

Our interview lasted for about five minutes, during which time she prepared me for what I might expect by way of rebuke and praise at times, both of which might come to me abundantly, and they did. But I had in large measure learned to evaluate such things properly and was not unduly affected by either. Inability to impersonalize these extremes was the reason so many who were summoned to her side, and who seemed promising, could not stand after a brief stay and had to return to their homes. They took her praise to themselves as a heavenly benediction and her rebukes as personal condemnation.

My first interview was remarkable in that it was the first and only time that I ever saw or heard of our Leader becoming embarrassed or unpoised for any cause. It came about this way: Mrs. Sargent had introduced me by saying, "Mother, this is Mr. Rathvon of Boulder." Perhaps not understanding clearly, she greeted me warmly, "I am glad to see you, Mr. Boulder." Noting an amusement which we could only partially suppress, she became momentarily flurried but in a moment was as serene as ever. After Mrs. Sargent explained matters, she appeared as amused as the rest of us had been and, like all who have a true sense of humor, she enjoyed a bit of wit whether it was at her own expense or not.

Day-to-day conversations and routines

More early impressions as recorded at the time are to be gathered from the following extract from a letter written to my wife soon after my arrival:

Sunday, November 22, 1908

Our talks when we gather in the library before and after meals, as well as at table, are just what any other Scientists [who are] up to date might talk about. The Yale-Harvard game yesterday was discussed by all the men, Calvin Frye included, within half an hour after it was decided. The topics of the daily papers, including Rockefeller's testimony, etc., are subjects of comment. I have had the floor much of the time telling about Colorado at the table and have to be on guard that I do not do too much talking; but they will ask questions! Mrs. Sargent, this morning, said she was glad that Denver re-elected Ben Linsey to the Juvenile Court, showing she is awake to what is going on. After all, Mrs. Sargent and Calvin Frye seem to be those of greatest weight in the whole establishment—more indeed than all of us put together.

Mr. Dickey is kept very busy with correspondence;[126] the rest of us are known as "workers," and outside of the regular hours of "watching," which is but another name for treating, we can do as we like, observing the rules of the household never to be outside of bell range—telephone or jump bell, either one—which means practically staying in one's room. We are on watch four hours each day, one in the morning, 9–10, two in the afternoon, 2–3 and 4–5; and one in the evening, 7:30–8:30. We then shut our doors and get down to hard work.

The subjects for each watch are given us, covering the needs of the hour. We are, of course, careful to keep our thoughts off our Leader and handle as best we know the topics that are given us.

Overcoming separation

December 19, 1908, Extract from letter to E.S.R. [Ella Rathvon]:

Well, I had an interview that will be of uncommon interest to you, for it will enable me to communicate some things that heretofore were not communicable. You remember I said I would wait an opportune time and then say something about you. I went right at the matter, as nearly as I can recall, somewhat in this fashion: "Mother, would you object if I were to impart to my dear wife at times some of the good and helpful things you are constantly giving us? She is working bravely in Colorado to overcome the claim of separation and is making it much easier for me here than if her work was not so well done. I know some things I could tell her would help us both."

"By all means, tell her such things and give her my love this night. And you must both know that what you are doing and giving is not a sacrifice, but an offering."

As nearly as I can recall it, these are her words, and it has made me glad to know that at least a part of the restriction of silence has been removed.

This is a copy of E.S.R's letter[127] to our Leader in reference to our Leader's message to E.S.R. in the foregoing interview:

Boulder, Col.
Jan. 22, 1909

Dear Mrs. Eddy:

It gives me great joy to tell you that the sense of separation is being gloriously overcome. Indeed I feel it safe to say it is overcome, and the full realization of its nothingness was brought to me by your message, sent in my husband's letter, that what we were doing was "not sacrifice, but offering." Then the burden vanished, and the joy that came to me is indescribable; I wish I could tell you how ready and happy I am to be of service to you. Each day it is a greater privilege to make this offering of love, for I have long cherished the desire to give you positive proof of my gratitude for your noble, selfless labor in behalf of suffering humanity.

Meeting this claim of separation has been the supreme test of my life, but by the grace of God and your messages of love and encouragement[,] I have been able to stand the test, and have proved the truth of your inspired utterance in *Miscellaneous Writings*, that "time and space, when encompassed by divine presence, do not separate us" (p.110).

With continued assurance of my loving allegiance to you, beloved Leader, and to our Cause, believe me

Gratefully yours,
Ella S. Rathvon

Sayings of our Leader

Editor's note: The following section consists of Rathvon's notes from lessons Mrs. Eddy gave her workers and from his conversations with her. The initials W.R.R. refer to Rathvon himself. The initials E.S.R. refer to his wife, Ella, who joined the household in September 1909. A few of Ella's notes, indicated by her initials, are interspersed. The heading "Sayings of our Leader" is Rathvon's own description of this section of his reminiscence.

November 28, 1908

"We must master every form of error in ourselves even to the last. I have done it for others in the past." [Mrs. Eddy] then told of a man with a crushed limb run over by a railroad train and carried into a hotel. She treated him and he got up and accompanied her to the door. She also told of a child laid out for burial who was taken out of her coffin and healed.

December 11, 1908

"Jesus proved—that is, demonstrated—his power. I have experienced and demonstrated over much. Now it is old age. You will not be spared this unless you profit by my example. Your opportunity is that of the listener to music played by a master. Could he play it without first having had the experience? Could a great mathematician work his problem without experience?"

December 13, 1908

W.R.R. asked, "How can I best improve Sunday?" Answer: "By realizing your spiritual identity." She then asked all of us, "What is the scientific signification of Sunday?" Various answers were given, none of which were wholly satisfactory. She then said, "Just what it says, a day of Light and Truth and Love, the day of Soul governing man. Is man spiritual? He is, then let Soul alone govern him." Called back. "When you leave me, I often think of more because I am then nearer to God. I opened *Science and Health* this morning at 260, line 7." (She read this passage impressively without glasses.)

W.R.R.: "How can I best serve you this day, Mother?" Answer: "By best serving God."

December 14, 1908

W.R.R. said, "I never want the day to pass without a word of good from you, and to tell you tonight how we are working for you." She replied, "I am speaking to you always, for I am sending out good to all mankind. I know you are working for me, bless you."

December 15, 1908

We had a long lesson, beginning with forty years ago when she first began to write Science. Many deserted her, and friends endeavored to persuade her to quit, but she kept on, subsisting at times "on an apple and a piece of bread. All who came were healed, and many who did not come. The dead were raised. Now, why am I thus? Do you know of anyone showing greater love? You must love more to help me. To love more, you must get rid of more self. The unselfed love is only what helps."

December 23, 1908

"If one stands on the shore in water knee deep and sees another buffeting the waves far out, is it just to say that the one is not harmonious and the other is? I am going through those things which may never come to you and which you cannot understand."

"Obedience is the only course. Being close to God brings obedience. If we do not obey, we are standing out against God and will be made to obey. I have found it so every time. I have not yet overcome the belief of life, substance, and intelligence in matter, or I would not be here. After Jesus overcame it, he was seen as perfect. I do not want you to see me as in the body but as having overcome it."

"We see the spiritual only as we unsee the material, and in proportion as one is done, does the other follow. Bonjour!"

December 25, 1908

"Good morning and Merry Christmas to all. Mass to Christ! Thanks are idle if not expressed in deeds. Thanks to God must be manifestations. Christ was manifested." After speaking to her of my wife, she said, "I feel the work both of you are doing. It is one of the most gratifying things of my life. Give her my love."

December 26, 1908

"We are either Scientists or senseists, which is it? 'Choose you this day whom ye will serve' [Joshua 24:15]. You must uncover error, know it, and put it out. I have not yet overcome it, but I will." Speaking of Christmas, she said, "I have tried for years to observe it but was always prevented. Christmas should be every day to the Scientist. If an issue comes, it must be decided for God. You must not put upon me the burden of deciding what *Science and Health* declares."

January 1, 1909

"Begin the New Year by doing, not talking. Talk is dangerous if it satisfies us and thus prevents us from going further and making our demonstration. If it does not prevent, it may hinder. The tongue may lie, but healing the sick is no lie. Wrong thought leads to wrong action and vice versa. If one is done, the other will do itself, just as the little boy in school who whistled and, when spoken to by his teacher, said, 'I did not whistle. It whistled itself.' I want you to see me active, sound, right, not showing signs of impairment or age or loss. See my real self as God guides, directs, and demonstrates me. See me as God sees me." Read Proverbs 2:10–11, *Science and Health*, p. 227:14.

January 9, 1909

"It is a trick of the devil to make something of nothing. It is the sublimity of the [D]ivine to make the something, everything.

The things we most count upon and rely upon here will cause us the most suffering until we no longer rely upon them."

January 9, 1909

"I am struggling with the claims of old age and death, and if I undertook to handle them as presented, I could never meet them; but I just hold to the allness of God, that there is nothing else, and I want all of you to do just the same.

January 11, 1909

"Evil has its compensation in suffering. Good in blessing, love in loving. We gain nothing by dying except seeing the unreality of it all. I have no use for the smiling kind who say with their lips 'God is all' and sit with folded hands doing nothing in the way of proof. It is a lie to say that which implies proving, if we prove it not."

January 14, 1909

Mrs. Eddy was speaking of her career, her mission, and her qualifications for executing it. Among other things, without any suggestion of self-exaltation, she said, "I am different from other mortals in many respects, one of them being that I more frequently get out of God's way."

January 14, 1909

Yesterday after Adam Dickey had been gone for several hours, our Leader called the rest of us in and said, "We are all one family and when my parents would go away, we children used to get together and say to each other, 'Now you'll be good to me while they're gone, won't you?' So we must all be good to each other while Mr. Dickey is away."

February 1, 1909

"I am trying to separate myself from a sense of life, truth, intelligence, and substance in matter. You will understand, therefore, what I mean when I say that I do not want all of you to come in to see me so often."

February 2, 1909

"I ought to be spared from deciding business matters. Hereafter I want them to be decided by McLellan and Frye. I do not want to be annoyed by them."

February 4, 1909

"Do you realize what you are doing for the world in helping your Leader? Could any greater help be given to the Cause than by helping its Leader—its Mother? If Jesus' students had watched with him, he would have made his demonstration nineteen hundred years sooner."

February 8, 1909

Our Leader said that "sleep in Science is not necessary." She spoke of preaching her best after nights without any sleep. She was joyous and vigorous, the best yet, and said, "Am making way-showers of you."

February 18, 1909

"The reason I have been able to carry this movement on is because I have gotten nearer to God than any other mortal. It could not be done otherwise."

Later: "What is the highest attainment one can cherish?" Various answers were given but none satisfactory. She answered herself, "Healing the sick. That requires the abandonment of everything. Away go automobiles and all else material. I gave up everything and I healed the sick. I saw a man crippled so that when he moved he was almost doubled up and had his hands on the ground to assist locomotion. I saw him seated on the curb, with his head between his knees, on my way to a patient. As I passed, I placed my hand on his head and said, 'Do you know that God loves you?' At once he straightened up, erect as he ever had been. One of my students was watching the incident and called the man to her, who exclaimed, 'Have I seen an angel?'" Through her healing she said she brought the world to her feet.

February 24, 1909

"After reading aloud to her from the *Monitor* of women suffragettes being arrested, she said, "I have always insisted upon my students obeying the law; nothing could have been accomplished by the methods these women take.""

February 24, 1909

"They threatened to blow me up with dynamite at one time if I did not stop preaching, but that did not move me, not a bit.""

February 27, 1909

"I am working a rule I never did before. I have the battle with old age and death. God will show me the way and I will show you. I have given the world what they could understand, but they are not ready for this last problem. You must help me work the rule, and then you will not have to go through what I am now. See this all as a dream; then wake up to see its unreality."

March 2, 1909

"We must see the perfect man, not a sick one. If you saw me as God made me, I would not be here. Now I want you to tell me my faults. Why am I here?" Various answers were given. W.R.R. said, "Because you believe you cannot do for yourself what you have done and can do for others. If I were there, you could raise me in a minute." She replied, "Thank you, dear."

March 3, 1909

"No word in the Bible is so much misunderstood as *love*. Its best definition is to be seen in results. It transforms the unreal into the real. We can have it without naming it."

March 3, 1909

When her students came telling of the shortcomings of others, she would say to them, "Now tell me something good about them."

March 6, 1909

"You must be able to handle and destroy every form of error whether it appears in storm or elsewhere. The same power that overcomes sin, sickness, and death can control the weather. When a Leader is taken down in battle, who is to carry on the conflict? All of you. Each of you, and I expect you to do it."

March 16, 1909

"Everything I have gained has been through suffering, but there is no necessity for sin or suffering. No justification for anything but the actual and real."

March 21, 1909

"Drop the touch of error. There is nothing to oppose the right. If we give enough reality to the good, there is nothing left of error. Now let us hold on to that."

March 23, 1909

Recently we were considering the question what a Scientist should do under circumstances where personality was not only aggressive but malicious. Mrs. Eddy said, "Know that he has no power, and live as though he was not."

March 26, 1909

"Our work is to disbelieve error. That being done, there is no need for argument, nothing to argue against. Now, tell me something." W.R.R. gave her *Science and Health*, page 393: "Mind is the master of the corporeal senses, and can conquer sickness, sin, and death." She replied, "What is the use of authority if you do not exercise it?"

March 26, 1909

"We are all in the infancy of Christian Science, and some allowance must be made as infants are not expected to talk as grown-ups." She then spoke of [a child] whom she was trying to get to say "aristocratic" and who said, instead, "a-wrist-to-scratch-it."

"A sense of humor is a great aid to a Christian Scientist."

April 4, 1909

"Working out of materiality is God's means of disciplining me. If I suffer for it, that is my fault. God does not send the suffering nor the sickness."

April 9, 1909

In her chair while manifesting a fine mental and physical condition, she opened her Bible at Isaiah 66:6–8, which she asked me to read. Later she said, "We must divest our sense of birth from travail. We are giving birth to children of our thought constantly, and such must be without travail. There is nothing new to God. Now, our work is to find out the old. We might put the word *new* out of our vocabulary. There is no place for it in our calendar. Let us substitute for it the word *now*." She then read, herself, from *Science and Health* and continued talking, "Man never started existing. You and you and you and I are forever one. There is but one Principle, and as we learn to know [its] ideas, we get to understand the universe. There is no age, no youth. Man is as old as God. Realize this and we will never grow old. The day dream and the night dream are ever unreal. This seeming life is a dream."

April 11, 1909

"What is the supreme test? Giving up all—family, friends, business, income, everything. Some of you have done it (pointing to me). I have to give up my belief of pain. Is it easier to give up than belief of pleasure?" Adam Dickey answered, "Yes." She replied, "No. There, I caught you, for neither is anything, hence there is nothing to give up. Tell me something." I replied, "According to divine Science, man is in a degree as perfect as the Mind that forms him" [*Science and Health*, p. 337]. She replied, "We are all one in the infinite, and there is but one infinite, the infinite One."

April 20, 1909

"You six are to be the exponents of Christian Science to the world. You were sent here by God. Nothing should stand in your way. Is there any love that is not spiritual? Is there any human affection? When I scold, I cannot see any good in mortal mind, none whatever. All my students who have left me did so because of my scolding." I then asked her, "Must we never praise those whom we teach?" She replied, "Yes, praise the good always."

May 1, 1909

After speaking to her of an incident in Boulder, she said, "Give your dear wife my love, and tell her God will bless her for the good work she is doing. God will bless all the wives who are helping their husbands here."

May 2, 1909

"Moses leaned on his staff, matter, and when he threw it away, it turned on him. Not until he took it by the tail without fear did he master it. The one who is afraid of matter is better off than the one who is not. The one who handles and demonstrates over it is better than either or all, for he knows there is nothing to fear."

May 5, 1909

"Never before have I had a household so uniformly satisfactory. Not a discordant note in it."

May 8, 1909

Th[is] remark was made in our Leader's presence: "It is a perfect day." She then asked, "What is a fine day?" and replied, "One in which you can get closest to God. I have had some of my best days in stormy weather."

May 9, 1909

She said to me on return from her ride, "I want you to take what recreation you like. There is an extra horse in the stable, and when I am out, you can use him, or the 'mobile, or whatever you like."

May 20, 1909

Speaking of herself, Mrs. Eddy said, "When I went into the presence of sickness, I couldn't stop declaring the [t]ruth until the case was healed. I knew the [t]ruth. Truth is conviction."

May 22, 1909

"The book will endure forever."

May 29, 1909

Speaking of exercise, our Leader said, "When you came to Christian Science, you gave up tobacco because it was scientific to do so. Exercise should likewise be discarded." Adam Dickey replied, "I gave up tobacco, but I did not shut myself up in a room. Should we do so?" She replied, "You must not ask me what to do and what not. I have to handle Mary. You must work out these things yourself. I was once a victim of hygiene and physiology. When I learned Christian Science, I was told to get away from them gradually. I dropped them suddenly and sat up all night preparing my sermons that I might deliver them without notes the next morning. You must not think I have demonstrated all I teach. I am telling you what I do for your own good, not because I like to scold you. You may wonder why I take my ride. It is not for exercise or diversion but to show mortal mind that I can do it."

June 16, 1909

"When things come hardest, you must stick tightest. Ask me questions, just as if you were in my College." I asked her, "Why can I cure another's failures and he, mine?" She replied, "Because you are afraid of what he was not afraid, and he afraid of what you were not."

June 16, 1909

"Like children who are growing and fret over it because they do not understand, I have learned to leave it to God and wait to understand Love."

June 16, 1909

"Those most unselfish are nearest God."

June 27, 1909

I read to our Leader from the *Sentinel* of June 26 relating to the experience of someone getting results from declaring his divine sonship, etc., in working out a problem. She said, "No such experiences ever came to me. I reached the result without the intermediate steps. If anyone was said to be ill in the next room, I would not have to treat. I would just know the [t]ruth about them, and they would seem to be no more sick or dead than you are. I cannot tell how I do it, but I have none of these experiences recorded by others, though I enjoy reading them."

"It came to me as a voice out of heaven, 'You have all in God and God in all.'"

The Pink Room at Chestnut Hill

July 4, 1909

A little incident occurred this morning which will serve to illustrate how keen our Leader's thought is to detect and direct when there is need of uncovering or instruction. We were all gathered with her in the Pink Room, she asking us questions and expounding Science to us as she alone can do. At times her leadings were so profound that we found a sense of difficulty in keeping pace with her thought. At others, through a flash of wit or a quick, pat comparison, a bit of advice or a homely incident from her own experience, we were traveling side by side with her, learning of God's goodness through the simpler things, as children at their mother's side.

One of the group, in his answer, used the quotation from *Miscellaneous Writings: 1883–1896,* "Error found out is two-thirds destroyed" (p. 355) and added something about destroying the other third. Quick as a spark came her admonition, "See that you do not trust too much to that two-thirds!"

July 26, 1909

In the carriage ride today, our Leader noticed some little children climbing the hillside and remarked, "They remind me much of my disposition even as a child. I was always fond of climbing to the top. No hill was too high. I wanted to reach the top and look over. It has always been so in spiritual matters also." While enjoying the beautiful trees and shrubbery of her reservoir drive, she remarked, "Every leaf upon every tree declares perpetually that God is Love."

July 26, 1909

"Your thought being with God is more powerful than all else."

September 12, 1909

One of us asked our Leader today in the Pink Room, "Can you destroy error by denial?" She replied, "No; the right way is to realize the omnipresence of good, and when that is done, there is nothing left to be denied."

Later: "Your giving up your wives and husband could not be borne by me if I did not know that by giving up all, you are gaining more."

September 16, 1909

We were gathered about her in the twilight. As she sat in her chair in the bay window with no light but the tiny lamp on her desk, she said, "I can recognize each of you without aid of material illumination by turning away from the material to the spiritual, from man to God. So I can distinguish between Dickey and Tomlinson, and between Tomlinson and von Rath." This was a surprise to me for I had never told her that von Rath was my ancestral name. She did not seem at all surprised, but merely said, when I mentioned it to her, "No one ever told me."

September 18, 1909

In speaking of the overcoming of sin, our Leader said, "Sin is to be handled by knowing there is no sin and no sinner. So with sickness. No sick individual to heal. No personality can injure anyone in this household. Do not handle the individual, but know the nothingness of the claim. Realize the allness and supremacy of God, knowing there is no opposite."

September 28, 1909

Mrs. Eddy remarked, "There is neither youth, maturity, nor decay. I do not have to eat pork or potatoes or beefsteak for strength. If we knew enough or demonstrated enough, we could prove there is no need of eating."

October 13, 1909

"I want a revival in your religion. Turn your thoughts away from materiality."

Later: "A mother should teach her child there is no sin. When too young to understand, it should be silently voiced to the child while in its mother's arms. Had I known this, it would have saved me much with George. Shall I give you a present this morning? It is this: There is no sin."

October 27, 1909

"I do not know why I do many things except because God tells me. When is as important as how."

October 27, 1909

"Goodness and beauty go side by side. Beauty is a thing of life, not apart from nature. The principle of good is inseparable from the principle of beauty.

November 27, 1909

"The right thing done at the wrong time is no longer the right thing."

December 12, 1909

(Sunday) All hands were in the Pink Room grouped about our Leader in the center who was looking well in a new gown and being her own loving self. After the Communion Doxology was sung by us all, she asked for audible prayers from each of us in turn; afterwards we sang three verses of the "Mother's Evening Prayer."[128] Then she gave us a most illuminating talk on our duties and privileges. She said, "You have been called here of God for the special purpose of carrying on His work. You are here to prepare yourselves for that high calling. This is a preparatory school where you are learning to lead the Cause. Now, what is the first thing for you to learn? Anybody answer." Adam Dickey replied, "To know there is nothing but God and His idea."

"That's it, dearie," she said, "and when you really know that, then there is no sickness to heal and no sin to destroy. Get out of your thoughts every word that suggests a belief apart from God. Every word."

December 24, 1909 (E.S.R.)

Good lesson. "Not so much what God does for us as what He is."

December 25, 1909

We were told that, during the coming year, we must manifest more of kind generosity and affection and that we must love God more, not only for what He does but also for what He is. Late that night I was called to her bedside when she said to me, "Do you know by what it is that I heal the sick?" I replied, "Through your knowledge of God." She said, "No, that is not it." "What is it then?" I asked. She replied, "By Love."

February 13, 1910

Home is not a place, it is a power. Going home is doing right. If you cannot make a home here, you cannot anywhere. I am glad all of you, so many, are going with me homeward, and we will all meet there. Blessings immortal, eternal, infinite, come not through personality, but through understanding Principle.

February 27, 1910

We were told that we were being prepared to take her place and we would be expected to take it sooner or later. "It might be a thousand years," but it would be some time, "for I have a higher work to do." Each of us was then given opportunity to promise to stay here as long as she would want us, as she said, "I have taught you all God allows me to teach you, until you come up to where I am."

March 20, 1910

"You are here preparing to take a strong position before the world. There is a high purpose to be fulfilled by you in healing the sick and reforming the sinner, but you are now getting ready for the higher office of teaching and preaching and carrying on the Cause in other important directions. We owe much to God, but He will allow us to pay the debt little by little if we keep the interest paid up. We do not have to wait until we pay all before we pay anything."

April 9, 1910

"When the fear of lying awake is overcome, you will sleep."

April 22, 1910

"We are not suffering for the Truth, and a lie cannot affect us."

"Do not depend too much upon your understanding, but let your upper-standing hold you."

"It is not time that heals—it is Truth that does it."

"Home of Soul, where sense has no claim and soul is satisfied."

May 14, 1910

(Sunday) In speaking of our singing on Sundays as expressive of things spiritual, she said, "It is possible that it may be heard by our dear ones who have preceded us. Their voices may unite with ours. They are not changed or disunited. We are forever inseparable in Mind."

Later: W.R.R. referred this morning to the whole world studying the same [Bible] Lesson at one time and [said] that any of them would esteem it a privilege of a lifetime to exchange places with us for one Sunday. "Yes," she replied with a smile. "The effect of this mind concentration each Sunday cannot be estimated. You who are here are but a moiety, but you are representative of the infinite multitude who are singing the praises of God through the universe."

May 28, 1910

"We should forget failures and disappointments. We experience a recurrence of evils and suffering because we do not forget them. We are often deterred from undertaking things because of a remembrance of past failures." (See *Miscellaneous Writings*, p. 130.)

May 28, 1910

"There is no death to Truth, Life, and Love. Always begin with Mind as the groundwork of your treatment."

"Your greatest need is to destroy your greatest temptation."

June 1, 1910

"A hundred liars have no more power to harm than one, and it has no power."

June 6, 1910

"In your arguments, do not admit any opposite to God."

"A denial of anything is an admission that it has a claim to existence."

June 23, 1910

"Demonstrating a truth is what Science is. Talking it without demonstration is what Science is not."

"If you do not get happiness where you are now, you will never get it."

June 26, 1910

"God always has headquarters."

"He gives us power as we assimilate the [t]ruth."

June 30, 1910

"I sometimes think there is as much love in expressing it as in having it."

July 3, 1910

"I lost him (husband) because I thought too much of him."

July 8, 1910 (E.S.R.)

Talk on belief of age. No growing old—neither young nor old. There is no "too late" nor "too soon" with God; all is the eternal now.

"Self-knowledge gives us knowledge of others."

"The strongest tie I've ever had, apart from love of God, has been my love of home."

"I want you all to feel this is your home, and if you do not and I can do anything to make it so, you must tell me and I will do it."

July 18, 1910

"The demonstration of health is health."

July 31, 1910

"If you know a thing theoretically, you are responsible for it practically."

"The victory is as certain now as it will be a century hence."

"Consciousness materialized is corrected by consciousness spiritualized."

"If all do not prove it, one must."

"You cannot make sour sweet, except you put in enough sweet."

July 1910

Not quite a year ago, in giving to us the scientific explanation of that passage in John (9:4) where Jesus said, "the night cometh, when no man can work," Mrs. Eddy said, "A temptation comes to all that we cannot do our work. If we yield, we are in the night. This is what is meant by 'the night cometh, when no man can work.'"

August 5, 1910

"I've had to learn. If blessings wouldn't do it, kicking would. I've had both."

August 20, 1910

"God clothes you in garments of righteousness and holiness. See that you put on these garments as soon as they are ready for you."

September 3, 1910

"When I saw my duty, hell couldn't keep me from doing it."

September 11, 1910

"Depersonalize self. To personalize thought limits spiritual growth." (See *Miscellaneous Writings*, p. 282.)

September 11, 1910

"He sets us free on the cross, not on the crown; that known, the cross becomes the crown instantly."

"When we gain the scientific sense of matter, there is no matter."

September 25, 1910

"There is never a time when there is not something for you to do. Doing that something opens the way for God's blessing."

October 2, 1910

"Mortal mind does not increase in wisdom; wisdom decreases mortal mind." (See *Science and Health*, p. 426.)

Question: Are beauty and harmony as reflected in things material, beneficial or injurious?

Answer: (Our Leader) "That depends on their effect upon you."

October 5, 1910

"The Cause is not dependent upon man or woman, and God will take care of it."

October 8, 1910

"I was brought up to believe that religion should always be solemn and altogether dolorous. I know now that it should be just the opposite, and we should have good cheer."

October 9, 1910

"Divinity always seems strange to humanity until replaced by familiarity. Until its strangeness is taken away, it is not profitable."

October 16, 1910

After the last line of the Doxology was sung, our Leader said, "There is endless instruction in that. Endless, but beginning here and now."

"You are here growing and ripening like a choice plant in the sun. What you are here doing for me, you are doing for all, and what you are doing for all, you are doing for God."

October 19, 1910

After singing "Guide Me, O Thou Great Jehovah" [with us], our Leader said, "When a child, I would go off by myself to sing and pray. I would never accept the words 'Feed me till I want no more.' Even then I did not want to reach a point where I would have had enough spiritual food. The more we get, the more we see there is to get and the greater our desire for more. If we did not expand, we would burst." E.S.R. [Ella Rathvon] suggested, "Feed me now and evermore," and our Leader replied, "That's very good."

October 23, 1910

"God can institute nothing that is not self-existent and eternal."

November 6, 1910

"When working for all, you are doing good work for yourselves."

"God is giving each of us the experience best adapted to lead us to Him."

"What you need more than self-forgetfulness is self-nothingness."

November 27, 1910 (E.S.R.)

Our Leader said, "Turn your thoughts to Principle, not to me. You lose your answer from God by looking to me for the answer."

November 28, 1910 (E.S.R.)

Another good admonition from our Leader: "When ministering your daily tasks, do not think that you have done something through matter, but know that God has done it through Mind."

Mealtimes and evening entertainment at Chestnut Hill

Certain practices in ordinary use in religious families were somewhat different at Chestnut Hill. For instance, there was no established rule for asking a blessing or saying grace before meals.

In Jesus' time grace before meat was customary, being one of the ancient Jewish practices recorded in the Old Testament which escaped Jesus' denunciation when "the traditions of men" were being substituted for "the commandment of God" (see Mark 7:8). We do not know whether Jesus followed this custom habitually, but there are several instances given in the New Testament where he gave thanks before serving others with bread and meat.

At times Mrs. Eddy would pass the word that we were not to have any religious observance at all before our meals. At other times she would tell us to have silent grace, so we would follow that practice until, after a season, down would come the word that she would like each of us in turn to recite some appropriate Scriptural passage, and after awhile it would be something from *Science and Health*. I can recall two from our Leader's pen that were frequently used. One was from *Science and Health*: "In that perfect day of understanding, we shall neither eat to live nor live to eat" (p. 388). The other was unique in that it is altogether scientific and has been given worldwide publicity, yet it does not appear in any of her published writings. It is easily remembered and is good to have with us if we are inclined to go too far when hungry and an appetizing dinner is spread before us. Here is what she authorized to be stamped on the back of her souvenir spoons that at one time had such a large sale: "Not matter but Mind satisfieth." So we had a great variety of pre-meal observances from one time to another. This to me was another evidence that Mrs. Eddy did not desire her followers to adhere strictly to any one form of religious observance at the table or elsewhere.

One of the features to which my thought turns often with pleasant recollection were the evenings when, after our Leader was settled for the night, the five of us—Mrs. Hoag, Mr. Dickey, Mr. Tomlinson, my wife, and I—would go down to the sitting room adjoining the kitchen and there sing together with Mrs. Hoag or Mrs. Rathvon at the piano. What our voices lacked in melody, they surely made up in volume, for I recall quite clearly Mrs. Hoag once turning to us and saying, "Why must you sing so loudly?"

Mrs. Hoag and Mrs. Rathvon sang soprano. Mr. Dickey stumbled along under a heavy load of base, while I clawed the scales toward the high notes, trying to contribute a thin tenor, and the Reverend (as we called Mr. Tomlinson) wobbled around in every direction. If we didn't make music, we certainly did produce a joyful noise.

Studying and revising *Science and Health*

Our Leader's attitude of deep respect, almost reverence, for *Science and Health* and her lack of familiarity with many things it contained was indicative of its divine origin. She would, like the rest of us, frequently find new phases of significance in familiar passages, which although signally helpful had not yielded to her all the richness they contained. Her unfolding recognition of the hidden treasure which that book holds should be a forceful rebuke to those deluded individuals who feel they have outgrown Mrs. Eddy's teachings or have exhausted all they contain.

While at Chestnut Hill, the following incident was related to me. In one of her earlier classes our Leader asked those present if they knew anyone who fully understood her writings. A man got up and said, "I know someone who does." "Who?" asked Mrs. Eddy before he had ceased. "Mrs. Eddy, herself," the man replied. "She does not," she said. "She understands only what she has demonstrated, and that is no further than the A, B, C."

Mrs. Eddy's occasional revisions of parts of her textbook, *Science and Health*, in her later years were not comprehensive but limited, and were for the avowed purpose of making its ethics and practice more simple and more readily understood. With a few notable exceptions, she added nothing new, but by changes of phraseology, inserting a word here and a sentence there, she clarified whatever may have seemed ambiguous or obscure to the casual reader. She was ever conscious of the limitations and restrictions with which she labored in her endeavors to express a spiritual idea in ordinary language. She refers to this on page

349 of *Science and Health,* where this statement occurs: "The chief difficulty in conveying the teachings of divine Science accurately to human thought lies in this, that like all other languages, English is inadequate to the expression of spiritual conceptions and propositions, because one is obliged to use material terms in dealing with spiritual ideas."

She was convinced that this clarification of thought would ever continue. In speaking on this subject in April 1909, she said to me, "Even through eternity the ethics of Christian Science as set forth in our textbook will ever become clearer and clearer." She was ever learning and would have her followers progress with her.

It was her practice on retiring at night after her bedside light was adjusted, with *Science and Health* before her and pencil and paper at hand, to write down such changes as she believed would tend to simplify or clarify whatever she then thought needed it. Sometimes weeks would pass without any change being made, but when she felt she was divinely guided to make an alteration, it was at once recorded and in the morning was given to one of us to take to her publisher without delay.

This night revision was in marked contrast with her methods of writing the book originally, as it is a well-known fact which I have heard her mention a number of times, that in writing *Science and Health* her pen traveled rapidly without her being able to recall afterwards much that was written, and that her ability to write disappeared with the sun.

On one occasion in July 1909, I was speaking to her about the remarkable correlation between her writings and the Scriptures on so many vital points, and asked her if in writing she went from one book to the other. She replied,

"Never. I would seat myself and write and write without leaving or interruption. Whenever the sun went down, I could do nothing further."

Mrs. Eddy was a close student of her own writings, the margin of her copy of *Science and Health* being sprinkled with pencilings, comments, cross-references, and correlative texts. I have seen her face illuminated as by a new discovery when one of us would find some apt passage and take it to her. I have met many devout Christian Scientists, but I have never known anyone who held the textbook in greater reverence or who studied it more faithfully than its author herself.

Music at home and in church

In November of 1909 a new Victrola was brought to the house, and all of us, including our Leader herself, enjoyed the music it afforded. For a while she used it daily, and on one occasion (February 13, 1910) she [listened to] the record of "Home, Sweet Home." After it was through, she spoke to the Victrola as though it were an artist singing for her benefit, and said, "Thank you, Mr. Singer Man, but I prefer my own choir to the choir invisible." She had a very pretty affectation of talking back to the voice the record reproduced, which displayed her natural playfulness if nothing else.

In the early days of Christian Science churches, it was quite the thing to follow the fashion of orthodox denominations and have an imposing choir, and while First Church, Chicago, was building its new edifice in the early '90s, the plans provided no space for the choir, which was quite an innovation. In course of construction, someone asked Mr. Kimball, who was most active in First Church at that time, what was going to be done about space for the choir of his church. He answered in his characteristic way, "We are engaged just now in fighting the world, the flesh, and the devil. When we get through with them, we will be qualified to take up the church music problem."

This brings to mind an incident Mrs. Eddy related to me showing how the so-called artistic temperament crept into the church choirs in her young days as well as in later times. She was walking along with her friend when they passed someone they both knew. Mrs. Eddy spoke but her companion did not. Mrs. Eddy asked in some surprise, "How is it you did not speak to her; you know her, do you not?" "Oh yes," was the reply, "but we sang in the same choir together for a while."

The *Christian Science Hymnal*, which was revised in 1909, had Mrs. Eddy's approval although not her close supervision as to words or music, with one or two exceptions which I can recall. When it was all ready to go to press, no tune was found for her poem "Mother's Evening Prayer" that was wholly satisfactory to her until the one that now appears in the *Hymnal* as Morecambe (No. 207) was submitted and suited her fairly well. As she desired to have the music of her hymn conform as far as possible to the sentiment of the words, she changed the last line of the first stanza so that the notes for the words "on upward wing tonight" would ascend instead of descend as originally written and as they were retained in the other verses. This change was made, and it so appears in the present edition of the *Hymnal*.

Journal excerpts

Editor's note: This section consists of excerpts from a journal Rathvon kept while at Chestnut Hill.

Thursday, January 14, 1909

The newspapers of New York and, in fact, all the East are making much of our Leader's gift of $500.00 to the Newton Hospital. It was another one of those right things at the right time, for which she has been noted. Then, too, it shows to the world that Christian Science does not advocate indifference to human suffering as has so often been alleged. The people of Newton have been well disposed toward our Leader ever since she came to dwell here and are now more appreciative than ever.

Saturday, January 16, 1909

The more I see of our Leader in the various sidelights of her wonderful mentality, the plainer do I understand why she was the chosen bearer of this message to the children of men. Never was there another like her. An outstanding evidence of it all is that those who have been longest with her and closest to her, and who have endured the most and been rewarded no more—save by close and continued companionship—than others less favored: these, I say, are the ones who pronounce with least hesitation the conviction that she was God-sent and God-governed. The day is coming, and may not be far off, when the tremendous significance of things daily occurring—in which we are the background, the stage setting as it were—will appear to all, and we may then wonder if we made the most of our opportunities.

Saturday, January 16, 1909

I have been here but a short time, yet I see the necessity of impersonalizing the generous praise that is extended when one has performed some particularly worthy thing, as well as treating in the same way the rebukes and reproofs that at times seem unduly severe. The exultation of the one and the depression of the other are both fraught with danger and can only be nullified by recognizing that they are not intended to be personal.

As an instance of the necessity of keeping our poise in our work, I would relate how, upon [my] going to our Leader this morning, she called me "faithful one" and said she would give me a new name—"Faithful." I like it well enough and hope it will stay with her and that I may prove it to be no misnomer. But it is just such little instances as that, when taken too seriously, that have uplifted one to the skies in a state of ecstasy from which the tumble to earth is disastrous.

Thursday, January 21, 1909

I have just had a remarkable interview. Calvin Frye called me after supper and said, if I had not been in, I had better go and he would remain in the hall. It was his hour for remaining in the room, but whether he was sent out for a purpose I do not know. I was received with the most unreserved graciousness and asked to take a chair, something never done before. I was at her side for more than fifteen minutes, holding her hand while she did most of the talking. She was at her best, in the most joyous mood, told me of some of her early reminiscences.

Then she spoke of the satisfactory outcome of the New York affair,[129] and I praised her for the wise fashion in which she handled it all, how the Field wondered at her leniency and now saw the wisdom of it as they have of other moves of hers. I said, "Mother, you are a General." She seemed much pleased but, not to be outdone, replied, "Well, if I'm a General, you're a Captain." Then she went on to tell me how she was pleased with my work, how she had seen things in me that she liked, and a lot more of similar praise that gave me much to meet.

Friday, January 22, 1909

Speaking of quick demonstrations, our Leader today related a case "somewhere in Massachusetts years ago—I wish I had kept the place and date—where a man came to me for help." Cancer in its advanced stages. She described it in detail, and it must have been a horrible case. She treated and looked again, and it was gone! One side of the man's neck was as sound and smooth as the other.

Sunday, January 31, 1909

A great lesson to be learned here is impersonalization. Never was there louder call or greater need to know that both good and evil must be separated from whatever personality expresses them. The call of the hour is to know only the good and its God-sent message—to see that what would pass itself off as an evil thing is no thing whatsoever and, when seen [as nothing], is made nothing and dismissed.

That one who has been made the mouthpiece of God—and who for forty years struggled against awful odds that such message might be delivered without contamination or chance of adulteration—that such a one should be made the target for the assaults of the one evil is not surprising. That such attacks should be subtle and insidious is in keeping with the characteristics of mortal mind, today more devious and arrogant than ever before in history. It then behooves us to discriminate, differentiate, separate, and above all to be patient and not disturbed over appearances.

Perhaps if all in this household were as far advanced as is our Leader, the wall of defense would be so stoutly built that error of no kind could find entrance or lodgment. They seem far enough along to protect themselves, as a rule, against such shafts as may be aimed their way, but to [every] one that is sent to pierce the armor of the soldier in the ranks, there are a thousand shot at our Commander-in-Chief. Is it to be wondered that an occasional shaft should find brief abiding where the archer would have it stop? It is for us to see it as sent by the enemy and pluck it out of our own consciousness, where its presence is known, guarding meanwhile the individuality of our Leader against all aggressive suggestions that would blind us to the source of the attack. This is a vital part of our work here—work that needs to be so well done that no matter how aggravated may appear the error, we can see it wholly apart from the true individuality and, recognizing its origin and nature, can destroy its effects. Only nothing can come from nothing, or better still, nothing but nothing can come from nothing.

February 1, 1909

In answer to an "Everybody Call" this a.m., a remarkable letter was read from a Scientist in England relating how Bishop Wilberforce, Archbishop of England, I believe, in a late sermon in Westminster Abbey, London, quoted from end to end "My Prayer in Christian Science" and advised his congregation to get it and study it closely.[130] The shops where it was sold were overwhelmed with orders and soon sold out. Later, one of his parishioners went to him and said that she was going to leave and become a Christian Scientist. "You have taken a step forward," he replied.

Sunday, March 21, 1909

There is no rank here. Deference is always paid to any preferences expressed by anyone, particularly by Calvin Frye or Mrs. Sargent, but there is no rank, or grades of rank, in the household. Each one has certain work to do which must be done without a taskmaster or supervisor standing by to see to its enforcement. Otherwise the term of service is quickly ended. Occasionally a case occurs where such liberty and freedom is too much for the individual and malicious animal magnetism handles him to his undoing.

March 31, 1909

It was quite the usual thing for Mrs. Eddy to invite us to ask her any questions that might occur to us, and today I asked her, "If a practitioner has a patient who does not respond to treatment, but later does so under another practitioner, was the failure in the first instance the fault of the practitioner or of the patient?" She replied, "It may have been neither, but was God's occasion." Then I asked her, "If a patient does not improve under my treatment, is it wrong for me to turn him over to another?" She replied with emphasis, "Certainly not." I then told her that I knew of a practitioner who does not keep a patient who shows no signs of improvement after two weeks' effort and asked her if that was the right thing to do. "No," she replied, "for it is challenging God."

Saturday, September 4, 1909

It has all come about in the most natural way, and inside of two hours yesterday afternoon, Ella Hoag was on her way to Toledo and Ella Rathvon installed in her place. In the morning, Ella Hoag consulted with me several times about the phraseology of a note in which she proposed to bring the matter to the notice of our Leader. She was to present the note in person, in which [she] stated her husband's insistence on her return home and recall[ed] the instructions given by our Leader (that she should find a substitute) before Ella was named. Adam Dickey opened the way for Ella Hoag to present the matter after the drive. Our Leader naturally demurred at the first presentation of the thought of losing her "old worker," but after being assured that everything would work out well, she assented. At 4:10 I passed the word to Ella [Rathvon] by phone, and by 4:45 she was here, bag in hand. She helped Ella Hoag pack up and then settled herself comfortably in Ella Hoag's room without a jar. The household [workers] are happy at her coming, though very sorry to lose Ella Hoag, who is beloved on all sides.

The change is a notable and perhaps momentous one. Neither of us regards it with anything but serenity, for it is one of the many that have come to us without any effort or attempt on our part to accomplish something and [that] have worked from the very beginning harmoniously and irresistibly. We see in it the hand of Principle, by [which] alone we desire to be guided and directed. The opportunities before us are unique and we will do our best to improve them. The senseless law has always been held, and still is in some quarters even within the house, that husband and wife could not stand long side by side here without one or the other becoming upset over the rebukes which might be given the other. This we know will not prevail with us.

There are three reasons why we are not apprehensive of either of us being upset. First, that if any rebuke is needed by either, we will both be glad to have it given. Second, that if there is undeserved severity displayed towards either, we both know enough of Christian Science to see it as malicious animal magnetism and not as emanating from good, and will therefore give it a proper value as absolutely nothing. Third, that by our standing closely together, we can help each other, rather than our being here together proving a hindrance or an invitation to malicious animal magnetism. So, on these points we have no apprehension but are rather glad of the opening to break this law.

Another worthy field for demonstration open to us is to refute to the world the lie that is being spread throughout the Field that our Leader wants to separate husbands and wives. Ella Hoag's long retention here—and her thus being kept from her aged husband—is quoted in support of this false rumor, [with] Adam Dickey's case and mine as corroborative. Now by Ella Hoag's returning home and Ella and I standing fast side by side, this lie will be dealt a two-fold blow.

Sunday, Sept. 5, 1909

The entire change from one Ella to the other which was made quickly and imperceptibly, without stopping the

William and Ella Rathvon at Chestnut Hill

machinery for a moment or shifting the load, indicates that it was brought about and completed by Principle and hence cannot be reversed.

Friday, September 24, 1909

We need to handle constantly what malicious animal magnetism endeavors to intrude to bring about mental inactivity. I am not disturbed about it, for I see it is the result of the peculiar, not to say abnormal, manner of life we necessarily have here. Every possible physical comfort, not to say luxury, is supplied. But there are certain mental routes to be travelled certain hours of every day and night, with varying changes on the same themes between times. In a certain sense, we are hemmed in by tradition on all sides, but I have broken more of them than any who have preceded me. As a result there is more liberty manifested, and this is even being noticed in the Field, and they are rejoicing with us.

Wednesday, September 29, 1909

It was my watch last night, but by suppertime conditions were not promising so that Laura Sargent declared she had better take it herself. By eleven we were all called. The climax of the New York situation has been reached, Augusta E. Stetson having been notified of her degradation, card removed from the *Journal*, and authority to teach rescinded. Her attitude is one of guarded compliance, and no one can tell what she has really planned to do. We are holding steadfastly to "no reversal" and, I believe, will win out. There are also indications of a renewal of activity on the part of the "Next Friends'" attorneys, all of which may have contributed to the unsettled state last night.[131]

Thursday, September 30, 1909

My watch last night was a good one throughout. On my watch I did much mental work, treating aloud and talking the truth with force, not to say vehemence. Later, I did some exercises in thought concentration, attention, direction, and constructive thinking generally.

Thursday, October 7, 1909

My watch last night was a peaceful one. Laura Sargent has of late declared repeatedly that never before was there such a united household and never had the usual problems yielded so readily and completely.

Wednesday, October 13, 1909

Just before starting for the afternoon drive, our Leader asked Irving Tomlinson and me to accompany the carriage in a hired buggy as a measure of protection, which we could not understand at the time. Later in the day Adam Dickey received a story from Archibald McLellan that his daughter overheard a conversation in the street cars to the effect that a woman had been offered a large sum of money to run her auto into our Leader's carriage and tear off a wheel.

Wednesday, November 24, 1909

I had a talk with our Leader after supper as she sat in the twilight looking out on the snow-covered thoroughfare. She spoke of my coming a year ago, the starting of the *Monitor* at that time, and what our newspaper had already meant to the world. She alluded to the predictions of failure then made on all sides and pointed out to me that all first steps of an important nature she had taken in building up our movement were against the judgment and advice of those about her. I said, "Where would the Cause have been today, Mother, if you had minded ridicule, or even the speech of the people?" She replied, "It was always so at the beginning of each new move, but soon the faithful ones thronged to follow me."

Sunday, December 19, 1909

After singing several hymns and the usual stand-up prayer by the Rev. [Irving Tomlinson], we were given a most helpful talk in which the importance of our positions here was enlarged upon. She said, "The work which you are here being prepared for will reach all over the earth. You were placed here for that purpose, and your heavenly Father is caring for you even as a material father watches over his children. It is a special God-given privilege to be in this house. The program of the hour rests upon you to help me, and that without my telling you. You are to be afraid of nothing."

We were also told that when a rebuke may be thought to be directed at any individual, such is not its destination or object. Instead it is aimed at the error which at the moment needs the rebuke.

Friday, December 24, 1909

"Mother, Mr. Kinter and I had a talk last night about conditions in the Field, and a question came up which I would like to leave with you. Are not Christian Science treatments worth as much as those of the doctors of medicine?"

"Of course they are," she replied with emphasis, "Why should such a question be asked?"

"Because, Mother, the world does not think the Christian Scientists themselves regard them as of as much value as they make such a small charge for them. It belittles them in the eyes of many people who are apt to take one's own estimate of himself and his ability."

"Then they should charge more. Why don't they?"

"Mother, they would be glad to do so if they had some authorization from you. But they are charging just what they did twenty-five years ago when they based their charges on what the physicians then charged. Since then, everything has advanced until now the physicians get fees much larger than we do."

"How much larger?"

"Well, they get two dollars, three, and sometimes more; but would it not be well to authorize them to charge just what reputable physicians do in their respective localities?"

"Certainly, and you may write Mr. McLellan and tell him that is my wish."

Sometime in 1909

A child was brought by its fond mother to see our Leader. During the call the devoted mother, holding her infant in her arms, spoke of the mother love as approximating the divine in purity and unselfishness. Mrs. Eddy corrected her and pointed out that a mother's love is centered on her child because it is hers and is not therefore unselfish. She said that only the mother who loves other children as fervently as she does her own, manifests the love that is unselfed. It was a lesson in the impartiality and universality of the Love that is divine which we may profitably remember.

Wednesday, February 9, 1910

Mrs. Eddy was always interested in the occurrences of the day, particularly so far as they bore directly or indirectly upon the progress of Science. Early this month someone told me a good story of the *Monitor*'s work, which I repeated to her today much to her satisfaction. It was about a man who was under the belief of consumption and was ordered to go to the White Mountains. In passing through here and making his transfer from one depot to another, he was delayed at South Station. While waiting, he called a newsboy and asked him for a paper, saying, "Any one that's good will do. I don't know anything about the Boston papers." The kid looked him over for a moment, sized up his physical condition, and said, "I guess you need *The Christian Science Monitor*," and handed it to him. The man read the editorials and finally turned to the Home Forum page. There, an article marked "Hope" caught his eye and held it, for hope was something he had lost. He read it and got his first inkling of Science. He wanted to know more and sought the telephone directory. The only thing he could find listed was The Christian Science Publishing Society, so he called the operator there and said to her, "Say, what do you do when you're sick?"

"Why, call a Christian Science practitioner and get well," was the reply. "Well, connect me with one of them quick, will you, please?" She gave him Commander Blish's number, but the woman answering said he was out, to this man's great disappointment. He explained his case and she agreed to help him at once. The result was so satisfactory that he thereupon postponed his trip to the mountains and went to a Boston hotel instead. He began treatment with Blish the next day, and in three weeks he was a well man.

He then started to hunt the newsboy and had a gift of twenty-five dollars ready for him. Our Leader was much interested in this story when I told it to her and said, "I would like to add another twenty-five for the boy if he can be found."

Sunday, March 13, 1910

We had the usual prayer and singing and afterwards a talk on the line of God's scourging them that He blesses and loves. Later in the day, some scientific talks were given us, of which I will set down statements without respect to association or order of presentation. "As students, you are to kindle your light to make the way clear for all travelers, and then you are to go forth bearing this light. The rod may turn into a staff, but both are essential to growth. 'Thy rod and thy staff they comfort me' [Psalms 23:4]. You give me thanks for what I teach you, but the thanks I want most is to be expressed in knowing that I do not suffer from teaching you. At the time of my writing *Science and Health*, if I had been as scientific as my words, I could never have given the book to the world." To the question, "Why how is that, Mother?" she answered, "Because I then could have seen nothing but God and His idea."

March 23, 1910

Today our Leader told of a reminiscence following her return from the South after her husband's passing. She said, "When I was in the South with my husband, I saw for the first time an infant school that interested me greatly, as we had nothing of that kind where I had been living. After my husband died, I returned to the North and opened such a school, the first of the kind in New England. I had forty little children, among them the little boy of my brother-in-law, Mr. Tilton, a prominent manufacturer. One day he was passing [by] and speaking of it afterwards said, 'I looked in the window and saw a long row of little hats hung up orderly in a row, and looking farther I saw as many little heads bowed upon their little hands, all repeating the Lord's Prayer, "Our Father," and my boy was among them.' He had been an infidel, but the sight of those little children at prayer was too much for him, and he never afterwards was known to scoff or ridicule religious faith."

Friday, April 22, 1910

The more I ponder on this situation, unlike anything ever seen in the world before, the surer I become that the eternal truths that have reached mankind through the pen those fingers guided and [that] have brought health and happiness to uncounted thousands and will ever continue to bless, are not of man but of God. The human individual held the pen, but that was all. She has repeatedly told us that she did not know what she had written after she laid down her pen, and I haven't the slightest doubt of it.

I can well understand how she could sway those whose service or support she needed, for a more lovable person could not be found in the pages of history or in the hearts of men. If God had embodied in this remarkable personality all the grace and righteousness that He has given to man through it, we would all be worshippers of the creature instead of the Creator. "But to have this treasure in earthen vessels, that the excellency of the power may be of God, and not of us" (see II Corinthians 4:7).

Saturday, April 30, 1910

[Responding to questions about a By-Law,] she asked, "Why did I make it so?" When no one could say, the up-pointed finger settled it, and she said, "It was from there. Keep your finger on your lips and do not meddle."

Saturday, August 20, 1910

The week has been a quiet one with little out of the ordinary. The nights have been good, and kindliness and good cheer have marked the days. Last evening in our tossing the softballs about, the three of us, Maudie,[132] Adam Dickey, and I took up our stand in plain sight of the bay window, thinking to [provide] our Leader some diversion, as the night before interest was manifested. It was an immense success, Adam Dickey walking on his fingertips, among other stunts. When afterwards we went upstairs, we found our audience pleased to the point of mild excitement, and we were complimented on our nimbleness and proficiency.

August 20, 1910

On Friday at the drive hour, the electric current was off so that the elevator was out of commission. Calvin Frye and I, therefore, carried our Leader in her chair down the front steps, which was a performance I undertook without the slightest trepidation but found relief when the bottom step was reached. We were starting down face forward when our Leader stopped us and had us turn the chair about so that she did not have to look forward as we went down. The stairs are easy in angle, but nevertheless the responsibility was great, particularly as I trod on Mrs. Sargent's skirt at each step, she insisting on holding the back of the chair as we went down.

Wednesday, July 6, 1910

The most marked change of any since my coming here has been taking shape in the past three months. It portends a metamorphosis of some extraordinary nature which I must believe is for the good. There is a general softening and broadening. The nights are quieter than for years and years, I am told, and the days are full of rest and quiet. I would like to see more vigor mentally and physically, more interest in things that were once the center of thought, but these may be but incidental in the working out of the problem that I feel is under way. There is little or no physical ailment, the many things that we have had daily to struggle with having disappeared into their native nothingness.

Monday, July 18, 1910

After a quiet day, late this afternoon all hands were summoned, including Mrs. Dickey. We found chairs grouped around the couch, a most unusual thing which seemed to promise a long session. It was. Our Leader was at her best so far as poise, acumen, and graciousness entered into the interview. She kept us all busy answering questions, while with her it was thrust and parry all the time. I never saw a better or more wonderful exhibition of clear skill.

December 3, 1910 (E.S.R.)

"I have all in divine Love; that is all I need." Spoken by Mary Baker Eddy, and so far as I know, they were her last audible words.

December 3, 1910

Mrs. Eddy retired somewhat earlier than usual. All of us had been mentally active throughout the day in combating the manifestations of error that were apparent in the early morning.

It was before midnight when grouped around her bedside stood Calvin Frye, Mrs. Laura Sargent, Adam H. Dickey, Irving C. Tomlinson, my dear wife, Ella S. Rathvon, and myself. For the last time we were gathered in that little room, which today retains undisturbed [in] its simplicity and homelikeness.

We were aware that a momentous event in the world's history was apparently occurring, yet not one of us conceded its reality nor consented to its necessity. It was the eternality of Life and not the belief of death which was uppermost in our thoughts and which we endeavored to realize to the very depth of our being. As the moments passed, in the embrace of a quiet sleep, she gently emerged from the scenes of her earthly trials and triumphs and serenely entered anew into the service of the Master in broader fields of more glorious possibilities.

Sunday, December 4, 1910

Early this morning, at 3:00 a.m., Alfred Farlow was sent for, and the six of us prepared a statement to be given out to the press through Mr. Farlow tomorrow. We also arranged about the church services. James Neal has been in the house, a most helpful mentality. First he brought the medical examiner, Dr. West of Newton, and afterwards the undertaker and his woman assistant. There has been no difficulty anywhere. Watchers are guarding the gates from reporters. The day has been reasonably quiet, all bearing up well. Am convinced that naught but good can come out of it all. God's hand supports and "underneath are the everlasting arms" (Deuteronomy 33:27).

Thursday, December 8, 1910

We returned from Mt. Auburn Cemetery at two o'clock, and now I find myself beginning a new era. My knowledge of the Science of being is fixed and set beyond all shaking or unseating. I can hereafter speak with authority about things which heretofore I believed but did not know. Both Maudie and I made prodigious sacrifices in abandoning home and friends and family to take up what so many had failed to hold, and we have never for a moment regretted the step.

December 10, 1910

(Extract from a letter written by W.R.R. to Judge Hanna)

Your letter came late this afternoon, and before I put out my light, I want to write a line or two to you even though it contain but a very little of what I would say to you if we were face to face.

In the first place let me thank you most heartily for your words of assurance and comfort. They match the many that have been coming to us from all directions the past few days and have made the momentous events of the past week much easier to bear. It is most gratifying and inspiring to note the spirit of confidence and certainty that breathe through them all. Not one word of dismay or despair has reached us from any source whatever. No allusion to that illusion called death—it has all been life, life, life, and that abundantly. You will be pleased to know that the same spirit is manifested in the household from one end to the other. With two exceptions none of us know what the next step will be or where it will lead, yet there is not the slightest sense of uneasiness or perplexity. And what is more, there has been no harrowing grief or despondency. We are conscious of a great void, an emptiness that is indescribable but not irremediable, and all are mightily impressed with the need of higher consecration to the work that is opening up before each one of us. We know we have not lost our Leader, for she lives and ever will live, and in her books we find what she would most have us know and do.

Mr. Dickey as a Director will remain here in Boston. Mr. Tomlinson this morning resumed his place on the Bible Lesson Committee, which he had only temporarily vacated, but the rest of us are quietly making our demonstration while disposing of the many things which demand attention as the outcome of the week's occurrences.

Christian Science Monitor *delivery trucks and drivers in front of The Christian Science Publishing Society*

The far-reaching vision of our Leader's final publication

Prior to the appearance of *The Christian Science Monitor* in November 1908, such a thing as a daily newspaper owned and issued by a religious organization was regarded as impractical if not impossible. This was the unanimous opinion of non-Science newspaper people, one of whom went so far as to declare that its title alone would prevent its survival and that a ship flying such a flag would be on the rocks before it could get out of the harbor. Some of them even stood on shore waiting to pick up the wreckage. But they have all sought cover long ago, for according to their standards, the impossible has happened. The calamity they expected never came, and our craft is today sailing along majestically with the flag flying at its masthead, saluted respectfully even by those journals who still cling to outworn methods and unworthy ideals. They have seen the impossible come to pass. And instead of its being a constant source of tremendous expense to her Church, it has become on its own merits an outstanding business success.

Our own corps of operators, editors, writers, news gatherers, and the force of technical workers, pressmen, typesetters, stereotypers, etc., were recruited as far as possible from the ranks of the movement, and they of course were hopeful, if not altogether expectant, of the success of the paper. Their training in the newspaper world, however, caused them to gauge success by financial returns while, on the other hand, our Leader declared the true mission of our paper to be "to injure no man, but to bless all mankind" (*The First Church of Christ, Scientist, and Miscellany*, p. 353). They measured success in terms of dollars; her aim was salvation: from sin, sickness, and all error.

On one side stood alone a devout woman, consecrated to the noblest ideal that could actuate a human deed—a woman totally without technical knowledge or newspaper training who had probably given little or no study to the physical and material side of the enormous problem she was facing—and on the other side a corps of trained experts in the various lines of journalism, intricate and involved as they were. But she had what the others did not have—that is, a lifelong training in the ways of learning God's purpose and of adhering inflexibly to its execution.

Standing firm on the *Monitor*'s name

From the very day that our Leader announced *The Christian Science Monitor* as the name of her newspaper, there were grave misgivings at the Publishing House that the new venture, seemingly weak as it was, could not carry the added weight of the name "Christian Science," and whenever occasion offered, our Leader was asked to reconsider her determination, but without avail. Experienced newspapermen confidently declared that success for the paper was doubtful in any case, but with the words *Christian Science* in the title, failure was certain. They [made comments like these]:

+ "People won't buy a daily paper that exploits religion."

+ "The man who buys a newspaper prefers to take his religion and his news in separate doses and on different days of the week."

✦ "Frankly speaking, most people fight shy of whatever has anything to do with Christian Science. You will drown your newspaper before it has a chance to swim if you hang the words *Christian Science* on it at the start."

These views were shared to a greater or less extent by us at Chestnut Hill with a single exception. That exception was our Leader herself. The rest of us feared. She knew, and her knowing was the outcome of that perfect love which casteth out fear. She saw more clearly than anyone on earth saw in that day that the words *Christian Science* in its title would not only add prestige to the paper but would draw to it the attention of thousands who would read it to learn something about the religion of which they had heard so much. She cared nothing for the voice of men if she could hear the voice of God.

The first copy of the *Monitor* to come off the press was taken out to our Leader at Chestnut Hill by Mr. McLellan, the then Editor, and Mr. Alexander Dodds, the Managing Editor, on the afternoon (November 24, 1908) before Thanksgiving Day. I remember well how carefully, almost reverently, they handled it as they spread it out on the desk in Mr. Dickey's room, where several of us were awaiting its arrival. It was late in the day, and the lights were on when our Leader was told it was ready for her approval. Word came that Mr. McLellan was to take it in to her at once, and we urged him as he left to make one more appeal in support of the forlorn hope that our Commander-in-Chief might after all change her mind and see fit to eliminate the words "Christian Science" from the title of our paper. He left the copy with her and soon came out, saying somewhat

Christian Science Monitor *delivery trucks promoting "A Daily Newspaper for the Home"*

dejectedly, "It is of no use; the name of our paper will have to remain *The Christian Science Monitor.*"

The value to the Cause of that one woman's unalterable decision becomes more and more apparent with the lapse of time. Already we can appraise its effect in enhancing the public's appreciation of the paper and their increased respect for Christian Science and its Discoverer and Founder.

Our Leader's ongoing interest in her paper

Mrs. Eddy was closely interested in the successive steps of the paper's development, outlining and directing its policies but entrusting the mechanical and business sides of it to her chosen associates. Where technical experience was needed, she had little to say; where wisdom, vision, and a reflection of divine intelligence were requisite, she alone spoke, and her word was law. [The following] incident will illustrate how confident she was that others could well do material things without her participation and, on the other hand, how necessary it was for her and for her alone to decide quickly and finally matters of policy and the larger affairs in which Principle was involved.

The matrix, or mold, from which the first copy of our *Monitor* was printed was sent out to the house for Mrs. Eddy's inspection by the Manager, who quite naturally supposed it would be of interest to her, showing as it did the original of every imprint and letter on the paper. It was a curious looking object, and as I took it in to her, I expected she would be more than casually interested. "What is that, my dear?" she asked. "Why that, Mother," I said, "is the matrix from which the first copy of our *Monitor* was printed."

"Indeed" was her only comment as she glanced at it and resumed her reading. She did not give it a second look, and I thereupon retired, crestfallen, and took my matrix with me. But far different was her attitude on the weightier matters of our paper's ethics and fundamentals.

[For] more than two years that followed [the first issue of the *Monitor*], I had daily opportunity to note Mrs. Eddy's interest in its progress and her watchful solicitude for its permanent success. She read it daily, a first copy off the press being sent each afternoon to her house for her personal use. She was especially interested in the constructive and helpful news of the day, the metaphysical article on the Home Forum page, and the editorials, each one of which bore the name of the writer rubber stamped on her copy before being sent to the house. Thus she knew the authorship of every editorial and metaphysical article.

The *Monitor*'s role in Christian Scientists' lives

[In June 1910, about a year and a half after the paper

began,] Judge Smith[133] and I discussed the *Monitor,* what it is, what it is not, and what it may be made to be. He agreed with me that it must be made a paper Scientists want for what they get out of it, and not merely subscribe for from a sense of duty or obligation. He believes editorials may be made more scientific; that is, they should touch things more from the viewpoint of the Scientist and less from that of the simply good citizen.

As I see it, we can hardly expect a busy Scientist to read closely every issue of the *Monitor* from first page to last, but he can glance through each issue, note the captions and headlines, and then read such parts as hold particular interest for him at the moment. This, I take it, is enough to qualify one to be regarded as a *Monitor* reader. This indeed was our Leader's way. Each afternoon she would look over the paper, reading those parts which interested her especially and giving brief attention to the rest so that, when she was through, she had an intelligent concept of the whole and a thorough familiarity with such parts as she cared to read. She was a rapid reader and had the faculty of gathering much in a short time—a faculty that all of us may develop to our advantage. Her comments upon what she had read or observed were interesting and illuminating.

Among these things which we are in danger of dissociating from our Leader are our periodicals. Years ago, whenever a *Journal,* a *Sentinel,* or a *Monitor* came into our hands, Mrs. Eddy came into mind. She was back of them. They were the children of her thought, her chosen agencies for promulgating the [t]ruth and for blessing mankind. We would no more think of them without thinking of her than we would think of the White House without thinking of the President. They were inseparable. If not a part of her, they were at least close to her.

The Christian Science Monitor was the demonstration of the Discoverer and Founder of the religion whose name it bears. Upon her rested its creation, upon us rests its success. She did not fail in her part. Fellow Christian Scientists, let us not fail in ours.

The *Manual*—our enduring guide

After I was in Chestnut Hill for a short time and [had] studied the *Manual of The Mother Church* as our Leader desired us to do, I was at first puzzled, then perplexed, and finally apprehensive that she had apparently made no provision for [certain] sections of the *Manual* to function after her signature or assent could not be had. We decided it would be best to speak to General Henry M. Baker about it as he was legal adviser to our Leader, as well as her cousin, and a regular visitor to the home.

"You need not be at all uneasy," were his reassuring words. "It is a matter of common law in a case of this kind, where it is physically impossible to carry out specified conditions by the one named, that the next in authority assume that jurisdiction. And in this case the next in authority is the Board of Directors of The Mother Church. Any competent court in the land will uphold the *Manual* just as Mrs. Eddy intends it to function whether her signature is forthcoming or not." His few words that afternoon lifted a great load for me.

Our Leader's priorities

I had not been long associated with our Leader before I noted a pronounced reluctance on her part to be consulted about the details of the business of her church and the material affairs of the movement at large. We were naturally desirous of sparing her and would defer as long as possible bringing to her notice matters which might cause her distress even to consider. "Let the Directors attend to it. I cannot be annoyed by material affairs when the world so greatly needs my spiritual support"—these words were often spoken expressing her attitude on such occasions.

The sacred duties arising from what she has characterized "the great demands of spiritual sense" (*Miscellaneous Writings*, p. 204) were never neglected nor deferred by her, however depleted her physicality seemed to be. [But] her reluctance to give thought to material affairs was evident. She dismissed it all by saying, "The Cause of Christian Science is not dependent upon man or woman, and God will take care of it."

During the last years, 1909 and 1910, she relaxed somewhat her direction and control of the operations and undertakings of her Church but never delegated to others the regulation of its policies. What should or should not be done, she determined. How it should be done was left to her representatives.

On the other hand, her interest in world affairs and in the more important phases of her message to mankind and its imprint upon the thought of the day never lagged or diverged. She was keen and alert about anything that promised to affect humanity for the better in a large and lasting way. Exploration, discovery, and invention claimed her attention in so far as their substantial results were important, but the means by which they were attained she cared little about.

Mrs. Eddy was alertly interested in the more important

of the world's daily occurrences, but her thought was ever turning from the things about us to the things beyond us, from the things that are seen to the things that are not seen. And although she was always considerate of the comfort and well-being of those about her—no mother could be more loving and thoughtful—yet Mrs. Eddy's closest companions were ever her own thoughts, which when expressed in words disclosed how steadfastly and continuously she dwelt in "the secret place of the most High" [Psalms 91:1].

Stern rebuke and loving patience

In my two years' daily association with our Leader in her home at Chestnut Hill, I frequently heard her rebuke error vigorously, vehemently, forcefully, but never once did she upbraid the erring one for past mistakes that were sincerely regretted or past failures that were honestly re-tried.

In this we have another instance of how closely she followed the methods of the Master Scientist, Jesus the Christ. We are told his rebukes were fearful, and we know his talks to his disciples were impressive and forceful, but nowhere is a word recorded to show that he remembered their past mistakes or recent failures. And what records some of those rugged men must have had before the consciousness of Love's omnipotence entered their lives, softened their hearts, and taught them to forget as well as to forgive! How often their blundering feet must have slipped backward in their efforts to go forward! May we not conclude that Jesus knew then, as we know now, that the man who takes three steps forward and falls back two arrives before the man who never starts.

We will today do wisely and well to follow more closely

the course our Leader took when she was confronted by defection and disloyalty. Where true repentance and sincere contrition followed a transgression, she patiently turned the transgressor to the "universal solvent of Love," wherein even the "adamant of error" is dissolved (see *Science and Health*, p. 242). On the other hand, if the error was obdurate, Pharisaical, or defiant, none could be more stern or fearless in rebuking and denouncing it.

A gracious hostess and patient teacher

In enumerating the graces which characterized Mrs. Eddy in her later years during the time when I was at Chestnut Hill, I would name her faculty of putting at their ease all with whom she came in contact. On occasions I have talked with visitors downstairs in the library, waiting for an appointment with her, who were extremely apprehensive and uneasy over the prospect of speaking with her for the first time [but] after a few moments in her presence were completely composed and serene.

I have noticed, too, that in conversation with her, one would be incited to voice only the good, with a clarity and understanding far beyond [his] ordinary ability. She seemed unconsciously to radiate intelligence that was reflected in a degree by those to whom her thought was directed in an interview, yet never was there any indication or suggestion of anything weird or uncanny about her. She was just a lovable, womanly human being possessing traits and proclivities that were sublimated to an extraordinary degree through her recognition of spiritual realities— omnipotence, omniscience, and omnipresence.

She was inclined to be brief, if not curt, with those who

would undertake to impress her from a selfish motive with the profundity of their knowledge of metaphysics or familiarity with the letter of the Scriptures. On the other hand, I have repeatedly seen her take pains to make clear some elementary phase of the truth of being that was puzzling to the sincere student. To her there was no such thing as a little truth. Obviously, she habitually realized that "All is infinite Mind and its infinite manifestation" (*Science and Health*, p. 468).

Keeping our Leader fresh in thought

Do not become forgetful of our Leader; keep her memory ever green. Think of her not merely as an outstanding, majestic figure of the past, but as an ever-present, ever-enduring influence for good. Love her for what she has done for you. Emulate her consecration; exemplify her wisdom, her vision, and her courage. Honor her, if you will, for her unwavering devotion to the one supreme object of her life—to show mankind that the way to salvation lies in the supremacy of Spirit over every material condition. Think of her in terms not of the past but of the present. See her as speaking to you now through her books and her writings, which need no date, for their truths can never grow old and yet were never new.

Mrs. Eddy was the most divinely human personage I have ever known. She was like the rest of us in many things, and in others she was as far above any of us as the stars above the earth. She enjoyed being with people, but far more did she enjoy being alone with God. She was interested in the progress of world affairs but was always more intently absorbed in bringing the affairs of Spirit into the range of human consciousness.

The earnest Christian Scientist is reminded at every turn in the road of progress that Mrs. Eddy is not a figure of the past, existing for us only in memory, but that she is the loving, vivifying influence of the present whose provisions for our permanent welfare are with us wherever we may go and in whatever we may be doing. Every time a Christian Scientist, young or otherwise, opens his textbook, says his daily prayer, studies his Bible Lesson, attends Sunday School or church, visits our Reading Rooms, hears a lecture, reads our periodicals, or makes a demonstration great or small, he has a reminder before him of our Leader's loving consideration of his needs and of her thoughtful means of supplying them. Let him, then, recognize her as ever belonging to the present and not to the past. One does not think of sunshine or light, truth or love, as pertaining to the past, but to the everlasting present.

*Bas relief marble
sculpture of Mary Baker
Eddy by William Frederick Pope*

Endnotes

Introduction

[1] *We Knew Mary Baker Eddy, Expanded Edition, Volume I,* p. 266–267.

Taking Class with Mary Baker Eddy
by Jennie E. Sawyer

[2] The title of Mary Baker Eddy's primary work changed in 1883, so depending on when Sawyer's husband purchased the book, it may have been titled *Science and Health,* or it may have been called *Science and Health; with a Key to the Scriptures.* Not until the sixteenth edition, published in 1886, did the title assume its present form: *Science and Health with Key to the Scriptures.*

[3] Students at this time often went through class multiple times with Eddy.

[4] After The Mother Church was reorganized in 1892, the concept of branch churches began to unfold. Before then, during the time Sawyer refers to, there were no rules for Christian Science churches, which resulted in some confusion and disagreement in the Field.

[5] Each teacher of Christian Science holds a meeting annually to which all students he or she has taught over the years are invited. This meeting is called an association and includes an inspirational address prepared by the teacher. These excerpts from

Sawyer's association addresses contain recollections of comments made by Mary Baker Eddy. Sawyer continued to share her recollections in association addresses long after Eddy's passing in December 1910.

Lessons from Our Leader
by Victoria H. Sargent

[6] For information about changes to the title of *Science and Health*, see endnote #2 for Jennie Sawyer's reminiscence.

[7] "Mother" was a term of endearment for Eddy used by many early followers. In 1903 she requested that she no longer be called "Mother." (See Article XXII, Section 1, of the *Manual of The Mother Church* by Mary Baker Eddy.) Nevertheless, many of those closest to her, especially those working in her household, found it difficult to let go of the name that so aptly characterized their love and respect for her.

The Human Side of Mrs. Eddy
by Janette E. Weller

[8] For information about changes to the title of *Science and Health*, see endnote #2 for Jennie Sawyer's reminiscence.

[9] The National C.S.A. refers to the National Christian Scientist Association. Formed in January 1886, the NCSA was an association of both Mary Baker Eddy's students and students of teachers who had passed the Normal course in the Massachusetts Metaphysical College. The association met annually in various cities— New York, Boston, Cleveland, and Chicago—until 1890 when Eddy suggested that the NCSA disorganize or adjourn and meet again in three years. It reconvened for the last time in 1893 in Chicago at the time of the World's Parliament of Religions associated with the Columbian Exposition (World's Fair).

[10] After quoting this piece of correspondence, Weller adds the following note: "For a full appreciation of the above letter, it is essential to read the first article in *The Christian Science Journal* for July 1895."

From Seafaring to Healing
by Joseph S. Eastaman

[11] "The Travail of My Soul" series appears in the January, February, March, May, and July 1892 issues of *The Christian Science Journal*. The May article is published in full here, along with an excerpt from the July article. (Though the July article is part of the "Travail" series, it carries a different title: "Early Lessons in Demonstration.")

[12] The very first First Members were the charter members of The Mother Church, The First Church of Christ, Scientist, formed in 1892. There were originally twelve; four were members of the new Board of Directors—Ira O. Knapp, William B. Johnson, Joseph S. Eastaman, and Stephen A. Chase—and eight others: Julia Bartlett, Ellen L. Clarke, Janet T. Colman, Mary F. Eastaman, Ebenezer J. Foster Eddy, Eldora O. Gragg, Flavia S. Knapp, and Mary W. Munroe.

One of the very first acts of the new group was to admit twenty others to serve with the original twelve as First Members. Over time, Mary Baker Eddy appointed others to be First Members as well. These First Members shared the responsibility of conducting church affairs with the Board of Directors and Eddy.

On January 10, 1901, the First Members relinquished their role in church government; on March 17, 1903, their designation became "Executive Members"; and on July 8, 1908, they were disbanded.

[13] For information about changes to the title of *Science and Health*, see endnote #2 for Jennie Sawyer's reminiscence.

Lives of Glad Devotion
by Mary F. Eastaman

[14] For information on First Members, see endnote #12 for Joseph Eastaman's reminiscence.

[15] See Psalms 84:10.

Seeking and Finding God
by Julia E. Prescott

[16] The "Next Friends" suit was filed on March 1, 1907, by William Chandler in the name of Mary Baker Eddy's biological son (George Washington Glover II), her adopted son (Ebenezer J. Foster Eddy), and other relatives and "next friends" against several men in key roles in the Christian Science movement, including Calvin Frye, members of the Christian Science Board of Directors, and others on Eddy's staff and in the movement. The suit alleged that Eddy was incompetent to manage her own finances and affairs and that the group of men named was taking advantage of her. In the end, this attack on Christian Science and its Founder was foiled and the case withdrawn (in August 1907) for lack of grounds after a group of experts concluded, upon interviewing Eddy, that she was perfectly competent.

Proving the Truth of Christian Science
by Emma A. Estes

[17] Christian Scientists who had taken Primary and Normal classes and had qualified as Christian Science teachers could form Christian Science Institutes for teaching Christian Science in their cities. The first evidence of these institutes in Eddy's correspondence dates from 1885. Advertising cards for Christian Science Institutes first appeared in *The Christian Science Journal* in 1886. Teachers often advertised themselves as the "principal" of the Institute. Beginning in January 1905, at the direction of the Trustees of The Christian Science Publishing Society and with

Eddy's consent, listings for Institutes were no longer published in the *Journal*, and the Institutes themselves were soon discontinued. Teachers then indicated their status in their practitioner listings.

[18] Most likely these weekly meetings were a predecessor to today's Wednesday testimony meetings.

[19] Estes is mistaken here. There were other branch churches in 1889. For example, First Church, Oconto, Wisconsin, was founded in June 1884.

[20] When Estes heard that other cities were holding regular Sunday services, she added them to the Cincinnati Institute's schedule. Since Eddy had not yet ordained the Bible and *Science and Health* as the pastor of the Christian Science Church, services were conducted by an individual, such as Estes, who delivered a sermon based on Christian Science texts.

[21] Estes is referring to the following letter, which is part of the collections of The Mary Baker Eddy Library (L12746):

> Pleasant View
> Concord, N.H.
> Aug. 22, 1899

> Miss Emma A. Estes, C.S.D.

> My dear Student:

> I have been recently informed that you are being reported as disloyal because you did not leave your [F]ield of labor in Cincinnati and come to Boston, as I suggested in a letter written to you last Jan. You replied at the time to that letter stating the difficulties in the way of leaving your [F]ield at that time[,] and I replied in substance through my secretary that you had better remain where you were.

> I do not, and never did, consider that an

act of disobedience, nor that you were ever
disloyal to our Cause since the day you
first entered my class.

May God prosper you and comfort and
support you in your labors[.]

With love[,] mother

Mary Baker Eddy

N.B. Give my love to your dear church[.]

Mother

Gems of Instruction and Encouragement
by Lida W. Fitzpatrick

[22] In 1896, Eddy added a By-Law to her *Church Manual*
indicating that students could not take Primary
class instruction from more than one teacher. For
the current wording of this By-Law, see Article XXVI,
Section 7. An exception was made for pupils whose
teachers had strayed (see Article XXVI, Section 8).

[23] This is the passage referred to on page 442 of the 268th
edition of *Science and Health*: "Christ changes a belief of sin
or of sickness into a better belief, that melts into spiritual
understanding wherein sin, disease, and death disappear.
Christ, Truth, gives mortals temporary food and clothing
until the material, transformed with the ideal, disappears,
and man is clothed and fed spiritually." The wording
in the final edition of *Science and Health* (also on page
442) is almost identical: "When Christ changes a belief
of sin or of sickness into a better belief, then belief melts
into spiritual understanding, and sin, disease, and death
disappear. Christ, Truth, gives mortals temporary food
and clothing until the material, transformed with the
ideal, disappears, and man is clothed and fed spiritually."

[24] The "Mr. K" mentioned here may be Edward Kimball,
who served periodically during these years.

[25] This is the wording in the final edition of *Science and Health*: "To prevent disease or to cure it, the power of Truth, of divine Spirit, must break the dream of the material senses. To heal by argument, find the type of the ailment, get its name, and array your mental plea against the physical. Argue at first mentally, not audibly, that the patient has no disease, and conform the argument so as to destroy the evidence of disease" (p. 412).

Privileged to Serve Our Leader
by Joseph G. Mann

[26] The Grand Army of the Republic (GAR) was an organization for American Civil War veterans who had fought on the Union side.

[27] For brief background on the "Next Friends" suit, see endnote #16 for Julia Prescott's reminiscence.

[28] Mann is likely referring to Eddy's biological son, George Glover, but Eddy had an adoptive son as well, Ebenezer J. Foster Eddy, who, like George, was among the "Next Friends" hoping to prove Eddy's incompetence.

Golden Memories
by Clara M. S. Shannon

[29] For background about Christian Science Institutes, see endnote #17 for Emma Estes's reminiscence.

[30] For information on First Members, see endnote #12 for Joseph Eastaman's reminiscence.

[31] "Voices Not Our Own" is on pages 8–9 of the final edition of *Retrospection and Introspection*. The only difference in content between the two articles is the inclusion of a poem by Mrs. Hemans at the end of the final version of the article.

[32] The booklet *Christian Science History*, first published in 1899, went through a number of editions and revisions.

At Eddy's request, it was widely distributed and used to counter falsehoods about her and the history of the movement that were being circulated by Horatio W. Dresser, Josephine Curtis Woodbury, and Frederick W. Peabody. On June 29, 1906, its publication was discontinued. The booklet is part of the collections of The Mary Baker Eddy Library (V03420).

[33] The precise identity of this young man is not known, but he did not go on to play a parental role in George's life.

[34] Mary Glover married Daniel Patterson in June 1853. The accident referred to occurred in February 1866.

[35] In mid- to late-1866, after Daniel Patterson's second instance of infidelity within a matter of months, Mary ended their relationship. Soon afterward, she began using the name Glover again, though she was not legally divorced from Patterson until 1873.

[36] Mary Glover and Asa Gilbert Eddy were married on January 1, 1877. Though referred to as "Dr. Eddy," Asa did not have medical training. In the nineteenth century, use of the title "Dr." was commonly given to those practicing some form of health care, regardless of whether or not the individual had an academic degree from an allopathic school of medicine or a medical license associated with federal or state regulations.

[37] Early submissions of Mrs. Eddy's manuscript were rejected by publishers until W. F. Brown, a Boston publisher, agreed to produce the book if Mrs. Eddy covered all printing costs. The process was fraught with difficulty, however; the printer made changes to the content that seriously affected the meaning and also introduced many careless errors. These difficulties coupled with Mrs. Eddy's corrections and revisions caused more than a year to elapse between the publisher's receipt of the manuscript and its first appearance in print.

[38] The full title is *In Quest of the Perfect Book: Reminiscences and Recollections of a Bookman*. It was first published in Boston by Little, Brown and Company in 1926.

[39] In his book *Mary Baker Eddy and Her Books*, William Dana Orcutt explains the nature of the printer's difficulties, along with Eddy's response:

> As a result of Mr. Wilson's high personal and professional standards, the volume of work steadily increased, requiring enlarged facilities and increased personnel. The business horizon looked particularly bright in 1894, but unknown to Mr. Wilson, his partner for some time had so mismanaged the financial affairs that the whole business structure had become impaired, and the Press faced bankruptcy. As the finances had been entirely in this partner's hands, and as Mr. Wilson had implicit confidence in his ability, the precarious situation had remained undiscovered almost until the crash came. (p. 48)

Orcutt adds that Eddy wrote Wilson a check (as did many of his other clients) to help him recover from his financial difficulties.

[40] *Science and Health* editions 226 through 262 all came out in 1902; of these, the 226th was the most significant revision.

[41] The Committee on Publication (referred to here as the Publication Committee) for The Mother Church is appointed by the Board of Directors and has the responsibility to "correct in a Christian manner impositions on the public in regard to Christian Science, injustices done Mrs. Eddy or members of this Church by the daily press, by periodicals or circulated literature of any sort" (*Manual*, Article XXXIII, Section 2).

[42] The Busy Bees, a group of children aged twelve years and under, were organized by Maurine R. Campbell in 1890 to raise money for the construction of Mary Baker Eddy's room (often referred to as "Mother's Room") in the Original Edifice of The Mother Church. In June 1891, each of the 52 Boston Busy Bees was given a small beehive bank for storing the money collected on behalf of the building project.

On January 6, 1895, the Original Edifice of The Mother Church was dedicated, and the Fund for building and furnishing the Mother's Room was closed. In total, 2,600 children had contributed almost $5,000.

In June 1898, Eddy asked the Busy Bees to disband, but to show her appreciation for the children's generosity, she established a trust fund with $4,000 of her own money that would pay a dividend to each of the Busy Bees upon reaching "legal age." The sole condition of the trust was that the children should remain loyal to Christian Science. The trust was closed on June 6, 1935, when all the Busy Bees that could be found had received their distribution. Also in appreciation for their efforts, Eddy dedicated *Pulpit and Press* to the Busy Bees and offered them the opportunity to purchase it for half price, which meant that she did not earn any royalties from those sales.

[43] On page 553 of Margaret M. Pinkham's *A Miracle in Stone: The History of the Building of the Original Mother Church, The First Church of Christ, Scientist, in Boston, Massachusetts, 1894,* (Santa Barbara, CA: Nebbadoon Press, 2009), the author describes the inscriptions above and leading into the Mother's Room:

> The white door ... is overhung with a white marble tablet on which is inscribed in letters of gold the word LOVE. The entrance floor was attractively patterned in mosaics with the inscription, inlaid in front of the door,

Mother's Room
The Children's Offering

In 1904, the tiling in the entry to the room was changed from "Mother's Room/The Children's Offering" to "Rev. Mary B. Eddy's Room/The Children's Offering."

Later, the November 21, 1908, *Christian Science Sentinel* (p. 230) announced a new By-Law under Article XXII in the *Church Manual*. It read, "*Closed to Visitors.*—Sect. 14. The room in The Mother Church formerly known as 'Mother's Room,' shall be closed to visitors." Mrs. Eddy added the following comment to the notice: "There is nothing in this room now of any special interest. 'Let the dead bury their dead,' and the spiritual have all place and power.—Mary B. G. Eddy." The original copy of this notice is in the collections of The Mary Baker Eddy Library (L07016). In the final edition of the *Manual*, this By-Law is Article XXII, Section 17.

[44] This is the first verse of William Williams's Welsh hymn "Guide Me, O Thou Great Jehovah," which was translated into English by Peter Williams. An adaptation of this appears as Hymn No. 90 in the *Christian Science Hymnal*.

[45] In his reminiscence included in the first volume of *We Knew Mary Baker Eddy, Expanded Edition*, John Lathrop describes this man, Oscar Norin, known at the Concord State Fair for jumping from a great height into a tank of water:

> Mrs. Eddy asked to witness the exhibition of high diving, and so her carriage was driven through to the side of the pool of water where the diver, dressed as Mephistopheles in red and with tail, was to dive down from a height through a hoop of fire into a small pool of water. Mrs. Eddy had told Judge and Mrs. Hanna, who

accompanied her in her carriage, that she looked upon the exhibition as an example of overcoming fear and wanted to see it. The moment arrived, and the diver from his lofty height poised and gracefully dived downward through the fiery circle into the water, coming quickly to the surface. He walked out and up to Mrs. Eddy's carriage, bowed low to her, and ran off. Mrs. Eddy had invited the First Members of The Mother Church to be present, and most of us were so intent watching her keen interest and pleasure that we missed the actual dive. When the man in red disappeared, Mrs. Eddy turned to Judge and Mrs. Hanna and said, "I beheld Satan as lightning fall from heaven" [Luke 10:18]. (pp. 267–268)

For another account of this feat, see "The Concord State Fair" on page 411 of the October 1901 *Christian Science Journal*.

[46] Matthew 18:15–17 is commonly known as the Matthew Code:

Moreover if thy brother shall trespass against thee, go and tell him his fault between thee and him alone: if he shall hear thee, thou hast gained thy brother. But if he will not hear thee, then take with thee one or two more, that in the mouth of two or three witnesses every word may be established. And if he shall neglect to hear them, tell it unto the church: but if he neglect to hear the church, let him be unto thee as an heathen man and a publican.

Climbing the Mount of Revelation
with Our Teacher
by Laura C. Nourse

[47] Nourse's "In Transitu" appears on page 493 of the January 1890 *Christian Science Journal*. Three verses from this poem are the basis for Hymn Nos. 197 and 198. Other verses from the poem are the basis for Hymn Nos. 392 and 393.

Correspondence and Other Exchanges
with Mary Baker Eddy
by Septimus J. Hanna

[48] Other notable points in Judge Septimus Hanna's service to the Cause include his delivery of Mrs. Eddy's address to the World Parliament of Religions held in conjunction with the Columbian Exposition (World's Fair) in Chicago in 1893; becoming a First Member of The Mother Church in February 1895; taking Normal class from Eddy in 1898 (Hanna's wife, Camilla, also attended this class); and publishing *Christian Science History* in 1899. For more information about the latter, see endnote #32 for Clara Shannon's reminiscence.

[49] The Christian Scientist Association was the association of students taught by Mrs. Eddy.

[50] L05197.

[51] For information on First Members, see endnote #12 for Joseph Eastaman's reminiscence.

[52] For brief background on Augusta Stetson, see endnote #120 for Adelaide Still's reminiscence.

[53] On August 20, 1898, Mrs. Eddy directed Publishing Society Trustee William McKenzie to publish "a weekly newspaper" that would be for the "dignity of our cause and the good of students." Regarding its name, she said, "Please name it a little more graphically[,] e.g.[,] *Christian Science Messenger*" (L04871B). Then on August 23, she wrote to Hanna,

the Editor, about the newspaper's name: "'*Leaflet*' is too meaningless for our use so I suggest *Messenger*. I hope it will prove a guardian *angel*" (L05228). In the end, *Christian Science Weekly* was the name chosen for the first issue, published in September 1898. Three months later, in January 1899, the *Weekly* was renamed the *Christian Science Sentinel*.

[54] L05231.

[55] This is the poem that appeared in the first issue of the *Christian Science Weekly:*

> A Dedicatory Poem
> By Mary Baker G. Eddy
> The Discoverer and Founder of Christian Science
>
> And the eyes of them that see shall not be dim, and the ears of them that hear shall hearken. — *Isaiah*
>
> Thou All in All, of every age,
>   And rising, radiant sphere—
> Help us to write a deathless page
>   Of truth—this waning year.
>
> Help us to humbly seek and sow
>   And reap Thy wise behest—
> Whate'er the boon, a joy, or woe—
>   Knowing Thou knowest best.
>
> Aid the soul-sense to soar and sing
>   Above the tempest's glee;
> Give us the eagle's fearless wing,
>   The dove's to mount to Thee.
>
> All-Merciful, how faint, unfed,
>   Is every hungry heart;
> Give us each day our daily bread,
>   In knowing what Thou art.
>
> Pleasant View, Concord, N.H.,
> August, 1898

An earlier version of this poem titled "Invocation for 1868" appears on p. 28 of *Poems* by Mary Baker Eddy.

[56] This letter effectively announced the end of the Obstetrics classes; two days later, on March 10, 1902, the By-Law "Officers" (Article XXVIII, Section 1) was adopted, which prohibited the teaching of obstetrics.

[57] These are the 27 Bible Lesson topics Eddy established: God; Sacrament; Life; Truth; Love; Spirit; Soul; Mind; Christ Jesus; Man; Substance; Matter; Reality; Unreality; Are Sin, Disease, and Death Real?; Doctrine of Atonement; Probation After Death; Everlasting Punishment; Adam and Fallen Man; Mortals and Immortals; Soul and Body; Ancient and Modern Necromancy, alias Mesmerism and Hypnotism, Denounced; God the Only Cause and Creator; God the Preserver of Man; Is the Universe, Including Man, Evolved by Atomic Force?; Christian Science; Thanksgiving

For many years the Bible Lessons consisted of six sections. The Bible Lesson Committee continues to follow the original, flexible directions given by Mary Baker Eddy.

[58] Mrs. Eddy did not end up using 385 Commonwealth for her "winter home." On July 24, 1894, about two weeks after this letter, she wrote Mrs. Hanna again, saying, "I love my home here [at Pleasant View] too well to leave it for a season ...."

Blessed by Serving Our Leader and Her Cause
by Edward E. Norwood

[59] Norwood's healing appears under the heading "An Expression of Loving Gratitude" on pages 694–695 in the chapter "Fruitage" in *Science and Health*. This excerpt from that testimony indicates the severity of his ailment: "All my life had been spent in semi-invalidism, and I seemed destined to a continuance of suffering, but in three weeks after beginning to read

Science and Health, to my joyful surprise I found myself a well man, sound physically and uplifted spiritually."

[60] L04875B.

[61] This is Frances J. King, a student of Mrs. Eddy's who lived in Tennessee.

Happy Memories of Mary Baker Eddy
by Anna B. White Baker

[62] Other members of this class recall Mrs. Eddy entering after the students were assembled. See, for example, page 268 of Edward Norwood's reminiscence.

[63] It's likely that Baker is referring here to her own husband, Alfred E. Baker, who was a graduate of Hahnemann Medical College in Philadelphia.

[64] The term *Mental Science* was used by the general public and the press to refer collectively to various mental healing methods that sprang up during the latter half of the nineteenth century; Christian Science was typically included in this group. Unlike many of these systems, however, Christian Science is based on Jesus' teachings and makes a sharp distinction between the divine Mind and what Mary Baker Eddy called "mortal mind." For these and many other reasons, Eddy explained repeatedly that Christian Science had little in common with the mental healing systems of her time, including those that became part of the New Thought movement.

[65] L10483.

Invaluable Instruction
by Mary E. Eaton

[66] Eaton's father's testimony was published under the title "Free Indeed" on pages 252–255 of the July 1898 *Christian Science Journal*.

[67] For information on First Members, see endnote #12 for Joseph Eastaman's reminiscence.

68 This is the thank-you published on page 530 of the March 7, 1908, *Christian Science Sentinel*:

> To Miss Mary E. Eaton, C.S.D.
>
> You will accept my thanks for your multiplied favors, flowers, and friendship unceasing.
>
> Lovingly yours,
> M.B.G. Eddy

Memorable Encounters with Mrs. Eddy
by Charles D. Reynolds

69 Reynolds's first year in the healing ministry is recorded in his article "A Year's Experience," published on pages 339–345 of the September 1900 *Christian Science Journal*.

70 For information about workers' use of the term "Mother," see endnote #7 for Victoria Sargent's reminiscence.

71 Reynolds's testimony about this healing appears on page 287 of the August 1936 issue of *The Christian Science Journal*.

Serving Mrs. Eddy—An Invaluable Experience
by Minnie A. Scott

72 Scott's work involved planning and preparing household meals, ordering supplies, and assisting Eddy by preparing her bath and warming her bed, for example.

73 In addition to the security services described here, John Salchow served as night watchman at Pleasant View for three months beginning in autumn of 1903. However, his primary jobs were handyman and groundskeeper during almost a decade of working in Eddy's household. For more information about Salchow, see his reminiscence in the first volume of *We Knew Mary Baker Eddy, Expanded Edition* (pp. 366–427).

[74] For brief background on the "Next Friends" suit, see endnote #16 for Julia Prescott's reminiscence.

[75] A version of "Evil Is Not Power" appeared as an editorial in the November 2, 1907, *Christian Science Sentinel*. Mrs. Eddy amended that article and had it reprinted the following week (November 9), with a correction to that version appearing one week later (November 16). She continued revising the text before it was published as a leaflet, and then after she had made even further revisions, it was issued once again. The final version, published in December 1907, appeared in pamphlet form only, not in the periodicals. Copies of the *Sentinel* articles and the published pamphlets are in the collections of The Mary Baker Eddy Library.

Memoirs of Mary Baker Eddy
by Adam H. Dickey

[76] While serving in Mrs. Eddy's household, Adam Dickey wrote a friend about an exchange he had with Eddy that demonstrates his importance to her. His letter reads, in part:

> ... I usually go in every evening before she retires and say good night to her, and so often she has detained me, telling me of early experiences in her career and of things that led up to her great discovery.

> One night I said to her, "Mother, I just came in to tell you how much I love you." She took both of my hands in hers, and with such a tender look, she said, "Well, I never could tell you how much I love you." I think I am having an experience that has fallen to the lot of few, outside of Laura Sargent and Calvin Frye.

[77] Mrs. Eddy referred to mental murder in *Science and Health* four times: pages 164:17–23, 419:25–28, 445:2–8,

and 447:5–11. Two examples from these may help the reader to glimpse something of what Mrs. Eddy meant. On page 164 she wrote, "If you or I should appear to die, we should not be dead. The seeming decease, caused by a majority of human beliefs that man must die, or produced by mental assassins, does not in the least disprove Christian Science; rather does it evidence the truth of its basic proposition that mortal thoughts in belief rule the materiality miscalled life in the body or in matter." And on page 445 she said, "Also the teacher must thoroughly fit his students to defend themselves against sin, and to guard against the attacks of the would-be *mental assassin*, who attempts to kill morally and physically. No hypothesis as to the existence of another power should interpose a doubt or fear to hinder the demonstration of Christian Science."

[78] This "record" refers to the diaries Dickey maintained while at Chestnut Hill.

[79] The current *Church Manual* at the time this letter was written was the sixty-seventh edition, issued December 23, 1907. It includes this By-Law titled "Opportunity for Serving the Leader," Article XXII, Section 10:

> At the written request of the Pastor Emeritus, Mrs. Eddy, the Board of Directors shall immediately notify a member of this Church to go in ten days to her, and it shall be the duty of the member thus notified to remain with Mrs. Eddy twelve months consecutively, or three years consecutively if Mrs. Eddy requires or requests it. A member, who leaves her in less time without her consent or who is discharged, shall be dropped from the Church. Male members, who remain with her three years consecutively, shall be paid semi-annually at a rate of twelve hundred dollars yearly in addition to rent and board. Female members shall

receive one thousand dollars annually with rent and board. Those members, whom she teaches the course in Divinity, and those who remain with her three *consecutive* years, receive the degree of the Massachusetts Metaphysical College, if they are considered by Mrs. Eddy prepared to receive it.

[80] The change in terms of service was actually made a year before Dickey picked up the *Manual* in a Chicago Reading Room. The shift occurred between the fifty-ninth edition of the *Manual* issued in 1906, which stipulated twelve months of service, and the sixtieth edition issued January 8, 1907, which stipulated twelve months or three years of service, consecutively. The "new *Manuals*" he found in the Reading Room were most likely the sixty-seventh edition, quoted above in note #79, or possibly the sixty-eighth edition, issued January 31, 1908, which also stipulated twelve months or three years of service consecutively.

[81] The address Mrs. Eddy gave on this occasion is reprinted on pages 251–253 of *Miscellaneous Writings: 1883–1896*.

[82] For background on the "Mother's Room," see endnotes #42 and #43 for Clara Shannon's reminiscence.

[83] Dickey is partially mistaken about Calvin Frye's background. As *The Life of Mary Baker Eddy* by Sybil Wilbur explains, Frye was from Lawrence, Massachusetts, and worked "in the Natick mill as an overseer of machinery" (p. 277). He was a member of a Lawrence Congregational church when he became interested in Christian Science. For more information about Frye's ancestry, his education, and his selection for service in Eddy's household, see *The Life of Mary Baker Eddy*, especially pages 275–278.

84 By the time Mrs. Eddy was living at Chestnut Hill, her finances were being handled by a Trust for her estate. However, Calvin Frye retained responsibility for paying the household staff's salaries.

85 Ruching is a ruffle or pleat used to trim a woman's garment.

86 Dickey wound up working for Eddy as both a mental worker and a secretary.

87 The paragraph referred to on page 187 of *Science and Health* reads, "The valves of the heart, opening and closing for the passage of the blood, obey the mandate of mortal mind as directly as does the hand, admittedly moved by the will. Anatomy allows the mental cause of the latter action, but not of the former."

88 This sentence concludes the chapter "Christian Science Practice" in *Science and Health*: "Christian Scientists, be a law to yourselves that mental malpractice cannot harm you either when asleep or when awake" (p. 442).

89 These verses read as follows:

> Wherefore lay apart all filthiness and
> superfluity of naughtiness, and receive
> with meekness the engrafted word,
> which is able to save your souls. But be ye
> doers of the word, and not hearers only,
> deceiving your own selves. For if any be a
> hearer of the word, and not a doer, he is
> like unto a man beholding his natural face
> in a glass: For he beholdeth himself, and
> goeth his way, and straightway forgetteth
> what manner of man he was. But whoso
> looketh into the perfect law of liberty,
> and continueth therein, he being not a
> forgetful hearer, but a doer of the work,
> this man shall be blessed in his deed.

90 "No more Communion," Article XVIII, Section 1, first appeared in the seventy third edition of the *Church Manual*, which was issued in May 1908. On July 8, 1908, the By-Laws pertaining to "Executive Members" were repealed. For more information about Executive Members (originally called First Members), see endnote #12 for Joseph Eastaman's reminiscence.

91 The winter of 1909–1910 in Chestnut Hill, Massachusetts, was quite severe with sixteen inches of snow on December 26, 1909, and seven days of single-digit temperatures between December 28, 1909, and January 5, 1910.

92 Lida Fitzpatrick also refers to the physical threats Eddy encountered early on when she spoke publicly about her discovery. In a journal entry dated April 1, 1907, Fitzpatrick records Eddy's recollection of those times: "When I was introducing this work and they would throw stones at me through the window—and never touch me—and said there was dynamite under the building where I was to speak, I went right along, and I screamed Truth all the louder; if they screamed, I screamed all the louder, until they stopped."

93 In *Message to The Mother Church for 1902*, Mrs. Eddy describes receiving the title for *Science and Health*: "Six weeks I waited on God to suggest a name for the book I had been writing. Its title, *Science and Health*, came to me in the silence of night, when the steadfast stars watched over the world, — when slumber had fled, — and I rose and recorded the hallowed suggestion" (p. 15).

94 As part of her dedicatory message to First Church of Christ, Scientist, St. Louis, Missouri, Mrs. Eddy wrote, "Enjoying good things is not evil, but becoming slaves to pleasure is" (*The First Church of Christ, Scientist, and Miscellany*, p. 197).

95 This drive to view The Mother Church Extension occurred on February 6, 1908, and was reported in the Boston newspapers the following day. Two and a half years later, on July 29, 1910, Mrs. Eddy requested to be

driven by her Boston house, 385 Commonwealth Ave. From there she would also have been able to see the dome of the Extension.

[96] Mrs. Eddy's dominion over "mortal mind's antagonistic beliefs" (i.e., "the enemy") illustrates Jesus' words to his disciples: "Behold, I give unto you power to tread on serpents and scorpions, and over all the power of the enemy: and nothing shall by any means hurt you" (Luke 10:19).

[97] CONSTANCY

> When starlight blends with morning's hue,
> I miss thee as the flower the dew!
> When noonday's length'ning shadows flee,
> I think of thee, I think of thee!
>
> With evening, memories reappear—
> I watch thy chair, and wish thee here;
> Till sleep sets drooping fancy free
> To dream of thee, to dream of thee!
>
> Since first we met, in weal or woe
> It hath been thus; and must be so
> Till bursting bonds our spirits part
> And Love divine doth fill my heart.
>
> From *Poems* by Mary Baker Eddy (p. 3)

[98] Dickey is mistaken here. The invitation concerned a Memorial Hall at Lincoln's birthplace, which opened November 1911, not the Lincoln Memorial in Washington, D.C., which opened in 1922.

[99] This saying has been attributed to Michelangelo since at least the eighteenth century, but no original source for it has yet been located.

[100] The letter Dickey wrote (at Eddy's direction) regarding the statue included this decisive message from Eddy to the Board of Directors:

> No picture of a female in attitude of
> prayer or in any other attitude shall be

made or put into our Church, or any of
our buildings with my consent. This is
now my request and demand: Do nothing
in statuary, in writing, or in action to
perpetuate or immortalize the thought of
personal being; but do and illustrate, teach
and practice, all that will impersonalize
God and His idea man and woman.
Whatever I have said in the past relative to
impersonation in thought or in figure, I
have fully recalled, and my Church cannot
contradict me in this statement. (L01466)

[101] At this time, Alfred Farlow served as a one-man
Committee on Publication. For more information
about the duties of this office, see endnote #41 for
Clara Shannon's reminiscence.

[102] The word *cicatrized* first appeared in the fiftieth edition
of *Science and Health*, published in 1891. This edition
was a major revision of the textbook; it included the
first appearance of marginal headings as well as several
new chapters. *Cicatrized* was changed to *ankylosed* in
the 1910 edition.

[103] When Mrs. Eddy called her staff together, it was
generally for the purpose of teaching them about a
metaphysical point, thus the use of the word *class* here.

[104] In the final edition of *Science and Health*, which reflects
the revision Dickey goes on to describe, page 221
begins, "I knew a person who when quite a child
adopted the Graham system to cure dyspepsia. For
many years, he ate only bread and vegetables, and
drank nothing but water." As the passage explains, this
individual was completely healed through Christian
Science.

[105] For information on First Members and Executive
Members, see endnote #12 for Joseph Eastaman's
reminiscence.

My Years in Mrs. Eddy's Home
by M. Adelaide Still

[106] Still also notes Mrs. Eddy's references to herself as a pioneer on pages 30 and 50 of *Retrospection and Introspection*, Eddy's autobiography.

[107] Duties associated with "table work" typically included waiting on the table, serving food, collecting and keeping track of dishes, and tidying the dining room.

[108] For brief background on the "Next Friends" suit, see endnote #16 for Julia Prescott's reminiscence.

[109] The *American Heritage Dictionary of the English Language*, fourth edition, gives this definition for *alienist*: "A physician who has been accepted by a court of law as an expert on the mental competence of principals or witnesses appearing before it."

[110] Mrs. Eddy likely delivered this comment with irony in her voice since both her biological son, George Washington Glover II, and her adopted son, Ebenezer J. Foster Eddy, were among those who filed the "Next Friends" suit. (See endnote #16 for Julia Prescott's reminiscence.)

[111] According to *Bartlett's Familiar Quotations*, the phrase "splendid misery"—from a letter Thomas Jefferson wrote to Elbridge Gerry on May 13, 1797— refers to the difficulty of being president compared to the relative ease of being vice president. Jefferson wrote, "The second office of the government is honorable and easy, the first is but a splendid misery."

[112] Solon Spencer Beman (1853–1914) was a renowned Chicago architect, well known in the Christian Science community. He designed the first seven branch churches in Chicago, as well as Chicago's Grand Central Railway Station and Blackstone Memorial Library. His son, Spencer Solon Beman, continued as a famous architect and designer of Christian Science branch churches.

[113] A longer excerpt from this letter is included in Judge Hanna's reminiscence on page 238.

[114] The 1907 edition of *Science and Health* referred to here is in the collections of The Mary Baker Eddy Library (B00479). The piece of paper Still mentions has been removed from the book and is in the Library's manuscript collection (L14628). Most of the note is in Still's handwriting, a verbatim transcription presumably of what Mrs. Eddy said, but the last seven words—"Science that God's supply is on hand"— are in Eddy's own handwriting.

[115] This eighty-first edition of *Miscellaneous Writings*, published in 1908, is in the collections of The Mary Baker Eddy Library (B00394). In it, the phrase "lose with God!" has been crossed out and "to know that you can lose nothing which is real" has been inserted with a caret (^) underneath the line and alongside the passage in the margin. In addition, tucked into that page is a small slip of paper with the entire phrase written out. Both the marginal note and the slip of paper appear to be in Laura Sargent's handwriting.

[116] Baker is referring to the various difficulties Mrs. Eddy faced in settling the land and funds for building the Original Edifice of The Mother Church. For a detailed account of these problems, see chapter 2, "The Land and Its Ownership," in Margaret Pinkham's *A Miracle in Stone: The History of the Building of the Original Mother Church, The First Church of Christ, Scientist, in Boston, Massachusetts, 1894,* (Santa Barbara, CA: Nebbadoon Press, 2009).

[117] See *Manual*, Article XXII, Section 11.

[118] The correct date of this visit by George Washington Glover III and Andrew Jackson Glover is July 16, 1910.

[119] Evelyn Tilton Glover was born on January 12, 1880, and married Warren Schell on January 14, 1902. She died on August 17, 1903. They had no children. The photograph Still mentions is in the collections of

The Mary Baker Eddy Library, but it has no writing on the back. It appears that Eddy actually wrote this note on a calling card that was then tucked behind the photograph in the frame. That piece of paper is also in the Library's collections and reads essentially as Still indicates: "My darling granddaughter—passed on" (L14280).

[120] Augusta Stetson (1841–1928) was healed of sorrow and extreme exhaustion while listening to a lecture Mrs. Eddy gave in 1884. Soon afterward, she studied with Eddy and went on to become a Christian Science practitioner and teacher. In 1886 she went to New York City to help organize a church there, where she also served as pastor. Stetson never realized her promise, however. Pride and ambition led her to obstruct those she considered rivals and even to aspire to Eddy's place. In 1909 her membership in The Mother Church and her standing as a practitioner and teacher were revoked by the Christian Science Board of Directors.

[121] "Consistency" appeared on page 270 of the December 5, 1908, *Christian Science Sentinel.*

[122] Still's guess that Mrs. Minnie Scott wrote the letter is incorrect. The letter's author is not known, but it could not have been Scott because she was no longer working in Eddy's household at Christmastime in 1909. Eddy's response to the letter first appeared on page 350 of the January 1, 1910, *Christian Science Sentinel* before being included in *Miscellany.*

[123] Ira Knapp passed on November 11, 1910. Adam Dickey replaced him on the Board of Directors ten days later, November 21, 1910. Dickey's appointment was announced in the November 26, 1910, issue of the *Christian Science Sentinel* (p. 250).

[124] "The Mother's Evening Prayer" is one of the seven poems by Mary Baker Eddy that have been set to music and are included in the 1932 *Christian Science Hymnal.* The words of this poem may also be found on

page 389 of *Miscellaneous Writings: 1883–1896* and in the collection of Eddy's poetry titled *Poems*.

[125] The first version of this sentence appeared in 1886, in the sixteenth edition of *Science and Health*, where it read, "The maximum of good is to-day met by the maximum of evil." It remained in this form through the thirty-fifth edition in 1888. That same year, in the thirty-sixth edition, the sentence appeared this way: "The maximum of good is to-day met by the maximum of suppositional evil." The wording changed again in the fiftieth edition (1891) and in the 226th edition (1901) before assuming its permanent form in the final edition of *Science and Health*, where it appears as two sentences that read, "The maximum of good is the infinite God and His idea, the All-in-all. Evil is a suppositional lie" (p. 103).

Treasured Time at Chestnut Hill
by William R. Rathvon

[126] Regarding correspondence, Rathvon included this interesting incident in his reminiscence: "Many freak letters came daily, some grotesque, others ridiculous. I recall one letter from a foreign land just addressed 'Eddy, Amerika.' It reached its destination all right— an evidence of the efficiency of our Post Office Department and their recognition of the greatest of that name on this continent."

[127] This letter was published in the "Letters to our Leader" section of the January 30, 1909, *Christian Science Sentinel* (p. 431).

[128] For information about "Mother's Evening Prayer," see endnote #124 for M. Adelaide Still's reminiscence.

[129] This refers to the planned new edifice for First Church, New York, which was intended to rival The Mother Church in magnificence and stature within the movement. In response to discussion of these intentions in the press in late 1908 and early 1909,

"Consistency" and "One Mother Church in Christian Science" were published under Archibald McLellan's name in the December 5, 1908 *Christian Science Sentinel* (p. 270). For Eddy's comment on the situation, see "The Way of Wisdom" in *Miscellany* (pp. 356–357).

[130] This particular anecdote has not been confirmed, nor is it clear what "My Prayer in Christian Science" refers to, but the respect for and interest in Christian Science described here is correctly attributed to Albert Basil Orme Wilberforce (1841–1916), a well-known Anglican clergyman in England in his day. Correspondence from Ralph B. Scholfield, a Christian Science teacher in London, England, indicates that Mary Baker Eddy inscribed a copy of *Science and Health* to Wilberforce. Scholfield also wrote that his own Christian Science teacher, Mabel S. Thomson, often quoted this comment by Wilberforce: "God in Christian Science was the finest concept of deity that has ever come to the mind of man." In addition, Evelyn Heywood, C.S.B., told Scholfield that one of her uncles was Wilberforce's curate and that, when she was a child, she met Wilberforce and heard him preach. Heywood also told Scholfield that Wilberforce presented Eddy's statement "What Our Leader Says," found on page 210 of *Miscellany*, to his parishioners as a Christmas card one year.

[131] The "New York situation" refers to Augusta Stetson's efforts to usurp Mrs. Eddy's place. For brief background on Stetson, see endnote #120 for M. Adelaide Still's reminiscence. For brief background on the "Next Friends" suit, see endnote #16 for Julia Prescott's reminiscence.

[132] "Maudie" was Rathvon's nickname for his wife Ella.

[133] Clifford P. Smith, a former judge and lawyer from Iowa, was a Trustee of the Christian Science Publishing Society from June 19, 1908, through September 12, 1911.

Partial Bibliography

Works Cited and Mentioned—Published by The Christian Science Publishing Society

Christian Science Board of Directors. *Christian Science Hymnal*. Boston: The Christian Science Publishing Society, 1932.

Christian Science Publishing Society, The. *We Knew Mary Baker Eddy, Expanded Edition, Volume I*. Boston: The Christian Science Publishing Society, 2011.

Orcutt, William Dana. *Mary Baker Eddy and Her Books*. Boston: The Christian Science Publishing Society, 1950, 1978.

Wilbur, Sybil. *The Life of Mary Baker Eddy*. Boston: The Christian Science Publishing Society, 1938.

Works Cited and mentioned—Written by Mary Baker Eddy and Published by The Christian Science Publishing Society

Christ and Christmas

*Christian Science versus Pantheism**

Manual of The Mother Church (abbreviated *Church Manual* or *Manual*)

*Message to The Mother Church for 1901**

*Message to The Mother Church for 1902**

Miscellaneous Writings: 1883–1896* (abbreviated *Miscellaneous Writings*)

No and Yes*

Poems

Pulpit and Press*

Retrospection and Introspection* (abbreviated *Retrospection*)

Rudimental Divine Science*

Science and Health with Key to the Scriptures (abbreviated *Science and Health*)

The First Church of Christ, Scientist, and Miscellany* (abbreviated *Miscellany*)

Unity of Good*

---

* These works are included in the compilation *Prose Works* other than *Science and Health with Key to the Scriptures*.

Index

Page numbers in bold refer to images.